MW01486838

DAILY FLIGHT PLAN

A Daily Meditation in Memoir

Mike C.

MYSTIC SUNSET PUBLISHING

JACKSONVILLE, FL

This meditation in memoir is a collection of the author's communications
with his sponsees in AA. They include interactions with family and
friends and life events. Some events have been shifted on the timeline for
flow purposes only. Some names and identifying details have been
changed to protect the privacy of others.

Edited by Lynn Skapyak Harlin
Cover Graphic/Layout/Design by Shannon Cavanaugh
Cover photo by Pexels
Published by Mystic Sunset Publishing

1st Edition
November 2019

The information contained in this book is the author's personal
experience and should not be considered a substitute for the advice of a
qualified medical professional specializing in addiction disorders.

MYSTIC SUNSET PUBLISHING

P.O. Box 16952
Jacksonville, FL 32246

Printed in the United States of America
2468097531

DEDICATION

I dedicate this book to my children as a living amends. They had to endure my alcoholism during the most important years of their lives. I was missing family life out chasing a career and robbed them of time and love. A special thanks to my son Michael Dean who passed away from ALS at the age of 56. He inspired me to write again and taught me the real meaning of one day at a time.

ACKNOWLEDGEMENTS

Heartfelt gratitude goes out to the entire fellowship of Alcoholics Anonymous. AA saved my life so that I may be of service to my still suffering alcoholic brothers and sisters. I received unconditional love from the very first day of sobriety and hopefully this book will pass on that love to others which was freely given to me.

My Jacksonville Team, consisting of my two daughters, Shannon and Diane doing editing, artwork and the logistics of getting this printed. It was a team love project and I am truly blessed to have such a wonderful family

Lynn Skapyak Harlin did the first level of edit for us and removed some annoying habits from my writing. The second level edit, and publishing effort, was done by Tracy Dot Com Collins, a fellow traveler on the Road to Recovery.

FOREWORD

Mike C. asked if I would help get this project off the ground and I gladly said yes. The only problem was I had no idea what I was doing. But I had said yes, so it was going to happen. I began reading and editing and worrying about the next steps.

In the meantime, at my cornhole shop, I had a very friendly client named Dana Hammett come by to pick up her order. She told me about her friend Tracy who was having a birthday party and book launch who wanted to have cornhole at the event. My sister Diane and I said, yes, of course, and Dana hooked us up with Tracy. Dana gave us a little back story on Tracy and her book about her first year in sobriety. My sister and I just looked at each other.

We showed up to Tracy's event a little early to deliver the cornhole games and no one was there. We wandered around a little until we ran into Tracy in the parking lot, unloading her car. We offered to help, and she accepted. I grabbed a case of beer out of the car, which then spilled out to the parking lot onto my feet and proceeded to spray beer all over the place. Hi, Tracy Collins, nice to meet you!

Tracy invited us to her party, and we attended. She had a little auction set up to raise money for a charity she is associated with which helps fellow alcoholics. One of the items was one hour with her editor. I looked at my sister and said "Well, if this isn't a sign, I don't know what is." We bid and won.

I thought I would just email Editor, Lynn Skapyak Harlin a few pages of Mike's work, but she wanted to meet. I went to her house in Jacksonville, we sat in her little back room filled with books from authors she had edited and books on recovery and talked. Lynn, like Mike, has been in recovery for 25 years. The coincidences didn't end there. Both Lynn and Mike were heavily involved with POW recovery movement during the Vietnam War, and likely, nearly crossed paths during those years.

I hope Lynn and Mike get to meet in person one day.

Shannon Cavanaugh
Partner at Mystic Sunset Publishing
Jacksonville, FL

ABOUT THE AUTHOR

The author of these daily messages for each day of the year is Mike C. As an active member of Alcoholics Anonymous, he got sober in Hawaii with a sobriety date of April 21, 1994. After 11 years in the program, he moved to Thailand, and these short messages began as a method for Mike to keep in touch with men he sponsored in recovery. Over the years, he has added sponsees from over 10 different locations all over the map. The writings offered here are selected from 10 years of carrying the message of AA.

Mike is a retired military officer and a combat pilot with 30 years of service. In addition to being an alcoholic, Mike suffers from PTSD from his years in Vietnam, Laos, Thailand and Afghanistan. He shares his experience, strength and hope to include the loss of his son to ALS disease in 2017, a life-threatening accident in 2013, and the loss of a close friend also in AA.

He stresses to the people he sponsors; prayer, readings and meditation upon awakening every morning. The use of a gratitude list is repeated in the pages that follow. The idea of this book is to read one page, every day, over a cup of coffee. Here is a list of the books Mike reads every single morning:

Alcoholics Anonymous, 4th Edition (commonly referred to as "The Big Book")

Daily Reflections, Also an AA publication

Body Mind and Spirit, A Hazelden Publication

Twenty-Four Hours A Day, A Hazelden Publication

Around the Year by Emmet Fox, A Harper One Publication

A New Day, A Bantam Book

The Twelve Step Prayer Book, A Hazelden Publication

Here are the 12 Steps of Alcoholics Anonymous that are suggested as a program of recovery:

Step 1: We admitted we were powerless over alcohol—that our lives had become unmanageable.

Step 2: Came to believe that a Power greater than ourselves could restore us to sanity.

Step 3: Made a decision to turn our will and our lives over to the care of God as we understood Him.

Step 4: Made a searching and fearless moral inventory of ourselves.

Step 5: Admitted to God, to ourselves, and to another human being the exact nature of our wrongs.

Step 6: Were entirely ready to have God remove all these defects of character.

Step 7: Humbly asked Him to remove our shortcomings.

Step 8: Made a list of all persons we had harmed and became willing to make amends to them all.

Step 9: Made direct amends to such people wherever possible, except when to do so would injure them or others.

Step 10: Continued to take personal inventory and when we were wrong promptly admitted it.

Step 11: Sought through prayer and meditation to improve our conscious contact with God, as we understood Him, praying only for knowledge of His will for us and the power to carry that out.

Step 12: Having had a spiritual awakening as the result of these Steps, we tried to carry this message to alcoholics, and to practice these principles in all our affairs.

January 1

CONQUER YOURSELF

I was one year sober and made my first trip away from my home group to see friends in Las Vegas. For some crazy reason, I opened the drawers and found next to the normal Gideon Bible a black book on Buddhism. I picked it up and opened to the intro page and it had a list of Buddha sayings. Two of them hit me between the horns. "**Blood stains cannot be cleaned with more blood; they can only be cleaned with love.**" I needed to see that one because I had spent my entire adult life trying to extract blood from my enemies. Love my enemies. There is a concept for world peace. But the one that made me sit down and meditate is: "**A warrior is not a true victor even if he has vanquished one thousand enemies in a thousand cities until he conquers himself.**" There it is in black and white; I had been fighting everything and everybody and the enemy was me. That one sentence started 20 years of study in the teachings of Buddha and I found all of it to compliment the 12 Steps very well. In my imagination, I was a dragon slayer; and the reality was, I was the monster. My whole life was a fight, so when I got sober, I thought it was just another battle to be won. How about not fighting anymore? What? That's all I knew so I had to rewire my thought process to not fighting.

Now the problem was identified. It's me. Now how do I conquer the man in the mirror? The 4th Step is a huge chunk of the work to be done. When I viewed my character, I could see what I thought was an asset was really a liability. After a few years I came to the awakening the entire 12 Steps were the method of defeating me and declaring victory over my former self, and the birth of an entirely new improved version of me. In my Morning Prayer and meditation, I step on top of the carcass of the defeated person I was before I entered recovery. I keep the image of the old me very green, so I don't forget who I can become again if I do not stay vigilant. I know there is a monster still inside me all caged up, but the gorilla is hibernating just patiently waiting for me to wake him up. So today, when I see a fight brewing, I can sidestep the anger and let the thrust go on by without engaging. This makes me victorious every time.

I gave up the life of fighting city hall, my bosses, nasty people, for a life of conquering myself on a daily basis. Losing all my enemies brought real freedom for this warrior.

January 2

LOVE IS THE ANSWER

The path of love is open to everyone. No special talents or skill needed. No entrance fee, no dues to be paid, no professional training. Love will heal you. Love will comfort you. Love will guide you. Love will illuminate you. Love will redeem you from sin. My Higher Power is love. We all have a loving God who is there for us. Love is the answer to any question I have. My day starts with love and ends with love and is full of love from sunrise to sunset into La La Land. I sleep with the angels in the arms of love.

This is from my *12 Step Prayer Book*: '**Love is patient, Love is kind. Love is not jealous; it does not put on airs; it is not snobbish. Love is never rude; it is not self-seeking; it is not prone to anger; neither does it brood over injuries. Love does not rejoice in what is wrong; but rejoices with the truth. There is no limit to love's forbearance, its truth, its hope its power to endure."**

 Then there is the 11th Step Prayer: "**To love, than to be loved**." I made a trip back to Vietnam on an "amends" trip back in 2002 and my former enemies embraced me with love and forgiveness. A lesson I hold close to my heart. I share my meeting with former enemies every morning and I love them all. Today I have no more enemies. Here is another offering from my inspirational reading: "**Love is friendship that has caught fire. It is quiet understanding, mutual confidence, sharing, and forgiving. It is loyalty through good times and bad. It settles for less than** perfection and makes allowances for human weakness."

"Love is content with the present, it hopes for the future, and it doesn't brood over the past. It's the day-in-day-out chronicle of irritations, problems, compromises, small disappointments, big victories, and common goals."

"If you have love in your life, it can make up for a great many things you lack. If you don't have it, no matter what else there is, it's not enough."

January 3

THOUGHT LIFE

There is so little we have control over in our lives, but we are in charge of our thoughts and attitudes. We are always thinking no matter how hard we try to stop. The wheels are always in motion up there in our grey matter. Even when we are sleeping our brain is working away. As my sobriety increases my ability to remember, my dreams have increased greatly. Some super long movies play in my theater every night. OK forget about the sleeping part and when we are awake we can control our positive or negative polls going on in our thoughts. Lately my spiritual readings talk about nipping bad thoughts in the bud. They advise not to dwell on resentments, revenge and indignation to the point of obsession. These thoughts take us off the beam and out of the Sunlight of The Spirit. The longer we let these thoughts block us from God the more we place ourselves in peril. My readings warn that if you plot the murder of your enemies, even though there is no action, you are guilty of murder. If you look with lust at another man's wife, you are an adulterer right then even though it is just a thought. Yikes. Guilty as charged your honor.

I have read the following passage in the Big Book a thousand times but just now it has enriched significance: "**Our thought-life will be placed on a much higher plane when our thinking is cleared of wrong motives.**" Our thought patterns can be channeled and programmed in a good spiritual way until it is from the heart. If my mind strays, as it often does, I quickly stop that thought and think of God in some way. If it is a particularly bad thought, I say a prayer. The good news is my routine of one quiet hour in the morning groves my thought life in the proper direction, at least at the start. As soon as my path crosses a disagreeable person all bets are off and I pull out my imaginary 22 caliber pistol. I have since thrown away that pistol mentally and think of ways to love this asshole. Not successful at this level of love, at least I am not a murderer as defined by my spiritual teachings. Wow, I have a long way to go in my thought life. I have allowed my thoughts to wander into dangerous areas thinking my fantasies to be harmless. Wrong.   If I clean up my thinking, then good positive actions will follow. How many sleepless nights I have had in the past rehearsing my revenge over all my resentments. What a waste.

The secret is to feed my brain with good nourishment, eliminate the news channels and useless garbage entering my thought life. I continue to seek a higher plane like the Big Book clearly states.

January 4

GOD'S LESSONS FROM NATURE

In my spiritual readings there has been a focus on knowing God more by learning the clues He has given us in nature. The creatures God has put on this planet with us all have spiritual messages. For example, a dog (God spelled backwards) is a loving companion to humans, honest, giving unconditional love to those who nourish and care for them. We hear stories of hero dogs all the time, saving children from drowning and rescuing people from fire. So why do we humans fall short of doing what a dog can do instinctively. One of my favorite prayers has this line: "**Let me learn the lessons You have hidden in every leaf and rock. Make my hands respect the things You have made and make my ears sharp to hear Your voice.**" I am trying to do just that, open my mind to the messages God has given us. When you stand over the Grand Canyon and see thousands of years of this planet, I feel God right there and see

His work for us to learn.

Emmet Fox has entire passage called "Claim Your Wings," he talks about the simple caterpillar who has limited range on a few green leaves. This little fuzzy creature has 9 sets of legs and tiny eyes but is clever in camouflage in order to survive. The steady diet of leaves become boring and the caterpillar has strange stirrings inside for a new life. Fox likens this to a "divine discontent" the caterpillar yearns for a more interesting, finer life. Our fuzzy friend weaves a cocoon and undergoes an amazing change of life. At the right time a butterfly emerges to claim his wings, fly free and extend his range for miles and miles. God made this beautiful butterfly in 18,000 different species all in bright color so we would take notice. We too can claim our wings and change our life and reach an entirely new level of freedom. For us, when we were drinking we were caterpillars crawling around in a limited circle. We do the 12 Steps and we undergo a metamorphosis and get a new life. The caterpillar is gone, and a useful colorful creature is born. A sober alcoholic on a spiritual path, Fox calls this the "True Self."

Nature gives us a ton of clues to get closer to God. God is in each of us and I need to remind myself of that when I get upset with another person. Nature is easier to understand if we could just remain teachable.

January 5

IT'S TOO HEAVY

In the old days I used to try to carry the weight of the world on my shoulders. I was responsible for what my country was doing, my organization was doing, my entire extended family was doing. It was so heavy I had to take a drink or twelve to handle it all. When I finally got sober and on the road to recovery, I was relieved of my duties as chairman of the universe. I got fired. I was stripped down to what I am responsible for and those things that are beyond my control which is just about everything but my attitude. The weight was lifted when I admitted my powerlessness. The shoulders heaved a sigh of relief when I surrendered. I quit, I give up, I cannot carry this heavy load anymore. My Higher Power does ALL the heavy lifting in my life today. He is all Powerful, He is all Strength. Why not let God handle the burden? He can, and I can't, simple as that. I am tired, weak and ill and lack capability. Now I have learned to turn it over to the Tireless One, the All-Powerful, the All-Wise and the All-Resourceful. That Power was available all those years and I missed it until now.

Now I work on staying weightless. Every so often I look at myself hunched over, because I have loaded up my shoulders again, because I thought I was in charge, that is why I say that 3rd Step prayer every morning. I was always a "take charge guy" and that is not an asset, it can be a defect. I used to say "I am captain of the ship" until the ship went down like the Titanic. I was into self-government, but nobody elected me. I was a dictator. Now I am out of government, mine, my country and the world at large. I am not up for election either. I take my direction from my Higher Power and adopted the principles that AA provided for me to follow. My baggage has been dropped, my inventory disposed of and my arms swing free. I was carrying a big bag of rocks that was totally unnecessary and too heavy. I do have control over my attitude, so I have an "attitude adjustment hour" first thing every morning and my Higher power provides me with the inspiration for the next 24. He has been up all night. God loves me and wants me to be happy, joyous and free, of that I am certain. All I must do is let go.

Here in Thailand the street vendors trying to sell something will often call me "boss." I reel every time I hear that and laugh out loud and thank God I am not the boss of anything anymore except my own sobriety.

January 6

WHO IS YOUR TEACHER?

Before every meeting I say to myself "Who is going to be my teacher today?" It may be a guy I really don't like but I need to keep an open mind, look for the message and forget about the messenger. I would like to think that I am teachable and possess an open mind but lately I have discovered my focus is narrower than it needs to be. In other words, my mind is open but not to all the things that will help me grow more. **"We know only a little"** from page 164 of The Big Book, is a very important sentence. I need to stay humble in my search for information and growth. I get surprised by who my next teacher might be. My children have been my teacher lately. My enemies have taught me many things I needed to learn. The hardest part is to improve your listening to learn the maximum. When someone else is talking I am talking in my head at the same time, "Yeah, yeah, I know, I know, so what." I need to shut that inner voice down when the messages are coming in. Not easy. Just because I have been around the block a few times and have lots of experience does not mean I have all the answers and possess all knowledge.

It's not only people that can be my teacher today. I try to learn from nature and all God's creatures with whom we share this planet. I see animals protecting their young and have super tricks for survival. My dog would comfort me when I was sick, that's amazing. Technology is a bit intimidating to me. I go in an electronics mall and I have no idea what 90% of all the stuff in there does. However, as I learn more technology, it enhances my learning. My buddy "Google" has a treasure trove of information. Most of all with new technology I can communicate with more friends and family in a more intimate way.

Who is the greatest teacher of all? God is. The problem here is there is no voice, no video, no graphics. Just quiet meditation and really listening for His message is the only way I can learn from God. I work my 11th Step every day to improve my learning by constant contact with my Higher Power, the ultimate knowledge. When I pray and read, I am talking. When I meditate, I am listening and learning.

Think outside of the box or get in the box.

January 7

YOU ARE NOT OK, I AM NOT OK, BUT THAT IS OK

Yes, the inmates are in charge of the asylum. We gather together daily in our meeting room all insane members of our fellowship. Luckily, we don't all act up at the same time. There is always a wrench for every nut. I admit I am insane and am pretty sure all the members I share an hour with are insane because they tell me all about their insanity. I am not OK, and they are not OK but somehow, thru the grace of God, it works wonders and that is OK. My thinking is faulty and therefore I ask God to direct my defective brain and He does. I get clarity usually in my morning hour of quiet meditation and prayer. I must tell my brain to shut up and listen. If I let my brain go on its own, it spins up to warp 9 and has no direction. As my pilot instructor told me years ago "Mike you have plenty of airspeed, but you have a problem with direction." True to this day I admit.

From my own experience, I can tell you my insanity is in check the more I do my program. But if I start skipping meetings, I soon lose my mind. It is insidious like the creeping crud. I tend to get off balance and become a drunk without the drink in my hand. Sober yes, nuts absolutely. I must remember my insane behavior that got me into a black horrible bottom is still in me. It won't go away. I am not cured. It takes constant attention or else I endanger myself to return to the insanity of my past. The biggest problem with my insanity is that my mind tells me that I am not insane and it's a big fat lie I tend to believe. Now I can spot the danger signs if I start developing a resentment or snap at somebody. Whoa. Sit down and chat with another alcoholic or make a meeting, pick up the phone, give myself a time out and say a prayer or 12. My brain has a positive and a negative and if I am not careful the minus signs can ruin my serenity and take me down a dark path. Am I insane? Absolutely but that's OK as long as I stay on the Road of Happy Destiny.

Now it is not my job to determine if you are OK or not. I need to accept you as you are and love you unconditionally and that's OK.

8

SUCCESS AND FAILURE

Success and failure are largely a matter of definition. I thought my ability to drink huge quantities of alcohol was success. Weaker chaps got sick and in trouble, but I could successfully drink more than anyone else. Little did I suspect I had failed my body by acquiring such a high tolerance and I was on my way to terminal alcoholism. I thought my climb up the corporate ladder made me a success, but I later could see, it made me a failure at family, life and marriage. Some of my "success" was really failure and my failures turned out to be successes. I failed the breathalyzer test the cops gave me, but it successfully got me into treatment. One of the best things that ever happened to me but at the time I thought I was a loser forever. I could have stayed a loser if I didn't accept defeat and surrender. My ability to define success and failure was a failure. This program has taught me how to do the job much better. If I let others define my success or failure I am doomed to failure. In my country USA most folks define success by how much wealth you have accumulated, the clothes you wear, the house and neighborhood you live in. After being on a spiritual path for a few years this all seems very silly. If St. Peter is really at the Pearly Gates and you show up there for an evaluation, he is not going to ask how rich you were. A more likely question is going to be, "How many people did you help?"

In the morning I wake up and thank God for being alive one more day. I am sober, healthy, and happy, so that's four successes right there. I look at my gratitude list of 64 successes, do my prayers and meditation in the first hour every day I rack up well over 100 successes in a row. As I progress during the day, I might make mistakes but at least I had a good start and the errors are usually minor. All those failures of the past go into the success column if I can use it to help someone else or at least not repeat my past failures. "In God's economy nothing is wasted." I truly believe that. My wasted years are useful to make my sober years the best they can be. All of us who hit bottom, recovered from the dark pits and found a Design for Living and a Higher Power are tremendous successes. We are very few out of all those eligible for this wonderful program. One drink and failure consume us like a dragon, sustained success requires us to do some basic things to stay on top of the world.

I often say that I ran out of failures, so success was the only option left. If a dark past is gold, then I am indeed a very rich dude.

January 9

THE WEEDS IN YOUR LIFE

Taking a weed wacker to your weeds just makes them grow back even stronger. Same in life, if you just brush off the top of a problem it does not go away and weeds in our life need to be taken out by the root. I learned all about weeds growing up before Roundup weed killer and weed wackers. One of my many chores was yardman for the family. I found out that weeds multiply at night. I know that they can be so strong as to bust up sidewalk concrete and cause cracks in a brick wall. Whenever I hinted that I would like to go play baseball my mother would point out that the yard had a lot of weeds that needed attention. After all what would the neighbors think. Weeds stifled my baseball career and I was chained to the massive lawn full of dandelions. To make matters worse, my sisters would blow on the fluffy white dandelion puffs and send thousands of seeds into the air. I would scream at them which enhanced their enjoyment. One time I put extra effort in to totally removing every weed from the yard and guess what? No appreciation, no extra credit, no thanks nada. The lesson I learned is it made me satisfied I could set a goal and accomplish a tough task.

Even in the military I could not get away from weeds. I oversaw base beautification and weeds were a problem, so we bought gallons of Roundup weed killer. Problem then became the chemicals seeped into the groundwater and caused contamination.

There is no shortcut to weed pulling. You must get down on your hands and knees to do the job right. (Hint)

In adulthood, the weeds in my life were resentments, broken relationships, unfulfilled potential and sins of selfishness. So eventually my "garden' was such a mess I did not care anymore. Once I got on the road to recovery and started my 4th Step I could see the "weeds" had smothered my garden. Doing the complete 4th and 5th Step finally got to the roots of my "weeds" and they got jerked out of the ground and discarded. Then in sobriety I learned that weeding my garden is a lifelong process just like the lawn of my youth. They crop up all the time and need to be dealt with before it becomes a big problem. My morning prayer and meditation keeps my garden looking very nice and my 10th Step searches for "weeds" before they grow into trees. If I have a broken relationship I try to find a way to break the ice and get into a "let's talk about it" mode. I want flowers in my garden. Also, I want to share my lovely garden with my friends and family.

January 10

SPIRIT VS. MATTER

Most of my spiritual readings focus on departing the material world to enter Nirvana or Heaven if you prefer. As I look at my gratitude list there are just a few items of "matter" and the bulk of the rest of the list is spiritual principles or descriptions of spirit. Most of the writers on this subject, such as Emmet Fox, say God is Spirit along with Truth, Principle, Love, Soul, Intelligence, and Life. I can see my prayers are asking God to find His will, not mine. God is all powerful and I am powerless, so I know He is a loving Father who wants the best for me and all I must do is my best to listen for His guidance. After all God is not limited, He has no beginning and no end but us human beings are very limited and can be defined in "matter," so why not tap into this power source for my energy and spiritual wellbeing. I know if I seek harmony with my surroundings, the people in my life and my Higher Power all will be serene and peaceful. It's easy to describe but difficult to attain all the time. In my own case, there are times like a fine symphony and times like chaos and everything in between. That process of claiming quiet time, gives me my best shot at peace and love.

I know that my material world will end but my spirit will live on after my body fails to operate. I try to push away shiny objects and things made of "matter" and view it all as just "stuff." I try to concentrate on love, helping others, learning, truth, principle and living life to the fullest. I must remember no matter how much "stuff" I accumulate it is not enough if I don't have love. The 11th Step prayer I say every morning is a list of spiritual goals and not one word about "matter." The longer I concern myself in the spiritual realm the better I feel. I would rather fly with the angels than drive a Mercedes. I feel better doing an act of charity than eating a big steak. Of course, the big difference between spirit vs. matter is things of the spirit cannot be measured, and things of matter can be weighed, touched, given a monetary value. Thus, some folks find spirituality beyond their grasp since they cannot see things of the spirit world. The rest of us are fortunate to have acquired faith and believe in the Great Unseen.

When faced with a problem I say to myself "Is this a problem of a spiritual nature or is it about matter?" If it is about matter, it doesn't matter.

January 11

RELAXATION AND FUN

For most of us, fun was off the table when we were hitting bottom and we were out of the game of fun so long we need to reprogram ourselves. In my case I never did have a concept of fun my entire life. My parents took fun away as a part of growing up. There was homework and chores and they never ended, so picking up a baseball glove and going outside to play was for the neighbors, not for me. Even when I played sports it was pain and pressure to win and do well, not a giggle in the gym ever but serious stuff. So as a teenager in the military, no fun at first but after the basics and schooling were over drinking was the first "fun" in my life. From that point on fun and alcohol were directly related and I could not have one without the other. In the military life it was a standard joke when things were going bad especially in combat. I remember coming back from a mission where we took a hit and one us got nicked and there was blood all over the windows and the second aircraft guiding us back to home base broke the eerie silence by "Are we having fun yet?" Even the word fun was a joke because there was no fun. I had to re-define fun in sobriety, thank God.

One of the secrets of handling tough problems is to stop thinking about them. Relax and not struggle. Get your mind off the problem all together. Think of God if you can. Pray, do anything but screw yourself into the ceiling trying to solve the riddle and just give yourself a headache. We all suffered mental blocks from time to time and for me I change the subject in my working mind and put it on the shelf for God to work on. For the first time in my life, a few years into my sobriety, I learned relaxation is part of recovery. I needed to relax my mind to meditate to listen to my heart and tell my brain to take a walk. The art of relaxation had to come first before I could attempt "fun." I am lucky to have my angel by my side who has no problem enjoying some fun every day. He takes time to play with me every day, to joke and poke fun. I am easily amused, so fun can be to pet Lucy Lu, a street dog who loves me unconditionally, for about 4 minutes.

Then there is a beggar lady whose baby girl knows me very well and gives me a million-dollar smile and likes me to pick her up and show her new heights. Priceless.

January 12

THINK OF GOD

Every meeting we read "How It Works" and the last line **"That God could and would if He were sought."** I have heard it thousands of times, but do I really seek God when I should? Of course I do, during my morning prayer and meditation, but what about the other 23 hours a day? One of my spiritual teachers writes about **Think of God** whenever you need Him especially in challenging circumstances. In other words, control your thoughts and call on God for a spot assistance. Further he writes **you can't, but God can**. God can do the heavy lifting that is beyond our limited capability. The secret is we must make the call, do the seeking with no dictation of the ways or means. If I really seek God I will find Him. Not just in the quiet of the morning when I am alone but during a train wreck. It need not be that dramatic, but I am conscious of the need to think of God during the day as events unfold. I got to put this into practice recently when I was in the waiting room outside the ICU in the local hospital. My friend was getting CPR for the second time and I was mentally preparing for what to do if my friend is disabled. I need to do A, B, and C, OMG what if he dies? "Stop it." I told myself and thought of God. Shortly thereafter my friend was out of ICU and returned to the living. My fears were unfounded.

We do have control over our thoughts and can channel them. So exactly how do I think of God? It will be different for every person, but God is not an old man with a big white beard. He is not Charlton Heston. I see God in nature. I take my thoughts to the surf crashing on the beach. I see fields of orchids, all colors and varieties. I see the creatures of the forest. I see the Grand Canyon. I see my favorite dog look me right in the eye and rub up against me for some love. I get out of myself, my pity, little problems and call on God as I see Him. The results are astounding. When I return to earth and open my eyes the problem has either gone away or I can see a solution that wasn't obvious before. We own our thoughts, so thoughts of God will always be productive and helpful. All I have to do is make the call and God is always there. If I look for trouble I will find it. If I look for God's will for me I will find that also.

January 13

HABITS INVENTORY

We all are creatures of habit and resist change. How many years did we drink and drug and refused to change? Now in recovery we have stopped the "killer" habit and have the courage to change. Now might be a good time to check our routine and do a habit inventory. I have shared with you many times my habit of doing one hour of prayer and meditation and it is my daily connection with my Higher Power, but can I improve on that hour? I added some new readings to my "habit" and it put some new fire into my spiritual thinking. I also added some new prayers to my daily prayer and it put some spice to the list. My point is, when doing your "habits" inventory; some good habits can be made better. I have to laugh at myself, I sit in the same chair in my favorite coffee shop, the same chair at meetings wherever I go even if I haven't been there in 10 years. Maybe that tells me something about my character defect on flexibility. I drink 3 cups of coffee at the same times every day, now knocked down to 2, shooting for one.

I exercise every day, same time, same place and same routine. Now I am looking for advice as to doing different exercises and adding or subtracting time on the treadmill. Maybe do some swimming. I'm always looking for more healthy choices. Thailand is great for fruits and vegetables. In the USA they serve French fries with everything. Unfortunately, I have a habit of eating everything. Then I learned it is OK to not eat everything you are served. It was a new concept for me. My good friend says, "If it tastes good spit it out." I don't go that far but I know 3 minutes of pleasure eating ice cream costs me 45 minutes on the treadmill so the payoff is just not worth it. I can tell you from experience my eating habits had to change with my advancing age. I love hot spicy food from all my years in Asia, but my mouth is not the weakest part of the chain. I had to adjust. I can see that some of my habits are tied to my defects. Certain people just bring out my sarcastic side and I have learned to resist the temptation to put people in their place and let God do justice and I keep my big mouth shut. I have good habits and bad habits but looking at them as an inventory helps me immensely.

Sometimes the habits we have put us in a rut and we fall into mundane time wasters. A review of our routine can replace good for best.

January 14

TIME IS MY FRIEND

The way we view time is largely dependent on our attitude and our situation. Time flies when you are having fun and it is slow as a snail when we are waiting for the doctor. To so many people time is the enemy, a battle to fight, and a reason to lose your temper or raise your blood pressure. However, we are the blessed ones to have learned to divide time into 24-hour chunks, 8 of which is sleeping, so there is just a short burst to deal with. OK in our 11th Step "we consider the 24 hours ahead" thus an action plan for those few hours. So, my suggestion is to focus on your attitude toward time because it is the only part you have control over. The tick of the clock is constant. No matter what, we wish it to speed up or slow down, it marches on. If we accept the rhythm of the clock, then we are ready to make friends with time. Most of my prayers have goals for doing better, helping others and bringing positive things to the day. My first hour of prayer and meditation is well spent because my Higher Power and I have a good start programming the next 24 doing His will not mine. Next, I have a list of specific items to attend to.

My time inventory goes like this: go to my home group meeting, 2 and 1/2 hours includes the meeting before and after etc. (I love this time). Do my daily exercise, 1 hour (hate the process love the results). Work on my taxes (ugh. one hour and stop). Visit a friend in the hospital (1 hour no fun). Take time to read a great book (1 hour or so. I love this). Go shopping for essentials (I hate this with a passion). OK you get the idea. I try to mix the fun stuff with the not so fun stuff. The process of making a list seems to work on my weak brain to get stuff done. I check my list at night and surprisingly I complete my 24-hour plan most of the time. If

I have a leftover, then it goes to the top of the list tomorrow. I make sure nobody wastes my time on unproductive activity like when I had a boss who sent me to strange places to work long hours for no result. I am the captain of my clock. I don't go to crappy movies or read trash. I don't watch CNN, Fox or internet garbage, a massive time waster. Time is currency so I try to spend it wisely. Time is more important than gold. If I am stuck waiting for the doctor or an airplane, I thank God for the extra time and send a message or two, read a book or just plain meditate.

I thank God for all the hours He has granted me for 8 decades. Decades of my time almost went down the river in a bottle, so I have learned to treat time as my friend.

January 15

HAVE FAITH IN YOUR FAITH

All of us have come a long way from desperation to a life of hope. We are the lucky ones. We won the lotto of life really. For each one of us, there are 10 human beings floundering around in the same disease we have without the knowledge we have on how to recover. All of us had at least a tiny bit of willingness in order to stop our insanity. From that small beginning we began the journey of faith in a Higher Power of our own description. Nobody gave us a "god" to follow. We were given the freedom to design our own concept of a power greater than ourselves. This faith has proven to be a valuable gift (yes, it is on my gratitude list and should be on yours also). My faith is not static by any means. It is a growing, changing internal strength that makes my life fun, happy, joyous and free. My days are all care free because of my faith. **I know that everything that happens is supposed to happen no matter what I think at the time.** Down the road, sometimes years later, I say "Ahh ha that's why that happened. I thought it was a bad thing and it turned out perfect, thank you God."

I don't know about you but for me my faith was zero when I started my program. All those members having a good time at my first meeting started the ball rolling on faith. They had stayed sober for years and were happy about it. So I had faith they were telling the truth and not only were they successful, but they wanted to help me and I believed them. That faith paid big dividends right from day one. They taught me about prayer so I did it. My faith began to have steel beams. I had faith God would provide and when I needed to find work desperately, I prayed and the phone rang immediately. Wow. Then life became a dream once I did all 12 Steps and started sponsoring people. I could see, graphically, faith in a Higher Power is well founded and became part of my solid foundation on which to rebuild my life all new. Today my faith grows and is an active part of my program. **Have faith enough in yourself to believe that you really have enough faith to move mountains.** It's time to spread your wings. Once you were a caterpillar and now you are a butterfly with freedom to fly anywhere you wish.

"You have come a long way, baby." Your faith can take you to new horizons you richly deserve. So, go move a mountain or two. Only you can limit you.

January 16

ACTION FROM GRATITUDE

You all probably think I will never stop talking about my gratitude list. You would be right. That list is just as important as my copy of the Big Book. I use both daily. I like to think of prayer as my spark plugs to fire up my engine every morning and the 64 items on my gratitude list are my pistons, my own Higher-Powered engine to spur me into action.

My list is not productive if I just gaze at it as nice to possess all these gifts. No sir, the list is part of my action plan to inspire me to do some good during the next 24 hours. I check my list.

I have "family" on it and it reminds me to pray for my sister having a cancer node removed. I'm sending her an encouraging message right now.

I have "friends" on my list. One of my close friends has been in a bad mood and acting out in anger. I plan on bring him a cup of his favorite tea to the meeting this morning and have funny opening line to try to cheer him up and have a decent conversation.

On my list is "health." I have been drinking 3 cups of coffee every day, which is a great improvement from 5, but today why not cut down to 2 for better health? Not so much the caffeine as the cream and sugar.

See I have some good stuff for my plan today by using my gratitude list as a prompt.

My point is, my list is from my past, but it is all about progressing into the future today. When I say the 11th Step prayer (the spark) I have looked at my gratitude list and fired up pistons, "family," "friends" and "health" and that is just a sample. In my daily 10th Step I can see where I need to make some positive adjustments but also, I did some things very well, so my negatives are switched to positives. My positives give me confidence I am on the right path and need to continue. A newcomer from Russia was in the meeting yesterday and I was inspired to show her a blank 3 X 5 card. She gave me a blank look. I asked her if she had ever done a gratitude list. She had never heard of such a thing. Imagine that. I pulled out my list and we started filling in her list. We managed to fill in her card up with about 20 items. I was giving explanations with each line item. "What's that?" (Language disconnect) "Self-esteem I tell her." OK I am not there yet." The whole process was 12 Step work, carrying the message and I was delighted to have a new gratitude list customer. Encounters such as this one lights my fire.

My message is that gratitude is not only progressive but contagious and seems to have a multiplier effect.

January 17

FASTING

Many of the great religious leaders have advocated fasting of all sorts.
Some health experts offer ideas on fasting from food and water. I
remember in the old days when I needed to take a physical once a year
and I was required to fast from food and drink from 8 p.m. until the
medical folks took my blood at 7 a.m. the next morning. I hated not
having my coffee to start the day, so I carried a thermos and poured
myself a cup while the blood was still coming out. It drove the MedTech
crazy. But worse was the no alcohol ban for 24 hours before the physical
and in later years I just couldn't comply with that fasting rule. Nobody
ever called me on it, so I shortened my "fast' to just a few hours and even
that was tough. My spiritual readings are talking about a different type of
fasting altogether; mental fasting. This is a new concept for me and I
have tried it and really recommend giving it a try. This is a fast from
problems, negative thinking and bad encounters with others,
nonproductive reading and viewing. In other words, fasting from fear-
based inputs is not spiritual in nature. You try to consume only that
which is love based and keeps you in the Sunlight.

I start my day by prayer and meditation being careful not to turn on the
TV or the computer. The first hour is always positive, spiritual, gratitude
based and thus love centered. I need to communicate with my family, but
I screen the method. I don't buy into what the computer pops in my face.
Another school shooting with a teenager armed with automatic rifles
opens upon his classmates. How is this going to help me? What can I
learn from this news? How does this make me feel? OK this news will
not do a thing for my soul. There is nothing to learn and it makes me sick
to my stomach. All negative inputs. I choose to fast from this garbage. In
fact, love news is very hard to find. Even a wedding in the UK, the news
is about 3 ladies wearing the same dress and a sideways glance from one
royal member to another. Do I need to know this? Where is the love?
You will not find it by watching the news or the internet. OK people.
There is one guy who turns red in the face at the sight of me. I fast from
this guy. I cross the street and go to places that greet me with a smile and

a nice word or two. I do spend time with a friend who laughs and jokes with me. I enjoy the positive inputs.

When you are in the midst of a problem, the idea is to take a "fast" from the problem and stop thinking about it and pray. Ask God for help. Then you will be amazed at how the problem either disappears or a simple solution presents itself. Try it, you will like it.

January 18

FEELING EITHER FEAR OR LOVE

The more I study spiritual principles, the simpler they seem to be. People are looking for the secrets of life and there are no "secrets" but the obvious seems to pass us by without notice. My latest reading had me thinking for 2 days now and I am amazed at the simplicity of the following true statement: **"Really there are only two feelings that a human being can have, namely love and fear. All other feelings, so-called, will turn out upon analysis to be either love or fear." (Emmet Fox, *Around the Year*, May 20)** What? Can it be that simple? What about anger, hatred, jealousy, criticism, egotism? Fear, fear, fear is the root. I look at my own ego trips for a sample. When I was self-promoting, I was trying to prove I was the better of my peers, I feared I would not get the recognition I thought I deserved. I almost got myself killed by my ego trip all based on fear. I had to beat my own drum so as to be noticed for fear of losing respect. Ego is all about fear when you boil it down to basics. I have been looking for an exception to feelings not love based or fear based. I am stumped. It is simple. Once I am in the realm of "fear" then I am out of the Sunlight. I am in the dark side of negative thinking. Yikes.

 I wake up with an overwhelming feeling of gratitude every morning. Gratitude = Love. Love is one line item of the 44 on my gratitude list but when I examine my list all 43 other items are rooted in love. My prayers are positive (Love again) my meditation is positive (Love) my readings are all spiritual in nature and full of love, happiness joy freedom. OMG I am a love bug for sure. Fox goes on to say: "**Joy, interest, the feeling of success and accomplishments, the appreciation of art, are allotrope forms of love. The great difference between the two feelings is that love is always creative, and fear is always destructive. It is for us to decide which of these two feelings shall hold sway in our lives.** If you keep this in mind and look at our 12 Steps you can easily see the love side and not one fear step. The only thing I can control is my attitude, so I make sure it is positive and soaked in love, then my thoughts are positive happy thoughts and from all that comes action. I pray that all my actions have a love base.

I want the rest of my life to be creative, useful and helpful to others. Subtraction of all my fears will help me reach my goal. My first 50 years were all fear driven so I hope the next 50 are all love driven.

January 19

FORGET ABOUT IT ALREADY

Since resentments are the number one killer for us alcoholics, we need to focus our attention on forgiveness in equal measure. If we really want to be happy, joyous and free we must master this art of forgiveness or we cannot stand in the Sunlight of the Spirit. I have heard and am sure you have also the phrase: forgive but don't forget. I heartily disagree with that philosophy. If we want total freedom, forget about it already. If we don't wipe it off the board then, to my way of thinking, it is only partial forgiveness. I hear the words of forgiveness but does that forgiveness come from the heart or just in speech? Not only does it need to be heartfelt but wiped from the mind, so it does not come back to life later on. I have had many opportunities for forgiveness and I don't review the event again. It is gone forever. The problem with resentments is that it goes both ways. Both sides have a part thus forgiveness has two parts also. The stream flows both ways.

I had a significant spiritual experience in 2002 when I made my amends trip to Vietnam and Laos. I traveled 2,000 miles in both countries to all the places I lived and fought. Some places I lived for a year and others I was there less than a day. In combat, sometimes a day is a lifetime. I was not proud of some of my behavior in those places under the umbrella of war. I fully expected to find hatred from my former enemies and some backlash from being an American military guy coming back to the place I had inflicted great damage. To my surprise that was not the case. I found my adversaries not only to be forgiving but to be loving. "Love thy enemies," where have I heard that before? It freed up my soul in ways I cannot explain, and it affected me so much I decided to live here. I had a huge resentment against the Vietnamese for torturing my fellow pilots, but I learned in their culture once you are captive you are no longer a human being with human rights. It was not easy, but I had to let it go and forgive my fellow military adversaries as they had forgiven me.

All the spiritual leaders stress forgiveness as necessary. It is addressed clearly in the 11th Step Prayer I say every morning. Forgiveness has been part of my recovery for so long I forgive everybody in advance.

January 20

STATUS QUO

"If it's not broke don't fix it" is a nice cute phrase for your car but in recovery this does not apply. It is broke, and it needs daily fixing or else we get into trouble big time. I remember in my first year I felt so good I just wanted to stop and chill out. Like, "Hey dude don't change anything, stay where you are in this happy zone and enjoy the cruise." That attitude was almost fatal to my recovery. You are moving away from your last drink or you are moving toward the next drink, but you are moving, like it or not. If you plan on treading water in this program you might drown. Your disease is progressive, so our recovery must be progressive, or we are floating downstream into troubled waters. If you skip one meeting, no problem; skip two, no problem...oops. This alcoholism is like the creeping crud. It sneaks up behind you and smacks you in the head. For me, I do Step work every day, no exceptions, no resting. If I needed to take one pill a day to stay alive, I would not miss taking that pill. Well, my spiritual routine is keeping me on the path, so I am not going to forget to take my medicine.

The big problem with this disease is it is telling you, you are OK you don't have a problem. Don't believe the lie. I see a lot of members with 30 and 40 years of sobriety get into the "elite" status and leave the service work to the young ones. They stop sponsoring pain in the butt newcomers, they stop reading the literature. They are staying sober but become preachers and forget they are equal to the newly sober. For me, I seek new literature to spark my brain in the spiritual learning business. I want new ideas to spice up my words to you guys and not say the same stuff over and over. If I am done learning, then I am done. The more I learn the more I define my ignorance. I do not have the answers, but I seek God in other people and in the world around me to receive the hidden messages in every cloud, every flower, every creature. I want to keep moving forward, keep learning, keep finding new ways to help others. The status quo is not for me. This process of newness has a side benefit of keeping me young and fresh.

"Inaction rots the vigor of the mind." (Da Vinci). Understanding God is a lifetime endeavor and there is so much more to learn I need to keep busy and get closer to God before the last curtain.

January 21

THE DEATH GRIP

I learned a long time ago to let go and let God. Having a death grip on anything will result in poor results. How about this quote: **"Love is like an egg, the more you squeeze the more you lose."** This is so true raising kids. You want the best for them but if you have a death grip on their activities you might choke out the growth they need. Letting your children make their own mistakes is tough when you know a better way. My kids grew up just super fine without my monkey wrench twisting their lives. In love relationships I made every mistake in the book using a death grip on my mate until they made an escape. What was supposed to be love, turned into a hostage situation. My poor young wife was stuck in a little 28 X 8 foot trailer with no car or money and pregnant. I couldn't figure out why she was crying all the time. Ten feet of snow outside the door and I was at work 16 hours a day. I put my needs over common sense. I had no business getting married without any resources and taking her to a God forsaken part of Maine. When I went to college I forced her to go to college also. I had to let go of that one when she quit the first day and was home with her feet up smoking a cigarette. It took her awhile, but she made her break for freedom.

When I was a kid I was fascinated by butterflies. I noticed when I caught one they would fold in half and stop moving. If I held them too long they died and the beauty of the butterfly was lost. I think nature has messages from God and the message here is leave the butterfly alone to fly free and share its beauty with all who can see its flight. Same with some flowers, if you touch them it shortens their life and some delicate ones die altogether. When I was learning how to fly an airplane, I was going to make that piece of machinery do what I wanted it to do. So I had a death grip on the stick. My teeth were clenched. My legs were at full power against the rudder and I had the throttle in my white-knuckle grasp. I pushed the beast around with my neck muscles about to pop. The instructor told me to let go of everything. He told me to take my hands off the stick and throttle, put my feet flat on the floor. You could almost hear the aircraft give a sigh of relief. It flew straight and level all by itself without my input, just great. I never forgot that lesson and the one piece of instruction taught me to be a top pilot. I let God run the controls in my life today and let go of my old ways.

Some of us have a death grip on some of our character defects and refuse to pry our fingers off the choke hold. I pray to God to help me let go.

LAUGHTER THE BEST MEDICINE

Life would be pretty dull without some laughs every day. I have read how a good laugh is good for your health. I know for sure it is good for my heart and mind. Having a good sense of humor is not something you learn but a character asset either you have or you don't. In my experience it is a by-product of a happy life and being right sized. Rule 62 "Don't take yourself too seriously." We are the biggest joke of all. I remember my first meeting where I stood on the outside viewing the group before the meeting started. They were hugging and laughing, two things that seemed very strange to me. This sober thing is serious stuff I thought. Thank God I was wrong 100%. I gave them a good laugh by my stupidity during that first meeting and some members still talk about it. Soon I was laughing along with my home group and it made the hard work of getting started on the road to recovery much more enjoyable. The meeting before the meeting is always a fun time to joke around.

I like Victor Borges's quote, "The shortest distance between two people is laughter." It breaks down tension and levels the field. It is a great ice breaker. Everyone's sense of humor is as different as our fingerprints. It is a non-hostile communication as long as harm is not intended. Humor can be negative if it is used to berate or humiliate and hurt someone. Sarcasm is not funny in my opinion. When I work with someone, I try to make them laugh and put them at ease. Laughter is a big fear reducer and opens the mind. I cannot sing but I can laugh. Laughter is my song. Laughter lingers on with a super aftertaste that is sweet. I put cream and sugar in my coffee so laughter is the cream and sugar of my life. It takes out the bitterness. Laughter liberates my soul and makes my troubles shrink. When I think fondly of someone I think about their laugh and that makes me closer to them and their memory.

When I was a kid, we got Reader's Digest and they had a little 2-page article called, "Laughter Is the Best Medicine." And if I read nothing else, I read that. Try it, you will feel better. I promise you.

NO SECRETS

The 5th Step is so important that most advisors say you might not be able to achieve long term sobriety without doing a complete 5th Step. There are no secrets too bad not to cough up when you do your 5th Step. Holding back is not a good idea I have found in my experience. I saw folks who just can't tell their deepest darkest secrets and carry them to the grave. They are denying themselves complete freedom. For sure God knows and you know so just one more part of the step is required. When I hear a 5th Step I say, "OK tell me what you don't want to tell me and get the worst out on the table first." I have done enough of these to tell if my boy is holding back or not. Alcoholics know when we are getting BS since we all are expert BSers. I usually start with questions like "Did you murder anyone?" Of course not so the rest is easy dude. Let's drop the bag right here and now. That 4th Step is heavy and this 5th Step is going to take the weight right off of your soul, heart and mind. It might hurt but you will feel so good when you finish.

The person you do your 5th Step with is someone you feel confident will be open minded and keep your secrets. Most people use their sponsor, but it does not require a sponsor, just another human being. I cannot stress the importance of doing a total job too much. I have seen cases of long term sobriety members going out after 15 to 20 years all because there is a secret or two buried in the inventory that didn't come out. In my case, I found I needed to go back after a few years and do an additional 5th Step because I had forgotten whole episodes. (It was a function of coming to sobriety late in life.) If I go to meetings regularly I really do a mini 5th Step when I share at meetings. I share my recent failings, resentments and character defects as they pop up in my daily living. I love sleeping with the angels and I can't do that if I have a dark part of my heart and mind. I want a clean slate all the time. It helps my goal of weightlessness.

After a whole career of secrets behind the green door, I love blue sky, clean air and an open heart free of any garbage from the past. Ahhh.

January 24

JUST DO IT

I use the Nike tagline when I work with somebody on the 4th Step. **JUST DO IT.** Had one guy ask what type writing instrument should he use? What weight paper? What color? He stalled until he quit and never did stay sober. I know I was guilty of procrastination and that's why I preach to get into motion. The 4th Step is the first time you actually do anything! This process is the heart of getting all the way to Step 9 all in one action of beginning your inventory. This document is what you will use for your 5th Step, your character defects will be in living color for Steps 6 and 7. Your 8th Step, list of persons harmed, is part of your 4th Step inventory. This is key to a big chunk of your recovery.

What I recommend to my guys is use a legal-size pad and start with the first thing in time that you did, like steal candy from the 7-11 store when you were 6 years old. Put the person or persons involved in one column. Use a timeline from as far back as you can remember to the present. **You might as well start now because your inventory will not get any smaller. The longer you wait the more inventory you will have.**

The next point is to write it. I made the mistake of letting one person do it on the computer. It was a bad idea. The voice recordings not a winner either. **The physical act of writing your inventory on paper gets it out of your head and that takes the power out of the wrongs we have done.** I know of no shortcuts to putting pen to paper. Just do it. Seeing it in writing clears out the fog you have been in for years

OK when? My recommendation is in the morning after your prayer and meditation when you have no special time for your next event. Like a weekend with nothing else on your schedule. If you get a good flow going you want to keep up a head of steam until you run out of gas. I also recommend you read the 4th Step prayer.

"Dear God,

It is I who has made my life a mess. I have done it, but I cannot undo it. My mistakes are mine, and I will begin a searching and fearless moral inventory. I will write down my wrongs, but I will also include that which is good. I pray for the strength to complete the task."

It has been my experience that once you get started it will flow along. After the first session, sleep on it and pray some more. Then round two will go smoother and if you are not interrupted you will know when you can say "complete." This process will set you free. Trust me.

January 25

SHINE YOUR LIGHT

The great thing about this recovery business is the visible change to the unspoken messages of your face, your actions and your demeanor. I remember from childhood the saying "don't hide your light under a bushel." If I soak my morning in prayer and meditation my face has a glow, so says my best friend. What we are inside our heart just naturally comes to the surface. If we are happy, joyous and free it shows. We smile. We laugh. Our eyes are bright and loving. This program is good for the complexion and your health too. When we do our inventory, we get right sized and all the acting is over, the masks are in the garbage. We are the real deal. We need not say one word and people can read us like a teleprompter. You put out signals "approach with caution," "leave me alone," "come talk to me I am approachable," "I am in a bad mood today," "I am happy to see you," all get transmitted as soon as you enter the room. I always say it is interesting in AA rooms to see members enter and without a word they say "Look who's here" OR "Hey here I am." Like it or not you do shine something, so hopefully it is light.

We all know somebody we admire by their humility or kind acts. My all-time hero is my Aunt Jerry. She did not have a selfish bone in her body. I never ever saw her do anything for herself. I observed her at family functions and she was in 100% service role. She did not sit down and chit chat, she was cooking, cleaning and tending to everyone's needs and requests. At Thanksgiving she would not eat until everyone else had their fill. Then she would find a quiet corner and have a small dish of leftovers. She was totally dedicated to the welfare of her family, three sons and their families too. I never heard her say one bad word, ever. I never heard her gossip or talk bad about anybody. It just was not in her makeup to have ill will about anything or anybody. She was a saint and everybody loved her. Her sister, my mother, was just the opposite. Why am I telling you this story? My Aunt Jerry wrote me a letter dated March 3, 1993 which I still have. She said, "Michael you need to do something about your drinking" If it was anybody else I would tear up the letter and curse the sender but coming from her it turned me around and I accepted the fact I needed to get help. Her light shined on me. The rest is history.

The point is that to be helpful to others the lights need to be on to attract the person needing help. I work on getting closer to God every day to improve my heart and my manner, my actions, my face will follow.

January 26

FLYING BLIND

When you fly from A to B it is not anywhere you damn please, it is at a specific altitude and on a very narrow radio beam heading. It is not the wild blue yonder at all. It may be in total darkness and thick clouds, flying blind. Following your instruments carefully will insure safety and you will not run into another object, like a mountain. Some faith is required. Faith that you have the skill to follow instrument rules, faith that the instructions from the ground are correct and faith your instruments are working properly. If you stray too far from your assigned flight path or designated altitude the ground controllers will violate you and you may even lose your license to fly. You see where I am going with this?

In our recovery we need to stay on the beam. There are some spiritual truths we need to follow to insure safe travel down the road of recovery.

At times we cannot see the road ahead for whatever reason and our faith in our Higher Power guides us in times of "blindness." The Steps lead us in the right direction, and if we are off the beam, the road gets rocky and speed bumps knock us off the Path. If we are angry and harbor resentments we are in the weather, blinded by our negative thinking. In those times we need to go to the basics, pray, go to meetings and share your feelings. Talk to your sponsor and other members. Get back on the beam as soon as possible.

We have all kinds of laws we know to be true, the law of gravity, in our program we say "If you don't take the first drink you won't get drunk," a simple rule but all who go out have forgotten the basic law. Back a few years ago a 4-star general named "Big George" took off in a jet with his aide in the back seat. He was so arrogant he thought he could outrank aerodynamics and rolled the aircraft right after takeoff and crashed a 12-million-dollar machine and scattered body parts all over the Saturday morning shoppers at the end of the runway. **"For us to drink is to die"** If we forget the laws we will be in the same boat as Big George.

This recovery business requires some discipline and compliance with spiritual principle. My daily morning meditation keeps me on the beam and if I stray it only takes small adjustments to find the center of the Road.

January 27

LOOSEN UP

It was kind of a surprise to see the Emmet Fox topic of "Loosen Up" since he is from the 1930's thinking. His point is, **"to be tense is the surest way to fail in any undertaking great or small."** This is very profound and so true. It applies to recovery also.

All I need to do is put in small gentle inputs and loosen up. Same in sports. When I first took up golf I was doing great with no lessons, no teacher, but I got to thinking I was very good at this game and began adjusting my grip, watching my feet placement and soon I was terrible and my score got a lot worse. Super athletes are almost effortless at their craft. Being uptight at anything dooms us to failure.

So it goes with the program. We want to progress on the road to recovery, but if we become impatient, we lose heart and our enthusiasm. Many meeting rooms have a sign **Easy Does It** which reminds me it took decades to cause all the damage I did and I am not going to fix it overnight. In fact, the rest of my life might not be enough. I see in my spiritual reading the saying **"Wear the World as a Loose Garment"** and that reminds me not to be uptight about the ills of the world around me. I am powerless over wars, hurricanes and murder. If I worry about the bad news around me then it's like an anchor tied to my butt. A lot of how loose we can be is in our personality. The Type A personality who is aggressive, impatient, assertive and controlling has much difficulty staying loose. (Guilty as charged.) Or Type B personality who is not a leader but does not get upset readily and much more laid back than a Type A. As a recovering control freak I work hard on letting live and letting go of my standards as applied to others. My definition of what is "right" is not shared with everyone else. If I push my agenda it brings retaliation from my fellows. I must remember that everything that happens is supposed to happen no matter what I think. Go with the flow. My days of paddling upstream are over, I hope.

If you can treat your activities as fun and accept difficulties as part of the game, then you can enjoy life so much more.

January 28

GOD'S BANK

The problem with money is there is never enough or if there is, you are afraid of losing it. Fear seems to go along with money one way or another. The Promises really addresses fear and not the amount of money you have or don't have. The path of recovery is all about getting in touch with your Higher Power and trusting Him for everything including financial wellbeing. I can tell you with 100% assurance; spiritual wellbeing happens first then financial woes go away later. When I first got sober my debt was staggering. I was using 12 credit cards like smoke and mirrors and was only paying interest at bare minimums. The chickens were about to roost, and my biggest fear was to crash and burn because of $350,000 in the red. I saddled up to a guy in the program who was a millionaire and showed him my numbers. Surely, he would come to my rescue. I said, "Frank look at my situation here, I am screwed." He looked carefully and said, "Yeah Mike you are screwed." Big lesson here. You have to be self-supporting and maybe do a stint in the streets but other AA members are not going to bail you out nor should they. I have seen a lot of bad blood between AA members over money borrowed or owed, it was ugly stuff.

I tightened my belt, went to meetings, did the Steps and after a morning meeting I sat in my living room, soon to be gone, and said out loud, "Dear God I cannot go another day without a job." And the phone rang. It was a former student of mine who remembered I had some safety experience and his construction company needed a safety engineer for a large highway project. I went down to the trailer where the project manager's office was for an interview. The big boss looked at my resume and commented that he needed a guy with at least 5 years of construction safety experience. I took a deep breath...this is a program of rigorous honesty...right? My program kicked in. I said, "I really don't have construction experience but I have 28 years of destruction experience." He almost fell on the floor laughing and I was hired on the spot starting the next morning. See prayer works. Slowly I crawled out of my horrible debt as I kept up my spiritual program. That job led to another one right after the construction was finished. Today my bank book is my gratitude list. That's where all the riches are listed. That is the real deal in value. Possessions and money is just stuff. I am only a steward of some stuff and that is temporary.

I bank at God's bank, always open 24/7, and all my needs are met at His bank. My balance sheet/gratitude list shows me I am indeed quite wealthy.

January 29

IS YOUR SHADOW CROOKED?

I just love proverbs and here is one of my favorites from the Chinese: **"If you are standing upright, do not worry if your shadow is crooked."** What we are and what people think of us can be quite different. I would add to the proverb, "standing upright and doing the next right thing." I now know the only person I really need to impress is myself. I need to be happy with what I do, how I act, where I am headed and be at peace in my heart. Other people are going to judge me and declare my shadow crooked indeed but how they judge me is none of my business. In my professional life what others thought of me determined if I got promoted and continued climbing the corporate ladder. I would do things I didn't want to do in order to fit the mold expected of me and bend myself into a pretzel to gain approval by my bosses and peers. When I looked back on my past I realized I was a total imposter. I wasn't who I said I was, I wasn't who I wanted to be. I had so many masks I lost my real self and my self-respect. I didn't like what I had become and was not in touch with reality or the proper image of myself. My 4th and 5th Step set me straight.

Today I am where I want to be, doing the best I can with the daily help of my Higher Power. My shadow is not important. In my group there is one member who is anti-American and anti-military. You can guess where I stand with this dude. When I share, he either closes his eyes or rolls them. He has not spoken to me in 5 years and we go to the same coffee shop every morning. Once a year I say hello and last year he made a guttural noise so who knows maybe someday he might respond. I am very happy with this relationship and when he shares in a meeting I can't hear or understand his accent so it's all good. However, I do dress appropriately, shave and come to meetings early. Why? To show that newcomer I care about this program. I am approachable and available. I joke and show my happiness with the way I act. Every guy I sponsored has made some kind of judgment of me and my program before asking me to sponsor them. My shadow is important only to help others. I am not running for political office. I don't have to be a phony anymore. If I

34

get your approval that's great and if I don't that's OK too.

Some egos require a shadow even after death. When you die there is no more shadow, but some egotistical people are worried about their legacy into perpetuity. That's why our traditions ask that no group be named after any person living or dead. Good idea, aye?

January 30

NEED A MIRACLE?

Most people think of miracles as the parting of the Red Sea. To me we are surrounded by small miracles every day. A miracle is something that happens outside the laws of order and reason. An example out of my own life, I was flying in a hostile combat environment with no place friendly to land. Survival questionable. I landed at an enemy held airfield rather than crash land. Survival not possible. I was out of gas, another big problem. I found one gas barrel; it was a small miracle but I had no tool to open the machine's tight seal. I fashioned a tool with the butt of my gun to open that barrel and was able to fuel the plane. Prayer had begun long before I made up my mind to land under fire at this place. Several things happened in a certain order that allowed me to escape with my life along with a Lao observer and the airplane. I was listed as dead in some circles and missing in others. All agree it was a miracle which happened back in 1969.

More recently a neighbor had given birth very prematurely to twin girls. One did not survive, and the second girl was 2 inches and a couple of ounces, sort of like a tiny mouse. This little miniature person spent 6 months in an incubator and now today is a quite normal 3-year-old girl. The doctors gave zero chance of survival, but this cute smart little lady is a delight to see and watch grow up. A miracle of a great gift to the family and all who prayed for a good result.

If you are in the need of a miracle, I suggest you start with prayer. I am alive today because my prayers were answered many times over, I know prayer works. I have no doubts about that. In 1979 I was in the hands of an enemy bound and determined to kill me. Again, prayer was the key factor in my second hostile escape. You need not look any further than the mirror to look a miracle in the eye. Think about how many alcoholics don't know there is a different path available. How many other alcoholics are going to die a miserable death without any hope of a happy life? You and I are a very small minority of the total population of alcoholics that are in recovery. We are not only recovery but a whole new wonderful path with a spiritual design for living. A miracle I would call it for sure. I find a lot of "coincidences" are God's way of being anonymous but sending another miracle for us to witness if we would just open our minds to accept these "fortunate events." God is doing for us what we cannot do for ourselves. I believe there is a message from God in every rock and leaf and I try to receive His messages in whatever form they come.

I enjoy life as it unfolds because I know everything that happens is supposed to happen. I expect miracles and I find them all the time. It is the spice of my life.

January 31

I AM MAKING MYSELF SICK

When I was a kid in grade school, when I was afraid of a test coming up in school I could make myself sick. My temperature would be high enough my mother would let me stay home. It was her I was afraid of and the repercussions if I did poorly. Fear made me sick. We all know that Body, Mind and Spirit are all connected and if one system goes haywire the other two soon follow. If you are sick or prone to being sick you might ask yourself the question, "Am I the one making me sick?" We all have a part in it for sure. If I feed my mind nothing but bad news, then soon I am bad news. If I read all about sickness, soon I itch and feel woozy. The internet stuff about health is crap. "If you have one of these seven symptoms you will die soon." Delete. In my morning meditation I feel great because in the morning it is the best I am going to be all day. I am rested, my mind is clear, my motives are pure and I am too happy to permit the presence of trouble.

No better case study than my son Mike. He was diagnosed with ALS early 2011 and he accepted the fact it was a fatal, no cure disease. He was in a test group of 25 ALS patients for some trial drugs. 60% were dead after two years and the rest were all dead by year four except my son. The doctors were amazed and wanted to do all kinds of tests on Mike's body to determine why he was still alive. First of all, Mike said he is the head decision maker on his medical team and he would not allow these biopsies to be done. He told them, "How are you going to test my attitude?" He was right on. His attitude of positive thinking, stress free activities and surrounded himself with love, friends and family. He made it to April 2017 which is some kind of record. His mind and spirit carried his body many extra wonderful days and years.

If you keep talking about your aches and pains, you will ensure that you will always have them as you enjoy rehearsing them. The body will try to heal itself. If I stay busy and get out of myself and my ills God restores my body back to good health.

February 1

IMAGINATION

Einstein said that "Imagination is more important than knowledge." Nothing comes to be unless it is imagined first. The Golden Gate Bridge had to be imagined before it could be built. Cars and planes had to be imagined before they were invented. Actually, Ben Hur could have raced around the track in Rome in a Thunderbird if they could have imagined it back then, but limited thinking made it take a lot longer. The rules of aerodynamics were as true in 100 B.C. as they are today, but it took until 1903 to "imagine" manned flight. So it goes with our limited thinking. We can't produce what we can't imagine. When I was drinking my imagination was warped. I thought all the flashing lights outside my door meant the Prize Patrol was delivering my $10 million when it was the cops with a warrant for my arrest. When I was a kid, I had a super hyperactive imagination but over time it got crushed by failure, disappointments, my parents, my teachers and finally alcohol squashed my ability to imagine. My imagination turned into nightmares. When I hit bottom, imagination was just another thing that went blowing in the wind.

To take a real example out of my own life, I became a jet pilot through imagination. By a fluke I got a ride in a jet trainer T-33 aircraft while I was in college. I was given a chance to fly the machine and enjoyed myself to the point I made up my mind to be a pilot. I was scheduled to be a logistics guy and was sent to college for that assignment. The big hurdle was to convince the Air Force to switch my assignment and prove I was qualified medically and pass a pilot mental score test. I went against all odds to find a way to make my case. I kept the image alive and through luck and some help from the medical staff, I got into pilot training and became a top gun. Little did I know at the time, as a "normie" that becoming a pilot led me down the road to become a full-blown alcoholic. After that happened my imagination went into hibernation along with any other kind of growth. Now in sobriety my imagination can come back into play as part of my life. I have from day one imagined long-term sobriety and it has come to be a reality. I imagined a wonderful relationship with a near perfect lady and that has happened too. I imagined a great relationship with all my family and that is 90% true also.

Now when I hit a rough spot, a negative thought or a budding resentment, I imagine God, usually through nature, and it works wonders in channeling my imagination toward God and His will.

February 2

THE KEY

When I sat in the deep dark bottom, I created for myself, my options were bleak. If I continued to drink, death was knocking at the door, yet I had to drink in order to function. I could not, not drink I had to keep going. I thought I could just drink myself to death but even that didn't work. I just got sick without the benefits of being drunk. I was painted into the corner with no way out. Stopping was impossible. Suicide looked like a way out, but my value system screamed at me I did not have that right. I was screwed. My ex-wife to be was pushing me into treatment and that sounded absolutely disgusting. God sent me a tiny sliver of light called willingness; the key. Of course, at the time I had no idea that this little tiny bit of willingness was the key to open the door to recovery. It was just like "guess I will try this since I have no other brilliant ideas of how I am going to get out of this mess I am in." At my first meeting I was not really willing and almost made my escape when my soon to be sponsor grabbed me before I could make a run for the exit. That first hour in AA swung the door of willingness wide open never to close again.

Needless to say, "Willingness" is on my gratitude list because without it I would not be writing to you. Most likely I would be a distant memory of a few family members. Then with that tiny start I was willing to do the Steps, I was willing to do whatever it takes to not only stay sober but to grow up with a new set of principles. A "do over" God granted me, a gift I certainly did not deserve. You can't buy a pound of willingness, unfortunately. Either you have it or you don't. If your mind is closed and you say, "I can't." Then you can't. End of discussion. I keep that in mind when I work with others. If my prospect has a closed mind, I am wasting my time and his. But if I detect a hint of willingness then I press on to try to help. There is a story about how small a mustard seed is, and once it grows a mighty tree is the result. I liken my recovery to the mustard seed that got nourished by the fruits of this program. My tree is a couple of decades old and can take care of storms and high winds. My willingness has grown and grown some more over time.

Since willingness worked so well in getting me on the Road of Happy Destiny then why not have willingness to try new adventures, try new skills, and open some doors which were closed because my mind was closed.

February 3

CHANGING DECK CHAIRS ON THE TITANIC

On a Southwest flight one passenger asked to change his seat. The flight attendant loudly told him, "Sir, all the seats will arrive in LA at the same time." It reminded me of an old timer share about us alcoholics often switching chairs on the Titanic. Dropping one obsession just to take up a new one will still put us to the bottom of the ocean. I can only speak for myself, but it is very clear I am an obsessive person. My entire life has been extremes, super highs and horrible bottoms. In my young life I was obsessed by climbing the ladder of success. Well I did that, but at what cost? It was a heavy price for my family as I stole time from them in pursuit of the brass ring. I just could not figure out why I was so empty inside when I had the beautiful blonde by my side, a luxury car, fame and plenty of money. My obsession lacked any spirituality and thus the ship went into the icy waters. Of course, alcohol was part of my culture and duh, that went too far also. The big problem with obsessions is you don't see it the way others see it.

When some of us put down the drink we pick up something else. Food, sweets and smoking are more common and of course to excess is bad for us but not as bad a picking up another drink. My doctor tried to put me on valium and the treatment center raised hell and said I am trading one addiction for another. I am happy I never took drugs because knowing myself I would be an addict. Even luckier, I never learned how to smoke because I was track team guy. OMG the pain of stopping smoking I see in others makes me so grateful my obsessive self-did not even touch a joint. All my other obsessions, like being a serial groom, were enough to work on for the rest of my life. I became an adrenaline junkie and I did so many dangerous things to get my "fix" and that almost killed me. However, I went back for more and volunteered for special ops missions nobody wanted because they were sane. Today I am off the adrenaline, food, booze and racing cars.

I accept my obsessive nature and have turned my obsessions into prayer and meditation, attendance at meetings, service and helping others. I am very obsessed with AA and it works for me.

40

February 4

WHO AM I?

Sounds like a simple question: who am I? In my own fog, at my bottom, I had no clue as how to answer that question. Layers of my disease took me so far away from reality for so many decades I lost the real person I was. The thought of doing a personal inventory was like Greek. I would have gone my entire life without ever doing self-examination if I did not find the rooms of AA. The first time I saw Step 4, I was baffled by the necessity of a "moral inventory." I had spent most of my adult life behind a façade of some sort, like a uniform that said, "I am authority, I am boss, I am a leader" and in reality, I was none of those things but I had been filling those roles for so long I believed it myself. Self-deceit is the worst lie of all. I couldn't handle the truth. My false roles were much better than the real deal for sure. Down deep I knew I was a fraud. My mission was not to be exposed. The actor in me was doing a pretty good job until the alcoholic incidents pulled down the curtain on my play acting. My boss said. "What the hell are you doing in my company?" You got me dude.

We all have learned we need to change the person we were when we were practicing our disease. OK, change from what to what? The need to view graphically our entire inventory becomes a necessary part of the process of change. Once I saw the list of resentments closely akin to a telephone book and wreckage of a bulldozer in a demolition derby I saw the mountain I needed to climb. Just the willingness to change was a good enough start and reality slowly became obvious through all the fog. That bag I was carrying around for decades suddenly got lighter and that encouraged me to press on and do a complete job. I knew, no matter how painful it was, that this was good for my recovery, good for my soul. One action that made a big step in doing my inventory is going into my den where a whole wall was full of awards, plaques of accomplishments and photos of me next to jets and shaking hands with important people. It had nothing to do with the real me anymore, so I boxed up the whole batch and trashed all the trappings of the past. I said this is now and I am just another bozo on the bus trying to stay sober and improve my life.

Today I know who I am. I am the right size. No more masks to wear, no more acting, no more inflated ego. That's freedom.

February 5

EQUALITY

One of the most attractive aspects of our program is no one person is better than another. We are all alcoholics with only today as our sobriety. No matter how many years of continuous sobriety we are one arm's length away from a drink. No boss, no president, even our sponsor is just another alcoholic not our superior. I came from a background of a very ridged pecking order. If someone was of higher rank, he was automatically better than me and could order me around. Of course, I was better than everyone below my rank. If we had the same rank then we would have to check date of rank to see who was boss. Terrible system. In AA we all have the same date of rank...TODAY. I guess it is human nature to form a pecking order to see where you fit on the "better than and less than scale" The neighbors drive luxury cars so they must have more money. Most of us come from a material world where we line ourselves up by wealth and not good spiritual qualities. We have already learned the lesson about possessions and a fit spiritual condition.

Equality is a basic spiritual principle. I am reading Emmet Fox and he goes to great length to explain the relationship all of us have with one another. We are all joined together as part of the whole. Children of God are all equal in every way. That is why the AA principle of all-inclusive, no leaders, only trusted servants works so well. Some trusted servants think they are more "trusted" than others and become arrogant in their service roles. That huge ego we all came into the program with will rear its ugly head occasionally. Our program, at it's very base, has a key spiritual principle that can change our lives in and out of the rooms. If my goal is to get closer to God then why not start with my fellow human beings, my brothers and sisters. I must learn to love all mankind, not just in words and theory but deep in my heart. The closer I get to them the closer I get to communication with my Higher Power.

I could have been a goat farmer from Sudan when I came out of the egg, but I was born in a relatively rich country. Do I have more opportunities than a Sudanese goat farmer? Yes. Do I have more resources? Yes. Am I a better person? My spiritual principle tells me I am not. If I should ever cross paths with a Sudanese goat farmer, I should hug him as my brother. World peace is possible if everyone could adopt this simple law of love.

February 6

YOUR BODY YOUR TEMPLE

We often talk about where to find God. Some find it in nature, others in the vastness of space in the universe, but why not our own bodies? A truly amazing collection of water, blood, bone and assorted elements. It is our house of spirituality. It is our God given temple. I often say if my body is a temple then I am Angkor Wat, somewhat ancient. We had no choice in how tall we would be or the color of our skin or our eyes but after that we had plenty of choices as to what to put in our bodies and how we decorate our temple. When we were in our disease, we were killing our body with poisons of all sorts, eating terrible stuff and breathing bad air. All of us are very fortunate to have survived the things we did to our bodies. Speaking for myself, once I put the drink down my body improved dramatically. I had high blood pressure, was 60 lbs. overweight and could not swallow anything larger than a pea. So today all those things reversed by the grace of God and this program.

You have often seen me quote one of my daily readings Body, Mind and Spirit. You need all 3 in harmony to enjoy all life has to offer. I find it a work of God how wonderfully we are designed and the body's ability to heal itself. The doctors wanted to give me a knee replacement 7 years ago. Absolutely necessary they said. Well I got 3 shots of WD 40 for the joints and I have been pain free for all 7 years. I have taken over the job of being the chairman of my medical team. Prayer is my best medicine. Today I am very careful about what I eat. I exercise every day to keep my weight down and work my heart muscle. A lot of damage has already been done but I am enjoying controlled decay. I have found my spiritual routine and my readings help my body respond much better. In my experience I might feel a little down, a bit sick and tired but if I go to a meeting my body responds to the spiritual uplift. I cannot carry the message if my body is in the shop. It's not pretty by any means but all the parts still work albeit with rust and a slower pace.

God has forgiven me for all the abuse I heaped upon my body over the years. Recovery is not only for our addiction and obsessions but for better health and some longevity we don't deserve. Thank You God.

February 7

EMPATHY

Sort of a follow-up to humility is the subject of empathy. One of the biggest attractions of our wonderful program is everyone has gone through the same thing to finally find sobriety. Just by definition all those who went before us have empathy for the still suffering alcoholic. When I think of the people, I know who are truly humble another characteristic they all have is empathy. They identify with the person they are listening to and communicating with. I know when I was losing my son to the incurable disease ALS, I had a fellow member who lost his brother to ALS. He gave me some insight and a book written by a survivor of ALS. Then in my home group a longtime member lost his son to a drug overdose. That made me grateful that my son's death was not a horrible accident. Then when my son passed another very good friend of mine lost his son a few days before mine passed. All this empathy eased my pain so much I could endure the inevitable.

It is easy to understand empathy with someone who has had the same painful experience but what about those people you have no shared scenario? I give myself a poor report card in empathy when I get upset with someone who has made me angry in one form or another. I don't have enough information to be angry. I have no idea what that person has been through to make them so mean and hateful. For all I know this person was put in a closet and beaten by an evil stepmother with a high heel shoe for 10 years. I need to have empathy for others and try to feel their pain even though I haven't had the same experience. I haven't much tolerance for depression because to my mind you cannot be grateful and depressed at the same time. So, Mike's formula says depression is selfishness and anger without enthusiasm. OMG, I got attacked on that joke not very funny to some. Depression is real this guy shouts at me. Plus taking medication on top of the problem I have my opinion that there is no chemical solution to a spiritual problem. Thus, my empathy was zero in this case. I have softened my thoughts on this and many other matters and keep my mouth shut since I am not a doctor.

To me empathy, humility and love are all interwoven into a perfect personality. I am pretty good with love and OK with humility but empathy needs work. Pray for me.

February 8

OH, IT'S HARD TO BE HUMBLE

When I was in Hawaii I had very good friends who had a Bluegrass group. One of their songs was "Oh It's Hard to Be Humble When You Are Perfect In Every Way" all tongue in cheek of course but a grain of truth in this song. A bloated ego can paint a false image in one's own mind and humility is off the table. Most of my spiritual readings on the subject of humility boil down to being an honest you. Not more than, not less than, just be yourself with addition or subtraction. My constant contact with my Higher Power keeps me in the humble zone, it lets me know how little I am in the bigger picture and how powerless I am over just about everything but my own attitude. If I have a humble attitude and a correct self-image, I open the door to accepting the world as it is and my bit part in that world. I can't do everything, but I can do something without applause or praise. If my ego needs to be fed, then all my humility is gone with the wind.

"Humility is knowing there are forces outside ourselves, like the

grace of God, and family and friends who helped shape our lives. **There is no humility without gratitude."** *Body, Mind and Spirit.* We all know about HOW, Humility, open-mindedness and willingness. I often talk about my gratitude list, and when I review, I am humbled by the gifts I have on my list.

Over 20 years ago I met the Dalai Lama in Honolulu by chance. I instantly felt at ease with this man and he talked to me like he knew me already. He made me feel comfortable and we had a short talk as if we were lifelong friends. Afterward I thought it was spiritual aura of a great teacher, but I now know what was so attractive about him: humility.

Humility is like a sense of humor, either you have it or you don't. You can't study about it, buy it, or borrow it. It is a byproduct of love, gratitude, caring for others and thank you God our program will lead us to humility if we let it.

February 9

SELFISHNESS SELF, SELF

The root of our problem is selfishness, so says the Big Book. I would add, it is the trunk, the branches and the fruit. Selfishness makes me sick to my stomach. I know I work on my own daily and what I see in other people is the selfishness I don't like in myself. I see selfish behavior at every meeting I go to. Someone brings cookies and some guy takes two handfuls while others get none. Another guy talks for 15 minutes eating up the clock for a still suffering alcoholic who needs to share but is unable. The group departs without putting away the chairs and cleaning up. Put money in the basket? Maybe tomorrow. It upsets me when it hurts the unity of the group and is harmful to the members. The only thing I can do is set an example even though nobody follows my lead. I can only do my level best to be unselfish in my words and actions. So many of my prayers attach selfishness and focus on helping others. It sets the tone right off the starting block every morning. Reading spiritual books and meditating get my focus outward instead self, self, self.

There are so many forms of self, hard to list them all, but let's just say self-centeredness to make it easy and all inclusive. No surprise is it? Our disease is a selfish one. When we were drinking, there was no one more important than me. Feeding that gorilla inside of us took all our effort and resources. We often hear in meetings somebody say, "I wasn't much but I was all I ever thought about." Our founders know selfishness was our inner core and it had to change for any chance of success in staying sober and becoming useful human beings again. Looking at the 12 Steps it is easy to see they all work on the selfishness we all have in common Finding a Higher Power and communicating with Him is key of course. Then looking at our inventory the selfishness is a continuing theme in all our past dealings. Getting into service is getting out of self, sponsoring others is out of self in short, thinking of others. None of us are at the center of the universe so the humility which comes from long term sobriety chips away at our selfishness that has calcified in stone.

For me the further I get away from me the happier I become. My joy is seeing the results of others progressing and knowing I was there to see it.

February 10

INTIMACY

Intimacy was off the table for me for years and years leading up to my final bottom. No wonder I had to learn all about intimacy all over again. The funny dilemma for me was that I wanted to have people in my life, but I didn't want them to get too close. I had an imaginary bubble around me and I didn't like anybody in my "bubble." They could smell the alcohol and see my blood shot eyes. Keep your distance please. Finally, that got to be too much trouble, so I just isolated myself from other humans. Part of intimacy is honesty. If you can't look yourself in the mirror, then for sure you can't put forth an approachable countenance. If you can't stand yourself then nobody else can either. Thanks to the program you begin to like yourself and then you become attractive to others. Most important in 12 Step work is to be approachable to a newcomer. Doing a 5th Step is very intimate process. Trust, honesty, open mindedness, all are necessary in the sponsor relationship.

My very first meeting of AA I stood outside the room and observed the group. OMG they were hugging each other! Yuk. I was unhuggable and certainly did not want to hug anybody else. Luckily my soon to be sponsor spotted me trying to escape and assured me I was in the right place. Soon after I was hugging and trusting other members of my new group. Intimacy had a fresh start. I learned all about friendship and sharing my feelings. Every meeting of AA I get a chance for intimacy by opening up my heart to others and sharing what is happening in my life. I trust them, love them. They trust me and love me. That is the real deal. In my personal life I can be with my wife and we know each other so well that we can enjoy intimacy without saying a word. Just being in the same room is harmony for both of us. Intimacy has no secrets, no hidden agendas. Intimacy is not selfish or self-serving. It is love.

For me the biggest key to intimacy is the ability to listen and feel what the other person is feeling. If they can do the same, that is pure intimacy.

February 11

OUR FATHER

When you think of Father in a spiritual sense, He is a loving parent who wants the best for us. He is not a task master with fear as motivator. When we say the prayer "Our Father" it sums up the entire relationship. He is "our" Father not "my" Father, He is Father to us all with no one child better than another. All of humans have one Father the same Father. We are all God's kids. So many names are given to our individual Higher Powers. Even the Buddhist don't have a word for God, so they insert the word good and that makes sense to them. I was blessed. So many of the first guys I sponsored had a "God problem" and that was an advantage. Better to start from ground zero than have the wrong idea of spirituality, God and faith like I did. I was wrong on all counts. I had to be re-trained and adopt the AA way of designing my own Higher Power. I knew prayer worked so it was a sliver of faith to begin the process like training wheels. I had a "starter God."

Smart guys seem to have more problems connecting with God because they want tangible evidence, they want to see this God in a human way and of course that is impossible. Our little limited human brains cannot "see" God or anything spiritual you can put in a glass case. I like the Great Unseen from some of our literature. From the very first meeting I developed faith in the people I saw in the meeting because they all could not be putting on an act. They were happy, helpful, kind and downright nice folks. Then as I did the Steps, I could see this thing works and my faith went from a sliver of light to a burning flame. Time after time I called on my Higher Power to help me, guide me, and so I know He is there doing the heavy lifting and comes through 100%. Ingrained in my pea brain is that everything that happens is supposed to happen no matter what I think at the time. My faith grows and grows because the evidence in my own life is proof enough for me.

The concept of Hell is an invention of man. I bought into that fear until I didn't care if I went to hell where all my friends would be. As far as heaven, my belief is that this is heaven and most of us miss it or don't appreciate the heaven God has provided us. A pity.

February 12

COMMITMENT

One old timer told the story of "commitment" he said when he looks at his breakfast of eggs and bacon, the chicken is involved but the pig is committed. On my gratitude list the word "commitment" stirs my energy every time I see it. I am blessed I do have commitment not only to AA and staying sober but commitment to my family, friends and a host of other things too. I am "all in" every morning and talk to my Higher Power with conviction and commitment to do my best according to His will, not mine. I am committed to my home group by being in service and attending most every day. On time and clean shaven, well dressed, I show a newcomer I am serious about this program, in other words committed 100%. I am not a spectator; I do participate in the group conscience and maintenance of our meeting place. I put five times more money than most other members because to put any less would be less than a cup of coffee at Starbucks. I am committed to all the Steps and all the traditions like the 7th Step.

I am working with a guy right now who has quite a bit of sobriety however he does not go to meetings, sponsor anybody, not in service of any kind in or out of the rooms so guess what? He is all over the map crazy and wondering why. He has never committed to anything his whole life, never married, never worked for somebody else and fears commitment. I know in my own case I do daily maintenance of my spiritual condition and it is still not enough sometimes. This highlights my commitment as a blessing God gives me the strength to persevere, some tenacity and discipline. Thank You God. In my personal life I will climb any mountain for my friends. All my sponsees are my friends also so I will do anything to assist them in any way I can. My brothers and fellow survivors. In recent years all our family has travelled great distances to be together for family reunions. Alaska, California, Vermont, Florida, Hawaii and Texas then throw in old dad in Thailand. We all make commitments a year in advance to be together. Love abounds in these reunions.

Commitment is like a sense of humor either you have it or you don't. Commitment is a state of mind that brings me joy and happiness. I am doing the right things with the right people in the right place. All in.

February 13

PRACTICE, PRACTICE, PRACTICE

One truth about success at anything is practice. One cannot play the piano without practice. All great sports figures practice their skills, usually a lifelong endeavor starting at a very young age. Tiger Woods had a golf club in his hands almost from birth. His father drove him to be best golfer on the planet by practice, practice, practice. Practice is the price for proficiency. Examining my own inventory what have I practiced the most and from an early age? Ah ha drinking if it was an Olympic sport I could have been a contender! In my first 50 years I mastered no sport, no skill, no academic heights, only the art of elbow bending. Left hand, right hand, no hands, I could suck em up. Now all that practice took me into a blind alley I needed to redirect my entire practice routine. This spiritual path takes daily practice and I can see the results for my efforts in my life, but I also know I need to try to achieve higher levels by improving my practices by doing more not less.

This business of controlling my mind takes a ton of practice after going in the wrong direction for so many years. Now to make a complete turnaround is not an easy chore. I see the 12 Steps as levels of proficiency in my new spiritual path which require constant practice. My mind needs a new way of processing life in spiritual terms and positive thinking. A total makeover. I listen to my friends with 30, 40 years of sobriety and I am not there yet. More daily practice is required to get to their level of proficiency. There are a few folks with a lot of sobriety who do not have anything I want. So I pick my role models very carefully. In my practice routine I learned I need to do all the exercises, get in service, attend meetings regularly, work with others, read the literature, the whole nine yards, if I am to reach my goals. I need to do the same things over and over again with a little more improvement each time. If I can bench press 200 lbs. today, I will attempt 210 lbs. tomorrow.

Practice makes perfect, as the saying goes, but we will never be perfect however we can strive for a higher spiritual plateau by practice, practice, practice.

February 14

THE PAUSE THAT REFRESHES

Another of my favorite reading from Daily Reflections is: "WE PAUSE ... AND ASK" That gap between the time somebody says or does something to me and how I react is so important to my recovery. I had my hair trigger removed a long time ago. That quick response of the old days meant I was getting ahead of God. I forged ahead without talking to my Higher Power and always paid the price causing needless harm to myself and the person receiving my venom. The longer the gap the better. I have one in the back cooker that has been there a month! I call this the **GAP (God Authorized Pause.)** These days of harmony are mostly kind words and soft voices 99% of the time. It is that 1% I must watch out for and hold my tongue and let a cool breeze pass by before ruining a whole day. Why should I be in a hurry to act like an idiot? Saying nothing is a new habit I have acquired and I really like it. I also need to watch my face because I can really convey my thoughts without opening my mouth.

In Thailand there are a few great attributes that are attractive. One is a "good heart" and another is "jai yen" translated is cool heart. Being slow to anger is now part of my life. It has a great health benefit too. Good blood pressure, no headaches, no fist fights. When agitated I ask myself, "Will this be important a year from now?" So far the answer has always been "No." Another technique I use is to take myself out of the room and take a walk, say a little prayer and that works wonders. I put a smile on my puss and re-enter the room with a fresh attitude. What I have found is when I get closer to God the easier it is to deal with other people. I remind myself we are all God's kids and I am dealing with my brothers and sisters. Anger seems to be a thing of the past as my recovery deepens. I wasn't good at anger management anyway. It is good for me to slow my pace and give my heart a chance to whisper wisdom into my brain.

God's speed is the right speed, not mine. If I get ahead of God I am in trouble, so the GAP is good to apply to all matters I face during the course of the day. I may need to find a quiet spot and regroup and everybody will be better off.

February 15

REGRET THE PAST?

One of the biggest truths I've learned on the happy road to recovery is guilt, blame and regrets are all a waste of time and effort. Some folks have a past they can't live with. I, on the other hand, embrace my past. I needed to make every mistake I made and every drink I drank to get to my bottom and eventually to the first meeting. I thank God for my past and I know He already forgave me for my errors and damage, later I forgave myself so I could put my past into the plus column. If my past is gold, then I am one rich dude. All my mistakes are now in my "help" box to say, "I've been there too" when I am working with others. We all know we cannot rewrite the script. What is done is done but the lessons continue into the future so that has immense value. To really enjoy this new life with a road map, a design and some principles, the old life needs to be smashed, destroyed and trashed. The main point is never to see if lightning can strike twice and repeat the past mistakes.

We all know the definition of insanity. Every New Year I would say "this year is going to be different." In a way I was right. Every year got worse. Not my imagination of a new year. I vowed to drink better booze and consume more not less. That worked because after a while the drink stopped working altogether and it brought me to the dark hole and my turning point. I knew I would die soon because I had 2 close friends die of alcohol related problems and both drank a lot less than I did. Yikes. What little value system I had left in my brain told me that I was not allowed to kill myself. I turned right instead of left and the rest is history. I must be grateful to God for sparing my life. All the great stories I have would be lost forever. All my lessons learned would never get passed on. I have a gratitude list so rich in rewards from making that decision to turn right at the turning point. I have miles to go before the balance sheet makes it to zero, the breakeven point. Regret my past? Not one minute of it.

As my sobriety continues in time, more and more of my past that was forgotten and buried into my sub-conscience now leaks into my conscience mind and it is even more gold to be used to help others. I have a gold mine of mistakes.

February 16

FREEDOM

Nobody is more grateful about freedom than one who has lost it. Being in the hands of a North Vietnamese regiment surrounded by armed soldiers in Laos, my life was in question and I lost my freedom absolutely. No pilot in my group was taken prisoner or survived capture. I had no reason to think I would be the first. I was pretty sure they were not going to have happy hour upon my arrival in a camp and I would detox in jail. I prayed like crazy then and promised God all sorts of stuff that I didn't do. He pulled my fat out of the fire and 10 years later in Afghanistan I lost my freedom again to the secret police. Prayer worked once more but I continued my alcoholic life once I was out of the hands of really nasty armed folks. What did I do with my freedom? I put myself in a prison of my own, making drink by drink, brick by brick until I could not enjoy any freedoms at all. Thank you, God and AA, I am today free from the bondage of self and King Alcohol.

Then as some years of sobriety added up I realized I had freedom to do many things I never dreamed of before. I had freedom to go anywhere I wanted. I had choices whereas before I had zero choice. I had to drink and freedom went out the window. Today I know that one drop of booze and I will lose both freedom from and freedom to do what I want. My dream was to live in Thailand. For 13 years now I have been living my dream and I met my dream lady and look forward to happiness management every day. If both freedom from and freedom to are not on your gratitude list I suggest you add them and be grateful for the blessing of freedom. It is priceless and most of us paid a heavy price for our new-found freedom. In order to keep free, we have found that we need 100% commitment to our program and work on our spiritual condition every day. Our freedom is a gift from God and most of us cherish it dearly. Freedom is not free.

The biggest freedom of all is freedom from fear, knowing our Higher Power will protect us, guide us and love us. He is never going to give us more than we can handle.

February 17

ALL IN 100%

One of my favorite Daily Reflection readings is the 100% Step offering. We hear that Step One is the only one we can do 100% and we need to do the entire step. Many of us would and could admit we were alcoholics but so what? It took decades for me to complete the second half of the step, admitting my life was unmanageable until the evidence became overwhelming. The way I view this is I am 100% alcoholic, not 95% alkie and 5% normal. No sir I am the real deal 100% alcoholic from the tip of my bald head to my toe nails. No chance of changing that percent ever again. I was once a cucumber and now I am a pickle through and through and I will never be a cucumber again. I accept my condition 100% and I know what will happen if I ever forget my true nature. I do this program 100% to counter my 100% problem. I do my daily meditation and prayer, go to meetings regularly, sponsor others, confer with other alcoholics, I am in service. In other words, I am all in 100%. I do not know what I could subtract from my program that would be a danger so why not do it all. After all these years not only is it my habit, my routine but I love the process and enjoy all the parts of the program 100%.

When you have a good hand in poker or you are sure you have a winner you push all your chips into the center of the pot and declare "all in" so 100% of your chips are on that one bet. If you are wrong and lose you go home broke. If you win then you continue the game with maybe twice as many chips as when you started. In the game of living 24 hours at a time, I tell my Higher Power I am "all in" and push my chips forward. I am 100% committed, no holding back. I am a winner in the game of life every day as long as I do what I have been doing all these years. I am dealt a different hand each day and it still requires a 100% commitment no matter if it is 2 Aces or a 2 and 7. My Higher Power is in charge of the next 5 cards and I have never lost a hand or my sobriety. I do not need to do Step One again. If someone relapses there is a part of Step 1 that they missed.

When I hang around normal people, every once in a while, I feel like I am one of "them" but I must stay vigilant about my 100% condition and skip the toasting and wine tasting and not once have I been put down for not participating in "normal" activity.

February 18

PROBLEM SOLVING

One big benefit of our wonderful program is a whole new way to solve problems. What is the biggest problem I ever had in my entire life? Let me think. Oh yeah, my drinking problem. How did I solve it? I found a Higher Power and asked Him to help me with this problem and since I could not do it myself, I turned the problem over to Him who could. I could not, He could, so I let Him. Step 1, 2 & 3. Since it was a miracle I ever got sober and this method worked so well why not use the same technique on all my problems. I would be crazy not to go back to my Higher Power and seek help in all my life's peaks and valleys. As my recovery progresses the problems seem to be less and less. Most of my problems don't involve right or wrong anymore. What is right is very obvious nowadays. Most of today's problems are a choice between good and better. Or as some folks call it "luxury problems." Most important in this new method of calling on my Higher Power is faith. As I garner more time in the program I can see my faith keeps increasing as my connection to my Higher Power has gets stronger. No surprise there.

Today I will share my "back burner" method of dealing with life's bumps and rocks on the road. I take a situation and instead of twisting my brain in knots I put the thoughts surrounding the issue on my back burner and get it out of my immediate vision. I let it simmer back there without any input from my active thoughts and action. I let my Higher Power do all the heavy lifting and pray for the wisdom to see a solution clearly. I let my sub-conscience cook the stew and in the morning during my prayer and meditation the answers come through loud and clear. I hit my forehead and say, "Why didn't I think of that sooner?" Well, the reason was I didn't give my Higher Power a voice sooner. "The answers will come as long as your own house is in order." My subconscious is in better communication with my conscience mind all the time now. I get inspiration in my sleep and remember these nuggets when I awake. Before I could never remember my dreams or sleeping thoughts. This inspiration is like waves on the ocean but clearer as my spirituality increases.

I have done so many brain washings I'm now getting into new territory in my mind. Now my heart can connect to my feeble brain much better.

February 19

BRAINWASHING

I will never forget a meeting many years ago where one of the members declared that "This AA stuff is nothing more than brainwashing." An old-timer interjected, "Jim your brain needs washing." Much laughter with that exchange but there is a grain of truth in the joking. All our brains have been misused, misguided, soaked in booze, polluted, dirty, self-centered. My brain was like a puppy in the backyard racing around in circles with no destination or purpose. I really need direction and mental discipline. My brain can still spin up to 4500 RPM in a heartbeat, it has no clutch, no governor, no brakes. My thought life most definitely needed a scrub job. Today I feed my brain a breakfast of prayer, good positive readings and meditation. I catch my brain before spin-up and refuse to let negative thoughts control my first hour in conference with my Higher Power. My attitude gets an adjustment every morning, and if you want to call it brainwashing, I am OK with that.

We are powerless over almost everything, but we are not powerless over our thinking. We can control our thoughts if we work on it, and if it is difficult, we can ask God for help. I need to change the person I was before, so it starts with changing my mind. My mind changes then my body changes and my behavior changes. I can train my thoughts and increase my brain power. No action happens without the thought first. In the past my negative thoughts could rule the day with fears, resentments and hateful images. My brain is the darkroom where all my negatives are developed. In my alcoholic brain, negativity breeds like cockroaches until I am infested. Washing my brain is necessary to clean the decks for positive, spiritual thought. You can choose the topics for your brain to ponder. I get my topics from my readings to write to all you guys. I cook those thoughts for a day and night and you hear the result. Badda bing, badda boom!

We have two voices within. Even if your brain tries to deceive you, your heart will whisper the truth. But you have to be quiet and listen really well.

February 20

BLESS SOMETHING AND IT WILL BLESS YOU

I have found it to be true whatever you bless will bless you back and whatever you curse will bite you sooner or later. I heard in meetings, "I hate this disease of alcoholism." I bless the fact I am an alcoholic, I know what is wrong with me and I am happy to know I am what I am. A lot of drunks go through life never knowing what is wrong and thinking there is a way out. I don't curse alcohol, I bless the new life I live today and that was a result of my getting help for my disease. I am not happy with the wreckage of my past but I know through my recovery program how to deal with my dark past. I don't curse my past because it is the gold to help someone else. We are taught if you have resentment to pray for that person so in a way, to bless them. It takes the negative power out of the equation. At least you get this resentment out of your head and let God take care of the problem.

Cursing something or someone just adds more negative logs onto the fire. I want to put out the fire, not fan the flames. I know a number of folks who are overweight by society's standards, so they curse their bodies and go through painful times of dieting, pills, and weird stuff like stomach stapling. Ouch. This cursing of your own body just leads to depression and guilt of failure. Blessing your body, or the parts you are not happy with is a much better idea. All my overweight family and friends, I still love them just as much as if they were models. All of them have a good heart and some people are just built big all their lives. When I look in the mirror I say, "Hey it ain't pretty but luckily I am alive."

I need glasses, dentures and hearing aids but put it altogether and I am a love machine ready to rock and roll. I bless modern technology for keeping me functioning.

I like the saying, "Condemn the sin and love the sinner." Cursing inanimate objects is laughable. Curse someone and they will repay the negativity. I bless everything, so God bless you all.

February 21

BE STILL AND KNOW

More shall be revealed, so how about 65 years later? When I was a kid, I used to read the Oakland Tribune newspaper. Mostly the funnies and sports but there was a catchy article in the corner of the news section that always caught my eye and I never knew the significance of the message. It was a small one paragraph entitled "Be Still and Know" To me being still was crazy, life was perpetual motion in my little world. Action. Occasionally I would read the thoughtful message but most of the time I ignored the article. Today in my reading I find that it comes from Psalm 46 "Be still and know that I am God." There it is folks, Step 11 to facilitate your constant contact with your Higher Power is quiet meditation and prayer. The message can't come through noise and activity but only by "being still." That is impossible if you are worried, carrying resentments and fearful. The mind needs a rest from the turmoil of the world. To me, the best time for that to happen is early upon awakening. I catch my mind at rest before engaging in conversation with someone else or allowing any inputs like a radio or TV. Nada...quiet, be still.

I need to constantly re-affirm my belief in God and do my 3rd Step affirmation of "Thy will, not mine." Turning it over, for me, requires silence. I remind myself of my powerlessness first thing. I have faith, but I need to repeat that fact in prayer to set the table to receive God's message for the next 24. It always comes when I am quiet. If the birds of worry have made a nest in my hair, then I can't hear the message. Mentally I need to step out of my body with its aches and pains for a few minutes and fly my mind upward into the stratosphere. I stay in the clouds with the angels as long as possible before I put my feet on the ground and tromp around the neighborhood. Then and only then, am I armed against the unexpected. I know God and I know whatever happens is supposed to happen even if I don't think so at the moment. Ninety nine percent of all my inspiration comes in the morning when I am still. God to me is not a vague concept but a real power in my life. He is there for me so all I have to do is listen.

In a couple of places in the Big Book is says, "In your morning meditation...." I think our founders knew the secret to being still to know God.

February 22

A NEW DIMENSION

When I went to my first AA meeting, I entered a new dimension of a sober life. It was the most important day of my entire life so far. Everything turned around for the better and my recovery began. Then completing the 12 Steps brought that spiritual awakening that is

60

promised as a result of doing the Steps. This was a new higher dimension beyond my wildest dreams. Then and only then was I able to be useful to others. Having done the Steps, I could help another alcoholic do the same thing. When I began sponsoring other guys it took me up one more level. The book talks about the joy of seeing others get on the road to recovery and stay there is something very special. Absolutely true. Until you are doing that you can't understand what this dimension is all about. We already know one secret to a happy life is giving of ourselves with no strings attached and sponsoring others does just that. It is giving freely because after all it was given to us freely and with love. The love multiplies as we get our chance to pass it on.

This new dimension is a step above the first spiritual awakening where we felt peace of mind and serenity for the first time in our lives. Now we can see it happening to others not just to ourselves. We begin to enjoy the success of others more than our own. It is not about us anymore. Seeing the guys you sponsor achieve a new life is like the first child being born, and it is exactly what it is ... a re-birth of a down and out alcoholic just like we were once upon a time. This feeling is a departure from our deep selfish core that we all suffer from. Nirvana in Buddha terms is: complete selflessness. The loss of self to a higher good is the heart and soul of this new dimension. The people I sponsored thanked me many times over but my thanks go to them for asking me. The rewards I received are much more valuable than all the gold in the world. Priceless.

When I have suffered personal grief and tragedy, my sponsees sponsor me in my time of need. They always do a great job telling me what I told them but forgot.

February 23

BOUNDARIES

One of the biggest gifts of recovery for me was the ability to set boundaries and say "no." I can trace my problem back to my childhood where there was anger, shouting and rancor between my parents. I hated it and would hide in the closet and cover my ears. To this day if I see and hear people mad at each other and fighting verbally or even physically I feel sick to my stomach. And these are folks I don't even know. Of course, when it is family members fighting, it hurts double. So as a result, part of my character was to avoid confrontation at any cost. I would walk a mile to avoid a rough exchange of angry words. Then in marriage I would boast that we never fight. The reason we never fought was I had zero boundaries. I would back up and give ground on what I didn't like. I would suck it up rather than have a disagreement. Learning to disagree with love and consideration was new territory for me. It was no wonder my marriages (many) all failed. I would back up until the boiler blew and I would run away.

In sobriety I have a fence and if someone gets inside my fence, I let them know as gently as possible. I have had guys in the program, well-meaning of course, get inside my fence. I had one guy rip the glasses off my face to clean my glasses. I let him know he was inside my personal bubble and I like my glasses dirty. I told him I can see him clear enough. Part of the fellowship is other members getting into your inventory without permission. I had one visitor do that and I quickly bit his head off. Thankfully he went elsewhere to bother other people and never spoke to me again. Great result. I have the right to say "no' and not feel guilty about it. Most of us were people pleasers and turning people down on a request just might bring ill feeling but that is their problem. You need not provide an excuse or a lie as to why not. Eventually the other person will respect your boundaries and if they don't then that's too bad for them. Yes, I will reach out to help someone else, but I am not going to become their slave, drive them around, feed them and give them money. I did that once and 15 years later the guy is still not sober. Go figure?

I used to be a doormat and I finally got tired of being walked on. I am better at confrontation today, but I still don't like it because I am no good at it. Peace, Love, Tolerance, mo better, aye?

February 24

COMMON PROBLEM COMMON SOLUTION

When a lawyer is trying to negotiate between two warring parties, he will try to find some common ground and start from there. Two lawyers, on the other hand, try to find differences and problems that stretch out the proceeding to make more money. In sobriety I had to endure a divorce and at the final court date, my soon to be ex-wife, was dressed in a froppy black dress, no makeup and minus the gold and jewelry she normally wore to prepare for battle. She was on her third lawyer and I pulled the plug on both lawyers right before the time to enter the court. I said, "Let's find some common ground, what do you want?" Her concern was health care coverage. "OK how much do you need?" $300. "Fine" I said, "done deal." We wrote in the agreement, signed it and fired all the lawyers. Peace and serenity followed. We were in and out of court in 5 minutes without heartache and drama. Thank you, AA, for teaching me how to handle life's little problems. It is no wonder how close our relationships are in the fellowship. Simple, we all have so much in common.

We have no nationality in the rooms. We are from The Alcohol Nation, all for one, one for all. Politics is off the table thank God. Imagine having to belong to a certain party to belong. Our membership rule is plain and simple. There is one language of The Heart. No money is involved except what is in your ability to contribute but absolutely nothing is required, amazing but understandable. We found a common solution to our common problem, the Steps. Once we all do exactly all the same process the bond is even deeper. There are a million different ways to do the Steps and it may take years for some and just days for others, but the result is the same...long term sobriety. I know what the bonding of comrades in battle is like, but the bonding of alcoholics is even stronger. The Battle of the Bottle is just as deadly as bullets flying through the air. We are the winners. The battle is lifelong and hopefully we are never alone in the fight. The fellowship is my army.

Our society is successful because it has a divine purpose and is God centered rather than materially or politically driven. Only one purpose, one problem, and one solution. Simple aye?

February 25

LOVE GRATITUDE SERVICE

Once we arrive at Step 12, we have just begun our new dimension. Hopefully the gratitude list I keep harping on is part of your daily thought process and it leads to action. For me gratitude is my expression of love by translating that love into my behavior. Service, of course, comes in all different forms but all of it is doing something for others. Getting out of ourselves is the goal. The harmony of love, gratitude and service makes the 12th Step part of our daily life. In fact, after a few years it becomes part of the fabric of your life and the right action and the best action comes without a lot of thought or effort. You can get on the pink cloud of happiness and ride it into the sunset if you so choose. I don't separate my AA life from the rest of my life. That's too much trouble. Just one set of principles, I have acquired as the result of doing the 12 Steps, works 24/7 in and out of the rooms. When I review my past, I can see I have done a 100% flip flop on my entire life. Thank you, God, all for the better.

These three things add up to a spiritual awakening for me. Before I was spiritually asleep in fact I was flat lined. My pink cloud every day is my awakening, it is a spiritual awakening. I get "in the zone" with a thankful heart and an overwhelming feeling of love for my fellow man, my family, this place on earth and what is left of me as a human being. I can open my mind for messages from my Higher Power and that works 100%, no exceptions. All my inspirations, all my plans come while I am "in the zone" or better yet I am awake in every sense of the word. I have blocked out my natural selfishness and started my day praying to show my gratitude and asking what I might do for others. I give freely of myself, my resources, my time and my love, with no expectation of reward. I know God will provide all I need if I stay on the path He has laid out in front of me. I don't have to ask. I have no want list. My gifts in this life are way out of proportion of what I deserve.

As most of you know, I am a giant fan of Mother Teresa. This is from her:

The fruit of silence

is prayer

The fruit of prayer is faith

The fruit of faith is love

The fruit of love is service

The fruit of service is peace

February 26

NATURE

One of my favorite descriptions of GOD is "The Great Outdoors." Nature is God's artwork for all of us to enjoy. I can see spirituality in all of nature and I try to communicate with nature every day in one form or another.

One of my prayers is from an American Indian prayer and it goes like this in part:

Make my hands respect the things You

have made, and make my ears sharp to hear

Your voice

Make me wise so that I may understand the

things You have taught my people.

Let me learn the lessons You have hidden

in every leaf and rock.

God has shown us His love for us by giving us enough fruits, fish and vegetation to sustain us in a very healthy way. He has given us awesome beauty in nature for us to enjoy and all in living color. The amazing creatures God has sent to join us on this planet all have a message for us to learn. There seems to be a Great Design and it all fits together in a Great Plan. How can I not believe in a Higher Power looking at all the evidence in my environment?

I can talk about it, or paint a picture, but nothing beats the real thing as God made it. I soak up God's art every day in my nature walk. I can see God everywhere and try to absorb the messages of what I see.

February 27

ALL MY AFFAIRS

In keeping with my theme of simplicity, I have adopted one set of principles, one personality and singleness of purpose. I don't have two sets of guidelines for my AA life and another for my family/friendship life. I have found if it is good enough for AA, it is good enough for me too. This is a design for living which worked for me outside the rooms of AA. Simple stuff like "Do the next right thing" I really need "love and tolerance" with my insane fellows in the program but I need it with my family too. I have one sister who sent a blistering email to me and our other two sisters. It did our inventory loud and clear, but the funny thing is no one has heard from her in over in 11 years. All this stuff was 15 to 20 years ago that she still has resentments over. Wow, does she ever need a program. The spark that caused the venom came from our concern about her welfare since she was in a heavy fire area. Amazingly she is a therapist in the business of healing. My program came to my aid and I was able to make my 2 offended sisters feel better by my consoling them. I told my 2 sisters that sister #3 is hurting and we are not part of the solution. We have to accept her as she is and let it go. Arguing the points of error in this horrible email would just fan the flames. The delete button was the best option. I did not read all of my inventory and none of my 2 sisters. What my sister thinks of me is none of my business.

In my former life I would react to whatever happened or what somebody said to me by the first thing that popped into my head. Now this program taught me to pause and give my heart a voice before I shoot off my mouth or type an email. I see the entire world through a new pair of glasses. It is not a hostile world out there, it is full of love and joy and it is the same world. What has changed is my attitude. My program has given me serenity instead of worry and fear. Some of my family is scared to death about North Korea and I try to tell them we have no control over what they do, so losing sleep over what might happen is a waste of time, same thing with politics. The election is over and some family members refuse to accept the results. I tell them to wait 3 more years and go see a good movie. They don't appreciate my attitude and expect me to march on the capital. The gift of acceptance, I must thank AA for pounding it into my skull.

As I review my gratitude list, very few of those items were there before I got sober and I became a fully vested member of AA. It makes all my affairs go according to God's will not mine.

February 28

WHAT WORKS

The danger of anonymity being broken had a horrible example with a professional golfer. His drinking was public knowledge along with his smoking while playing a round of golf. He declared he was going to AA very publicly, and when he got drunk again, he announced to the world that AA does not work. He missed the point completely. The AA program does not work you; you work the program. It is not like electricity where you flip a switch and the light comes on. I have been to some meetings where at the end, everyone holds hands in prayer and when it finishes the group says. "The program works if you work it." AA just has a set of "suggestions" and we have found that if you follow these and change the person who drank into a new life then sobriety is the result for millions. There was a 60 Minutes piece on Betty Ford treatment center and one celebrity spent 30 days and $40,000 and then stopped at a bar 2 blocks from the Betty Ford Center and got drunk. "It doesn't work," he says. He and many others think you can buy sobriety and pay somebody to do the work you need to do. Unbelievable.

My friend who runs the fitness center where I went for many years in Hawaii told me on Dec 30 to take a week break because the place would be chock full of New Year's resolution folks. He knew his demographics. About mid-January all returned back to normal. People want a quick fix and it just doesn't happen. Same with AA. Some call it slowbriety because it takes a regular routine over enough time to see results. Like the lunacy of joining a gym and then sitting at home wondering why there is no weight loss. Duh. AA requires participation and not spectatorship. Attend regularly, be in service, share your feelings, read the literature, talk to your sponsor and other people in the program. Sometimes quickly, sometimes slowly, the lights will come on and the Steps will get you to the goal of long-term sobriety but more than that a new happy life. A lot of people call this "working the program" but IMHO this is not "work." Digging a ditch is work. This is changing your bad habits into good habits, reordering your priorities, getting in contact with your Higher Power. This is an enjoyable effort to me and not "work."

If you hear somebody say "AA doesn't work," you can agree with them. Be grateful you have found a way out of the dark pit into the Sunlight of the Spirit by steady participation.

February 29

ALMOST FAMOUS

There are lots of readings about the hazards of the limelight for us alcoholics and for good reason. I have seen a ton of sober alcoholics go on ego trips only minus the booze. One famous speaker came to Thailand to be the main speaker at our roundup and arrived like royalty and with demands on arrival. I knew from visiting his "Midnight Mission," in L.A. his office is in an ivory tower above the soup kitchen and you can only get to his place by escort. He was above it all and taking the credit for helping the homeless and desperate souls of the street, but he didn't mix with them. At the time of his big speech in front of 550 folks there was a bit of delay to bring in enough chairs from the dining area. He said, "You guys need to plan better when you have a world-famous speaker in town." I said: "We will keep that in mind when that happens." At least he laughed. Circuit speakers often have a problem with humility and lose sight of principles before personalities. We all have personalities, but we need not be super stars and gurus. None of us is better than anyone else. We are one drink away from disaster and then we fall right off the stage.

On my theme for this month "giving" it too has an anonymity factor. We need to examine our motives when we give. Is it to raise our stock with our fellowship? Is it a way to get applause we crave? Can we give without getting credit or do we demand a payoff? Our founders knew firsthand the dangers of the limelight and crafted the traditions just right for us alcoholics. Center stage usually produces political leaders. Not a good idea for us. No bosses please, only trusted servants. Servant is a very special term. In my former profession I was on stage a lot and was a circuit speaker, I know how bloated my ego became and fueled my alcoholism to gross levels. I was almost famous in my former life and I did not handle it well. I am a stagehand today out of the glitter and spotlight. Nobody likes a promoter and so we have adopted the "attraction rather than promotion" tradition. You work the program not the other way around. If a promoter gets drunk again it does our movement absolutely no good.

Every guy I helped was attracted to the way I act in the program not how I advertised the program. I was happy, and they were not. Simple as that.

March 1

THE KEYSTONE

Early on I saw the 12 Steps Illustrated and it showed the 12 Steps in an arch with Step 3 at the top as The Keystone. The point being that if you take away the keystone all 12 Steps fall to the ground in a heap. It took me years to really understand what the graphic was trying to tell me. Every morning I pause and concentrate on the short 3rd Step Prayer. I need to remind myself I am not in charge anymore. All my life I was an aggressive "take charge" kind of guy. Just another of my habits I had to abandon to get on the road to recovery. I can take charge of a big aircraft, but I cannot take charge of my life without the help of a Higher Power. All the gifts on my gratitude list are by the grace of God, I am not responsible for any of my wonderful gifts. As I cruise through the day I tend to think it is me at the wheel and I often have to stop and release the controls to someone bigger than little old me. Everyone who has relapsed lost the spirit of Step 3 and thus lost contact with their Higher Power long enough to take that first drink.

It is my belief that there is no one step more important than another. We need all 12 in harmony. The other 11 Steps need Step 3 to work and all is lost if you take back control of your drinking problem from your Higher Power. In my shares I don't talk about drinking at all. That is done, I have given the problem over to God and He has done a great job for decades so why in the world would I take it back? I hear folks talk about drinking as if it is a possibility. They are thinking about drinking. I don't think about it at all. It is history and it will stay part of my past if I work the Steps daily. I do have a living problem, relationship problems, resentments stemming from my alcoholism, but I know beyond a shadow of doubt, that a drink will not help. I have proved it time and time again. I quit sticking my hand into open flames, same principle here. A favorite saying around here is, "The most important thing I do today is not take a drink." To me they are considering it. The most important thing I do is my morning prayer and meditation, so I am into Steps 11 & 12 and I never have to do Step One again. Drinking is not on the menu.

The Third Step, Prayer, asks God directly for assistance, "Relieve me of the bondage of self," so you can get past selfishness to "bear witness to those I would help of Thy power." There you have it in a nutshell, when you are helping others a thought of a drink is impossible.

March 2

MISTAKES

It is very hard to stand on the sidelines and watch somebody make mistakes when you know better. We have a saying; we should not deny an alcoholic his misery. When I review my own inventory, I can see my mistakes are what woke me up and got me on the right path. I made every mistake in the book, but I learned my lessons thru all the beatings I took. My big mistake was thinking I could handle alcohol and those wimps who got into trouble with booze were just weaklings. Beaten to a pulp I had to admit I was wrong. I realized all my thinking was wrong because all of it was soaked in mind altering chemicals. When I finally got sober (I was a slow learner) and did Step 4, I could see a mountain of mistakes and a lifetime of damage. I read my deep dark past is valuable, so I surely am rich with my past. The biggest by-product of reviewing my past is humility and gratitude. I am humbled by my mistakes and am lucky to have survived my many errors.

What then, when it comes to helping someone else? The tendency is to try to stop your friend from making harmful mistakes and you want to get in his driver's seat and steer him out of harm's way. Bad idea. I am not a marriage counselor or a lawyer or any authority on anything except on how to drink too much. I need to stick to my expertise, "How to keep Me sober." That is all I know for sure. Once I enter into my sponsees' personal life and his work life I am on thin ice and need to remember my role. One guy I was sponsoring didn't secure his phone and his wife got all of his contacts including me. She called me and for one hour she did my guy's inventory and told me what I needed to do to straighten this dude out. She kept telling me I was his boss and no matter how I explained it she never got the point. She tried to draw me into controversy. "Don't you think he should be doing this and that?" I would not bite and not give her a chance to interfere in my relationship with my sponsee. I wanted to hang up but I assumed it was helping her vent and hopefully run her out of gas when she talked to this poor guy. I wanted dearly to tell him to run away from this lady but once again, not my business.

There is no satisfaction in saying "I told you so." I learned not to give advice and not "tell" anybody anything but only to share my experience. I have a treasure trove of mistakes to draw from.

March 3

AUTHENTICITY

Just added another item to my gratitude list: authenticity. Huh? I got this from one of my spiritual readings and what it means is to be real, be you, be honest and open. What you see is what you get. Of course, it wasn't always this way. In the old days I was one persona at work, directing the show, another person at home trying to keep family from revolting and still another character in the bar throwing the bull with the best of them. Mix all three of these personalities and it still was not me. I tricked myself into thinking I was somebody I definitely was not. With alcohol in my body that is somebody else. It looks like me and sounds like me but is a chemically altered guy. Certainly not authentic. When I did my inventory I could see some big chunks of who I really was. Yikes. Is that me? I really didn't like that person at all, so I had a choice, keep on pouring chemicals into my decaying body or do the Steps and change the person I saw in the mirror 25 years ago. One path was certain death and the other path was AA. Not really an option, but lucky I surrendered and with the smallest sliver of faith I am the real deal today.

There is a guy in the fellowship who is a doctor sometimes, an Army colonel sometimes and a Navy general fighter pilot sometimes. This dishonest portrayal of oneself does no good for anybody especially the impostor. Expanding a resume may get you a job but in the business of recovery and service we all need 100% honesty. The only thing important about my resume is I was a drunk, I came to AA, got a sponsor, got into service, did the Steps and changed the person who drank into a person who does not drink and is a decent member of AA and society at large. I need not make up stories to illustrate a point or impress my audience. The only person I need to impress is myself. What other people think of me is none of my business. My openness, my honesty and my positive attitude is what attracted the guys who asked me for help. Sobriety is very appealing once you have become a fully vested member by doing all the Steps and garnering some years of 24 hours at a time. In my case, years before I was happy in my own skin. I can live with myself today and not try to be different.

I am authentic, but it is fluid, I hope the real me is better today than it was yesterday. A work in progress,

March 4

CONDITIONING

I believe body, mind and spirit require daily conditioning. For me to stay alive I go to my little fitness room in my condo and get on the treadmill for about 35-40 minutes every day. If I miss one day I can feel the difference the day after my mini vacation. I like the treadmill because I can meditate at the same time for double duty. I used to walk the beach, but I fell too many times on broken stones and other hazards. I also am very careful about what I consume and try to nourish my body instead of adding unwanted fat or harming the temple that God gave me. (If my body is a temple then I am Angkor Wat) More important, however, is my spiritual conditioning. Many members say that our disease is doing push-ups just waiting for us to screw up. I look forward to my "conditioning" session upon awakening every morning. It is just like breathing clean air to me. I would no more skip the prayer and meditation than I would hold my breath until I pass out. It is my daily bread, my inspiration and my intuition. I try to add new information, new prayers and extra time to my conditioning program all the time.

If you can bench press 150 pounds now you can always bench press 150, you add 10 pounds until that is normal, then 10 more until you hit a limit. The same thing with your spiritual conditioning. You can keep adding "weight" to your spiritual bank account and get stronger spiritually. Some folks back off instead of increasing their routine and I would not recommend that. The more I am in the program, the more I realize how little I know, so I need to keep growing. I know that we only have a daily reprieve based on our spiritual condition, so I need to stay in shape or place myself in the danger zone. Maybe not taking a drink so much as losing my serenity and having an emotional slip. I read inspirational books like, "Sermon on the Mount" by Emmet Fox. Most of the outside thoughts of other writers lead right back to the Big Book and I have yet to find a conflict of thought from the study of religion or spiritual leaders. Religion is created by man and spirituality you can find through direct contact with your Higher Power.

My healthy body helps keep my mind working correctly and my spiritual health keeps the entire system in harmony, so I try to stay in fit condition with my daily workout.

March 5

DEPARTURE LOUNGE

Are you ready for departure from this life? My good friend Chicago Mike was sitting as a passenger in his family car with his wife driving. They were stopped at a red light totally innocent and not moving. A bus came into the intersection at a high rate of speed with no brakes. Mike was dead instantaneously and his wife had many broken bones and was pinned into the wrecked car. Maui Hank was driving himself to the hospital when his brand-new pacemaker broke open. He never made it.

Many more examples so I have learned to be prepared for lights out at any time. That's why when I see something that needs to be done I do it now. I have a "croak file" for my family that has what they need for my departure. A will, a list of worldly connections that need to be cut, important documents etc. My in box will still have stuff when I die but I try not to give more pain to my loved ones. Hank died with all that important stuff locked in a safe and no one had the combination. One guy in our group has his emergency phone number to his own cell phone. Don't think he will be answering. Our group has a lot of experience on what to do and we honor their wishes and their memory.

The point is that we never know when our time is up. I live every day as if it will be my last. Sooner or later I will be right. I cherish each day as a gift from God and squeeze every bit of love and enjoyment out of today. Today is the only cash I have for sure. If I see a flower I smell it, if I see a friendly dog I pat it, if I see a smiling person on the road I smile back. I will never pass this way again. When I sit in my meeting room every morning I think of it as the departure lounge. All of us are going to depart and several have already gone west. I try to let my friends know I love them today and try to learn more today and be of service today and contribute today.

Tomorrow is not a sure deal but if I live today as best I can then the door will be open for a great tomorrow if God gifts me one more day.

March 6

HARMONY

The last three Steps have no beginning or ending. They mesh together perfectly without having to dissect the individual parts of the Steps, In other words harmony. Since I am unable to sing or make music through an instrument, my harmony comes from the blending of prayer, some of which are poetic, and meditation mixed with self-examination into one sweet mixture. The first hour of quiet time is music for my soul and mind. What a sharp contrast from the old days of loud shouting and ringing phones to wake me up. I used to start my day with chaos and today I ease into the day with peace and serenity. If something happens to bring a sour note to the harmony, I learned to side step or deal with the problem and get back to the happy tunes. Nobody can ruin my day without my permission. I choose to stay in the zone and design my own orchestra. My close friends are in my band and their love and conversation are at the top of my chart. No longer listening to a distant drummer I can hear my Higher Power loud and clear during my quiet intermissions. The answers do come just like the book promises.

 If I look at my life as a work of art, I can find ways to decorate my tapestry every day. I can learn new ideas and expand my horizons if I make the time to grow. Those last 3 steps are growth instructions I have learned. If I don't keep growing, I am dying. If I am done learning I am done. If I don't help my fellow man, then when I fall nobody will put me upright again. I want my children and my grandchildren to view the mosaic of my life as one of love and happiness. I thank God for giving me enough years to paint a new canvas to cover over the drunken years. My material possessions are meaningless in the end. The only thing I really "own" is my attitude and my actions. I can channel my attitude in the positive direction with the last 3 Steps in combination. Before I take any action, I have already asked God to help me do the right thing. I address my selfishness and ego long before my interaction with others so I can blend into the outside world with harmony and tolerance.

My music is my own and I don't expect anybody else to dance to my tune or enjoy my melody. My routine puts me square into the comfort zone.

March 7

COMFORTABLE SOBRIETY

There are all kinds of sobriety and shades of sobriety, there is: white knuckle sobriety, sometimes sobriety, forced sobriety, raw sobriety, situational sobriety but I like the reading today **comfortable**

sobriety. Sobriety that accepts life as it is really is not as we would have it. A sobriety that lets go and lets God in. It is wonderful to be where I want to be with whom I want to be with and not have a "want" list of any kind. A comfortable sobriety is a grateful one, happy with what one has, and forgets what one does not have. I have learned to wear the world as a loose garment and not stew over the woes of the turmoil around the globe. I am powerless over terrorism and hurricanes so why let the negative aspects of the outside world ruin my serenity and make me uncomfortable. Once I know who I am, accept who I am, then I can be comfortable in my own skin. I try to let go of those things that are a threat to my comfort level, avoid controversy, process resentments before they take root and stay away from negative people. I have found if I try to do the next right thing, I am happy with myself and therefore comfortable.

By comfortable, don't envision me sitting on my couch. I have to be active and vigilant on a daily basis to enjoy my comfort zone. I got comfortable by doing the Steps over and over again. I got comfortable by connecting with my Higher Power every morning for years. I got comfortable by changing the person I was when I first walked into my first meeting. I got comfortable by doing the entire program, service, and helping others. I can deal with reality and truth today. I am old and I am comfortable with that because that is the truth but I don't have to think old or act old. I do have control over my thought life. I am learning new things every day, not trying to be teacher but being a student. I act young, hang around young people and play like a kid. When I was a kid, I acted very old so now is the time to get out my plastic pail and shovel and head for the beach. Being comfortable is directly related to my gratitude. As I review my gifts daily, I can feel rich and prosperous because it's true.

I learned a long time ago material stuff does not make me happy. Being in the Sunlight of the Spirit is warm and comfortable and to me is heaven on earth.

March 8

GO WITH THE FLOW

When I was only 13 years old, I adopted the attitude of "Rebel without a cause" and that got me kicked out of the seminary to be a priest. From that point on I decided to be different, a "maverick." I never liked crowds and I certainly wasn't going to follow the masses. When I joined the military at 17 it was against my grain to get in step, be in uniform, be disciplined. Somehow, I kept my rebel attitude and got away with my going against the program. I was the most unmilitary person I could be. "Go with the flow" idea would make me vomit. I enjoyed tilting windmills and breaking the rules. I was always swimming up steam. In my office I had a super big poster with a quote from Thoreau. "If a man does not keep pace with his companions, perhaps it is because he hears a different drummer. Let him step to the music he hears, however measured or far away." (God help me it still sounds good) A good friend of mine saw the poster and said, " Hey Mike you aren't even in the f*#ing band!" I took that as a compliment at the time but now understand what he was telling me.

When I came into the rooms of AA, I heard the joke about being unique just like everybody else. I thought myself special with a one-of-a-kind experience. I came to realize I knew nothing about a normal sober life. It was a program from Mars. However, I listened to the "Martians" who have tons of sobriety and knew my maverick attitude had to go. Lone wolf drunks need help from the group and require a sponsor and meetings. "Stick with the herd, stick with the winners, do what we did and you can be happy, joyous and free like us." OK I surrendered and gave the "program" a try. All those millions of alcoholics before me paving the way were successful and they were right. I had to prove it to myself and listen to wiser folks than me. I had to quit trying to break the rules and push the envelope. The "suggestions" of the 12 Steps and the 12 Traditions were hammered out by alcoholics just like me. Now I find similarities and disregard the differences. It is so much easier to go with the flow, let the stream carry me to my destination of a better more serene life.

I have learned firsthand; this program works perfectly, so I resist the urge to tinker with what works so well. For the first time in my life, I am following instructions.

March 9

DECLUTTER YOUR LIFE

When we did our inventory, we got rid of unnecessary baggage and dropped a lot of weight off our soul and mind. It felt so good to delete junk that was rolling around in my brain for decades. Then to do amends and find a new level of freedom by making it right with those I harmed, including myself. Only then did I feel so weightless I could fly with the eagles. Then I discovered I missed much of life while I was practicing my disease. There were hundreds of books I should have read, there were dozens of trips to the park with my kids I missed, there were birthdays, weddings, Christmas where I was missing in action. If you are still working, I encourage you to stop and retire as soon as possible so you can enjoy life and make up for lost joy. I thank God every day I am not working at a job 60 hours a week like the old days. My job blocked the sun out of my life for so long I forgot some basics of a normal life. Drinking made it even worse. I hurt everyone around me and I damaged myself.

My message; look at what you do and clean out blockage to the good stuff out there waiting for you. Travel, plays, read books, visits old friends, picnics, learn new ideas, help more people, smell flowers and pet dogs. I suggest you put things that waste your time in the "spam" folder and delete. If I watch the news more than a few minutes a day I am wasting my time. I learned a long time ago, "Don't try to teach a pig to sing, it wastes your time and it annoys the pig." I am not a teacher anymore, I am not qualified to do anything but share my experience and help others.

I declutter my physical surroundings. Paperwork multiplies at night, so I try to dispose of unnecessary paper. I have 2 keys, no wallet, no smartphone, no watch, no beeper, notebook, nada. Freedom from gadgets is wonderful. You see more birds, trees and mountains on the horizon. I see folks walking with their entire attention focused on their magic phone, bumping into other people and light poles. Crazy. Making complicated things simple is pure creativity in my book.

My first job as a kid was to take out the garbage and still today I love to take out the garbage and dispose of the clutter in my life. Ahhh, freedom.

March 10

NEGATIVE AND POSITIVE

When you look at a battery it has a positive side and a negative side to produce the power to run your gadgets. Same in life, I found you can find a flipside to everything and energy works both ways. Electricity is negative to positive in action to turn on the lights. You can turn a positive event into a negative experience as quick as a light switch. I knew a friend who came into a million dollars through the death of his parents. He was so happy at first but became fearful of handling so much wealth. He became paranoid everyone was trying to rob him and soon lost trust of all his friends. Sure enough he lost half the money in short order trying to invest it to be even richer. He is miserable to this day and cannot get over losing half his fortune instead of enjoying the money still left. Our brains can turn anything that could be positive into negative thinking as fast as electricity. Each of us has a combination of positive and negative thinking rolling around in our skulls. Which one is dominant, is up to you.

I don't let my brain run loose between negative and positive. I work on mind control every morning before my brain has a chance to take me to dark places. I fill my still sleeping brain with hundreds of positive inputs before it knows what is happening. My 8 prayers are positive, my 6 readings are positive, so a negative thought does not have a chance, at least for that first hour. In my experience how that first hour goes sets the path and tone for the rest of the day. Then of course life happens and if you turn on CNN the negative inputs begin but at least I can deal with them a lot better.

I am a "best case" scenario guy so I stay away from "worst case" people and negative thinkers because they can drag me down with them if I am not vigilant.

March 11

NO TEACHER NO BOSS

When I first came into AA, I was anxious to learn how to climb the ladder of success and become a leader and find a position fitting my age and experience. Needless to say, I provided a lot of entertainment to my first home group. I wanted my membership card and was ready to sign in on a log book to get "credit" for the number of meetings I attended. Ha ha. At my first meeting I wanted to meet the "boss" I was crushed to find out there is no boss. Well how does anything get done? I asked. I was told the "secretary" of a meeting has no authority only starts on time and finishes on time and the secretary has no more duties after the meeting is over. In the military they have rank and date of rank within each rank. I learned in AA we all have the same rank and that is "alcoholic" and the same date of rank "24 hours." Wow what a great idea. After I got the hang of it I could see the beauty of our perfect fellowship. In the military I was a leader and I had also been a teacher and professor. I had to be re-programmed to forget my old experience and re-adjust my ego.

When I read the part in the Big Book about the "director" the hair on the back of my neck stood up. That was me. I was the director who made everybody hit their mark. I learned it is not my show, it is God's show. I am not the director, it is not my theater, I have no control over the script. Unfortunately, some of us in service tend to creep into ownership. "My meeting" or "my group" really bad thinking. I have seen some people list their past service positions like a resume for promotion. I checked the AA catalog and they don't have merit badges for years of service or certificates of outstanding performance. The ego problems of the past can come to life again within the rooms of AA. Then some us, myself included, can't help being a "teacher" from time to time. You will hear in meetings "In order to stay sober you must do this or that." Since there are no rules or commandments, all that "teaching" is pure moonshine. The only thing I should ever talk about is my own experience, strength and hope.

I think one of the hardest concepts of AA to grasp is the group is the highest level of AA organization. The group conscience is God working for the group. It works and I love this way of doing business.

March 12

DO WHAT YOU DO BEST TO EXCESS

When I taught management, I used to stress the benefits of doing what you do best to excess. In other words, find your talent and focus on that to the point of excellence. Not so much to be a super star but to be part of a team with other members doing the same high level of performance to be the best you can be as a team. Take baseball for example; nine different positions with very different skills required. The catcher has to be a guy who can evaluate the skills of the 10 pitchers on the staff and know how many different pitches each pitcher has. Then he has to know the vulnerabilities of the batters facing his pitchers all 26 members of the opposing team and then multiply that times the number of teams in the league. A monumental task to say the least. Then he must squat in a very uncomfortable position and signal each pitch to try to keep the opposition from getting on base. This guy has to be smart as hell and a good athlete besides. Then, if he can hit the ball with any kind of decent average, they pay him millions of dollars. The not so smart guys you put in the outfield and hope the fly balls don't bounce off their heads into the stands for a home run.

A winning team has the right combination of expert members. In my own case, I really wanted to be a music man but I cannot sing. Once I bought a guitar and never could do anything with it. I am tone deaf and have zero musical talent but love music. On the other hand, I had a talent I did not imagine. I never really thought about being a pilot but as circumstances happened in the military I ended up in pilot training. My first check ride to see if I could graduate into jets I heard the check pilot report back to the boss I was a "natural pilot" and I was the best he had ever seen. I went to the top of the class in flying and found a talent I had no idea would present itself. I was never defeated in aerial combat and hang with the best pilots anywhere, Top Gun. (OK we are not going to discuss how it messed up my ego in this little piece). My points are several. Inventory your skills and focus on what you do best and not try to be something you are not. Then explore disciplines that you haven't tried and maybe you will discover a talent you never thought of before.

We all are on the AA team, a winning team for sure, so we can do our part in service by doing what we are best at. For me, I am best at sponsoring guys and not so good at visiting people in the hospital.

March 13

HOW OPEN IS YOUR MIND?

Humility Open mindedness Willingness, (HOW) are the essentials of our recovery, so let's take a look at how open your mind is. Open mindedness is a goal never to be totally reached. We all have little walls in our brain and a lifetime of prejudices that are in cement. Some of our values from childhood are grooved into our psyche for better or worse. Our brain is full of facts we believe to be true. Maybe if you examine them the truth has changed over time. For example, when I was young we were terrified of Russians. Nikita Khrushchev pounded his shoe on the podium at the UN and threatened the US "We will bury you!" I took that to mean he would put us all 6 feet under and kill us. It wasn't until years later I learned he really meant economically not by nuclear weapons. All my adult years Russia was the enemy of my country. So the word Russia or Russians sets off bells in my head. Well we have a Russian lady in our group and guess what? She is an alcoholic just like the rest of us and it is hard to believe I once was headed to her country in a B 52 back in 1962 during the Cuban missile crisis. What a lovely person she is. I had to reprogram my mind about Russians.

The goal is to accept change. All of us have a natural resistance to change, very human but in recovery we have to learn to embrace change and look for change. If we don't change, we are sunk. Those walls in our thinking can prevent us from long term sobriety and stop any form of happiness. We are the only ones who can break down these walls that have been installed into our cranium. Now the trick is to find the blockage points that impede our progress. When you find a negative thought, stop and inventory the negativity. "I can't" pops up all the time but maybe you can. We make our own limitations and often we underestimate ourselves. We see a task and it looks like a mountain too high to climb so we quit without trying. Our mind is one thing we can control. We can stretch our boundaries and make our best attempt and leave the results up to God. If we open our mind to learn new things and new ideas our life will be enriched and fun again.

When you get as old as I am you will find your head full of useless information and screwed up ideas. I use my "delete" button as much as possible to make room for new fresh inputs. Also, I find a lot of unused grey matter.

March 14

FINDING YOU

When you were out there drinking that wasn't you. That was somebody twisted and warped with mind altering chemicals but it wasn't the real you. Then you got sober. Was that you? Not even close, that still is not the real you. Until you change that drinking person completely you still haven't found yourself. It may take years to wipe away the damaged soul you once were into the beautiful person God created way back in the beginning. The first inventory exposes some big chunks of truth about who you are at that time. Some of us can't handle the truth and avoid Step 4 & 5 all the way to the grave. But as the song goes, "Getting to

Know You" you can now establish a sober relationship with yourself. It can be the start of something really big or it can stop right there unless we continue for the rest of our lives. Every anniversary I look back at some of the stupid things I have done but I keep chipping away at the block of stone I started with. How many years have you been going the wrong direction? You are not "cured" overnight. Some of those character defects may never leave us or they may sleep awhile and surprise us unexpectedly.

OK, you have been sober for a while, doing the next right thing for X years now. Is this the real you? No, not yet. "Adversity introduces one to himself" a quote I keep close to my heart. When everything is going our way, of course life is wonderful. Then life happens, someone close to us gets killed, a friend commits suicide, the love of your life runs away with your best friend. Any one of these events would knock Mother Teresa off her spiritual path, so us fragile humans take a blow to our serenity and happiness. Now we are getting to the real you. How you react to adversity will show you how far you have come or how far you need to go. Just like this gent who has been off my radar for years comes back to town and starts his horrible behavior all over again in my sandbox. I thought I had a good measure of love and tolerance. Hmmm maybe not yet a candidate for sainthood.

Now you found yourself. Are you done? I say no. Down deep you may have some art in you, maybe not in a painting but in some other pursuit. There are so many things you can grow into and improve the quality of your life as it is now but you have to find the real you first. Good hunting.

March 15

EAT THOSE WORDS

The problem with speaking is that once the words are out there you do not get to edit or delete what you just said. I have said things folks make me eat decades later and again and again. Sometimes what you say may be more painful than a bullet. What comes out of your mouth is bad enough but if you are angry it really goes south in a hurry. I know when I am upset my brain is like a loose cannon and rational thinking is off the table. Nothing good ever comes out of my speech when I am disturbed. Something is wrong with me, and when I speak, I confirm that fact. I know to keep my big mouth shut. When it comes to a war of words I lose. I think of the right thing to say a day later.

My old boss had a sign engraved in wood above his office door. "Take Every Opportunity to Keep Your Mouth Shut." Guess what, his career ended when he said something in confidence at a cocktail party in Washington D.C. He forgot to follow his own advice. I took his failure to heart and try to obey the spirit of that famous sign. We are powerless over most things but we do have control of our tongue. It does its best at rest. I learned I have a "delete" button in my brain right next to a "save" button and those things unsaid have brought me great success.

I utilize the GAP method before opening my yap. God Authorized Pause or rather wait and consider the impact or harm your next verbal message might bring. I used to have a hair trigger response to everything and thought my quick mind was an asset. No more a problem because it was my trigger and I removed it. I need not be in a hurry to make an ass out of myself. I know when I am a upset I am not the "real" me so letting a GAP happen has been a lifesaver and no black eyes since I got sober.

I would love to eat some of the classics that have come out of my loose tongue but unfortunately some are in print for all eternity. My advice is to pretend a scribe is taking notes every time you speak.

March 16

FIX WHO?

My role as a parent and boss in my job, in part, was to fix people. I thought I was pretty good at fixing other poor souls who needed my guidance. Of course, I not dare look at myself. After all I was the Dad and big boss so I looked down on my kids and workers. Oh boy did I ever have to drop that entire line of thinking. It is easier now because my kids parent me now and nobody works under me. My chain of command is simple now. God then me. That's the entire organizational chart. That is not to say I am completely cured of fixing others but now I am quiet about it and just wish in my mind so and so would stop swearing and smoking.

My daughter was a smoker by the time she was 12 and one day I saw her smoking with her buddies from a distance. I cruised down to where she was and she stuffed the lit cigarette into her coat pocket. She tried to blow me off but I kept yacking until smoke came up her sleeve. I advised her the coat was catching fire and she was cold busted. I made her sit down at the kitchen table and smoke the entire pack one after another. I was going to "fix" her from smoking forever. She was having too good a time, so I broke off the filters and made her smoke the fuzzy end with raw tobacco hanging out. Today she is 53 and smokes a pack a day. So much for that lesson! I learned early on I cannot fix anybody if I can't fix my own flesh and blood.

March 17

NEED HELP?

At some time, we all need help. Sounds simple and obvious but why is it so many of us refuse to seek help? In my own case, I was brought up to never have outsiders help, never ask for anything. I have since learned to reverse that thought pattern. In most cases there is someone who can help you with whatever your problem may be and folks are happy to help. In AA the oldest senior members I found to be very approachable and most willing to impart some wisdom. Sort of like the kid in the mail room getting a face to face with the CEO. What a good deal. Asking for help gives someone else the chance to give of themselves and they enjoy helping. Why deny them the joy?

Knowing where you are weak and seeking help is courageous rather than a shortcoming. I am so weak on the computer I just find a 6-year-old kid to help me out. It doesn't even embarrass me anymore but when they talk to me like a 4-year-old that hurts. When the car doesn't work I don't lift the hood and stare at the engine. I have no idea how anything works under the hood. I have a super mechanic in my speed dial. In fact, I have surrounded myself in experts in all sorts of different disciplines. I like to think of my circle of friends and family as a team. My team has been in first place for a long time. The AA group can be a great team when everyone participates and does what they do best for the team. The goal is simple. Stay sober and carry the message to the alcoholic who still suffers.

Help and be helped is part of my daily life which is totally different from the days of the Lone Ranger. Thank God.

March 18

THE GORILLA INSIDE

My computer has a little sticker that says "Intel inside" and sure enough the inside of my computer does magic beyond my intelligence to comprehend. If I opened it up, I would have no idea of what was in there. But since I know myself, I can look inside of myself and deal with my insides. Inside of all of us is good and bad. We can be sweet one minute and raging the next. The trick is to feed the good side and nurture that part of our makeup and try to handle the character flaws as they show themselves. I have a gorilla inside and he is in a cage hibernating. The gorilla will always be there and will never die but I try not to ever wake up this beast in my heart or let him out of the cage. Once the gorilla is loose then there is going to be a long dance. We will dance and dance and it will not be over until the gorilla says it's over. I have already been through the dance of death many times and I am done dancing. The beast in me has been nice and quiet for a long time but that doesn't mean he isn't in there waiting for an opportunity to cause havoc.

The reading today talks about "pruning" to grow and that is a perfect analogy for the 10th Step. A daily pruning job to make just a little more progress on self-improvement. I have a friend in Hawaii who has a little 26 inch Bonsai tree which is 130 years old. He clips away at tiny little twigs and leaves every day. The tree is absolutely beautiful and shows the loving care of the owner. We are just like that tree we are beautiful people who need daily care to stay that way. We often hear "pain is the touchstone of spiritual growth" which I believe 100% but pruning is just small daily changes not so painful. A little nip here a little behavior modification there and progress not perfection is good enough for one day. The first big inventory in Step 4 is sort of like passing a watermelon, it really hurts but feels so good when you are done. As it says in the Big Book page 71: "You have made a good beginning. That being so you have swallowed and digested some big chunks of truth about yourself." I just love this line, what better word than chunks. My message is, the daily pruning will ensure the gorilla stays in hibernation.

Don't wait for someone to bring you flowers, you can decorate your own life and add a garden of gratitude to your new house of recovery.

March 19

INSTANT STEP 10

You all have heard me talk about doing Step 10 every morning in my hour of prayer and meditation and then again at night just before I sleep when I thank God for another wonderful day. However the 10th Step, I learned, is whenever it is needed throughout the day. Plus you can do more than 1 or 2 you can do a dozen if need be. I call that the "instant 10th Step." Most days it is pretty easy because I didn't do too much so there is not much inventory to review. I do it anyway to keep my street squeaky clean. There are rough times like yesterday and my "instant 10th" took more than one hour. I would never ask my sponsees to do something I haven't done myself. So here goes a real demonstration of my 10th Step as an example for your reading pleasure: This dude I haven't seen in a couple of years enters my home group meeting 30 minutes late. He does not live here and I processed my resentment about him long ago. Seeing him triggered the whole ball of wax all over again.

He screwed up a guy I was sponsoring and he told tall tales of his heroics as a 2 star general and a POW all bull sh**. I almost came out of my chair until a fellow member stopped me.

I was really upset to see this guy in living color again. Tenth Step tells me that if I am disturbed there is something wrong with me. I say to myself, hey what the hell is he doing in my home group? Wait a minute, I don't own the meeting I go to on a regular basis and it belongs to all the members of AA of which I am just one. What the hell is he doing in my country? Whoa baby I am just another guest in this country and so far they have not made me in charge of immigration. He looks so arrogant. Oops there goes my judgment button. He comes in late and starts passing notes and whispering to people. OMG I am doing his inventory and not mine as the 10th Step proceeds. I realize my wrongs and this guy doesn't even know how pissed I am nor does he give a rip. What are my fears? Well I am afraid he might ruin a newcomer beyond repair. Again, I am powerless over this guy and what he does, except I don't need to hug him and take him to lunch. I should thank him for making me realize I need to work my program all day every day. He will return to his home country soon and be out of my air space. OK not my air space.

So ends my demo of a 10th Step. Most days are happy, joyous and free but life happens no matter how long you stay sober. Thank God we have a process to handle life on life's terms.

March 20

THE 12 STEPS OF LOVE

Love today means so much more than when I was a practicing drunk. My old idea was, I love you and I want to be loved back in equal measure or else the deal is off. Since those crazy days I have learned to have NO strings attached to my love and my acts of giving. I have no expectations for love given freely especially knowing I was loved freely when I was at my worst. In fact, I have learned to have no strings attached to anything. It is so much easier than keeping books on what is owed back to me.

Love is deeper than I imagined when I first started this journey of recovery. Each of the 12 steps takes me to a new level of love which was beyond my comprehension until I did the Step. I developed a new understanding of my Higher Power. I know God loves me and that is a cold hard fact. He has kept me around for 77 years through thick and thin. That is love. My faith has continued to grow and faith and love go together like a marriage. Trust, caring, unselfishness and helping others are all connected to love. Love is not selfish but when it has a selfish motive the love does not last. Trust me on this one. Love has no ceiling it is unlimited.

Remember your bottom? The thought of self-love probably would make you puke. Now as the Steps get completed you begin to feel better about yourself. Until Step 9 when the damage must be addressed as best as possible so you can feel like a whole person again on the right path. You can't love yourself until you know who you are. You have to love yourself before you can love somebody else. Any sooner and the chemistry is wrong. All of my previous relationships were doomed because I was in them, not even counting the other person's part in the deal. I was so selfish and ego driven all my relationships would be gone with the wind eventually. Now with a real meaningful set of principles in my life I can form great relationships because the love is from the heart, real and lasting. Service to others is love. Love is on my gratitude list as a separate line item but love is embedded in all the other items on my list. I am a regular love bug as one of my homies calls me.

At my first meeting they told me they would love me until I could love myself and I thought they were crazy. It took a few years but now I understand they were speaking the truth, with love.

March 21

VIGILANCE

If the doctor gave you a pill that you had to take every day or die, you would take that pill even if it was a bitter pill to swallow. The same thing applies to my AA program. I need to take my medicine every day to stay alive spiritually. Vigilance is on my gratitude list (eventually I will talk about every item on that list). If I am not vigilant about my disease I will die. I stick to my routine no matter what, storms, death, sickness, I still pray and meditate. My mind needs to be controlled or disciplined if you will. Things are just rosy most of the time and this lures me into a sense that I am OK. My disease never takes a vacation or a "time out." It is just waiting for my guard to go down and wham across the chops. My life before was chock full of bad habits. Today I am still a creature of habit but I have replaced the worst habits for good healthy ones. I enjoy my habits or discipline or vigilance whichever you want to label it. I know I cannot stay happy, joyous and free on yesterday's service, prayer and meetings. I need to do those things again today. I watch for HALT, not to get Hungry, Angry, Lonely or Tired. Usually those come all at the same time. I can't afford a slip, so vigilance is key to my survival.

Vigilance also applies to my sixth sense of avoiding danger before it happens. I have learned to be aware of the dangers to my serenity and peace of mind. I can avoid brash arrogant people and go a different path. I can say no to a party I know is going to have a drinking theme. I cannot go on a trip that puts my health in jeopardy. I try to keep alert and awake to all my surroundings. My antenna is always operating to spot trouble. If my AA program loses its priority, I am a lost soul. I have witnessed so many of my brothers fall back into the pit and die a horrible, nasty death. Unfortunately, you don't get a temperature or a red flag doesn't flash as you fall backward away from the things you need to do to maintain your spiritual condition. It is slowly eating away in an insidious manner until you crash and burn. This is a quiet disease. We need to be noisy about our recovery and share at meetings and talk to other alcoholics. This disease will tell you that you are immune to alcohol. Don't believe that ever, it's a lie.

I have accepted the fact I am an alcoholic, but I am OK with that. I know what medicine I must take every day without fail. Vigilance.

March 22

WHAT THE WORLD OWES ME

We have discussed amends at great length, mending fences, paying debts, repairing relationships to complete our 9th Step. What about the amends owed me? Sam owes me $100; my boss owes me a vacation; my bank owes me for being hacked; the baker only gave me 11 cookies when I paid for a dozen, on and on. I used to sit on my pity pot and mentally list all that was owed to me. My resentments went deep and I would add to my list of grievances to make sure I stayed pissed off. I resented my employer for not sending me to the places I wanted to go and let me fly the aircraft of my choice or even place me in the type command I wanted. They sent me where they wanted for their needs, the bastards. I forgot to be grateful to them for sending me to 2 years of college, paying me well and spending a million bucks training me to be a pilot. In my 30 years my employer sent me to 8 years of training and schools. Was I worth the millions they spent on my ungrateful butt? On balance I got the better part of the bargain for sure. OK here comes one of Mike's secrets to a great life: take all that is owed to you, the entire list and forget about it already.

One of my favorite spiritual readings is: "Take all the good things people have done for you and carve them in granite, take all the wrongs done to you and write them in sand." Great idea. If you play golf as poorly as I did you end up in a sand trap often. Those sand traps all have a rake close by for you to smooth out your mess as you hack away at your ball. I think my 10th Step every morning is my "rake" to cover up the stuff I wrote in the sand. It is so much easier to keep the balance sheet at zero instead of keeping a book of debts owed. I forgive everybody forever. That's real freedom. If someone "borrows" money from me I treat it as a gift. If I get paid back great, if I don't get paid back great, because I forgot about it as soon as I gave it. I bought an old junk car from a guy I worked with in 1962 and promised to pay him on payday. Well he got reassigned and was gone and I had no idea where he went or how to pay him. The car went away too. I never forgot my debt even though it was a small amount and in 1978 I ran into this guy by accident. He had not forgotten either and when I forked over the cash with interest, he was very surprised and it made me feel wonderful. It was a precursor to doing my 9th Step amends and in every case the experience was weight reducing. I can fly today.

I owe the world of AA for saving my life and the world owes me nothing at all.

March 23

ACCEPTANCE

When I was new, "acceptance" was drummed into my head. Page 449 in the 3rd edition. "Acceptance is the answer to all my problems." Thus, Acceptance is on my gratitude list because it is key to my recovery. Like Popeye says, 'I am who I am." BUT when we first get sober, we can't answer the question, "Who am I?" We have lost sight of who we really are. We have departed the world of reality and entered fantasy land or doomsday land. We hate ourselves and it takes a goodly amount of time to form a loving relationship with who we really are. I felt so unlovable at my first meeting and those happy idiots wanted to hug me. Yuk. Don't touch me for God's sake. I had to get all the way through the Steps before I even felt like a meaningful member of the human race. Finally, I could accept my status. I am OK, not less than, not better than. There is a rule not written down anywhere but a rule just the same, "No relationships in the first year." Why? Because you are not ready to love someone else until you love yourself. Wow when I violated that rule it almost was fatal to my recovery. The real you is buried pretty deep after years of being "out there." It takes a lot of prayer and 24 hours to unearth the real deal the real you. You probably forgot how to play, how to read a book cover to cover, how to stop and smell the flowers.

Your inventory got to the big chunks of who you are and you accept the good and the bad. Now how about other people? A lot more difficult because now you have a plan, a design for living, you have principles and boundaries. The folks you meet don't have a program, the poor bastards. Some have no principles or ethics. Accepting people, places and things as they are, not as we would have them. Easy to say but hard to swallow. Some of us go the other way from sinner to disciple and try to change other people in our lives and fix them because we love them and want the best for them. We know the best of course. The best thing we can do is leave them the hell alone and accept them warts and all. Not easy when we live and work with people who annoy us by their behavior. Let it go or get dragged down with them. Acceptance is the key that opens the lock to the chains of bondage and set me free.

It should be no surprise that the last Step in the process of grief is acceptance and moving on. My son set the perfect example when he accepted his fatal disease and went straight to acceptance.

March 24

A DO OVER

Every day I thank God for my new life that He has granted me. Not only is it new but 100 times better than the former life. Can you recall your last hangover morning? Holding your head and having nothing to look forward to? Viewing life as a big pain in the ass and resenting almost everyone you meet? Then, if you can imagine, an angel sat down beside you while you are holding your face like an accordion and this angel says: "Hey dude! How about we do this all over again? Wipe the slate clean and start a brand-new life with a bright future and love. Peace and serenity thrown in for good measure. You can be useful, happy joyous and free. So how about it?" You don't believe the angel and ask. OK what's the catch? "Glad you asked," says the angel. "OK dude all you have to do is give up and raise your hands in surrender, stop using the stuff that gave you the headache you have, find out who you are and what you have done (inventory) mend all your broken fences. Connect with a Higher Power and we will provide a lifetime of help. Now does that sound fair enough?" There you sit. Take the deal or continue in misery. Up to you.

I had two such angels appear before me right after my first AA meeting. They didn't look like angels but they were for sure. Now when I was born, my parents named me after an angel. And although I was no angel myself, I believed in them. I used to think I had two guardian angels watching over me. One day shift and one night shift. I envision the night angel sitting at the bar, unshaven, messy hair, cigarette with along ash hanging looking at me with disdain and saying to me, "Hey, I can't take this anymore, I quit." I lost my angels until those two angels from AA took me aside and promised me a "do over" if I followed their path and joined them. What did I have to lose? I took the deal, all of it, the whole 9 yards. My new life started about 25 years ago and that's how old I am in my mind. I believe in angels again and find them in all sorts of disguises. I feel young, act young, and only when I get a look in the mirror do I realize Father Time has had his way with me. I hang around other people, do my duties, help others and that way I don't have to look at myself. I am a very young man trapped in a very old body but my mind is young because it was not used much before.

Every morning I thank God for a second chance at life, a new start with a clean rap sheet, I pray I will do it right this time around.

March 25

THE ART OF RESPONSIBILITY

Now that we have been in recovery, we accept responsibility as a matter of normal life. Remember the last time you drove drunk? Where was responsibility then? I thank God that I didn't kill some innocent people when I was drunk driving. I know a prominent lawyer who was driving in a blackout. He killed a man driving who was driving with his wife. The amazing part of the story is after being convicted, the lawyer entered AA, did his amends to the widow. She, in turn, testified on his behalf at his first parole hearing and the lawyer was set free to practice law again. I thought when I became a full time drunk, I could drop the heavy burden called "responsibility." I wanted to be responsible for nothing but it just doesn't work. I was responsible for stealing time from my family and killing my body by abuse. When I was in a position of responsibility, I used it as a shield to cover my bad behavior. When I was flying aircraft with hundreds of people strapped in the rear, I was less than 100% responsible. I never flew drunk but let us say I was fuzzy. My amends were my chance for a "do over" and to take responsibility for my past behavior and mend my ways for future actions. When I do the next right thing, it is doing an indirect amends for all those years of doing the wrong thing. I don't have to think about being responsible today. It is part of who I am.

The next part of responsibility is sorting out what I am responsible for and what is not really my job or duty. This is not so easy or clear. I see a couple arguing on the street and the male hits the female in the face. Captain America wants to save the damsel in distress as is the nature of a red-blooded hero. Not so fast Captain. This is not America and the rules are different in a different culture. My gut was going one way and my heart another direction. Luckily the female decked the male and she drove off on a motorbike before the male could get off his butt. In AA I am responsible to help anyone who puts out his hand, that's easy. But when a member is abusing the fellowship to market his products what do I do? I could do nothing and let everyone deal with this guy on their own or call him on his behavior. This is where the art comes in. Discretion and diplomacy may be needed to determine just exactly where does your responsibility begin and end. The rule of powerlessness might help you in your decision. I wasted much agonizing over stuff I have no control or responsibility. I pray for guidance in the art of my responsibilities.

When someone I am trying to help drinks again, I used to feel responsible but I learned I cannot keep someone else sober. I do my inventory and ask myself what is it I did not say or did not do to help keep this guy on the road. For that I am responsible.

THE PROMISES

It is no secret the 12 Promises listed on page 83 of the Big Book come after Step 9. Once we have done Step 9 to the best of our ability those promises all come true just as advertised. I can verify it in my own case. After Step 9 you are into the last three Steps of daily growth and those will be part of the rest of your life, and that is a promise. My AA grandma Alice, now long passed away, taught me there are more than 50 more promises listed in the first 164 pages of the Big Book. She told me I need to keep reading the book for the rest of my life and find all of them. Some are not so obvious and you grow into the understanding as your years pile up. I know I am surprised that someone keeps going into my book and adding stuff that wasn't there before. I now realize it was me that wasn't there before. You want an example? OK then look at page 86 and you will find a sentence there: "Our thought-life will be placed on a much higher plane when our thinking is cleared of wrong motives." Sounds like a promise to me.

Your assignment is to find another promise and let me know what it is. I am not sure I have found all 50+ so I am willing to learn. The amazing part of this program is the hope in the process and all the sayings and stuff people keep repeating are 100% true. The old guys say, "It keeps getting better." I didn't believe it because I was floating on air the first few years after doing all the Steps. How could I possibly feel any better than this. My happiness meter is maxed out or so I thought. There were new plateaus and new areas of understanding that were beyond my comprehension. There were whole sections of my brain that had never been used. God is doing for me what I could not do myself. That fact came to me suddenly just like it says in "The Promises." The word "promise" was not a good word in the past life. It seemed that other people's promises never came to fruition. My promises were empty as well. This program offered a brand new set of promises but this time they are solid as stone.

If you are having trouble filling up your gratitude list, just read the promises and you will find a ton of treasure. That is a promise.

March 27

GET OUT THE CAUTION TAPE

I liken my bottom to a smoking hole in the ground with yellow caution tape all around the damage site. "Proceed with Caution," was good advice to all. I had dug a deep black bottom of despair for myself and could never get out of the hole without help. I got the rescue team of my homegroup to pull me out before I lost it all. To my way of thinking the first seven Steps filled in the hole so reconstruction could begin and not before. Then I wanted to live a life of a white picket fence but first I needed to mend the fences of those I had harmed. So the yellow tape came down and the outside world could proceed with relative safety in my direction. I always laugh out loud every year when the reading comes around to "Yes, there is a long period of reconstruction ahead" (Big Book page 83) Yeah like the rest of your life dude. How many years of destruction was I involved in? Decades of going the wrong way will take decades of amends and reconstruction. I can only start when I do the best job possible on my 9th Step.

 When I review my life before I got sober there was no plan, no design for my life. Stuff happened and I reacted to what happened. I was clueless and let the wind whip me around the world with no direction and no safe harbor in the horizon. I am lucky that circumstances treated me very well and I now know it was God working in my life even though I did not seek His help. The God of my understanding pulled me out of the pit of darkness and despair and the fellowship taught me how to live with a design this go around. A brand-new life is way past my imagination. When I did my inventory, it introduced me to myself the good the bad and the ugly. I was not Captain America or 007 as my gin-soaked brain conjured up but the real me, the truth. So thru owning up, growing up and cleaning up I can see the world with a new pair of glasses. I cannot thank all the people who helped me get through the Steps but I can pass it on now as a fully vested member of AA who has done all the Steps and continues to do them every day. Now my house is built on firm ground, the yellow tape has come down and I have the white picket fence of my dreams.

Life is wonderful today but I must remember the deep smoking hole that I came from and to which I could return if I pick up a drink.

March 28

RAW SOBRIETY

Not picking up a drink is AA 101 so let's move on and talk about living life on life's terms, service, recovery, helping others, self-improvement, growth. I listen to some guys in my home group who are sober but there it ends. I hear nothing of sponsorship, doing the Steps and progressing. They are happy to be sober and that is enough for them. Well in my experience, when these people hit a speed bump of life and their girlfriend leaves them, they get drunk again and can't figure out why. They have not changed is why. They are still angry, selfish dudes who never underwent the "change" the Steps promise. They are spectator's in the program and not participants. They are sitting on the bench watching the world go by without addressing their inventory and their faults. Making amends is off the radar needless to say. Every morning when I work on my "insurance" policy to make it through the next 24 hours, I am adding credit to my spiritual bank account, so when I hit a speed bump, I can handle the down side of life.

There is an old saying, "If it is not broke, don't fix it." For us alcoholics that is bad advice because it is broke and will always be broke. It needs daily fixing. There is no cruise control in recovery. You need to keep growing. If you quit rowing the boat you will go downstream sooner or later. Your disease does not rest so we cannot rest either. You need not be in a hurry but you need to keep moving forward. I have a good friend who calls it "slowbriety." Meaning it takes time and patience to work on all that needs attention. "Well I am sober and that's the point, right?" My answer: OK that is point 1 of 12 points. Just being sober is like a milk stool with one leg. The way I look at it is, I have no idea what part of my recovery program I could eliminate and not put myself in jeopardy so I do the whole 9 yards. I have been doing this for so long I enjoy every yard of the entire program, I don't want to subtract anything, in fact I look for stuff to add. The thought of a drink has not entered my mind as an option for decades. It is off the menu forever along with liver and lima beans.

This disease tells me I don't have a disease. Wrong. I have learned to keep moving away from my last drink or else I am moved toward another. Standing still is not an option.

March 29

UNCERTAINTY AND EXPECTATIONS

Fear of the unknown haunts many of us into a downward spiral. FEAR Future Events Appearing Real. The sun will come up in the morning, of this I am certain. It always has and no reason to doubt it but all else is up in the air. Before I got sober and learned about powerlessness, I had delusions of strength and power. I had a patch on my uniform with lightning bolts and a sword. Power. "Peace is Our Profession" my patch said. BS fear and intimidation that our enemies would be nuked was our profession. Insurance is nothing more than selling uncertainty. You can buy some peace of mind against the worst-case scenario. In times of uncertainty we have expectations of an outcome. We all know expectations are a resentment in the embryo stage. I used to lose sleep over expectations and the disappointment of losses. Thank God this program has given me some measure of emotional maturity to handle uncertainty. If I stay in the "now" then future uncertainty is off the radar. I have no control over uncertainty so why upset my serenity over what is out of my hands.

Now the way I deal with uncertainty is buy some spiritual "insurance" in my morning prayer and meditation. I gird my loins against the unknown of the next 24. I am prepared to handle what other people say and do to me. I divide up the workload for the day. I have to go to a meeting and meet a guy who needs help. I let God take care of the economy, North Korea, the floods in Houston and all other matters. He doesn't need my help. I have a family member who is crazy about nuclear war and has bought books on how to survive and is in constant fear of rogue governments. What a waste of a nice day. I do have family in Houston and all I can do is support them with a loving word and some prayer in their behalf. None of us control hurricanes but we can blow up a floatation device. I cannot change the wind but I can adjust my sails (read attitude). I let God do what He wants when He wants and try not to get ahead of God. Godspeed.

I have learned that everything that happens is supposed to happen no matter what my expectations or desires are. It's not my show.

March 30

ATTITUDE ADJUSTMENT

An old TV series called "The A Team" had a character in the rogue cast called "BA" that stood for Bad Attitude. The character never smiled and had nothing but negative things to say and called everybody a fool. We all know somebody like BA and probably steer clear of nasty, mean dudes whenever possible. We cannot change the tick of the clock, we cannot change anybody else, we cannot change our past but we can change our attitude. We are powerless over much of what happens in our life but we do own our attitude. We can choose to be happy, joyous and free. That hour upon awakening every morning I refer to it as "prayer and meditation" but I could name it "attitude adjustment hour." I read good, positive stuff, I say real meaningful prayers and get in contact with my Higher Power so how can I miss? Then of course there is my gratitude list that makes me smile and lifts my spirits as I gaze on the basket full of gifts God has given me by doing this program. Every day starts so positive there is absolutely no room for doom and gloom.

Do other people affect my attitude? Sure they do. That's why I pick a group of like survivors to spend one hour with every morning. They are my brothers, my friends. Not all of them like me, nor do I go have coffee with them afterwards. That's OK, I don't get angry. Selfish folks ruin my day. I hang with the winners and positive guys who make me laugh.

When something bad happens, I recognize my stinking thinking as my brain goes south on me. I have learned not to wallow in the s**** and get a quiet moment where I adjust my attitude and re-evaluate the situation. Can I do anything about this problem? Probably not, so forget about it. If I can do something then I need to think about the right course of action and even ask God for some help and courage. Talking to someone I trust, like my sponsor, helps adjust my attitude. Often I am too close to the problem to see it in focus. Attitude is one of those things that have no upper ceiling. It can always be improved and educated. Helping others improves my attitude, I can't help anybody if I have a bad attitude.

You can re-start your day anytime you need to change your attitude and get some wrench to adjust your loose nut.

March 31

BAND OF BROTHERS

I am sure all of you have seen films about combat and the bond of comrades in battle. It is a certain kind of brotherhood that comes from survival of life and death drama. Call it war in most cases. I can tell you from experience that my combat buddies are very close by this special bond of relationships forged in fire. AA is no different. Alcohol can kill you just as dead as an enemy bullet. The war against alcohol is a life and death fight just as intense as any gun battle. So it should come as no surprise that the friendships you develop in AA are lifelong loving relationships. We are the lucky ones. We are survivors. We are still alive and some of our alcoholic brothers have perished in the battles lost. We have a lot in common with all those folks we share meetings with. It is a band of winners, only if we follow some basic survival "suggestions." The Titanic sunk to the bottom of the ocean and we are all in a dingy together. Everybody has an oar and we all need to row (be in service) to keep our fellowship afloat. We can make it to the shore if we work together.

My very first meeting of AA, I met a group of fellow survivors and I am still in touch with 10 folks from that very first meeting back in the 90's. We are friends for life. In combat my life was saved by 2 men, they 12-stepped me into the program and saved my life again. Those 2 guys are in my life today. The only way I can repay them is to save some poor, suffering soul from the battle of the bottle. The guys I sponsored are very close friends and they really don't need me to work the Steps anymore, but we are close on a different level. Why is this bond special? Well, let's see. We all went through the same basic training, put down the drink, got a sponsor (some prefer the drill sergeant type or get a pussy cat like me) went through the 12 Steps, got in service and help others. So that is a lot in common. This is the common thread through all of us. That connection leads to love and a lifelong relationship. Trust me on this one. As I look at my email contacts, I can see that 90% are AA contacts and there are about 400 of those. I literally have friends all over this planet.

I am not in combat every day but the bottle can kill me just as dead as a missile. My brothers help me stay protected every day and I know I have an entire army covering my back.

April 1

EMOTIONAL SOBRIETY

I am wobbly. My Higher Power is my Rock and is my stable moment in time during that first hour of contact with Him. My whole life was based on "pleasing" others and bending over backward for approval and recognition. I finally learned not to depend on others for my happiness. As we learn, that is an inside job. Making other people happy does not always make me happy. The mood and whims of others no longer drive my attitude. I get my attitude and priorities straight in the morning and deal with others very carefully after that. Pleasing others almost got me killed. I tried to please my bosses and maybe get promoted for doing their bidding. It was "cool' to volunteer for dangerous missions and I did that to gain recognition and came close to denying my children of a father. I could have said no but I did not want to disappoint the big boss. A sure sign of low self-esteem is saying "yes" at every opportunity. It took some growth on my part because in sobriety I was volunteering for more service positions than I could handle. One old timer told me I was denying a newcomer the chance for service so let others step up to the plate.

After some work, I learned to be true to myself and stay within my ability and capability. In other words, "get right sized" and not try to be Superman. The secret to stability is in the process of giving instead of taking. Once you take yourself out of the equation in your actions then happiness comes from doing the next right thing and helping others. It is so much more stable than selfish pursuits. If I try to follow God's will and step back and leave the results up to God and let the chips fall where they may then for me that is stability. I am powerless over how people react to my actions good or bad. Sometimes I am not "pleasing" to others and I am OK with that now. Once I abort my principles for the desires of others I get slapped in the face every time. My instincts come from years of working this program. Am I right all the time? Of course not, but I try my best. I may need to make amends if off the mark but that is OK too.

My emotions used to be on a roller coaster, now the downs are short and the ups last a lot longer. If I follow my heart instead of my head the result is stability.

April 2

WHAT WILL THE NEIGHBORS THINK?

When I was a kid my parents drummed into me the idea that what the neighbors think was of great importance. The lawn had to be cut and neat because of the neighbors not because it looked good to us. We had to be quiet because we would not want the neighbors to think we were undisciplined. Our car had to be clean, not for our benefit but what would people think if we drove a sloppy car. The clothes we wore had to be fitting for public exposure. You know what? The neighbors never did tell us what they thought of us. My mother had a full formal living room that no one was allowed to use. I was in charge of cleaning, getting ready for a senator or the Pope to come by for a visit. Twenty years we never sat in that "living" room. My early life was all about appearances. Looking good was top priority. As a teenager I wanted a car to run and get me from A to B then I wanted to impress my friends, I got fancier cars and finally a Caddie. I had arrived, a car to match my ego and self-importance. Funny now I just want to get from A to B again.

When I first came to AA I heard "To Thy Own Self Be True" I finally got the message. "Appearances" have nothing to do with my insides. The only person I need to impress is myself and my Higher Power. I want to be acceptable and approachable in order to be of service to someone else. Sobriety is very attractive. If you are happy, joyous and free, it shows in your face and your actions. The women in AA taught me to dress well, shave and be on time for meetings. "Mike you aren't going to the beach. You are attending an AA meeting and you need to show that newcomer you care about this program." I do those things to be approachable by a suffering alcoholic. I learned not to compare my insides to others outsides. That rich guy over there may be miserable in his heart. In AA nobody is more important than another, there is no rank, no pecking order. We are all God's kids. Recently a newcomer said I was "inspirational" and I told him that I work on inspiration for one hour upon awakening every single morning of my life. I am constantly inspired so I should be inspirational, and it should show. That's my job. I accepted the compliment.

What other people think of me is none of my business. What I think of myself is top priority and I don't stop looking for improvement.

April 3

OMISSION

Some amends are very clear. Yes, I threw the family cat through the picture window. A specific action and reaction. The cat is dead, the window is broken and Mom has a broken heart over Fluffy. However, if you want to do complete amends you have to search your inventory for all the things you did not do but should have done. In my own case, I was a father of 4 children, but I really was in name only for much of the time. I was missing, gone of my own free will, essentially stealing time from my family. A sin of omission instead of commission. (there were those too). I used my military "missions" as a cover for my absence, but the truth is I volunteered for those "missions." So as my amends, I have spent 3 times more time with my family in the last 25 years than the 25 years before. I can never replace "being there" as they grew up but I am available now. One daughter lost her husband and my son passed, especially painful to the other daughter with 4 years invested in assisting my son pass away. My 3 grandchildren have some special needs and I am able to help in some ways I could not for my own children.

This amends process takes some deep thought and soul searching. The car you dinged and never left a note is easy to remember but stuff like metal anguish and forgetfulness. It is harder to recall what you didn't do than physical damage and financial debts. What I did as a husband and father was leave the child rearing to my wife while I was playing warrior. I was sober when she really needed help. She worked all her life and contracted cancer and could not work any longer, I was able to be there for her financially and spiritually plus being there for my kids as their mother slipped away. Making amends for sins of omission is just as rewarding as paying off a debt. I can say from experience all these amends I mentioned were especially uplifting and a large part of my recovery. It is by design that Steps 8 and 9 come after you are sober for a while and done your inventory. The help of your Higher Power in completing this task of mending fences is all important. If there is a doubt, whether you owe an amends, make it anyway. It doesn't hurt.

 The best way to make amends is to put yourself in the place of the other person. Try to take your slanted view of events out of the picture and put your dunce hat on.

April 4

SIMPLICITY

We often hear that this AA program is a simple program for complicated people. I disagree with that thought. We would like to think we are special, unique and thus complicated. Yes, we can complicate life if we choose and we can declutter our life as a course of action. I remember this guy who used to force his way into the speaker's platform to do his share. Most speakers talked for 5+ minutes but this man had one message: "Don't drink and go to meetings," period, end of story. He had 20 years sober and that was his simple solution. I was looking for more in-depth analysis but what he said is 100% correct. The one that grabs me is: "You won't get drunk if you don't take the first drink." Duh. Sounds stupid but everyone who ever relapsed must have forgotten the simple truth. I also like the Steps put in simple form. The first three steps: I can't, He can, I think I will let Him." Wow, so true, but those three Steps you will be doing for the rest of your life, simple or not. Or how about this one, for all 12 Steps, give up, clean up, make up and grow up. Again, very short and sweet but true.

Lawyers make a living by making things complicated. I would like to be the opposite of a lawyer (in more ways than one). I would like to have clear sky and a smooth road for the rest of my life. I did complicated, and it is too hard on the body, mind and spirit. It will make you old before your time. It will rob you of happiness and steal your valuable hours and days or even years. This is why the early morning routine of peace and quiet where I visit my Higher Power is so important. I get down to basics and not take on the troubles of the world. I don't take on the family drama of other people's inventory. It is just little old me and God. My chores are few and simple. I give over the impossible like world peace to God and I get busy with the possible like write a friendly letter. If I accept my powerlessness I can see, I can adjust my attitude and priorities and very little else. There is no burden on my shoulders, I have done all my amends, carry no resentments and the roof doesn't leak and I quit doing homework so I am free to enjoy the day.

I try to stretch my creativity in my new-found freedom, so making complicated stuff simple, to me, is real creativity.

April 5

DEEP AMENDS

I take this amends process very seriously. It has been so rewarding and brought new levels of freedom and happiness I could never imagine. Doing amends led to other benefits besides mending the fences. First of all, the Step says make a list of all persons harmed. Just because they are dead or unavailable does not exclude them from the list. Just make a list and worry about how, when, or if later on down the road. In my case, I did a lot of damage over a long period of time, so the list was extensive and some names I could not even remember but they went down on the list by description (the Navy commander I punched out in a bar in Japan for example) or groups of people (the VFW convention in Orlando who asked me to be speaker. Very slurred offering on their dime) or an institution such as the Catholic church where I was altar boy. I supplemented my lunch money with offerings out of the collection basket or the entire United States Air Force for short changing them in some of my work. It is not just Dick and Jane for my list it goes much deeper than individuals. There was a time when I was in a position of great responsibility and all my troops went down with the ship when I screwed up and got fired. Those poor folks went to the four winds and some of them would like to kill me!

By deep amends I mean you may have to spend some money in your quest to do a complete job. In my case I had to get on several airplanes and travel long distances to get to all the areas where I did my alcoholic damage. Then the next step is replacing amends for persons not found or passed away. Here is where creativity kicks in. For example, in Vietnam there was no way I could find all the people I had harmed 35 years ago so I found a young man in high school in Dalat, Vietnam who was a very bright student. Just by chance I met him in an internet shop and we developed a relationship that has carried through his high school year and with some sponsorship I was able to assist him into college at the University of Singapore. Today he is married and has a top engineering job. In the case of all the people I cannot find, I try to do some acts of kindness for someone else to replace the ones on my list who are unreachable. This process is wonderful for the soul. I feel like I have replaced parts of my soul scattered around my path of destruction and drunken behavior. This will be ongoing for the rest of my life because I am not sure how many amends I need to make to bring the balance sheet back to zero.

The bottom line on amends is I am willing to go to any lengths, swim any ocean or climb any mountain to make things right in the eyes of my Higher Power.

April 6

PROGRAMMING

In the old days I used to feel like I was on the end of a buggy whip and life just snapped me all about at will. I never had a plan or direction. Stuff happened and I reacted to it. When I first came into AA, I had no problem with the God thing but they kept calling AA a "program" and I did not want to be "programmed." My life was a mess and these guys wanted to change me. No way. As the fog cleared, I could see the need to be "programmed" by the AA program. Better stated, A Design for Living. My life before could be titled "The Rocky Road to Hell." I made a grand decision to undergo the "change," or in other words, do the Steps. Is it programming? You bet it is and I am happy to be re-programmed every morning and every evening. For the first time in my life I had some white lines that I needed stay between and have some structure and discipline. My entire thinking process had to be rebuilt from scratch. My attitude needed adjustment and priorities needed to be re-structured. All I had to do is surrender to my powerlessness.

I sit in the same chair every morning, at the same time and read the same 6 books and say the same 8 prayers. Never miss, never change the routine. Programming? Yes sir. The theme of the first hour every day is reminding myself I am not the director, it is not my play, and it is not my theater. I am but a bit player in the game of life. I ask for help and plan only the next 24 hours. I admit my powerlessness to my Higher Power and seek His will not mine. I did it the wrong way for 50 years and proved to myself I needed a "program." That first hour is all about getting out of myself and addressing my selfish ways. So many of my prayers are about helping my fellow man and being in service. Many more of my prayers have a happy story of hope, smiles and laughter. Goal setting to do the next right thing and focus on what is right and not who is right. I admit my faults and seek improvement.

I am so happy with this structure and discipline which led me down the Road of Happy Destiny. I enjoy my daily brainwashing because my mind can go south in a heartbeat.

April 7

HAPPINESS MANAGEMENT 101

Problems, problems. My problem is managing my happiness since I have so much of it. Time for my short course on Happiness Management 101. How do I stay so happy? First, when I wake up, I discover I am still alive and that makes me happy. I am in Thailand and that makes me happy because it is where I want to live. I have two feet to put on the floor. Since one of my very best friends has only one leg, I am very happy to have all working parts. I am very grateful as soon as I open my eyes and that is directly linked to my happiness. Then I consider where I fit in the universe. I have been fired as manager of the planet, so God is now in charge and that makes me happy. What a relief. I consider my part in world affairs, again I have no more place on the world stage and that makes me happy. What is my job today? Hmmm, help somebody else, that will make me happy. Do some basic exercise to keep all my body parts in relatively good shape and keep my joints lubricated. In short, staying alive makes me happy and taking care of God's equipment makes me happy.

Since I am happy, I smile and give every living creature I meet a smile and I get a thousand smiles back, so that makes me happy. I am too happy to allow the presence of trouble so I am basically trouble free except for all this happiness I need to manage. All luxury items to focus on. If I seek out a forgotten friend that makes me happy. To just take a walk and pet a few dogs and smell the flowers, that makes me happy. I get in touch with nature and enjoy God's artwork in my surroundings and that makes me happy. I find I am easily entertained by the company of some friends and listen to their conversation and that makes me happy. None of this would happen if I was not sober. That is Life Today 101. If I lose my sobriety, I can burn my gratitude list and watch my happiness go with the wind up in smoke. I can't forget, as I laugh today, I used to cry in my beer. My management technique is to care for my body, mind and spirit every day without fail. It is easy to do if I declutter my life from shiny objects, free myself from resentments and be of service to my fellow mankind.

I cannot change the world but I can do my best to be happy, joyous and free in my little corner of my world.

April 8

GOLD MINE

True enough for me, this program is a virtual gold mine. I hit the Lotto of Life. I am a winner for the first time ever. I would have to say the product is much more valuable than gold however. It was a second chance at life without alcohol. I never imagined giving up my nectar of the Gods (as I called it in those boozy days). This "gold" is not mine to keep I soon learned. I must give it all away, every ounce, the entire product must be passed on. I can't keep it unless I give it away. Huh? One of the program oxymoron's, the program dies if I am not in service and not available to the guy who needs help. My problem (a luxury problem) is I give but receive even more back. My basket is overflowing with gifts I must give away. It is a never-ending upward cycle of giving and receiving. As I look at my gratitude list, all 36 items are much more important than all the gold in Fort Knox.

Here I am at the gold mine and collecting some nuggets. Do I put some in my bag and call it a day? No sir. They tell me I just barely scratched the surface of the Mother Lode. I have come to believe this is true. The old timers said, "it will keep getting better" and with some years picking away at the gold mine I have to agree. The more I dig the more I learn and find out how much I didn't know. I had no idea ignorance could go so deep. I will be a gold miner for the rest of my days. We have to be the opposite of Midas and not hoard the gold or anything else for that matter. I work on a spiritual wakening upon awakening every single morning and I get it from somewhere. Either the readings or an intuitive thought or a prayer answered but I keep at it until it happens.

I have no doubt that the dividends earned from the gold in this program will last a lifetime and for generations yet to come.

April 9

ACTS OF KINDNESS

A big part of "thinking of others" is action. It's actually doing something for someone other than ourselves. I was taught, from the beginning, to perform random acts of kindness. I will never forget crossing a bridge in the Bay Area when the driver in front of me paid my $5 toll fee. I tried to find the car ahead of me not knowing which one was my benefactor but I smiled and waved to a lot of surprised motorists. It is contagious. Actually, it was 2 acts because the toll operator could have easily pocketed the $5. Once I had a sponsee who had an extreme case of selfishness and I assigned him to perform random acts of kindness and not get credit for them. If caught in the act the rule was to do two more. A very difficult task for this guy but he bought some flowers for his secretary and put them on her desk but not only did he get caught but she threatened him with sexual harassment. Needless to say, he fired me as a sponsor and we were both relieved. "No good deed will go unpunished," is one of the laws of nature. The point is not to derive some benefit from these acts of kindness. The benefit is you feel better about yourself. Reward enough.

To me, kindness is an attitude that needs to grow with time. Many of my morning prayers touch on kindness and giving. "Give every living creature a smile" for example. These days I smile all the time without having to think about it. I am looking for ways to give back. Even small things like picking up someone else's trash or helping someone with loading packages. Selfishness is our enemy and doing for others attacks that bad boy head on. Getting out of ourselves takes away aches and pains (read self-centeredness). Kindness can be in giving money but most kindness is the form of a encouraging word to someone who needs a boost, a smile to a stranger, a cheerful attitude of happiness. It is very attractive and contagious. It takes some time to change from a totally selfish bastard to Mother Teresa. It's one day at a time just like all other major personality changes.

Our entire program is built on giving to others, if we don't the program dies, and we die too. I can't change the world, but I can change my world by being a little kinder.

April 10

SICK PUPPY

"Ask Him in your morning meditation what you can do each day for the man who is still sick." Big Book page 164. Most of us take that to mean helping the alcoholic who has not yet achieved sobriety. It is true enough but to me it goes a lot further. In my way of thinking it means helping anybody who needs my help, alcoholic or otherwise. Even a step beyond, I include my fellow earth travelers who have been sober for a while. By "sick" I think there is all kinds of sick, emotional, mental and physically sick. I know I am a sick puppy from time to time. Luckily not often but still I am not banging on all cylinders all the time. So when I go to a meeting I don't know if I am going to help somebody or I am the one who is going to be helped. I try to keep an open mind and ask myself, "who is going to be my teacher today?" Or that guy over there looks so sad I will try to chat with him and see if I can get a smile. In any case I try to be approachable with a good attitude and a kind word or two. I can't help anybody if my body language says, "Stay away from me."

This business of "help" is very delicate. If I start telling someone what they should do all is lost. Doing their inventory for them is equally dangerous. Advice is cheap and usually worthless. Telling them, "Boy are you one sick puppy" will turn them off since they know their own sickness quite well. I just relate I have been down the same road as the person I am trying to help and give real examples of what I did about it. I only have my experience and I should not try to use someone else's story. I have no experience with drugs, for example, so I tell them just that. Most of all I like to sow seeds of hope and happiness. They can see I care about the program and I care about them enough to do whatever is necessary to help them deal with their situation. I never say I know it all because I don't. I know only a little but I have some tangible results after all these years of making many mistakes and still keep trucking.

I listen to what I have to say and sometimes I am only helping myself but thinking of others fills my life with rainbows.

April 11

INTUITION AND INSPIRATION

One of the fruits of this sober life is the gift of intuition and inspiration. As time passes, I rely on my intuition because I trust myself 100%. My experience and education are all mixed up in my personal blender and without fear blocking my way, inspiration happens all the time. I am not inspired every minute but it comes when it needs to come or better yet, when God tells me. Before I got sober the path to inspiration was completely off the table. I could only focus on staying out of trouble. I never connected the dots my troubles were caused by my drinking. Once the fog cleared my mind it started working like God designed it to do.

Most of my inspiration comes in the morning during my hour of prayer and meditation.

I start with an attitude of gratitude and humility follows on. The trick is to quiet my mind and stop the chatter from "the committee" and listen to my heart. Here is where my intuition clicks in. I have to translate the language of the heart into meaningful thought processes. The lights come on where darkness was before and I thank God for living in The Sunlight of the Spirit. Inspiration is not something I can force; it is like a surprise package in the mind. "Where did that come from?" I say to myself. The answer to that question is my Higher Power helping my thought-life. These special moments light my fire and spur my desire to get into action to follow up on the God given inspiration. I have never been disappointed when I have turned my inspirations into reality.

I use the "back burner" approach on tough problems and sleep on them without trying to solve the problem. I let go, let God and wait for a solution in the morning. Works for me.

April 12

RELIGION

When I was a young man, I thought myself religious since I went to a church sponsored grammar school and high school. I was an altar boy. I went to church every Sunday because my mother forced me to go even though she never went. As soon as I broke free from my parents and joined the military, I never set foot in a church for the next 30 years except for the occasional wedding. When I sobered up, I was without religion or spirituality. I had to learn you can have religion without spirituality and/or spirituality without religion. Many have both and my hat is off to those folks. Luckily this program does not require a specified religion or many of us would never achieve long term sobriety. When I heard the Preamble that states we are not involved in politics or religion I heaved a sigh of relief. If it is good enough for AA, it is good enough for me. I had zero concept of spirituality so all I did is follow the way my elders paved before me. I was happy to set aside my old ideas than did not work in my past.

In my travels I have spent many years in Islamic countries, Buddhist countries and Catholic countries. I have learned from all of them without having to join a particular sect. They all have the Golden rule, "Do unto others as you would have them do to you." They all have do not kill, steal, lie or harm others. They all say do the next right thing, just like AA principles. I need not go to 123 Elm Street to pray and participate in a spiritual ritual. My hour of prayer and meditation is 700% more than one hour every Sunday at St. Leo's. I do my confession at meetings with my fellow alcoholics and in my 5th Step. My good friend who is a deacon in his church treats me like a pagan for doing my worship at the kitchen table. I just can't buy one religion is best and all others are wrong. It would make billions of humans participating in the wrong religion. I don't feel the need to pick one to the exclusion of all others. The God of my understanding has done a terrific job of keeping me sober and providing intuition every single morning.

I heard it said people who go to church want to stay out of hell and alcoholics have been to hell already and don't want to go back. True for me.

April 13

WHAT AM I MISSING?

Reading about pride or rather the removal of pride from our way of life, I began to think of all the things I am missing from the old days. Stuff like guilt and blame. Both of those were a total waste of time and effort. How about hangovers? Do I miss those horrible mornings? Do I miss bad and scary mail or threatening phone calls? Do I miss watching my rear-view mirror for cops? Do I miss forgetting whole chunks of time? Not knowing where I was or what I was doing? Do I miss checking my car for damage/blood? Do I miss living life like an emergency? Carrying a weapon? Do I miss staying awake all night with a head full of resentments? Sleepless nights plotting revenge? Do I miss bankruptcy and fear of being homeless? Do I miss being so lonely I sought lower companions? Do I miss not being able to swallow anything larger than a pea and puking every meal? Do I miss having my health deteriorate so bad I was close to death? The list of things missing in my life goes on forever and makes me so grateful for finding my way out of the deep dark pit I put myself into.

How about material stuff? Do I miss my blue Caddie? Nah, means of transportation is not very important as long as I can get from A to B. Do I miss the blonde from hell that went with the fancy wheels? Nah, she was good looking to the outside world and it was more about feeding my ego than love. What did love have to do with anything back then? Do I miss the house on the hill with a view of the Pacific Ocean? Nah, I never looked out the window and enjoyed the spectacular view. It drained my bank account and was a status toy. Do I miss a staff of 30 people and 2 reserved parking spaces? Nah, I have no business in a position of responsibility. Do I miss being respected because of my position rather than anything earned? Nah. Do I miss my diamond studded watch as necessary bling? Nah, the time is posted everywhere, and I am not living by the clock anymore. No sir the spiritual path really does not focus on "stuff" it contains priceless items listed on my gratitude list. Do I miss anything from the old days? Not a whip.

What replaced all those things from pre-AA times? The answer is Humility.

April 14

ONE POUND OF HUMILITY PLEASE

I always joke in my home group that when the topic of humility comes up I should, by all rights, pass. Fighter pilots don't have humility and when a bunch of them are together it is an ego fest. The very first meeting of AA my new sponsor kept repeating ego, ego, ego, at every word out of my mouth. Clearly, I was not right sized. I had a distorted view of my place on this planet. As I did the Steps, I no longer talked about my exploits in an aircraft and addressed my alcoholism. I was a pilot I am now an alcoholic. My history has some great stories but my daily reality is living life on life's terms without juice to light my afterburner. My daily readings and prayer attack my ego buttons right up front upon awakening. I ask for help, I read what others have to say, I review my shortcomings and do my inventory. My gratitude list keeps me humble. All those gifts are from God not from my accomplishments. I am in awe of God's handiwork. Nature makes me humble.

You can't buy a pound of humility. Either you have it or you don't. It is not being a doormat or groveling in front of others. To me it is a true assessment of yourself. You are not the smartest or the dumbest, you are not the richest or the poorest. You are not an "est." You are what you are. What you see is what you get. Here is how I work on my humility. This program is a spiritual one and nirvana is to reach a state of selflessness. In other words, you are completely devoid of ego and material possessions. At this moment I have X money in the bank and live in a nice place but I am just a temporary steward of these creature comforts, and when I die, I will leave with zippo, nada and naked. I don't "own" anything. My soul and my good works are the only things that will proceed when my ticket gets punched. It is not about me. Life is not about me. I could be a trillionaire king and have the deed to an entire country but if I have no soul then all is lost. Life is about helping others and finding the path God has planned for you.

In our case, drinking keeps us from a spiritual path. This daily reprieve makes us useful, humble, human beings again. Thank you, God!

April 15

WORST CASE SCENARIO

When I was in the war planning business we had to present "worse case scenarios" as a prudent study for survival. Real life does not require us to be so negative as to focus on worst case. We can "what if" ourselves into paralysis. Our fear machine can cripple our ability to be happy, joyous and free. I know several family members with the "sky is falling" attitude. In fact, they make a list of all the bad news happening in the world and paint a picture of gloom and doom. All of these horrible things never happen but fear of them happening ruins their day or many days. I prefer best case scenario thinking. If we are doing our best then why not expect the best. I have found a positive attitude is good for your health both mentally and physically. I look for the sunny side of everything. Only occasionally am I in a bad situation, so I deal with that in the rare event of trouble. Why be in the scenario business anyway? Focusing on future problems ruins the present. God is in charge of the future not me. How can I get quicker than God?

Faith that God is the Master Designer is what I try to remember on a daily basis. I try to go with the flow and wait to be surprised. My guess as what is going to happen is pure moonshine. In my morning meditation I focus on what I do have control over and leave world crisis up to God. This process knocks the fear factor down to a very low level. God has brought me this far in great shape, He is not going to drop me on my head now. I have no input or control over North Korea's nuclear program. The President has not called me or sent me an email asking for my opinion on the G2 Summit. My job is simple, stay sober and help others. Good things have happened to me doing just that and only that, I am going to keep going on. When my attitude is negative, I get negativity back, when I smile everybody smiles back. I try to stay out of the scenario business altogether and keep my meaningless opinions floating in space.

I stick to what I know for sure, the sun will come up in the morning and if I do good things everything will be alright.

April 16

MY PIECE OF THE PIE

So funny, we can reduce the root of all our fears into fear of losing what we already have or fear of not getting our just rewards, our piece of the pie. Every morning when I look at my gratitude list, I can graphically see God has given me everything I need and more. I don't need to reach for the "pie." It's not my pie anyway. That list is one of the biggest fear removers in the world. No "want" list, no "bucket" list and no "wish" list. My faith in my Higher Power is not static, it grows each day as the evidence builds up that my life is wonderful. Way passed what I deserve. Faith trumps fear every time. Not always easy to let God do what He does without my help. I have a little sticky note that says: "Mike I don't need your help today. Thank you. God." Going with the flow is best rather than trying to change the wind or paddle upstream. I need to stick my oars in the boat and let the events of the day continue without me controlling anything. I cannot change the wind but I can adjust my sails, read: attitude adjustment.

The strongest belief I now have is everything that happens is supposed to happen. God is the Master Designer and even though things don't look too good at the time, there is always a reason not apparent to me. I was driving to Bangkok to see a VA doctor and I got stuck in the worst traffic jam of my entire life. Two hours not moving. Patience is not one of my character assets but I didn't resort to road rage but rather it gave me time to reflect on the reason for my trip. I realized the purpose of my trip, to get a bigger piece of the pie from my veterans' benefits. I felt my disability rating was way lower than many other vets I know who saw way less combat. Ego, selfishness, doing other's inventory came to light as I did my 10th Step in traffic. I should not have even been on the road to see this evaluation doctor in the first place. Then I injured myself in the taxi going to the hospital, blood running down my arm. OK God I get it, message received. My motives are not pure on this whole "give me a bigger piece of the pie" trip. Comparing my inventory to other folks' inventory is a waste of time and none of my business anyway.

Today I am going to close my eyes, have faith, and fall backwards into the arms of my Higher Power.

April 17

12 STEP OPPORTUNITY

Living in Thailand, there have not been many 12 Step opportunities but my sponsor always says, "You may be the only version of the Big Book someone encounters." On my last day in Mystic, there for my son's funeral, we went to my son's favorite watering hole and meeting place to thank the owner for all the gifts he bestowed on our family over the period of years. I never got a chance to thank the elusive owner but God put me there for a 12 Step opportunity. This friend of my son engaged me in light conversation and suddenly he said, "I have been watching you this week and I have never seen you drink." I told him I quit drinking over 20 some years ago. The conversation quickly went to my sobriety, why, problems, temptation, etc. He admitted he was an alcoholic who just can't get the program even though he has gone to a lot of meetings and some guy has tried to help/sponsor him. I gave a short experience, strength and hope speech as he listened drink in hand. He wanted me to change my flight and stay on and work with him but I pointed him to the local firehouse where there are about 50 sponsor worthy guys. Usually not a good idea to talk to a drunk who is drunk but he responded well and told me I changed his life. Time will tell if anything stuck.

I get home to my condo in Thailand to find out a long time resident and member of the fellowship is not only drinking and ingesting huge quantities of valium but is tossing empty beer bottles out the window into the property next door. Another home group member and neighbor and I went 12-Step calling in his condo. He had quite a few years of sobriety up to this point so it was easy to remind him that "For us, to drink is to die." Once picking up after a long amount of sobriety it goes back to bad stuff faster than electricity. He agreed and we made a date to get him to a meeting in a few hours. Show time and he was too messed up to even put clothes on. The next morning, I go by and he swears he did not drink the night before and is off the valium. I told him it is 7:30 a.m. and he has time to get showered and dressed for the daily 9 a.m. meeting. He looked me in the eye and promised me he was coming to the meeting. He did leave the condo at 8:30 (my spy report) and on the way he made a decision to buy 2 large bags of beer and get drunk all over again. By the time I returned home beer bottles were flying off his balcony and security and condo management was all energized to bring down the hammer. The easier, softer way was right in front of him but he chose self-destruction.

Was the 12 Step call successful? Yes, me and my fellow 12 Steppers are eternally grateful for our sobriety and we did not drink so that is success enough. Our drunk friend is alive still so there is hope and we are standing by to help if he makes a decision to let us help him.

April 18

TRUST

Probably our lowest trust level came when we hit bottom. I know I didn't trust myself so everything else was off the table in the trust department. My first trust from ground zero was a trust in my sponsor and my AA home group. They had no reason to deceive me and I could see they were doing just wonderful and I was hanging on to my butt with both hands. I looked at my last dollar and it said, "In God We Trust" and that sounded like a good idea and a starting point. I did trust my Higher Power and slowly I could trust myself to make it through a 24-hour period without a drink and finally the obsession was lifted from my shoulders and I could have a meal in a bar without having a panic attack. In the process of doing the Steps a lot of things were changing rapidly, faith, spiritual growth, good health, happiness and trust I was on the right path at long last. But what about trusting others? I have always been a rather positive person even while I was drinking. I trust everybody until they prove me wrong. Some folks go the other way and trust no one until they earn trust.

When I was a kid, I got a lesson in trust from an older kid who said he was going to stick a dart on my big belt buckle. I thought his aim was too high but he said "trust me" and the dart hit me between the eyes. I have learned to trust my instincts a little more than someone saying "trust me." My favorite line out of the "Animal House" movie was all the brothers hanging around the frat house and this poor freshman was looking at a 0.0 grade point average and the senior frat brother says, "Hey, you screwed up, you trusted us!" It is true, we need to be very careful with our trust and not get run over by scams and con jobs. I still think it is better to be disappointed occasionally than be untrusting as a general way of thinking. This is especially true in dealing with other alcoholics. I trust everyone will stay sober. When they don't, I still trust they can get back on the right road again. If I act like I don't believe in the guys I am trying to help the wrong message might go out. I want to be the picture of hope and encouragement to the struggling drunk.

In case you were wondering, yes, "trust" is on my gratitude list. I have been a trusted servant in AA from day one and repay that trust by giving of myself.

April 19

REGENERATION

Need a makeover? How about some new clothes, a fancy watch, new hairdo, maybe some Botox shots? Nah, that is not going to work. All external stuff won't change you one bit. The makeover we all need comes from the heart and radiates outward from true change or regeneration of the old you. The first thing changing the way I think. I know my thought patterns led me in the wrong direction for years so since the old way did not work I need a new "thinker." In the old days I never asked God for help, my process was doomed from the start. My best thinking put me in a downward spiral. I needed to build a new self, one with the assistance of a Higher Power this time around. I have to admit to my inner self that I need a total makeover by zeroing all my dials and release all my old ideas into outer space and form a mental ground zero. I must surrender to the pace of the Steps and use the stepping stone approach to my change. This is not a speedy deal to reverse all my old gears.

In order for this change to happen, I need to be at peace with myself and everything else. I have to stop fighting and go with the flow. Follow what has worked so well for my fellow alcoholics in recovery. I can see the light in their eyes and the smiles on their faces. I am "under construction." I know I am a good person down deep but I am in the clutches of this disease. My heart is OK it is my thinking that is sorely lacking. I was given a Big Book the first day at my first meeting and my new sponsor told me it was an instruction manual. At the time I was not into reading and his words flew over my head but later it all made sense. The first obstacle to my regeneration project was my ego. It became obvious to everyone else but finally I got it. My ego needed reduction in depth. I also saw my education and history of accomplishments were all meaningless. I had no spiritual center only self-centeredness. The difference is black and white. It's no secret that the 12 Steps will change you if you do them thoroughly, completely and consistently.

Today I am still a work in progress, my regeneration will take the rest of my life, this new life is wonderful because it has a spiritual center which was totally missing in my past.

April 20

GETTING TO KNOW YOU

In the old days, doing a self-examination was not going to happen. My impression of myself had nothing to do with reality. I am sure if you saw what people thought about me and what I thought about myself it would not match at all. I hid behind my past accomplishments, I was at the bar telling war stories to my troops and my boss came by and said, "That's great Mike but what have you done lately?" I laughed it off but after some thought I realized he wasn't joking. The answer was nothing. I was too busy covering my tracks to take an inventory of myself or review my goals. My attitude was of self-preservation and selfish motives. As I neared my bottom, I hated myself and what I had become, a hopeless drunk. For sure I didn't want to look at myself and all the damage I had piled up. It was too big of a mess and I did not know any way out. I needed one more drink or I would die and I would die if I drank one more drink. Catch 22, I was screwed. I did not want to know the real me.

When it came inventory time, doing the Steps, it was the first honest look at myself ever. I did not like truth but I knew I could change. I could reverse the flow and make amends. I could find a Higher Power and work on my spiritual condition and happiness came after that process. Pretty soon I was happy with my path and where I was going down the Road of Happy Destiny. In other words, I was OK with the world, with God and myself. I was able to form real friendships. It is not written anywhere but all the old timers said, "No relationships in the first year." and I endorse that completely. The first year there is so much change happening, if you are doing the Steps, you are not ready for prime time with a relationship. You aren't ready yet. You are not the "you" ready to mix your chemistry with somebody else. Getting to know you is a work in progress. I learned you might change so much the person you are with will no longer match your needs. You are a different person without alcohol. You may become a stranger to some when you get sober. I found this to be true in my own life.

The new "me" has talents that were buried and there are a million great things I've missed while in a fog for decades. I am chipping away filling in for lost time.

April 21

TENACITY AND FAITH

I had a very small list of assets when I did my inventory, but somehow, I was born with tenacity, maybe it is genetic. Faith was completely blocked out by fears of all kinds, some real but mostly imagined. Over the years my tenacity has paid off in big dividends, it has put gas on the fire. If you add a trusting faith you will be on top of the world, believe me on this. I am of the mind to keep going no matter what. If things look bleak that's OK because God is in charge of the future not me. He has done a great job and who am I to try to manipulate the future. Case in point; when I was in Laos, in combat where I was not supposed to be, I had to land my aircraft where there was no friendly place to put down so I landed at an airfield that had been overrun by the bad guys. I got the plane safely on the ground despite ground fire as the first step but after that I was out of ideas. I was smart enough to call for help and it came just in time to protect me somewhat. Here I was stuck without gas or a place to hide so I accepted the fact I was dead and it just had not happened yet. My tenacity kicked in and I decided to do stuff while I was waiting to get killed.

Faith. All this happened before I got sober but I did believe in God. There are no atheists in foxholes and this qualified as a different kind of foxhole so I prayed and made many promises to God. It paid off. I got help from world's best fighter pilot to knock out a gun that was about to eliminate me, I found a 55-gallon drum of gas and the inspiration of how to open the gas can was truly from God or else I would be have been dead back in 1969. I just kept going until I could fuel the plane with the help of my Lao back seater and fly out into a storm and darkness with faith that I wouldn't hit a mountain that was on three sides of the runway. That incident was a turning point in my life but it wasn't until I got sober that I could live up to all the promises I made to God in that near death experience. God took care of me and all I had to do was not give up. Today I believe everything that happens is supposed to happen no matter how bad it looks at the time. If I try to do the next right thing and leave the results up to God it all works out for the best. As I review my life, all the events had some lesson or reason for unfolding just as it did.

One event that happened today is another year of sobriety, so I could write this experience for you. Fifty extra years of life due to faith and tenacity.

April 22

GRATITUDE = HAPPINESS

When I wake up in the morning, sometimes my sleep is so deep, I am surprised to find out I am in Thailand. I say my first prayer, "Thank you God for another day, thank you for a night's sleep, thank you for where I am because I would not want to be anywhere else." Each day starts with gratitude and also my last prayer is, "Thank you God for another beautiful day in Paradise." Since we can handle only one attitude at a time, I try to make that attitude an attitude of gratitude. If I am grateful, then I am happy. I have learned not to chase happiness, it just comes as a by-product of doing the next right thing, of helping others, of open mindedness, of a grateful heart, of a good spiritual condition. All those things are connected in a very good way. My inventory of blessings far outweighs my problems. What a far cry from the morning I woke up completely disoriented, my head hanging over the bed and the sun coming thru the O of a bottle and I thought it was the eye of God to punish me. I was in a strange room I did not recognize and I was lost. I reached into an ashtray and pulled out a match book: Crown Hotel Seoul, Korea. OMG The O was a bottle of OB beer not the eye of God, I will never forget that morning and there was no gratitude back in those days and no happiness either.

Lately I let myself become unhappy with family health concerns some of which can be prevented. I had to pull myself out of my funk by reminding myself of my powerlessness. I am not a doctor and I am not a counselor so I can't be sticking my nose into my family's inventory. I grab my gratitude list and review my blessings. I can see God is not picking on me, just the opposite, He has filled my basket with gifts. My smile is back and the people I need to help do not want to see a gloomy face that turns them off. Happiness is attractive and contagious. A good laugh is like medicine for the soul. I have upbeat friends who care about me and comfort me in my low moments and bring me back to the Sunlight on the Road of Happy Destiny. I stay away from CNN and Fox News when my heart is hurting. There is nothing in the news to smile about.

Happiness is an inside job. I am in charge of my attitude therefore gratitude trumps all my problems.

April 23

THE KING AND THE PAWN

One of my favorite quotes is, "When the game is over, the king and the pawn go back in same the box." (Italian saying). Every once in a while, I think I am dealing with pawns. and even if I am not a king, I must be at least a knight or a bishop. I have to remember we are all God's kids and I am not better than anybody. My version of "right" just doesn't fly with others all the time. I left behind a life of rank and pecking order to this program where no one is better than anybody else. We are all pawns. No one person gets special moves different than their fellows. The pawn makes one square at a time. Our rank is the same, alcoholic and our date of rank is today, one day at a time. I know of no organization like that except our wonderful AA. It is a pity to see some pawns think they are better than other pawns and they forgot about the box. When I get resentment, I need to think about the fact I am a sick puppy and I am upset with another sick puppy. What I don't like most likely is what I don't like in myself.

When the game is over, I don't want to have any resentment not addressed. We are not in the Game of Thrones; we are in the game of life on equal footing with our fellow earth travelers. Some of us are more educated, have more wealth, or better health but all that is not important when the game is over. I have tried to make all my amends before the other person passes away or I pass away. The balance sheet should be zero. My car, my bank account is not coming with me. I came with nothing and will leave with nothing material. But I will leave behind positive love and good works for my family and friends. I hope they have a fun party when I am gone. Just another reason not to fire up any new resentment since my departure could happen at any time or somebody I love could go back to God. My friend Chicago Mike left us in a heartbeat sitting as a passenger in a car and got hit by a runaway bus that took him instantaneously. I never had a chance to say goodbye or how much he meant to me. It is a lesson I will never forget. I try to keep a clean slate with everyone because today may be the last chance to set things right.

In this new way of viewing life, we are all pawns and the game will be over when God says it's over. There are no Kings in AA thank God.

April 24

GROW UP

The old joke that old age is mandatory and maturity is optional fits some of us perfectly. When I was drinking, maturity was not happening. The years were adding up but spiritual growth, self-improvement and emotional maturity was out the window. When I finally sobered up I soon realized from my inventory I was not a grown up. I was a spoiled little kid with lots of years and no idea what a grown up should do. Relationship skills, I had zippo. Patience and tolerance? What's that? Love? Been lookin' in all the wrong places. My dismal failure was due to bad luck and bad bosses who had it in for me. My parents screwed me up by running a dysfunctional household. The church made me feel guilty about everything. Ooops. Maybe the first step in maturity is taking responsibility for my own life and my actions and quit blaming bad karma. When I looked at my inventory I could see clearly, I had been missing in action for any kind of growth. Luckily for me, spiritual growth was the first step and it came quickly.

This process of doing the Steps has given me a start in growing up. I have a long way to go but at least I know I am on the right road and have a road map. Admitting my immaturity gives me some degree of humility. I look at myself as a newcomer at each meeting and look for a gem that will help my recovery and give me ideas to help others. At my meeting someone referred to me as elder statesman but I told the group I am just old and never will be an "old timer." Part of being a grown up is to set an example of action instead of words. Talk is so cheap but walking the walk is best for me and those who are watching my actions. My parents wanted me to do things they never did so learning from that I vowed to do everything I expected others to do. I have put down my pail and shovel and climbed out of my sandbox forever. I got a late start but thank God I got a start. I do my best to make up for lost years of immaturity.

When faced with a problem I ask myself, what would a grownup do?

April 25

SELF-RESTRAINT

Self-restraint was a new deal for me and a necessary change to my bag of tricks. My hair trigger had to be removed and a pause button installed into my hard drive. Whatever I do in the heat of the moment or anger, the results are super bad if I don't stop and restrain any action. When I am upset it is good to write it down and leave it there on paper and not send it to anyone until I give it a rest. Later, when I look at my dribble, I am shocked at myself and happy I did not show my words to anyone. The delete button on my computer is my favorite keystroke. The delete button in my brain is my best choice also. When I am with a group of friends, I notice I tend to be sarcastic and I now dial that urge back because it is ego based and can be harmful even though it is intended to be in jest. I like to joke around but my new way is to make myself the joke rather than poke at someone else's hairline or big belly. Restraint of pen and tongue is always a better idea than shooting from the hip.

When I look back at myself in my working days and was in a position of leadership, I realize I talked way too much. I was used to holding forth and preaching the gospel according to King Mike. Geez. I have since dropped the idea that it is my job to enlighten everyone who will listen (or pretend to listen). In my home group our group conscience calls for a chance for everyone to share. That means when there are 30 people in the meeting it comes to 90 seconds to share. In almost every meeting some guys share for 5+ minutes which takes away time from the rest of the group. It has taught me economy of words. Quite often I pass or just fire off one sentence that I hope may be helpful to the alcoholic who is still suffering. Nobody is hanging on to my words anyway. I know what I have to say is not any more important than someone else's share. Just like when I write to you guys, I keep it to two short paragraphs. Nuff said aye?

Of course, I get angry just like everybody else. I let it simmer internally and let the steam pass for a day or two so I forget the problem. One of the benefits of getting old.

April 26

FELLOWSHIP AND FRIENDS

All my readings today were about the beauty of the fellowship and friends. Most of my friends come from the fellowship but not everybody in the rooms is a close friend. In recovery I have collected a ton of good friends and over a 1000 sober folks I am connected to through the program. A far cry from zero when I hit my bottom completely unable to form a relationship with another human being. My dog Stephanie was the only one who loved me unconditionally. That day 24 years ago, everybody at my first meeting loved me until I could love myself. It took some time but I formed a relationship with a Higher Power. When I did my inventory, I came to grips with who I really am and accepted the good, the bad and the ugly. Then I could have true relationship with myself then I could relate to other people and became open to forming lasting relationships. What a joy to enjoy laughter and experiences with others. Not only that but I need other people in my life. "No man is an island." My time as the Lone Ranger is over thank God.

Both the fellowship and my friends are on my gratitude list and they both are treasures to be enjoyed and enhanced. In the fellowship I have picked up gems from people I don't like and heard wrong stuff from people I do like so I try to keep an open mind and get the message, from whatever source, and handle the messenger separately. With my friends I share their successes and comfort them in their losses. I encourage and support them and they have done the same for me. I look at what I can bring to a relationship not what I can profit from. "He's my friend because he can get free tickets to the ball game." Nah. We have a true brotherhood just as strong as those formed in combat. Getting sober is a life and death deal. This is a we program not a me, myself and I program. Learning to be a good friend can be a new experience in love and understanding. My problem is I have so many friends that I don't always do a good job of staying in touch, a luxury problem for sure.

A friend is someone you know all about and you love them anyway. Be a friend to have a good friend in my experience.

April 27

THE MAGIC OF INVENTORY

I know of nothing more of a stumbling block to recovery than not doing inventory. I have seen it kill alcoholics and I have seen folks unable to "get it" because of an inability to do an inventory. I know in my own case I procrastinated doing a 4th Step and it could have been fatal. I got scared to death before I put pen to paper, but once I did, something magic happened. The process of getting my inventory out of my heart and my head and onto a piece of paper I experienced a new freedom and stepped up to a new dimension in my recovery. The weight of my past weighed so much that I was used to carrying it on my shoulders for decades. That weight was gone and I could jump over tall buildings and fly Mach 2, magic stuff. I had one sponsee do his inventory on the computer and I had my doubts but I went along with this guy. Well, sorry to say, he did not stay sober and I am an old fashion guy that believes in pen and paper. The writing of the words and seeing your inventory in living color is part of the magic I do believe. Typing doesn't do the job as well. You must hold the finished product in your hand and see graphically what was in is now out there. I have found this inventory a must to recovery.

I have taken a lot of 5th Steps and I can tell right away when a complete

4th Step has not been accomplished. In every case 100% scorecard those guys have not stayed sober. Half measures just will not work in my experience for me and the people I work with. The entire inventory must come up like a hairball. I knew guys with many years of sobriety go back out because there was something in their inventory that did not come out on their list and never shared in a 5th Step. Holding back can kill you. Trust me on this one, folks. When I do a 5th Step I ask the person to tell me what they don't want to tell me right off. Get it out of the way and it will be smooth sailing after that. If they lie, I can usually tell but I give them a second chance. Unfortunately, some stuff is so deep the person does not even know what is buried in their sub-conscience. I have found it is like an onion, peel back one layer and there is another one exposed. Keep peeling. You will be doing inventory for the rest of your life so not to worry if you missed something first time around.

I have also found that you need to do a new inventory when you have an "event" such as a divorce or broken family, etc. But magic happens every time.

April 28

RIGOROUS HONESTY

Tough subject, honesty. I was such a good little kid if I tried to lie my face turned beet red. A built-in lie detector but as I grew up and with lots of practice I could lie like a politician. Then a life in the military was one giant lie. In my drinking days a lie was necessary to cover my tracks, to account for my lost time and lost money. I knew when I started this program that honesty was part of the deal as it should be. I soon learned there are all kinds of honesty, cash register honesty, brutal honesty and rigorous honesty. OK cash register honesty is when the gal at Walmart gives you $2 extra in your change and you give it back to her so she doesn't come up short at the end of the day. That doesn't allow you to declare yourself "honest." Now brutal honesty. When I was about eight years old my mother came in from sunbathing and I said, "Hey, Mother you are getting fat." OMG big mistake. A 6-hour lecture and mental torture followed. I never called anyone fat ever again. Yes, I see fat people but I do not point out the obvious. Dangerous honesty. Your wife/girlfriend asks you if the lady over there is pretty? Do not answer that. Of course she is, but now is not the time for dangerous honesty. Say "I didn't notice" or change the subject. "Do I look fat in this dress?" Discretion and diplomacy is required not the brutal truth.

The honesty we need is rigorous honesty that begins with us. I can fool myself better than anybody. My inventory was the first attempt at real honesty. It is what it is and sugar coating it is not productive. Respect the reality not the lie. I lived in Fantasy Land for so long I believed it to be real. I could not recognize the truth until it hit me in the face. I thank God I woke up to reality with real people in real places. When we are honest with ourselves and others it is a kind of freedom. We don't have to remember who we lied to or review our stories to keep them all straight. I used to lose a lot of sleep reviewing my days of storytelling, so I wouldn't get tripped up. When you are drinking it makes that even harder. This is important when I inventory my motives with honesty. I can take 10 good motives and cover up one black evil one hidden even from myself. Of course, there are all manner of dishonesty, omission is my favorite. I could keep my mouth shut but there are times that is not the honest route. Rationalization and denial are less than rigorous honesty. Am I 100% honest all the time? Absolutely not but I try to improve my reality skills in my morning meditation.

I know I must confess my faults with my fellows to keep my street clean and stay free. To deny reality doesn't change reality.

April 29

TAKING A GEOGRAPHIC

Will moving away solve your problems? I have a lot of experience on this one I can share with you. In a way it worked for me when I was in the military. I moved 22 times in 30 years. Once I had been in one place for a while and my character defects became apparent it was time to move on. I was a "new guy" all the time. I was an expert at being a new guy but sooner or later I would be an "old guy" so I would move to keep fresh wherever I was even though I was rotten. Once I was a civilian, I just changed jobs to get the same effect without packing my stuff. One vivid memory I have is getting in my airplane and flying thousands of miles to a different country and leaving behind a messy relationship. The cockpit has a mirror on the top canopy for looking behind you in flight. I was airborne, happy to be leaving a bad situation, but as I caught my image in the overhead mirror, I saw a deceitful, dishonest and evil guy, me. I did not like what I saw and realized the problem was not going away and it was not behind me, it was rotting in my heart and soul. It was a mini spiritual moment I never forgot.

Most of us have learned that no matter how fast you go or however far you go, taking a geographic will not solve your problems. They go with you in your suitcase (read inventory). Hey wait a minute Mike. Didn't you move from Hawaii to Thailand? What are you running away from dude? OK fair enough. Since my recovery and sobriety come first, I had to ask the question: Is there good AA in Thailand? Can I be in service? The answers were yes to both and after making 12 trips to Thailand in sobriety I felt more "at home" in Thailand than anywhere in the USA. It took me some time to realize how spiritual the people are here and the atmosphere suited my program best in Thailand. In my morning meditation it came crystal clear that the move was right for me. Thirteen years later I could not be happier with my geographic for the right reasons. Then I met my bride of 14 years now (a new record) and I could not be any more satisfied. But I had to have my program as #1 priority or else it would have been wrong.

Wherever you go, there you are, the problem. If you do move bring the solution with you.

April 30

ANGER MANAGEMENT

Anger was at the top of my defects list when my inventory was taken. Anger is connected to fear and we all have had our share of that. But even more than fear, the ego was the fuel that fired up the anger engine. When I was a young man, I was an angry dude and that worked for me in the military but later in life it became a big problem. When I am angry, I say the wrong things and do stuff I would not normally do. The very same result of being drunk. Thank God I was not an angry drunk or my troubles would have multiplied. When I read in our literature that anger is the dubious luxury of normal people, I knew they were talking to me. I can't afford anger; the price is too high. I know anger is very normal but now I manage my anger instead of letting it go wild. I have removed my hair trigger to allow myself time to process my anger instead of shooting from the hip in a nanosecond.

What about when you are right? Wow, that is the worst kind of anger, justified. When you subtract the right or wrong from the equation you still have anger. That is the problem because I still handle being "right' all wrong. The good news is through this program there isn't much that makes me angry anymore. Acceptance puts out more of the old angers. If somebody steals my car, I still get angry but I now have GAP working for me as my anger management tool. GAP God Authorized Pause. The GAP is the period of time between what happens and my reaction to it. Hopefully a very long time so I don't make the situation worse. Some people count to 10 but I try to sleep on my anger and process it tomorrow. If I am angry it means I am not getting my way or my ego is bruised or I am losing something. So when all boiled down, anger is all about me. If I take me out of the problem the anger can look silly or stupid. Anger management takes care of itself in my morning meditation and starts my day calm and serene.

I have found that when I am in service or helping others, anger is never a problem. I am the source of anger, so the further I am away from me the better I am.

May 1

TOLERANCE

I used to be Mr. Zero Tolerance but this program has taught me peace and joy will not come to me without total tolerance. I cannot change people, places and things so the only alternative is to tolerate the things I don't like and accept my powerlessness. I have to remember I am a sick puppy and when I deal with my fellows in the program they are sick too. Maybe a different kind of sick but I need to love them but not co-sign their bad behavior when it upsets me. I have enough inventory without getting into somebody else's. I have my standards and they apply only to me. Since I am not a boss or a leader, I need not lay my rules on anybody but me. The only thing I can do is set an example. Action works better than talk. I tolerate every meeting, the same people talk too long at the expense of others who would like to share. I pass or make one short sentence.

We say love and tolerance is our code and they go together like salt and pepper. I need to have real love, from the heart, to be truly tolerant. Holding my breath and grinding my teeth is not real tolerance. We are all God's kids and everyone is my brother or sister. We are family. The only one I can change is me. Sometimes I need to change my attitude toward certain people who deserve to be choked to death. I need to take off my judgment robe and throw my gavel in the trash. I am not judge and jury or enforcement. My life is so much simpler now. I need only focus on my defects and sit in the eye of the storm when one of my brothers goes berserk. If I try to encourage instead of critique, be positive instead of negative and even if it does not help somebody at least I feel better. I learned other folks' views are going to be different and really that is what makes the world go around. Viva la difference. It would be very boring if we all were in agreement all the time. I am wrong often enough to know others have the right to be wrong.

A factor of tolerance is forgiveness. I need to forgive past acts of my fellows and not label them in a negative tone and hope they forgive me too.

May 2

MODERATION

Moderation?? What a joke! Folks like us did everything to excess and
that is what got us here in recovery. Moderation might as well be Greek.
Our entire life is very high highs and really low bottoms. Up and down
the roller coaster of life. What a ride and I want off. How about you? I
used to drink until I was drunk, eat until I was sick, gambled until I was
broke, partied until the lights went out, drove until the wheels fell
off. Now in this new life, moderation in all things is such a better idea.
Except drinking of course, there is no chance to achieve moderate
drinking. Sorry about that. Still a baby at this, I try with something
simple, food. I have learned to dial back at the table but stuff like a buffet
is trouble for me. Before I approach the buffet line, I have a little talk
with myself. "OK Mike, take it easy, skip the bad stuff, little portions
OK?" I proceed with great intentions and just take a little bit of this a
little bit of that and badda bing badda boom my plate weighs 5 pounds
and I was brought up to clean my plate. So my tummy hurts, I feel
ashamed of myself and have to add extra exercises to my workouts. Ugh!
Buffets are not for people like us.

Can I be excessive in AA? You bet. My sponsor was in service at 12
different meetings every week. He admitted ego was part of it and he was
told he was taking away opportunities for other folks to be in service. At
times, I have been secretary, treasurer, group service representative,
literature and clean up boy for my group because nobody else did it. I
learned to recruit and just leave stuff undone until someone picks up the
commitment. Worse than that is the AA folks who think they need to be
the police and enforce the traditions as they understand them. They
forget they are "suggestions" not law and order. When we do stuff to
excess there is always a price. If I exercise too much, I injure myself and
I can't keep my routine and the weight creeps back up. I am still prone to
overdoing so in my inventory I try to examine my behavior and look for
excess. Finding balance in my life is always a chore but I am getting
better at it all the time.

Having said all this, you can never learn too much, pray too much or love too much.

May 3

COURAGE

We say the Serenity Prayer so many times but how often do we really concentrate on the word "courage." I have learned that courage is not being fearless but taking action even with fear. It is very easy to do nothing and sit on the sidelines and be an observer and not be a doer. "I mind my own business" is what I hear a lot but the trick is to know what is your business and what is not. The unity of AA is everybody's business. Safety is everybody's business for example. We had the courage to stop drinking so why not other stuff? One our biggest fears is "change." We get in a set pattern or routine and we get uncomfortable with any change. So in my 10th Step inventory I look for what needs changing and address my fears or, in other words, muster up my courage.

When we undergo change there is a risk of failure. That is why in my morning meditation, I enlist my Higher Power to help me pick my battles. I ask God to point me in the right direction and consider my planned actions. If it involves other people, I need to be careful not to harm others just to further my plan for my benefit. Recently in my home group, I gave a little share about how much to put in the 7th Tradition basket. It seems here in Thailand the norm is 20 baht (and has been for 20 years) which is only about one half a US dollar. Being careful not to scold, I pointed out that in AA rooms around the world most contributions are USD $1 or 2. I explained it was a matter of conscience and in my own case, there would be no money without this program so I put in the max recommended by the Service Manual. My efforts to bring in more revenue to pay the rent was met with no change. One member told me I should have been a priest because I give guilt trips. So showing some courage may be met with hostility and resistance.

Nobody can feel guilty without their permission but still I know my courage may have a price and I ask for God's help with the fallout.

May 4

HOPE

"Hope is like the sun, which, as we journey toward it, casts the shadow of our burden behind us." (Samuel Smiles, don't you just love that name?). Most of us have known a deep feeling of hopelessness and the pain of no future. Now once we have known despair, we can help others in the same boat. I think about "hope" every morning in my 11th Step Prayer: **--that where there is despair, I may bring hope.** I couldn't give hope if I didn't have it myself. My basket is full of hope along with all the other blessings.

And there is this from *A New Day*: **It is the around-the-corner brand of hope that prompts people to action, while the distant hope acts as an opiate.** How true it is for us? We need to get into action and we were paralyzed by lack of hope and fear. Thank God, no more. For me, the hope came as I met the other members and the look in their eyes. The lights were on and smiles and laughter filled the room. They told me I could be one of them if I did what they did. I was sold. All I have to do is stay sober and when I did my 3rd Step, I gave my drinking problem over to God. I made a daily promise to my Higher Power not to drink today or ever again. I certainly do not want to break that promise. Why would I take back my drinking problem from God when He has done such a good job for all these years?

Hope is what colors my future, I need not live in the future. Whatever happens is supposed to happen so I can relax and let life unfold as it will in God's time and speed.

May 5

I AM RESPONSIBLE

We recently had an AA Roundup here in Pattaya and the theme this year was **I Am Responsible**. Our society would not continue like it has if we were not responsible for helping those who reach out. I know many hands reached out to me the minute I came in the door. The main speaker, a very articulate lady, gave a little talk on the last day of the Roundup on the topic of responsibility and how it ties into the part in the Serenity Prayer about **courage to change the things I can.** I really agree with her on the pre-step of safety, even before Step One. There needs to be a safe environment for recovery to happen. Doing my own inventory, I can remember times I saw predators come into the meeting hall. People who come to prey on the generosity of the fellowship. People who are borrowing money with no intention of ever paying it back. A room full of suckers as they view us. I have been victim a few times but more importantly when I see such people I need to have the courage to do something and not just sit there and watch them work the room.

Worse than the panhandler are the old timers that prey on new comers and grab them and try to make slaves out them. They have a brand of AA which is only theirs and they preach a bunch of BS. Most of the victims see right through these types but a new comer can be raw and very vulnerable. Then there is the sexual predator who swoops down on the new women and takes them under his wing. Real scum. So yes, I am ready to help anybody who reaches out and I am also responsible for doing something about an unsafe condition or an unsafe person who is using the fellowship for their own purposes. We have one guy who uses the meeting as an extension of his office. He is billing his company for hours which include the meeting hour. He preys on the fellowship to sell his product and the fellowship is part of his networking efforts. Our home group are all potential customers. He plays with his phone, texting the entire hour and leaving the meeting to answer phone calls.

Not only am I a responsible member of AA but I need to have courage to protect the other members from known threats.

May 6

HUMILITY

We all know folks who are truly humble and there is something very attractive about that very important attribute. You feel comfortable with humble people, they give you the feeling they are right with the world and they are right with themselves and all others they come in contact with. They encourage and do not criticize. They never one-up anybody but then again they don't belittle themselves. In other words, they are right-sized. Humble people communicate straight across, eye to eye not talking down or up. Humble folks listen more than they talk and allow you your point of view without controversy. Most of the humble souls I know have an impressive list of accomplishments but they don't wear them on their sleeve of hang them on the wall. You may have to dig a little to find the depth of their knowledge and experience because you can't see it from the calm exterior they all have. I learned from day one my pride was a liability and my attitude had to change. I was not a boss anymore and I had no rank in AA, I was just another alcoholic. Just another bozo on the bus.

My morning routine works on my humility by reading what somebody else wrote and praying to my Higher Power. Life is not about me. I am not the center of the universe; in fact, I am not the center of anything. I see myself as a single grain of sand on the beach of life. Life is a beach, right? From *A New Day*, **"True humility is not abject, groveling, self-despising spirit. It is but a right estimate of ourselves as God sees us.** What you think of me is none of my business but what God thinks of me is. My inventory showed me what size I am. I am not greater than or less than I think I am. It is what it is, warts and all. Solid humility leads to other good qualities: tolerance, kindness, understanding, open-mindedness, and patience. Humility and love are connected for sure. It is no wonder our program focuses on humility as key to a successful recovery. Arrogance just does not fly around other folks in the fellowship. Humility opens us up for more relationships and improves the ones we already have.

We get along better with ourselves and others. We can accept our limitations a little easier.

Humility is like a sense of humor, either you have it or you don't.

May 7

HEAVEN AND HELL

In all my study I have formed the opinion religion is an invention of man and thus heaven and hell is just so much false hope and fear as translated by man. Since no one has brought a video back from either heaven or hell there is no hard evidence that there is a puffy white cloud place for good people and a fiery furnace for bad people. I don't want to tread on your religious beliefs, this is my personal opinion and my ideas alone. If I could create my own image of a Higher Power then why not create an image of afterlife. My spiritual readings and study all talk about the cycle of life and death. We came from a very small organism at conception, we added water, nutrients and air to breathe. We grew into full sized human beings for a few years and at death we turn back into a tiny organism. "Dust to Dust" if you will. My teachers tell me the spirit is of God and the spirit just changes from a human body to the next level. To the gurus of "hell" they say it is unfulfilled desires that are not spiritual in nature but thirsts for gratification that never can be satisfied. Well, to me that sounds like drinking at the deep dark bottom where booze just did not work to fill the thirst. All of us have had a taste of "hell."

Forget about the "burn in hell" threats of past preachers and priests. Let's talk about where we are today in the peace and serenity of our new life in recovery. Sounds like heaven to me, ya think? Here is my philosophy: we are doing the next right thing on a daily basis, we pray, we ask for God's guidance and seek His will for us. We all are getting as close to God as we possibly can. We need not concern ourselves with heaven or hell. It is my opinion we are in heaven right now. I look at my gratitude list and there are more gifts from God than I can count, that's why I had to make a list. I can choose to stay in heaven by doing what I am doing daily or I can settle for less. I could go straight to hell by picking up a drink so that's not going to happen no matter what earthly tragedy I experience. I am in the arms of God and I am not going anywhere else. I am home in this heaven, I enjoy by the grace of God. All I must do is give, help others and stick with my fellow winners. My spirit will live on after my death by the actions I take while I am living, this I believe.

God is Love and my life is love centered and love driven. I choose to call my situation "heaven." I have no unfulfilled desires, no bucket list, and I trust I will be with other loving spirits when I transition. I don't have to wait for heaven.

May 8

WHERE TO FIND GOD

Heard at one of my meetings: "I define GOD as the Great Out Doors" and others say Good Orderly Direction which is a good one also. The reading about whether God is or is not, is simple to me. I know there is a God, no question. Each one of has a different concept of a Higher Power or God or many other names. God really doesn't need a name, He is. When I found myself in impossible situations, I prayed for God's help and He never failed me. Not once but many times. I find God in our environment every day. Nature is God's canvas of amazing artwork. I don't know how you could stand over the Grand Canyon and not believe in God. The earth is dissected, and color coded with eons of time on display for our inspection and education. The flowers of the earth take my breath away. Thousands of different flora so pick just one. Orchids. They come in so many varieties too many to count, different shapes and colors and they breed new hybrids' all the time. Who did that? You know the answer.

One famous author says she finds God in the garden. I go along with that but much further. I look at the creatures of the earth and find it awesome how each animal and insect have been designed for survival and propagation. The lizard with two eyes that work independently of each other. The giraffe that can forage above the rest of the competition. The dogs who have attached themselves to the human being and provided us love and companionship. (I heard one guy tell us that he hoped he could be half the man his dog thinks he is.) The earth is the size of a pea compared to some super large planets out there in space and yet we have the only life like ours with nations and conflicts. It comes to mind that God has given us all we need and yet we don't share our abundance and instead we fight with other nations. With all the gifts God has provided for us how can you not believe God loves us all? Down deep every person has some understanding of a force greater than themselves. Call it whatever you want and just for convenience most of us call this power God.

So, where do I find God? I find God in everything around me but most of all God resides in my heart.

May 9

AM I TWO-FACED?

Reading about Dr. Jekyll and Mr. Hyde brings to my mind all the inner conflicts over the right way or all the other ways. Many of my friends visualize two cartoon characters, one on each shoulder (a devil and an angel). One side says, "Go ahead and have a drink, nobody will know" and the character on the other side says, "you will know, and God will know." My favorite description is the old Indian Chief teaching the young braves the lessons of life. The Chief tells them, "Inside of each of us resides a white wolf and a black wolf, one is evil and one is good but as you mature only one wolf can survive." The braves ask, "Old Chief which one will survive?" The Chief answers, "The one you feed." This is what we do in our morning prayer and meditation, we feed the good wolf and starve the bad one. Before I came to the program the bad side always won the argument of the day. Down deep I knew I was on the wrong path but I kept on doing the wrong things. The role of badass fit me perfectly so I tried to be the badest badass ever.

Some of us learned how to wear masks or uniforms to maintain a split personality. Mean Joe Green put on a football uniform and became a monster who would knock your block off on the football field, but in reality, he was a gentle pussy cat. I used to put on a military uniform and act as if I was in charge and had my act together, but the truth was, I was an alcoholic sick puppy. I spent half my life being something I wasn't and the beauty of a sober life you develop only one personality with no mask to hide behind. The actor in us doesn't work anymore. Once we get sober the option of doing the next right thing is placed in front of us. No more double standards, no more faking it. Mr. Hyde has disappeared. The bad wolf is dead. Life becomes so much easier now that the inner conflicts are few. What is right becomes obvious to us and in times of indecision we have a Higher Power and a fellowship to assist us at those junctions. I don't argue with myself much anymore. The Right Road is straight ahead.

To the question of am I two-faced? No, what you see is what you get, warts and all. It is what it is. Old, sober, happy, joyous and free.

May 10

IT IS ALWAYS NOW

It is not always easy to stay in the "now" when all we have is the past which got us to "now." A bigger problem is the future and all the fears that go with gloom and doom on the horizon. I have some family members tormented by the future and the inability to accept what is. The statement "It is what it is." Simple but profound. We can't change what is, no matter how righteous we feel for what "should be." I have a family member I love dearly but she is a "worst case" scenario person and lives in total fear of events that have not happened and are not likely to happen. Her head is full of bad guys, rouge counties, possible deportations and resentments. There is no room for love or a positive thought or two. The sky is falling every day. North Korean missiles are on the way. Geez. I am going to try to sell her on the "best case scenario." In my experience people who expect the worse get their wish sooner or later but folks who expect the best (like my daily prayer says) usually get the best. Magic aye?

The Second Step gives us a concept of a Higher Power and with that comes faith to some degree at least. The only Rx for fear I know of is faith. I have faith that everything happens is supposed to happen. Not the way I would have it or think the way it should be but what happens has nothing to do with me. I am powerless over events so why get upset over things I have no control over. That's why dividing life up into 24-hour segments helps me stay in the "now." It is always now right now and in 5 minutes "now" is history and I can't change that either. It gets down to my attitude is always now so I try to keep now positive and light hearted. **"We are here and it is now: further than that all human knowledge is moonshine." from** *A New Day* **page 36.** It is self-imposed torture to agonize over politics and national behavior. We all have been fired from our position of Master of The Universe. We are the masters of our own actions and attitudes and that's about it. This is not a Burger King life "The way you like it." It has taken a lifetime of living to come to this moment right now. The point of power is in the present. This is where our actions get into motion. God will help me right now.

May 11

WHO ARE YOU CALLING CRAZY?

When I first came to the program and saw the 12 Steps, I had no problem with admitting I was an alcoholic and my life was unmanageable, I had no problem with God or Higher Power, I had no problem with inventory or restitution but insanity? No, not me. I was insulted. How dare these people call me insane. Don't they know how many degrees I have? I soon found out being insane means you don't think you are insane. Everybody else is crazy. Insanity is like "One Flew Over the Cuckoo's Nest." Insanity is those people walking around the streets talking to themselves. I learned that is mental illness and insanity is what applies to actions that are detrimental to oneself and others as in drinking. I heard the definition of insanity was doing the same thing over and over again and expecting a different result. Oops, that would be me. Thinking that it would be different this time but crashing and burning every time. I heard the story, "I didn't get in trouble every time I drank, but every time, I did get in trouble I had been drinking." Once again this was me.

I accepted the cold fact I was insane and had been insane for so long I couldn't identify the problem. Education will not curb insanity. Money cannot stop the insanity. I cannot "think" my way out of insanity. Since I am the source of the problem, I learned I needed outside help as Step 2 clearly states. Finding a Higher Power of some description, my own, is key to restoration. How about the nuts in the asylum? Somehow the magic of the fellowship is what most of us rely on to come out of the cuckoo nest. Thank God we are all crazy but not all at the same time. There is a wrench for every nut in the room. As I did my inventory and looked at my actions it was clear my actions made no sense at all. I endangered myself, my family my friends and society at large. I was going through life with a bulldozer piling up damage everywhere I went. Life was an emergency and constant chaos. Today I am a little less crazy but slowly I am getting closer to the goal of sane living.

I know I will never be totally sane and I am OK with that. I like being a little "off" it keeps my enemies guessing.

May 12

BIG EXTRA BENEFIT

We stay sober and help others stay sober as our primary purpose but this is only a starting point. When I first came to AA all I wanted is to get the heat off, then the idea to stop drinking followed. I would have been happy if that's all the program offered but there is so many other benefits I never dreamed of. One of the biggest surprises to me was real, meaningful and deep friendships. When I look back over my life I have no existing school year friendships. From 30 years in the military I have a handful of combat comrades but none as close as those I have found in the fellowship. Why is that? My guess is we have all had "near death" experiences and found a common solution to our problems. Our bottoms have been just as gut wrenching as combat. Having done both I would much rather do a couple of years of combat over taking a drink. I can do combat sober. The best people I have ever met have all been in AA. My friends in AA are gold! First of all, I didn't know how to be a friend until I got sober and changed my life and my attitude.

The fellowship is indeed the bright spot in my life just like the recent reading says. To see the guys I sponsor "get it" is like having my children graduated from college. This benefit goes way beyond what I expected. Sometimes the home group members annoy me but that's my problem. On my recent trip I was happy to get a break from the same guys every single day but about a week away I really missed them warts and all. Recovery is not a lonely business and we do need each other. That "need" turns into love after a while. My home group and the fellowship is on my gratitude list. I can find a friend anywhere in the world by going to a meeting. I am still close friends with 8 people who were at my first meeting. I don't have 8 friends from the 52 years of my life before that first meeting. Now I can't count the number of friends I have but easily over 100. These are friends who would come to my rescue if needed. Friends who come to the hospital when I am sick. Real deal friends who give unconditional love. One more drink and I could have missed this golden benefit.

I treasure my friends and work on making my friendships deeper and that is not easy because there are so many of them all over the globe.

May 13

BIRDS OF A FEATHER

Eagles hang out with other eagles, storks hang out with storks and us humans tend to hang with people like ourselves who speak the same language, live in the same place and have stuff in common. Same thing in AA, we need each other, we are birds of the same feather. When I was growing up I could never find other "birds" like me. I wasn't a nerd with a pocket protector and I wasn't cool with a 57 Chevy like the popular guys. My father never had friends and I was just like him. No friends to speak of. Bonding with a group just wasn't part of my young life or any of my family. OK how about teamwork? I was on the track team but what I did was individual not like basketball or baseball. After my first meeting of AA I felt I found some birds just like me at last. Also, I was given a service position so I was part of a team for the first time. I looked at the 3 legacies and saw Unity and Service and Recovery. The perfect triangle with equal sides and I felt the wisdom of our founders.

We hang together. We found what we need. Each other. All of are teachers and all of us are students. No one outranks another, we are all just alcoholics with a daily reprieve from drinking. No boss no sergeant of arms no leaders ahhh can this be true? Yes, it is. I have no blood brothers, but I have a room full every morning at my home group. I would do anything for them and when I was in the hospital they were there for me. Not only is it a fellowship but a source of lifetime friends. Real honest friends. As far as the business of keeping the group going we all have different skills and abilities. Just like a ball team some hit well and some catch the ball well. We all find our place on the team and it makes a winner. For the first time in my life I am part of a winning team. No super stars, no special treatment for anyone. I often mingle in other "flocks" and they just are not of my feather so I tend to spend my time with my AA friends and am most comfortable with my own "birds."

Being away from my "homies" for a few weeks made me realize how much I love them and need them as part of my recovery

May 14

CHILDHOOD

Psychologists tell us that our personalities are formed by the age of 2 and of course we have no choice over our genes. It sounds almost like we are doomed from the very start. Of course, we are powerless over our childhood. We did not get to choose our parents but we are not powerless to stop the chain of abuse and pain in our history. As we work our inventory, we can see how our character defects got their start and how our personality took shape from an early age. In my case I grew up with WWII, my dad was gone to fight the war. I listened to war on the radio and it was in my blood to find the military as my calling and get a shot at war myself. My childhood was without fun and games. Life was serious business and I was pushed to be the best and be competitive. To this day I have to really work on "fun." Thank God I am out of competition of any kind. Being just another "bozo on the bus" took some years for me to grasp. My parents tried to control every facet of my life until I could finally escape my dysfunctional household, it is no wonder I developed into a control freak. That character defect goes all the way to the bone but at least I recognize it.

This program is amazingly simple. Don't drink no matter what, seek help when necessary and chop life into 24-hour segments. When we step into recovery we are like children. Babies in a new wonderful world no matter how many years of life we have accumulated. The good news is we get a "do over" so we can see where we got off the path and into our addictions. It's OK to be childlike and admit our lack of knowledge and put on a new pair of glasses in which to view the world around us. It's OK to ask for help and find a sponsor to show us the Steps. Asking for help was forbidden in my family but now it comes naturally to tap the resources of a Higher Power and the fellowship. Today there are no trust issues whereas in childhood I was taught to trust nobody. This program taught me to love and in childhood love always had a string attached. Today there are still fears but they are natural fears to stay safe and alert which is better than a childhood ruled by fear. My early years were very scary, war, gangs, poverty etc. I am blessed to put that awful childhood behind me and start anew.

This new childhood is full of love, fun, a worthwhile place in society, spiritual growth, happiness beyond measure! Who could ask for anything more?

May 15

LESSONS IN RECOVERY

We all have an alcoholic past but after some years of sobriety we have a sober past also. Our disease is progressive, the good news is that recovery is progressive also as long as we stay centered in the program. Being in Hawaii where I got sober and re-visiting my original home group brought some recovery lessons to mind. I thought I would share some of those with you. My very first meeting was at the Wailana Coffee Shop in Waikiki at 7 a.m. on Tues/Thur and that has not changed. In fact, the very first waitress who had a big part of my surrender, Sylvia, is still waiting tables for the meeting. (She shouted ALCOHOLIC when I was trying to find where the group was gathered. Surrender followed. Dozens of people stared at me, so the jig was up!)

Lesson #1 was a lady named Lita (now passed away) sat next to me every meeting and one day I was reading a newspaper before the meeting and she told me, "Mike, put that paper away there is nothing in there that will help you stay sober." I have not brought anything to a meeting since. This was before smart phones, which today is a bigger distraction at meetings.

Lesson #2: When I was 6 months sober, I was installed as secretary of the meeting. One morning there was a very large group and I said, "Today we can skip reading "How It Works" to give more time for sharing." OMG, I violated the Holy Grail. Everybody jumped on my chest and beat me up. No, we are not skipping reading "How It Works" and ever since I treat the reading as a prayer and listen carefully or read it carefully when asked.

Lesson #3: Betty H and Cathy VW both taught me this: "Mike when you come to a meeting, you wear a nice shirt with a collar and be clean shaven. You show newcomer you care about this program." To this day I have never attended a meeting without a shave and real shirt. (I have seen guys come in with no shirt or under shirts. Yuk!)

Lesson #4: When you sponsor someone, you assist them in the Steps and matters of recovery. Yesterday I saw one of the first guys I tried to sponsor. Twenty plus years ago, this guy had me picking him up, moving him to another apartment, buying him meals and lending him money. Clearly, he was using me and when I caught him walking down the street with a 12 pack of beer, I severed my servant position having learned an important lesson. Sad to say after 20 years this guy is starting all over with court papers. But he did render an amends and some thanks for my support 20 years later, but it did my heart good.

It was a great trip down memory lane in sobriety, it made me realize I have come a long way. I had a good start.

May 16

RISK TAKING

I remember at my bottom I was so full of fear I would not risk driving because another DUI would put me in jail. I could not risk answering the phone for the fear of bad news since all my news was bad. In my last years of drinking I took no risks and my young life was nothing but high risk and my history was pretty much successful results from those risky years. After I got sober it was ground zero for risk taking despite my history. Why? FEAR, Future Events Appearing Real. My faith was starting anew so that had to come first before I could even think about risks. Having low self-esteem is a big factor in risk taking because when you view yourself as a failure then your actions are doomed from the start, at least in your mind. Then if you are overly concerned about how people think of you then it is difficult to risk looking foolish. But I have learned to do nothing and sit on the bench has zero benefit. **"Men who try to do something and fail are infinitely better off than those who try to do nothing and succeed."** *A New Day*

Now that we have been sober awhile, we have strength to try new ventures. We have a Higher Power in our corner who won't let us get too far afield. We are able to succeed more fully now that we have chosen the right path. Since we are now on firmer ground, we can push the envelope and expand our horizons. I know folks in the program who have gone from a high school education and at 40+ years old gone on to be lawyers and doctors after getting sober. Age and education need not be barriers to finding a new occupation. There was no need for forward air controllers to run air strikes in Hawaii. I had to find a different path. God provided me a job in construction even though I had zero experience in that field. But I took a risk in my interview and told the truth. My new boss laughed at my answer to experience. I said, "Mr. Zinc I have no construction experience but I have 25 years of destruction experience." He thought I would be just great and I got the job I sorely needed. That gave me credentials in the safety field that led to a better job in a treatment center where I belonged.

If we don't try to do something for the fear of looking bad to others, then we look bad to ourselves.

May 17

YOU ARE RIGHT WHERE YOU ARE SUPPOSED TO BE

Being in Hawaii, where I got sober, is bringing back memories from my early stumbles and falls. When I was just starting, I expected to be down the road of recovery a lot further than I was. Everyone just said, "You are right where you should be." It took a while to understand just what they were all saying. Everyone has their own pace of recovery and it has peaks and valleys it is not a straight-line deal. I made the mistake of comparing my progress to others and their program. I forgot it took me decades to get in the mess I was in and the solution does not come overnight. I could see the goal but finally realized it was a mountain to climb one step at a time, one day at a time and the road was slippery and jagged. Most of the guys who started with me were in their 30's and I was 53. I had more wreckage than most, the cleanup was going to take a lot longer. My pace was just right for me and I have a few more years before my sober years outnumber my drinking years.

As long as you are working on your spiritual condition every day you are traveling at God's speed. Your Higher Power is listening 24/7 and you are where you are supposed to be. However, one drink and you are not where you belong. All bets are off and Step One has a part you missed. Back to square zero. Staying sober is basic requirement and then whatever prayer and meditation you do is a positive action, then add a meeting or two and you are in the right place. Spend time with your sponsor and help another alcoholic and you are smoking down the Road of Happy Destiny. Obviously, the more effort the better the progress but you are the one to set the tempo. To ignore your family needs to go attend 5 meetings a day is not the spirit of recovery. Some balance needs to be found between recovery actions and basic life functions. I have heard guys blame their lack of progress on their location. Recovery has no location but your heart and soul. You can get sober anywhere and progress anywhere. If you live upstairs from a noisy bar, yes, it is time to relocate.

My past was a mountain of wreckage but now I have a sober past to measure the miles I have come from Day One Step One.

May 18

LISTEN TO YOUR HEART

One of the biggest steps in recovery for me was to understand the concept of heart talk vs. head talk. My head can mess me up so bad if I let it. My heart is good and is where the answers are imbedded. The benefit of prayer and meditation is the heart gets a voice and it can trump the crazy stuff in my head. The trick is to shut the yack, yack coming from your brain and let the intuition and goodness of the heart have a quiet moment to translate helpful information the lame brain can understand. The alcoholic brain is damaged and has no clutch. We all know alcohol kills brain cells and can cause "wet brain." It can wander around and take you to dark places very quickly. My brain tells me I am OK but I am not OK but I am getting better. My brain says I don't have a disease but I do. My brain is out to get me so my heart comes first. I have learned to stop the storm in my gray matter and rely on what my heart tells me. I have gone against my heart on occasion and always regret the results.

In Thai culture they have over 700 terms for "heart" and only a few for brain. They believe that all good or bad stems from the type heart you have. The best reference you can get from a Thai person is "jai dee" which means good heart A "cool" heart or a "hot" heart refers to your temper. Thai people speak very softly whereas in my native culture people talk loud and way too much. The heart talk has no chance. As you can tell my recovery has learned much from my adopted country and culture. If I am talking no learning is taking place no matter if it is out loud or just in my brain. It has taken me years to get my brain to stop talking and listen for messages from my Higher Power. I am certain God resides within me and not down the street in a church or a temple. My recovery depends on connecting my internal wiring to receive rather than transmit.

My brain is fast and furious and my heart is slow. I can tell when the brakes need to be applied and be still, be quiet and listen deeply.

May 19

HARMONY BEGINS AT HOME

Even on the road I have my 6 books of readings and no matter what or where, my first hour is one of prayer and meditation. In fact, being away from my comfort zone I need it more than ever. Traveling gets you into the HALT mode real quick Hungry Angry Lonely (not so much) and Tired (to the max!). In my reading this morning one hit the spot. Harmony begins within us. You cannot bring harmony to others if you aren't harmonious yourself. I remember in my past roles as parent and boss, I was always seeking harmony with my family and my workers and not achieving success. Now I know why in retrospect, I did not have internal harmony at all. There was always an internal war going on so how in the world did I think I could project harmony? Insane. I was trying to bring calm when I was in a personal storm. Not going to happen. Harmony requires thinking of all persons involved and finding common ground and making compromises where necessary. Not an easy task.

This wedding I attended brought the whole reading into focus. First of all, the bride (my cousin's daughter) and the groom come from great role model families. My cousin and his wife have been married 40 years and the groom's parents have been married 36 years. What was striking about the entire event was the groom is one of 5 brothers. They were like harmony in action. They all wore the same suits with vests and straw matching hats. They danced out to the ceremony like a Broadway show. They were one big extremely close tight family. That became obvious as the reception was a show of love. They operated like a professional dance troupe with fun and laughter. The atmosphere was contagious, and it was awesome to be part of the whole event. I look at my 5 kids and harmony does not come to mind. Two of my sons have taken themselves out of the family picture and all 5 have only been in one room once about 16 years ago. Big difference and my part in it started with divorce when my kids were young and the family began to be located all over the map. Harmony is a long-term effort.

Hopefully I have learned to promote harmony with my own internal serenity and sober actions at family events like this one.

May 20

CITIZENSHIP

When I was "out there" I lost my citizenship to planet earth. I was not contributing anything to society. In fact, I was net minus dragging others down and being a problem instead of a solution. I didn't belong in any group. I was on the outside looking in. I might as well have been an alien from outer space. I paid my taxes out of fear but that was my only civic duty. I performed no services for my fellow humans and neighbors. I was sort of a ward of the state. I was being paid for the past and doing absolutely nothing in the present and I had no future. If I was a car they would tow me to the junkyard. My first meeting I felt like I belonged with this group because they had the same history I had. For the first time in years I had a purpose, a group that made me a member. I was given a service position my first day and finally I could do something useful and positive. I was an alien among other aliens but they all seemed to be from this planet. Soon I returned to be a more reasonable human being by joining AA and forming new relationships from an entirely different viewpoint.

After being sober awhile some us can find our way to become useful contributors to projects of import. I know a lot of members who have gone back to college and become lawyers and professors. I know some who run for public office or city council. For a time, I was in the Rotary Club. (They have some traditions that mirror AA principles) The point is that now you have a new life how about giving back to the community that once shunned you. Give them a chance to love the new you. This spiritual life has a set of tools to be used in daily life. Before I only had a hammer so every problem needed a nail. Not so anymore. I can be a positive citizen and an active member of community affairs. This design for living we learned thru the program is not only good in the rooms of AA but also for our family and activities outside the program. Like Step 12 says, **in all my affairs.**

I am not two people one in AA and one outside AA. That's too much trouble, there is one me with my new tool kit.

May 21

CLOUDS VS. GROUND

The first time I flew over 55,000 feet and my two engines quit, as they were supposed to, it was so quiet and peaceful. I felt insignificant as I gazed at the planet from outer space. I didn't reach out and touch the face of God like the poem "High Flight" but I loved the spiritual feeling of being so high and looking down on earth as a place I really didn't want to be. It was full of reality, fears, resentments, problems, lies and betrayal. I would have preferred to stay in the quiet zone but of course reality was inevitable. My engines started, thank you, God and back to earth and reality. Yuck! Looking back on my life I was always reality challenged. I was a chronic daydreamer. Chasing rainbows instead of facing facts. The reading about having our heads in the clouds and our feet on the ground was very special to me. I have had many spiritual experiences and did not realize what they were until I had an awakening as to what spirituality was all about. As the reading suggests, why not both?

This is life today. I spend my first hour in the morning in the quiet zone, meditation and prayer. This is the best hour of the day, head in the clouds. I set goals for myself, examine my progress, get grateful, and think of others. It is all in preparation for reality, people and life's little dramas. All the spirituality and prayer in the world is worthless if it does not result in action. The spiritual daily tune up is my action plan for the next 24 hours. I never know what reality is going to deal me today. On the other hand, I have met people who declare themselves "realists" and shun the spiritual side of life and by and large they are grumpy, negative, doom and gloom types. The trick is to find a balance of spirituality and reality which works for you. In my previous life I could handle reality now I have a Higher Power and the fellowship to navigate me through real life's problems. No longer can I shut off the phone and pour a stiff drink and escape what is real.

I pray your cloud will bump into my cloud on the road of happy destiny.

May 22

RELATIONSHIPS 101

When I was growing up, both my grandmothers were divorced, and my parents should have been. The result was I never witnessed a real relationship. No role model for what a normal family was supposed to be. As I look back, I was great in school, English, math, social studies but I never got the course: Relationships 101. I was behind the door for

160

that course. I learned a lot growing up but relationships were not part of the curriculum. I had school "chums" but failed to have real friends. My parents had no friends. I had no idea how to be a friend. Then later sexual encounters required alcohol first 100% rule. Then the bar is where I formed friendships and we all know how shallow that is. Relationships were what I could get out of it instead of what I could contribute. Perfectly wrong. Marriage had no chance with me. I was not equipped to handle any relationship so why I thought I could handle marriage was insanity. OK then I kept doing it over and over again "It will be different this time." Famous last words.

My Relationships 101 course began when I made my first AA meetings. This overly nice gentleman declared himself my sponsor and poured unconditional love my way. That was a meaningful relationship. Then as I did my Steps, I developed my concept of a Higher Power and that was a key relationship. Then I learned to have friends I needed to be a friend and real lifelong friendships began. A little late in life but at least it happened and continues to happen. I cherish all my relationships and try to give love, encouragement and my time to all my relationships. I was hungry for a real marriage and I asked the married folks in the program about when my time would come. Margie, my relationship counselor, told me in my case it may take 10 years. OMG, I want to meet Miss Right Now. Oh no not possible, more growth was necessary for this dude. Sure enough, at the 11-year point, I was ready for the "real deal."

Looking back, I can see clearly why my relationships failed. They didn't have a prayer of a chance because I had zero knowledge.

May 23

LIFE HAS NEW MEANING

My first time reading the Big Book not much stuck except the part about the "director" that made my hair stand up because that was me. As the years have accumulated and I continue to read the Big Book I am surprised by the new things I find. I could swear somebody went into my book at night and changed the wording. But of course, it is me who has changed. Thank God I have undergone the change. They told me if I didn't change everything I would drink again and that was a horrible option. I keep searching for the 50+ promises and the one on page 89 is priceless. **"Life will take on new meaning."** Since our lives change little by little one day at a time it is hard to see the drastic difference between the old life and the new one. A whole new set of principles one could never imagine when one is drinking. The principle of instant gratification and trouble avoidance is not very noble. The complete absorption of self as the daily driving force of my existence is gone. What was black before is now white. A 100% flip flop.

What is the big difference? First of all anything "spiritual" was off the table when I was drinking. Today everything starts on a spiritual path. I am no longer the lone wolf. I have a Higher Power in my corner. I begin my day with an attitude of gratitude instead of damage control. I can process difficulties without anger. Helping others comes naturally these days where as before selfishness ruled the day. I have been given a "do over" by the grace of God and a chance to live two completely different lives. It is a gift in an old wrapping but the contents are so much better. I can use all those mistakes of the past to help someone else. The dark side of my life is not wasted. Nothing is wasted in God's economy. I love my new life and the new meaning which comes with it. I can sleep with the angels today instead of tossing and turning with nightmares of wrongs committed and people hurt by my drinking. Passing out does not count as sleep, so for more than 30 years, I never really "slept."

When I review the character defects, I start with 25 years ago, I can graphically see the amazing change my new life has brought.

May 24

HELPING IS A DELICATE MATTER

To me the 12th Step is about helping others in and out of AA. There are many ways to help but some help may be harmful if not thought all the way through. You can have the greatest of intentions but forcing your "help' down someone's throat may cause damage instead of improvement. The attitude "I have it and you don't" is the wrong approach with alcoholics and I suspect most people are the same way. When I am working with another alcoholic, I remind myself I am not better. Even if I have years of sobriety, I really only have the last 24 hours. The person I am helping is just like me and it could be me again if I pick up a drink. I am not the "boss" of anybody. I cannot order someone into sobriety. They must find their own path which may be different than mine. "My way or the highway" works in the military but not in AA. I know I only have answers for my program that have worked but everyone has to find their own answers. It is frustrating at times to watch someone you are trying to help keep running into brick walls. I have to allow others to fail.

Alcoholics are the most sensitive people on the planet. They easily get their feelings hurt so I have learned to curb my sarcasm and not make the person I am trying to help the butt of my jokes. I have hurt guys in the past in the attempt to be funny. I talk about my own trips and falls which are many. The book tells us not to talk "from a moral high ground" and that is very good advice. Nobody likes to be preached to and berated. No doubt you will hear bleeding deacons in meetings and it makes the audience gag. Nothing worse than a fellow with decades of sobriety but not enough days as in today. Talking down to anybody is a real bad idea. I know I can't stand someone who talks down to me. There are a few people in the program who talk down to everybody. I stay away from those guys and resist the temptation to put them down. My point is helping others takes some thought and prayer. Most of all it should be from the heart and with love. I expect no payment, not even a free dinner, from those I help. I give away what was given to me freely.

Not everyone I try to help can bond with my way of communicating. Sometimes the chemistry is great and other time not. I do my best and leave the results up to God.

May 25

IT'S NOT ABOUT YOU ANYMORE

When I was in grammar school, we used to sell Easter Seal stamps and it showed a young man with a crippled boy on his back and the caption was: "He's not heavy he is my brother." That image stayed with me my entire life and the message is the same as the 12 Steps. Helping others. When you first get started and begin the Steps, it is all about you. In order to get to Step 12 you need to surrender, find a Higher Power, give up, clean up, make restitution so it seems it is all about you. And so it is but the point is to get you to appoint where you are useful to the world at large instead of a net minus. One of the best years of my life is when I had a chance to be a caregiver for another member who was dying of cancer. I made up my mind to make a commitment to help my friend through all the problems of wasting away and finally death. It got me out of myself and made me grateful for life itself and the ability to be there for a person in need. I suddenly realized the point of the program "helping others." It is not about me anymore; I have done the work to make myself a fully vested member of society.

That is the awakening I came to understand after doing all the Steps. If I get out of my wants, my problems, my, my, my, and get into service to my fellow earth travelers. I am happy as a result. To know I am useful and doing the right things I don't need to focus on me so much as I focus on others. My two daughters have spent years caregiving for loved ones and I could not be more proud of their selflessness and sacrifice to their own wellbeing. To see the guys I sponsor make it through difficult times without drinking and grow in the fellowship is more heartwarming than winning the lottery. To see my home group care for others and go beyond the rooms and care for our members is a joy to be cherished. It all is done with love and love trumps all other emotions. I just need to turn off the selfish switch and turn on the help light by making myself available.

The further I get away from me and help you the better I feel about me.

May 26

VALUE VS. COST

There are some folks who know the price of everything and the value of nothing. Here in Thailand there is a very popular T-shirt with the words," No Money No Honey." It sort of implies that you need to have money in order to have relationship. True enough money drives the success or failure of many marriages and relationships but the point is missed entirely, love should have no price tag. If it does then it is not a meaningful relationship. Those with unconditional love are the keepers. The best things in life, I have found, cost nothing. Take "serenity" for example. Can you buy a pound of serenity? It comes from being in the right place doing the right things. It costs absolutely nothing. Faith, where is the store that carries faith? I have faith, if I remain on a spiritual path financial insecurity will never haunt me. The program taught me that money fears would disappear if I followed the Steps of the program and badda bing, badda boom, that is exactly what happened to me. I did the work and the rewards followed later just like the book says.

There should be no price tag on anything we do or give away. We need not look for a "payoff" for our acts of kindness. We don't need applause or even thanks if we really, give from the heart unconditionally. In my old way of thinking there was a string attached to everything I touched. If I do this for you then I expect you to do this for me. Now I cut all those strings so there is no "book" to keep, no accounting procedures. The things I cherish are priceless, they cannot be measured in a balance sheet. Happiness, good health, freedom are worth more than all the gold in Fort Knox. The further I get from the material world the better I feel. Money no longer drives me. I pity the poor guys whose hearts are attached to the stock market. Yikes! Being in service drives me, the relationships I have with my family drives me, commitment and loyalty is my cash. All the blessings God's grace has bestowed on me is totally priceless and cannot be measured. I am wealthier than all the gold in Fort Knox!

Of all my treasures, love on all levels is on top of the list, unconditional no strings love.

THE ZEN OF HELP

Before I got sober, I never would ask for help. Considering all the trouble I got myself into help was needed but not requested. Pray? What's that? Once I knew my name was going to appear on the police blotter so I called on a fellow classmate to pull my sheet off the daily report so my bosses would not find out. He saw the opportunity to do me in and eliminate me from the competition for promotion and he made extra copies so everyone would know I screwed up. So much for "help." When I hit bottom, help was the only way out since the Lone Ranger mode didn't work anymore. At my very first meeting this guy told me he would be my temporary sponsor. I was in no position to refuse, and if it was left up to me, I would never ask for a sponsor. I had no idea it meant "help," but that is exactly what I needed. My sponsor helped me get through the Steps and spent hours every week being a friend and confidant. My home group cradled me in their collective arms and nursed me back to relative sanity. There was help everywhere and I needed every ounce of it.

Today I don't get into trouble but I still ask for help every morning in the hour of prayer and meditation. My Higher Power is always there so I am never alone. Help is a small prayer away no matter what. Life is not an emergency anymore but I ask God's help to keep me from that first drink no matter the crisis. My spiritual condition is my #1 priority because, if I lose my sobriety, I lose my life. For this I need help. I surrender the fact that I am dependent on my Higher Power. Since He has done for me what I could not do by myself. When I go to an AA meeting there is a roomful of folks just like me who also have a Higher Power, and if I listen closely, I can tap into the lessons others have learned. For example, I hear about drugs and what happens to addicts. I never did drugs, but I have enough information from going to a lot of meetings that I would never be tempted to pick up. My group 12 Steps me every day. They "help" me by sharing their experiences. They also put life in perspective and I know my problems are small compared to my fellows. I accept help from many sources and am open 24/7 for assistance.

I allow help to be part of my life today and stay open minded to new levels of assistance. I know only a little.

May 28

SPIRITUAL AWAKENING

Step 11 leads right into Step 12 as you do your morning meditation the awakening just happens as a result. I get a spiritual awakening every single day when I do my 11th Step upon awakening. The heavens don't open up and a great deep voice bellows down to me but rather a inspiration or a new way of seeing things. A mind stretcher or missing piece of a problem comes to mind. A warm feeling I am on the right path or even an overwhelming feeling of gratitude to the point of tears of joy. I read looking for a spark which will push my envelope and pray for some guidance. If my mind is open enough the light shines in. The problems of yesterday suddenly are solved. Somewhere between the readings, the prayers and the meditation a spiritual awakening happens. It is during the plan for the next 24 hours things to do get on the daily agenda. At times there is an array of awakenings and others are one idea but it comes without fail.

There is something magic that happens after doing the hard step work of Step 9. The relief of making amends frees up the walls formed in your mind to a new dimension. You have done the clean up so now is growth time. All those years of zero growth are now over and your life has new meaning after a complete makeover. That's why the Step says very clearly "as a result of these steps." Now comes the meaningful part of the whole process. Now you are ready to be useful in helping other alcoholics. First part of Step 12 is key to being able to be fully vested to help others and is to be in the Sunlight of the Spirit. It may take some time before you get from day 1 to Step 12 but the gold is at the end of the process. The most important achievement of my entire life is completing all 12 Steps as outlined in the Big Book. I accept my powerlessness and adopt the power of the program.

Every morning I abandon myself to the Higher Power who I understand and remain happy joyous and free.

May 29

PROMOTION

There is a famous golfer whose behavior is well known who went public with his participation in AA claiming he was sober. A short time later it was clear that he was drinking and he publicly declared "AA doesn't work." Right there is the danger of breaking anonymity. Most people know this guy is more clown than a pro golfer, the damage is probably minimal. Recently he got busted for having 5 drinks halfway through a round of golf. At least he no longer identifies himself with AA. When I was in the Rotary Club all the members "networked" and had a running list of names, phone numbers and emails so the members could buy and sell from each other. I bought tires from one guy and lawyer services from another. In AA we network to help each other out with recovery stuff and hospital visits etc. It is not a promotion network.

I know that I am being watched and I may be the only version of the Big Book anyone meets. So, I conduct myself accordingly and give every living creature a smile. I am not selling anything but sharing my happy attitude. Every guy I sponsored picked me because I was happy and they were not. Attraction. I have seen predators come and take advantage of soft-hearted AA members and borrow money with no intention of repayment. I got taken by a guy who tricked me into thinking he was a good friend of a member in good standing. I find out this dude is a leech and it was too late. Years later I nailed him when his wallet was open and he very reluctantly ponied up. AA has its share of folks that counter our traditions but it will survive crooks and promoters. We will always have sober horse thieves, but if we are guardians of the program, we can take some hits and keep flying.

As I travel around, my smile is my passport and my attitude is my cash, so I need no logo.

May 30

THE LIMELIGHT

There are readings about the hazards of the limelight. When I joined the fellowship, I was shocked to find there were no presidents or poster boys for AA. The concept of anonymity was baffling at first but finally I got the message. Ego, ego, ego! Edging God Out. The message is the key to this program. Nobody gets endorsement money for sporting the AA logo on their shirts. There are no heroes because we all have clay feet, all of us are only an arm length from a drink. The primary purpose should never be overshadowed by a personality or front man. I can tell you from personal experience the limelight is dangerous for us and is intoxicating. You can't get enough of it and seek more applause. You pick up Time magazine and wonder why your picture isn't on the cover. You develop a "shtick" and keep adding cute additions to your act. You become a performer and even though the message is meaningful the real motive to feed that hungry ego. The ego has a thirst like no other.

In my former life I picked up a cause, namely the POW/MIA issue of our pilots in jail in North Vietnam. I could have been one of them but since I wasn't I felt guilty leaving them behind to be tortured for years while I was sipping martinis in the USA. I ended up speaking all over the country. It didn't take long before I thought I was a TV star and spokesperson for this cause. It even brought me in touch with a certain billionaire who was trying to find a way to release our guys in Hanoi by civilian intervention. My ego was out of control and I thought I could be a player on the world stage. I was drunk with ego and oh yea I was an alcoholic drunk also. Very dangerous chemistry. Bottom line, I got in big trouble. I forgot my place in life and I was way over my head. Guess what, I got away with it and got promoted 3 years early so it poured gasoline on my fire and I was off to the races again. I kept getting in deep kimchi as time went on and of course my progressive disease took me to my bottom. I have learned my lesson believe me.

I know humility is a requirement and being in the limelight is counter to my recovery. Being just another bozo on the bus is OK with me.

May 31

CONFORMING

I always described myself as a non-conformist, a maverick, a rebel with or without a cause. I never wanted to be part of the crowd or a joiner. I knew I was different so why be part of the herd? I marched to a different drummer. Unique. When I went to the seminary to be a priest I got kicked out for non-conformity. My violation was walking to town to see "Rebel Without a Cause" with James Dean, my hero. I soon was happy to get the boot and be with the girls instead of a lifetime of celibacy. This started a chain of civil disobedience on my part for several decades. In the military I never read a regulation or followed the rules. I not only got away with it, but it made me bypass my peers. I loved my wild reputation and found new ways to bend the system and be different. In my flying career I was charged with operating a flying circus. It was great fun, but my drinking finally tripped me up and the big bosses folded my tent. Then I could drink with wild abandon whenever I wanted and as much as I wanted. This non-conformist hit a black bottom.

When I finally made it to the rooms of AA, I planned to do it my way and break whatever rules they would present. It worked so well in the past why not with AA? The first thing I asked about was "who is the president and what are the rules" so I could replace the president and break the commandments. I learned no president, only trusted servants and they made me a trusted servant day one, then no rules at all. The Steps are suggestions, the traditions are suggestions. What? How can that be? How can I fight the system if there is no system? Perfect that Bill W and Doctor Bob knew about idiots just like me with terminal uniqueness. Then a line in *How It Works* got my attention. **"Some of us have tried to hold on to our old ideas and the result was nil until we let go absolutely."** Bill W was talking to me and my oldest idea was to fight everything, be a lone wolf and not conform to anything. I could see my fellow members were happy, joyous and free so I gave up my old role and decided to conform to AA "suggestions." It is the easier, softer way to go with the flow instead of forever paddling upstream. The Steps in order as directed worked a miracle on this maverick.

There is still some rebel in me but when it comes to AA Steps and Traditions I get in step with my group and am just part of the herd and that is a good thing.

June 1

GOALS AND DREAMS

In the old days my goals were like, don't forget to stock up on booze so I don't have to make a trip to the liquor store drunk. Don't run out of ice. My main goal was to stay out of trouble. I had no meaningful plan for the day let alone the future. Goal setting and dreams were foreign to me when I got sober. The goal line was behind me not in front of me. I think most alcoholics had lost the ability to set goals when they hit bottom and that is why staying sober for just 24 hours is the AA mantra. This works very well and keeping our focus on the 24 hours in front of us we can accomplish it. To me the St. Francis Prayer, we call the 11th Step prayer, is goal setting for being a better person. Thinking of helping others which was off the table when we were drunk. "Bring faith where there is despair," for example. This prayer is chock full of goals for spiritual living. I have read this prayer over 8,000 times but still have not mastered it. It has goals I may never achieve but I still try.

When I joined the military, I wrote down my goals and dreams in a letter to my mother. It was a 20-year plan. My mother kept the letter and produced it for a sit-down critique 20+ years later. Amazing that I hit all my dreams (a college education for example) and goals ahead of schedule. The lesson here is to write down your goals and the process of putting it on paper seems to perform magic. Is it not time to expand your new life with a fresh set of aspirations? The Golden Gate Bridge was built after the dream came first. I have set goals in self education to fill the gap of 30 years of drinking where I never read a book or took a meaningful course of instruction. Now is not too late to be teachable and expand your horizons. This new freedom outlined in the promises has no ceiling, no limits except self-imposed ones. All of us have cobwebs in the attic from years of non-use and abuse. After the "clean-up" we can move into the "grow up" stage that is carefully outlined in Step 11 & 12.

The joy of my new life brings me to tears of gratitude. Thank you, God, for this new life. I almost lost it all.

June 2

LOOKING FOR THE ENEMY

In my first year of sobriety I took a trip to Las Vegas to visit some lifelong friends. In my hotel room I just happened to open on of the dresser drawers and besides the Gideon Bible there was a black book on Buddhism. (I still have that book. The maid told me take it no charge.) On the intro page there were about 8 quotes from Buddha. Here is the one that grabbed me: **"A warrior who has conquered a thousand enemies in a thousand battles is not a true victor until he conquers himself."** I sat and pondered that phrase for a long time. I was a very spiritual moment. It hit me right between the horns. I considered myself a warrior and I had spent my entire life fighting. Even my job title had "fighting" in it. In Vietnam, my job was to look for the enemy, and every once in a while, I would catch my image in the cockpit rear view mirror, and I now know I was looking right at the enemy ... me. The search was over. I have always been my worst enemy and yet I was fighting everybody else on the planet and all institutions were on my hit list. I hated everything with alphabet soup, IRS, CIA, DOD, USAF, VC, and I hated my fellows not meeting my standards. I was one angry, hateful dude. Most of all I hated myself and what I had become.

In my very first meeting I heard, "I can cease fighting everything and everyone." What a concept. I surrendered, the fight is over, and the enemy is captured. Then this one line from Buddha changed my life. My eyes opened to the fact I needed to stop fighting the enemy out there and work on the enemy within. I needed to be conquered and my inventory was key and nobody else's faults were any of my business. I had enough on my own plate. So that began my journey of killing the "old" me and building a new me from scratch. My character defects can attack me at any time so now I am vigilant not to let any inner monsters loose again. I know the warning signs and I know my buttons. Every morning in my prayer and meditation I stand on the carcass of my former self and thank God the Fighting Mike is conquered. One drink and that dormant fighting machine will come to life.

Today all wars are over for me. I relax and take it easy and stay on the porch, my run with the big dogs is finished.

June 3

HABITS

Most of us are creatures of habit. I remember the old days. When I woke up, I had 3 options: A) beer, B) Bloody Mary, C) some of both all because my daily habit was to get alcohol into my system as soon as possible in order to shave. If there wasn't enough juice, my hands would shake so bad, I would cut myself to bits. Yuk! The first thing I learned in AA is all my old habits had to be changed. Drinking every day was the first bad habit to go but there were a bunch more to follow. In my prayer "Changes" that I told you about a few days ago has a line, **"I can change my list of priorities I can change my bad habits into good ones."** One of my many inventories is a "habit" inventory to check and see if some change or adjustment is necessary. For example, when I was working, I was drinking at least 10 cups of coffee every day. In sobriety I started with 3 cups in the morning and 2 in the afternoon then in recent history I am at 2 cups in the morning and no more than that. My heroes don't drink coffee at all. Maybe next year. I used a soft ball example, but you get the idea.

My good habits have brought me great happiness and I would not change those habits for the world. My hour of prayer and meditation have worked so well for so long why would I let up on what works. I am in the habit of going to a meeting every day. I am in the habit of a workout every day also. My habit pattern may sound very boring to an outsider but I have never been bored. Bad habits or harmful ones are super hard to break but the 12 Steps worked on drinking and the Steps will work on anything else that needs to be changed. Smoking is such a hard habit to break for example. I have seen folks with oxygen masks with a cancer stick out the side. Yikes. Very good habits turn into traditions which is a nice word for "habit." My home group has developed very kind and loving traditions that are not in the book. Our character defects are habits also. I try to keep vigilant to not let old habits creep back into my routine.

My habit pattern can always use a tune up and my prayers for goals inspire me to add good stuff until it becomes a tradition.

June 4

PURSUIT OF HAPPINESS

Some wise soul wrote "The sure way to unhappiness is to pursue happiness." I have to agree. I remember my days of "pursuit" driving a new Caddie, beautiful blonde by my side, fame, promotions, money but I was totally spiritually bankrupt therefore very unhappy. I looked at all the "stuff" and could not figure out my problem. The evidence said I should be happy and I was still in pursuit. One big thing missing in my life was helping others. That was off the table. Driven by ego and selfish pursuits the crash was inevitable. Thank God I found instant happiness in others at my very first AA meeting. They were happy and I was miserable. Solution: do what they were doing. Got a sponsor willing to guide me free of charge. I certainly was not looking for happiness at the beginning, I just wanted the pain to stop and get people off my back. Somewhere about day 10, all of a sudden, I had this strange feeling come over me, it was happiness.

I learned that happiness is not something you pray for or buy at the store. Happiness is a byproduct of doing the next right thing, being in the right place with the right people. Like a meeting of AA for example. I don't have to worry about happiness because it comes after staying on the right path. I have control over my attitude, so I choose to be happy. It is all connected to gratitude and humility. When I count my blessings then happiness is automatic. No pursuit needed. When I am right sized, not better than or less than there is no competition for status. Of course, we all know the secret to a happy life is helping others. Our Big Book page 83 in "The Promises" states: "We are going to know a new freedom and a new happiness." Keyword is new. I now thru the program enjoy a totally new kind of freedom and happiness that was not possible on the other path before I got sober.

I finally found out happiness is not connected to material stuff. The less connection with worldly possessions the happier I am.

June 5

THE RIGHT MEDITATION

Just like prayer I don't think there is a wrong way to meditate. There are a million right ways. I am not into incense and crystals but there are all kinds of literature and websites on meditation. Retreats and ashrams galore. For me simplicity works best. All I do is try to make all my committee members in my head shut up for quiet time. I learned when you are transmitting you are not receiving. If the voices in your brain are talking you are not accepting messages. I try to zero out all the dials, zero altitude, zero airspeed, zero direction, no motion, no noise. "Be Still and Know" was an article in a boyhood newspaper. Just now I understand the message. My prayers and my gratitude list, program my mind in a positive vein before I attempt meditation. I start from a feeling of peace and serenity. No "issues" are on the table. Putting my alcoholic mind in the silent mode took some practice but now I really enjoy the process and the results are stunning.

The authors of our Big Book state very clearly in two different places, "In your morning meditation" and I think they knew just what was necessary to do a good job. I love my mornings. Upon awakening I work on a spiritual awakening. No birds, no music, no TV, no phone, nobody else, no talking, just me and my Higher Power. My brain does not have a chance to spin up to 4500 RPM, while I begin my prayer routine. I know my heart has the "right stuff" so it is heart time rather than brain time. I need to give my heart a voice before my defective grey matter takes charge. The Sunlight of the Spirit is my sunrise every single morning and it fills my heart with love and gratitude. I know that I am the happiest man on this planet. I get a second shot at meditation during my hour in the gym on the treadmill. In fact, that is where I dream up my little piece to you guys.

I must admit it took some years to really feel the full effect of meditation, starting with 5 minutes at the beginning now up to a couple of hours.

June 6

THE RIGHT PRAYER

When I was a little Catholic boy going to confession, the priest would give me 10 Hail Mary's and 10 Our Fathers to say as punishment for my sins. To my young mind, prayer had a negative side, that was one of my old ideas that had to be smashed. Now I look forward to prayer and I know it works so I keep doing it. One of my sponsees wanted the "right" prayer and to my way of thinking there is no wrong or right way, just do it. The right prayer is the one that comes from the heart. My first prayer in recovery was short and sweet, "Dear God help me!" And He did. I say "Thank you God" many times during the day to tell Him how grateful I am. In the old days I only prayed when I was in deep kimchi. Now my prayers seek guidance, give thanks and sets goals for the day. I don't have to ask for anything, I have faith all my needs will be fulfilled so my prayers are on the positive side. In one of my spiritual reading it told me that prayer doesn't change God, it changes the person praying.

I know that I must change so the more I pray the more I change for the better. There was a lot of discussion in the readings about the synergistic effect of meditation, daily inventory and prayer done together. In my first hour in the morning all three get done but which order is not important. The Step 3, 7 and 11 Prayers are key to my daily routine. I remind myself that God's will first and foremost, I have character defects that need attention and the goals on Step 11 Prayer give me direction. I need to understand rather than be understood, comfort rather than be comforted. I read "Changes" which reminds me of my powerlessness. Also, it tells me my attitude is key, I can change that. I read "Take Time" which reminds me to take time to pray, play, read, laugh, think, give, work, be friendly and do charity. Then comes "Life Is A Celebration" it tells me to write a friendly letter, seek a forgotten friend, listen, speak my love, encourage another, show my gratitude, be kind, be gentle. The last one I read gives me a positive shot in the arm. "I Promise Myself" which I have sent to you all in the past. (If you want a copy I can email it to you) My favorite line: "Think only of the best, to work only for the best, and expect only the best." And it finishes like this: "To be too large for worry, too noble for anger, too strong for fear, and too happy to permit the presence of trouble." Wow.

I think any prayer is the right prayer, since doing this daily for thousands of days continuously these are part of my body, mind and spirit.

June 7

GROWTH

One of the most inspiring women in AA was my AA Grandmother, Alice C. Even though she has long passed away, her voice and lessons rattle around in my brain. With 50+ years of sobriety she went to at least one meeting a day sometimes two. The message to me is go to at least as many meetings as she does. Her clear message to me on several occasions was this: "Mike don't let anybody call the last three steps as maintenance steps. They are **growth** steps." I have come to believe her over the course of my recovery. I need to keep moving in my program, do more not less. If I am treading water I am in danger of drowning. Since our disease is progressive, we must keep growing in a forward direction to counter this progression. My recovery is progressive too, thank God! To me the 11th Step Prayer is all about growth...expanding my heart and my positive actions.

A lot of folks call November "Gratitude Month" which is great, but I have a Gratitude Day every single day. I review my gratitude list every morning and is part of my daily positive attitude. My gratitude is progressive just like my recovery and my disease. I seek new ways to help people, read new literature, open my mind to new ideas, learn something new and exciting. Life is a celebration but all the gifts on my list must be given away, the entire list, so when I depart this life, I have given it my all. Growing keeps me young at heart, happy joyous and free. I don't let up on my routine of recovery that has brought me this far and go on vacation, no sir! I enjoy doing an act of charity every day, comforting someone who is depressed, improving my friendships and being in service in and out of the AA rooms.

My personal 11th Step meeting every morning keeps me in the growth mode. When I am done growing, I am done.

June 8

LIVE AND LET LIVE

You will see this poster in many AA meeting rooms. **Live and Let Live.** Sort of like the AA version of the Golden Rule. Do unto others as you would like done to you. It reminds me I have my life, my way of doing things, my path, and I should respect different people with opposite ways and differing paths. My way or the highway doesn't work anymore. I am out of the business of convincing other people to change their ways, even staying sober. I can set an example without the lecture. In fact, keeping out of other folks' inventory and life works wonders for my recovery. I am too busy plugging the holes in my dike. Any professional credentials I have ever had are long expired. I am just another Bozo on the bus who stayed sober today. That's it. My opinion is worthless so why waste time expressing hot air. I don't get a bonus by signing up new members. I can, however, tell you how I arrived at the happy state I am in by following the Steps.

"AA is not allied with any sect, denomination, politics, organization

or institution; does not wish to engage in any controversy; neither endorses nor opposes any causes." Is that wonderful or what? Hey if that is good enough for AA it is great for me. I have adopted the very same stance. I am no good at controversy anyway so why get hot and bothered over stuff I have no control over. Nuts. I laugh when I see a basketball star endorse a political candidate. Stick to basketball dude. The internet has been driving me crazy with this US election coming up. (This too shall pass!) People try to pry an opinion out of me on this topic and I refuse to play. All I hear is controversy and opinion and not a lick of action. Do I hear love and tolerance? Ha ha. I don't belong to a political party as part of making my life simple and conflict free. So please don't ask. I used to be a champion of "good" causes in my younger days and it was frustrating and time consuming and now I have retired my sword of righteousness. My run with the big dogs is over. Thank God.

When I witness two people in a heated discussion it bothers me even though I don't know the subject or the people involved. I never did adapt to shouting. If that's a character defect I am keeping it.

June 9

SELFISH MOTIVES

In our morning meditation we review our 24 hours ahead and make our plans what to do with my time. Me, me & my stuff. All of our thinking comes from a "self" beginning. All of us are selfish to the bone. It comes free of charge with this disease. We need to take care of our sobriety #1 priority or else game over. Most of us seek a balance between selfish motives and other motives. Almost everything we do is in our self-interest even helping others and thinking of others. We do it because it makes us feel good doing the right thing. When we select an action there is usually more than one motive involved. I call the main motive the "headliner" motive we need to dig deeper for all the underlying motives, some maybe from our subconscious. OK example:

I build a school for kids in a country that really needs it. Headliner Motive: good

I put my name on the school. Motive: Ego

I write the cost off the school of my income taxes. Motive: Financial gain

I write a book about my school. Motive: Ego, need to be a hero. The book solicits funds for more schools. I buy a BMW and a new house.

(This fable is based on a true story.)

The point is it takes some thought to examine all our motives before we act. I am very good at wrapping a smelly rotten motive in sugar. The first test is to check for selfishness. Ah ha, there it is.

The main focus of my daily 10th Step is to curb my selfishness, be of service and think of others first.

June 10

JACK OF ALL TRADES

".. **and master of none."** In the old days I would hold forth on any topic. What a crock. Now that I am older, wiser and sober I have only further defined my ignorance. The more I learn the more I realize how much I don't know. Funny, when I finished 30 years in the military and got out with a severe pay cut, I needed to go to work to eat. I tried to find a firm that was involved with war planning. Nah. How about somebody that needed to hunt people in the jungle and shoot rockets at them, Nah. How about a pilot for vintage aircraft? Maybe, but was too drunk to take a flight physical. In short, I had zero marketable skills. Rats. Have another drink. I thought about writing a travel book about where to get good beer anywhere in the world. I knew how to get White Swan beer in Lahore Pakistan in a locked vault for "non-believers." Now there is a skill. Finally, God came to my rescue and I admitted failure outside the military and took a humble job way below my former level of Grand Pooh Bah. Rotgut gin made me even more stupid and brought me to surrender and find the rooms of AA.

In my new life of sobriety, I learned I knew nothing. I had to start over ground zero. I was taught to keep my mouth shut and listen. The only thing I can refer to as knowledge is my own experience. That's it. I can't talk about others or of book experience. Just what I know has happened to me and what works and doesn't work for me alone. It makes life very easy. I say "I don't know" all the time. OK so what do I know? For me only. I know if I don't take that first drink I won't get drunk. Duh. I know the 12 Steps worked for me, all 12 so maybe they just might work for you. I know that prayer works. I have tons of evidence on that one. I know I feel better after an AA meeting than when it started. I know doing the next right thing makes me feel better. For me, the secret to a happy life is helping others. I am an expert on keeping me sober, nobody else. I can only help you by sharing my experience strength and hope. Period.

I always used to preach, "Do what you do best to excess!" Staying sober and helping others is what I do best.

June 11

DARKNESS

The reading **"Nothing grows in the dark"** brought to mind some dark times. As you know from my writing, I just love The Sunlight of the Spirit. I enjoy the dawn of each new day so much. When I was up in the northern part of Maine in the winter time (11 months) I went to work at 6 a.m. and entered a building without windows until 6PM for 6 days a week. For 6 days I never saw one ray of sunlight. My skin was grey, and my spirits were dark as night. Those dark years made me grateful for the light of day. Where I live in Pattaya Thailand there are two cities. There is daytime Pattaya, for normal people doing normal things, and nighttime Pattaya, Disneyland for drunks. I tell people I am not allowed out at night which is a joke, but rarely do I venture into the lair of night creatures. In the morning I see some of the night crawlers who haven't found their rock to hide under. They look at me with disgust. "Yuck, all clean and sober, showered, dressed nice, smiling. Let me outta here." I laugh to myself and thank God I no longer live in the shadows. An old cowboy in Texas used to say, "Don't let the sun catch you drinkin' boy." There were drinking times when the dawn caught me unawares. Awful times.

What the reading is about is darkness of the mind and soul. That black abyss of depression and knowledge that you are on the wrong path and can't get off of it. You know the next thing you do is wrong, pick up a drink and you pick it up anyway. That is where the 11th Step Prayer gives us some ideas about darkness:

"that where there is despair, I may bring hope

that where there are shadows, I may bring light

that where there is sadness, I may bring joy"

These are gifts you can give with absolutely no resources. A smile costs you nothing. A kind word can turn someone's day around on the spot. The happiness in my heart full of gratitude can help someone else. All I must do is let the light that shines inside my soul come out where it can do some good.

I must remember sometimes when I am trying to bring light, some folks want to stay in the dark. OK, up to you.

June 12

INSIDES AND OUTSIDES

When most people go to buy a car, they look at size, color, beauty and sporty looks from the outside. But really, you drive a car from the inside not the outside. All the hours on the road are inside the car. There is too much attention put into how it appears to other drivers on the road. It would be better to read about the engine and safety of the seats than admiring the sleek contours of the body. Most big department stores have a massive display of cosmetics on the first floor when you walk in. All fancy names, Estee Lauder, L'Oréal, Clinique selling chemicals to make your outsides irresistible forget about your rotten black heart. If you want an inspirational book for your insides you will have to go to the 7th floor. Most of the commercials you see are about your outsides, your appearance and very little about your internal wellbeing. We all too often judge other people by their outsides and have no idea what is going on in their head and heart. Looking good and being good can be two different things. I know from my drinking days I would put on a fancy uniform and hide the real me inside a façade of authority but I knew inside I was a rotten banana.

Now after years in the program I work on my insides constantly and daily. If people judge me by my outside they will be disappointed. What other people think of me is none of my business anyway. I don't wear an Armani suit but I do wear a smile. I drive me from the inside. If I work on doing the next right thing my heart is at peace and I am in the zone of serenity. My program is about Body, Mind & Spirit. If I work on the spirit my mind is on the right track and my body follows a bit further behind. I do shave and wear a decent shirt every day before I go to a meeting so a newcomer knows I am serious about this program. It's not a stop on the way to the beach. Since I am happy from the inside it shows on the outside in my eyes and my ugly puss but newcomers know I am approachable. Funny thing my insides get better and better but my outsides suffer from Father Time and overuse.

Judging other people is a bad idea but judging them by their outsides is a real bad idea.

June 13

IT'S ME

The spiritual axiom that if am disturbed then something is wrong with me. This is true no exceptions. What? Do you know what he did to me? Do you know what he said? Makes no difference what he did, what matters is how you react to what he did. Yes, he was wrong but that is his inventory and there is nothing you can do about that. Only our inventory is what we can examine and it's very hard to swallow at times. Righteous indignation is the worst kind of being right. Yes, you are right. We all agree you are right but if you are disturbed you are wrong. Rats. If you strike with right on your side, you make 2 wrongs automatic. Running away from a fight is a fight won. That goes against my grain but I learned from experience it is true. I don't have to engage the enemy to be a winner. If a thrust comes, step aside and let the thrust go on by. It takes two to tango, but I don't have to dance.

I am not advising to be a doormat either but picking your battles is a fine art. You have the right to be respected but you cannot force an unreasonable person to respect you. Confrontation can be accomplished without anger and harm. You can bet if you push someone they will push back. The trick is to let go. Let go of this other person. Drop your resentment and fix you. Whenever I have a problem, I look for the solution. Answer: It's me! I am the problem and my daily inventory keeps me in the solution and focusing on my shortcomings and to forget about other people. I can always be more tolerant and more loving. When I am disturbed, I examine items of "self." Is my ego bruised? Are my motives selfish? Has someone dashed my expectations? Do I have fear of losing something I have? Somewhere in there the answer comes up. It's me, and I need to change and accept reality. Things just are not as I want them to be. I need to trust God and know everything that happens is supposed to happen.

I think being disturbed is a human function but how long I stay disturbed and my actions are up to me.

June 14

PERSEVERANCE

A good friend reminded me of a listing of some of the principles that go with the 12 Steps and I thought this would be a good time to share that listing with you guys. OK here it is:

1. Honesty

2. Hope

3. Faith

4. Courage

5. Integrity

6. Willingness

7. Humility

8. Brotherly Love

9. Self-Discipline

10. Perseverance

11. Awareness

12. Service

These are some principles of the Steps, good points to think about in your actions and experiences while doing the Steps. I know my disease is doing pushups in the background just, patiently waiting for me to get lazy and stop doing what has kept me happy joyous and free. I listen to those who have relapsed and 99% say they stopped going to meetings. Some never did meditate much and that stopped too. Then some "event" took them over the edge and badda bing, badda boom they got drunk. Magic. Sometimes fatal.

If I don't persevere, I die. Simple as that. I enjoy my routine of perseverance and look forward to my meditation, my meetings, my service, my sponsees. It's not work. I love to eat and I love to feed my spiritual needs also. I never skip a day of eating, so I never skip my prayers or my sober routine.

Why in the world would I stop doing what has brought me such happiness and serenity. Some folks do. Baffling.

June 15

PAIN

"Pain is no evil. Unless it conquers us" from *A New Day*. We all know pain and we accept it as part of life. We just must be vigilant enough not to give pain the power to destroy us. Three years ago I suffered the worst physical pain of my life, I fell, broke a rib that punctured a lung and collapsed it but even worse I severed my bowel. Poison was entering my body, enough to kill me. The doctors said it was amazing I made it and I am still recovering. The pain passed when I thought it was impossible. I had faith that God was going to spare me or take me and I was powerless over the situation except I had the will to live. Throughout the entire ordeal I thought about my fellow pilots who were captured and suffered torture every day for years on end. I was in the hands of angels and the best medical care in the world, not an angry enemy twisting a rope on my limbs until socket joints broke. I learned in POW training that the body can take only so much pain and it shuts off the brain and you are unconscious. Whatever physical pain you have there is somebody who has it much worse.

."·· pain was the touchstone of all spiritual progress." From *the Daily Reflections Oct 3*. Now when we look at emotional pain, we find it can last a lot longer than physical pain and hurt just as much if not more. The pain of the heart and mind can consume us if we allow it. Once again we have one thing we can control. Our attitude. Our focus. If pain is a problem your Higher power is on duty 27/7 and prayer works on pain better than booze or pills, I can tell you from experience. There is no chemical solution to a spiritual problem. Getting out of myself eases the pain and doing service, helping others is the Rx. Loss of a loved one is painful and is quite natural. Time to process the steps of grief is just plain human but sharing your grief with others divides up the pain. A pain shared is a pain halved. Get help. My fellowship helps me daily deal with the situation with my son. If I let my pain rule my thoughts and attitude I would be lost at sea. God is not going to give me more than I can handle besides He does all the heavy lifting.

Once pain passes you will be stronger, and you will grow.

June 16

GOD'S PLAN FOR YOU

This program of ours gives us a plan for living. In my previous life I had no plan and certainly did not consider God had an individual plan for me specifically. It wasn't until I worked the Steps for a few years I began to see a bigger picture than just staying sober one day at a time. Doing my inventory was not only the wrongs I had committed but my assets. Putting the assets column aside for a while until the amends were all made it is time to pull out our talents and put them to good use. When we are drinking, all that is not possible. but now we have our health back and our minds are out of the fog we can ask our Higher Power for new horizons and seek whatever God's plan is for us. When I was a young boy my teachers talked about "a calling in life." That ideal went away over time and there was no more "calling." But why not try to find that calling of our youth? In my lifetime before I got into recovery, there were very few times I was happy in my job. I was forced to move on to another job and never could stay in the happy zone for too long. I decided I am in the zone right now and intend to stay there.

I am sure God wants us to find a harmonious path in this life using whatever talents we possess. That said it follows we would also be happy following the calling of our hearts. In the search for finding out what

God's plan for me the first obstacle I noted was my immaturity at this spiritual life. All those years of my selfish disease no spiritual growth was taking place. I was so happy to be sober and that was enough at first but then I wanted more and my Higher Power was helping me grow to find my place in God's mosaic. I look at my fellow earth travelers and see all sorts of artistic and creative talents way past my abilities. With this late start in life I know I am not going to be a spiritual Dalai Lama. I am OK with my slow speed of my spiritual awakening and thank God I had one as a result of doing the 12 Steps. I can see how God laid out the events of my past to bring me to a state of usefulness and a joyful time for me that I am enjoying today. Late, but that's OK, I am where I am supposed to be doing what God intended me to do with the people I want to be with. Sounds like heaven to me.

I look at all the lovely people in my life as members of an orchestra playing 100 different instruments in harmony and I beat the drums for AA softly in the background.

June 17

NEGATIVE THINKING

Fear is the darkroom where all your negatives are developed. One of my many blessings is positive thinking is a way of life for me. I have a hard time understanding folks who are consumed by negative thinking. I was taught to glance at the negatives and focus on the positives. OK how do I do it? Simple, I look at my gratitude list every morning. Thirty-six positive items, gifts from God. I am truly blessed. I am a winner among other winners. Then I know the secret to a happy life. Simple, be in service to your fellows. Give away all these gifts to keep them and make them multiply. Worst case thinking will sentence you to gloom and doom forever. If you think you are responsible for all that is wrong in the world you imprison yourself. If you are ruled by fears then your faith may need an overhaul. If you pray for food but don't bring a basket then you have no faith. By the grace of God, you got this far, He is not going to drop you on your head.

My morning is so full of positive readings, prayer and meditation that not one negative thought has a chance with me. I refuse to be taken down. I avoid the grouch and naysayers at all costs. I don't listen to horrible news, and it is all horrible, hour after hour and let it fill my head with negative thoughts and images. I have very little control but I am in control of my attitude. If I have an attitude of gratitude then negativity is off the table. I try to wear the world as a loose blanket. Since I have no control over it so why let it drag me into a dark place mentally. I give every living creature a smile, I tell my friends they are important to me, I laugh a lot, I do an act of charity every day. I surprise someone by doing something nice when they least expect, my life is fun and happiness. How in the world can I be negative?

If I go about with a black cloud over my head, I would be of no use to anyone. That is against the basic principles of this program.

June 18

RECONSTRUCTION

Yes, as the Big Book says. **"there is a period of reconstruction ahead,"** (page 83). Like the rest of your life! It all started with destruction after years of drinking. I was digging a pit in the cold and dark until I hit solid rock and I could not go any deeper. The smoking hole in the ground is where I started when I hit my bottom. There was yellow caution tape all around the hole "DO NOT CROSS." First came the identification of the problem. Step 1, I was an alcoholic. Solution: get help and find a Higher Power. Step 2. Agree to stop fighting and let my Higher Power run my life. Step 3. Then to fill in the hole I needed to do Step 4 and 5 to own up to my mistakes and get to know the real me by a stark reality check. OK the hole is filled in and the yellow tape can come down. I know who I am and my defects in Steps 6 and 7 and all I have around me is wreckage. Steps 8 and 9 I begin to clean up the mess and build a mended fence around the foundation just laid by the first nine steps. Now I can start re-construction. This program gives me a big do over!

The Big Book is the basic blueprint for the new design for living. Now to gather some tools for the job. A lot of new tools never used before: honesty, spiritual literature, help from others in the fellowship, a sponsor, courage to change, willingness to do whatever it takes. So with plan in hand, the tools and God's help we can begin construction of a new better life. The new place will never be finished, it will always be under construction. A work in progress. But it provides shelter since it was built with solid principles and proven engineering. It is blessed with daily prayer and meditation. It has room for others who need help and is a warm and loving place to be. It can handle storms and disasters. It allows the Sunlight of The Spirit in from all angles. It is 100 times better than the original structure and the destruction of the old to allow the new was a wonderful transformation. Thank you, God.

This reconstruction needs daily maintenance because decay can come hard and fast if neglected.

June 19

WHATEVER IT TAKES

Early in my sobriety I saw some amazing acts of doing whatever it takes to right the wrongs we have done. One lady in AA, about 50 years old, was facing a drug charge and she was a repeat offender, she was facing 10 to 20 years in prison. At 50 years old that is pretty much a life sentence. Her public defender found out that the prosecutor lost his key witness to an overdose and she could skate free. She would have none of it. She told the group that she was guilty and would do the time if necessary. She said this is a program of rigorous honesty and she was going to tell the judge the truth and let the chips fall where they might. I wondered if I would have the courage to do the same thing and give up my freedom when there was an out. The judge was stunned at what he heard, this person told the unvarnished truth and admitted guilt. The judge gave her extended probation and she did not go behind bars. She went on to sponsor many other women in the program. She did ask us all to pray for her and we did. I have many stories of honest amends bringing wonderful results. I am responsible and this is an honesty deal.

Amends to me is a deep inside job of soul searching and planning to do a thorough clean up. I found the process is healing and rewarding. It took my spirit to a new level by doing deep amends. It required a lot of preparation and writing an amends plan for certain people. It is not easy to focus on just your wrongs and not the other person even if they had a part in the wrongs. "You threw a punch at me and then I broke your jaw." No no. Got to leave out the part of his throwing a punch. Just you breaking his jaw is the issue. The amends needs to be a speech not a dialog. You don't want to open old wounds and start the process all over again. The person you are making amends to may be hostile and angry so let them vent and resist fighting back. Not easy when they are wrong. Let them be wrong. Now is not the time to correct them. The mission is to clean up your mess. In my own case, I had years of humble living to pay back the massive debt I accrued as a drunk. I went from a Cadillac to a 15-year-old Chevette with a broken window. I went from a 3-bedroom house on the hill overlooking the Pacific Ocean to a rented condo. I went from chief of war plans to checking water temperatures in the local prison. I did whatever it took and I am better off for having done deep amends.

Hopefully these stories will make you look at your inventory to see if you have done a complete clean up. Be brave.

June 20

THE FAMILY

You have been sober awhile, but your relationships with family members are not as great as your program is progressing. Why is that? Maybe because they don't have a "program" they aren't the ones changing. Some family members are screwed up in our judgment. Why? Because we had a part in screwing them up, that's why. When newly sober the changes come fast and sometimes pretty dramatic but the family is not moving. I had to learn to focus on my own progress and stay out of my family's inventory. I had to realize they may still treat me like a drunk still drinking. The trust has been broken and it will take some time to repair. I need to remember all the damage I caused and I am fixing me but I can't fix them. Trying to tinker with their life is a real bad idea. That is hard when you are a parent or an older brother. Those roles are on hold. The only thing you can do is be an example of a tolerant, loving human being. Humility helps a lot also no matter what the pecking order might be.

In my own case, my family is very large and all over the map. The relationship was different with each person. All the way from constant contact to zero contact and everything in between. A spouse can be a special problem. In my first year I heard at a meeting what I needed to hear. This guy said, "The person you are with when you get sober may not be able to deal with the new person you will become by changing your life through this program." In my case, I found out that I was with a stranger after I got sober. I would have never met this person if I had been sober since she was the cashier at the local liquor store. I went often enough to start a relationship. I was able to release her with love and settled the divorce with no pain, no lawyers and no ill feelings. I still have a nice relationship with my two stepchildren from that marriage. The main thing is to have patience with family members and they will come around when they are ready, on their schedule. At least that has been my experience and I am still waiting for some to open the line of communication.

The main point I need to remember is, I was toxic in my relationships and the poison I put out will take some time to heal, maybe the rest of my life.

June 21

SPIRITUAL EXPERIENCE

Maybe all of us have had experiences but didn't recognize them as "spiritual." It is not a booming voice from the heavens that guide us or a burning bush that pops out of nowhere. Let me share some of my many spiritual experiences. The most recent was just a couple of days ago. I have told all my AA friends and sponsees if they want to talk to me come to a coffee shop at 8AM one hour before my daily meeting. Well, Tuesday was the 12th year anniversary of my home group Good Morning Pattaya and I bought a cake to celebrate the occasion. I changed my routine and drove right up to the meeting room and dropped off the cake and parked right there instead of the coffee shop as usual. It made no sense to walk over to the coffee shop and have to walk back for the meeting but a little voice told me "go to the coffee shop even if it is kind of stupid." The shop is under reconstruction and was a mess, and nobody was there but me. I was about to leave when there appearing at the door is a guy I have not seen in 4 years. I have been looking out the window every day for 4 years and this was the day he showed. That little voice brought about a spiritual experience. I have learned to listen to that voice.

A life and death spiritual experience happened to me before I got sober. I was forced to land my plane at an enemy airfield out of gas. I prayed to God and it looked like the end for me but my prayers were answered and events unfolded just perfectly for my survival. I did things that only some angel from heaven could have shown me. The escape was not in any manual. The most meaningful spiritual experience was my first meeting in AA. April 8, 1993. I was full of fear and expected to be humiliated and scorned. That one hour changed my life spiritually, emotionally and mentally forever. For the first time in 50+ years I felt I was in the right place. I was a misfit among misfits just a perfect place for me. My life took a reversal of direction that was spiritual in nature. I was reunited with a Higher Power who had been missing for 40 years.

Every day we stay sober is a spiritual experience. One day you were drinking and the next day you weren't and many days after. How did that happen? Magic? I don't think so.

June 22

SELF-PITY

We alcoholics have the worst things in the world happen to us, some are actually true. We tend to think our problems are mountains, when really, they are not so huge after all. My old home group had a guy, now passed on, who would rub his thumb and index finger together when a pity pot rant was under way. Joe what's that? Joe would say: That is the smallest violin playing "My heart bleeds for you." Most AA meetings are not the place to seek sympathy. If you spent a night in jail, there is a guy in the room who did 20 years in prison. One old timer in a meeting told the group if you are looking for sympathy you will find it in the dictionary between shit and syphilis. The point is there is no utility in self-pity. It is another waste of time. It can be intoxicating and self-perpetuating. Nobody likes a whiner.

The answer is the gratitude list. Once you review all your blessings you can see you are truly blessed and whatever is happening to you will pass. The deeper one falls into a pity pot it may lead to "poor me, poor me, pour me another drink," then into depression we go, the black hole of the soul. Get out and walk around the homeless people in your neighborhood. See how they live. My son was slowly losing his life to ALS...was he into pity? No way. He enjoyed every day given him. He did not want his family to pity him or feel sad. I am not into pity or sadness over what is going to happen down the road. Today is a celebration of life. Now. If I went around dragging my chin on the ground, I am of no use to anyone else. Now, that's a pity. **"My journeys are so long my legs ache and my feet are sore and I complained about it until I met a man with no legs." (Author unknown)**

Self-pity is like quicksand, the longer I wallow in it the deeper I get.

June 23

THE CHANGE

A guy who lives here in Pattaya with me went back to the USA on a visit and spent time with a retired military pilot from my past. My Pattaya buddy described me and my former compatriot said, "It sounds like a different person" That was the greatest compliment ever. Yes, I am a different person from 25 years ago. Thanks to God, the program and the fellowship I have undergone "The Change." One member I work with told me, he is sober and that is change enough. Well, stopping the drinking is a big change for sure but it is only a bare beginning. "Well, I am sober and that's the point, right?" Yes, that is point one of a thousand points. The rest of the Steps will slowly bring about a psychic change required for long term sobriety and a happier spiritual life. Unfortunately, so many of us stop at raw sobriety. Life is good, you can manage without alcohol and you feel better. Then some of us stop there. Cruise control will work for a while but sooner or later without the "change" we will crash and burn.

It takes courage to change. It takes a lot of prayer and work on our part to carve away at our wreckage. The amends part of my recovery was a big chunk of reshaping my personality and my priorities. I see so many of my fellow members with 30, 40 years of sobriety who have stopped changing. I know I need to keep moving, keep green, remember where I came from and how bad a bottom I hit. Little changes are hard to see results, it is frustrating at times when you feel you should be more at peace and serene. I was told from the very beginning I need to change the person who walked into the first meeting or I was doomed to drink again. I got busy because I know to drink, for me, is to die. I know I don't get to take a rest from this program because my disease is not resting. It is progressing but my recovery is progressing too if I keep doing what I am doing. Every morning in my hour of prayer and meditation. I come up with an action plan for "change" sometimes a little thing but I keep chipping away.

I like the "new" me a lot better than the "old" me and I owe it to "The Change."

June 24

MY NEW FRIEND

As I clean up my past and throw out the garbage you may come to realize, as I have, you are a new person. Hopefully as you subtract from your inventory and character defects you add all new good stuff. You can develop a new relationship with you. When we hit our bottom, we don't like ourselves even though we only think about our next drink. No surprise, our bodies were neglected, wrong diet, no exercise except elbow bending and toilet bowl hugging. The fog lifts and we start doing good things, eating better and repairing our minds, body and spirit. We discover we aren't so bad after all. The program brought me happiness and it came from doing the next right thing many days in a row and I began to like me again. I slowly am becoming worthwhile. The beating myself up part is over now, time to enjoy life and love myself.

"Don't compromise yourself, you are all you've got!" Betty Ford. So true when you think about all your trappings removed it is only you that you possess. A good friend of mine Jeff always says, "Take care of yourself" and I love that because sometimes I forget. If I don't love myself how in the world can I expect anybody else to love me? I need to remember to have fun, play and do something for myself. Before it was all destructive "fun." I have been to hell and back so time to heal in the sunlight and smell the coffee. Hey, I am stuck with me so it is much better to drop the attitude and get busy spreading the wings of the "new" me. This road to recovery has given me a second chance at life so I am grateful to God for the opportunity. I can't help anybody else if I am into self-loathing and unchecked character defects run riot. God brought us this far to do good things I do believe. Good things make me happy with myself.

"Today let me do one small, nice thing for myself." from *Body, Mind and Spirit*.

PERFECT

One of the most debilitating character defects one can have is perfectionism. Believe me I know firsthand. I grew up with a perfectionist mother who expected nothing less than first place from me. I was #4 in my class and that's as high as I was capable of but it was unacceptable and I was in misery all through grammar school. I was not living up to my potential was the mantra from my mother. Instead of enjoying a fourth-place finish in every test, I was plagued by disappointment from home. Then the military was even worse. every unit was the "best." Every man was rated as top of the heap. 99% of the people in the Air Force were in the top 1%. Very fuzzy math and the mottos were "Zero Defects." "The Finest Squadron" etc., etc. Being a perfectionist sets one up for failure, resentment and unhappiness. I was so obsessed with perfection I dropped many master's level courses when it became obvious I would not score an "A." It took extra years to complete my masters because of this insanity. If someone would have told me that when you finish the paperwork says "Graduated" no magna cum laude nada. Straight "A's" did not cut ice with anyone.

Perfectionism does not exist; to understand it is the triumph of human intelligence; to expect to possess it is the most dangerous kind of madness." from *A New Day*. This program taught me to understand "Progress not perfection." If I did not ditch the idea of "perfect" I could never have completed the Steps. the inventory and amends alone would be a mountain too high to climb. As in the past, if I could not do it perfect, I just didn't do it. My amends will never ever be finished, my character defects are still around but just being in the game is good enough. There are no gold medals at the finish line. Trying my best is surely not perfection. Now I can live with a "C" on my report card. Even when I was top gun the pressure of staying #1 was horrible. I became a target and I was never able to enjoy the high perch. All my energy was spent on maintaining my front runner position. Now just being in the middle of the herd is hunky dory. The only thing I must do perfectly is not pick up that first drink or pill. Everything after that I leave the grading up to God and my job is to strive for better instead of "just good enough."

It is a matter of seeing what is important, perfection is too time consuming and it makes everybody around me go nuts.

June 26

ALL

One big word in the 8th Step jumps out. **ALL twice.** "Made a list of **all** persons we had harmed and became willing to make amends to them **all."** Guess our founders wanted to make sure we got the point. This is a giant task for some of us, I know it was for me. What I had to do is get a calendar and try to recall my life from the stone age until the present. No easy exercise because of my extensive travel and many different locations of residence. To make matters worse I was in positions of leadership and, as such, wronged whole groups of people. In short, I was a menace to mankind. I preached a manifesto of "drink with me or get lost." Some followed me right into the bottle and the downward spiral. Some lost their lives to alcohol and I had a part in that. Just because someone is dead doesn't mean I don't put them on the list. The rules don't say "living only," the rules say **ALL.** So, my list was not only long but went back in time 55 years deep. Yikes. So how do I find all these people. I learned to pray and meditate on my list and some people needed to be found with research and some were long distances away. The rules didn't say "within a 100-mile radius" the rules say **ALL.** So, the globe became my area of operations for my amends. I am happy I understood the word all.

For those who had passed on I wrote letters, especially for folks like my father who never saw me get sober. They were not sent or read but it helped to clear my soul of the wrongs I had done by putting them on paper (not a computer...real pen and paper) and exposing the wrongs to the light of day. I wrote letters to those I could not find in my search, but they are still on my list. And as I travel, I remain willing to do my amends if I get the chance. Recently I found a person I had harmed in 1967. The amends process is so rewarding, the amends not only were received well but has rekindled a friendship on a different level, a spiritual one. In fact, all of my amends have brought love and understanding. I live in Thailand because of an amends trip. Like I said before, my deep amends put me in a plane many times to accomplish the mission. I started my trips to Vietnam, Laos and Thailand back in 1999 and the effort was so fulfilling I made the move to live here. Instead of dropping bombs I am part of the community giving back as a sober person with love in my heart. Did I finish my list? Not even close, but I try indirect amends to my fellow earth travelers in place of those I missed.

All is such a big word and though I made my list 22 years ago, I still add to my list as forgotten harms pop up from years past.

June 27

FORGIVENESS = FREEDOM

Nobody appreciates freedom more than someone who has lost it. I lost my freedom in combat twice just to give up my freedom to alcohol after surviving a dangerous profession. Freedom is in bold letters and underlined on my gratitude list. To me, my freedom came on 4 different levels. First, I was able to go 24 hours without a drink then a week without an obsession to drink. Great sense of relief was only the beginning. The second level was dumping my past by the 4th Step inventory and sharing with my sponsor in the 5th Step. The weight of years of heavy wrongs lifted from my shoulders was wonderful. Then the amends portion of my recovery in Step 8 & 9 was the third level of freedom to patch up the harms done, in part, to all those people in my life. This brought on a new sense of weightlessness to my soul. Finally, in order to keep on this high, I do a 10th Step every day to keep my street clean and enhance my freedom. The biggest hurdle to my amends was forgiveness. I had to learn that to truly enjoy freedom I need to forgive all of everything.

Probably the hardest forgiveness comes from family relationships. I found this to be true in my case. Some broken relationships go on for years and the longer they go the harder it is to kiss and make up. So you are hurt and it is not your fault. The other family member has harmed you, robbed you, lied to you etc. etc. This is the worst situation. being right has nothing to do with forgiveness. Being right does not help you at all. I learned who is right is not important but what is right is. Forgiveness is the right way to go down the road of freedom. I had to put aside resentments and harms done to me in order to open my heart to forgiveness. There are two family members that have cut me off for 9 years running. (Nothing personal, the rest of the family is cut off also.) If I get the chance I will embrace these two family members because I forgave them a long time ago. It was not easy mind you. It took a lot of prayer and soul searching to accomplish the task. Forgiveness is one of the few things I have control over. It is my attitude and I choose an attitude of forgiveness. The flip side is I have zero control over anybody forgiving me. I can do my amends but I need to leave the results up to God. I can't force someone to forgive me. I do know that God has forgiven me a long time ago.

I have learned that my freedom is so precious, holding back my forgiveness just weighs me down.

June 28

LISTENING DEEPLY

Listening is like any other skill and it can always be improved. I would like to think I am a good listener but to be honest sometimes I am downright lousy. It is easy to let our own thoughts drown out what is out there to be received. Very easy to miss the gem you needed to hear. Just like in meditation, I try to quiet my own inner voice. "Shut up and listen fool." If I think I know better than the person speaking then all is lost. Might as well leave the room. If I think I know what is coming I do my own "voice over" Yeah, yeah, got it, done that, been there yada, yada. I am not listening deeply at all. I am doing all the talking, even though not out loud, and missing the message altogether. It is really bad when I open my mouth and interrupt the person talking and take over the conversation. Rude dude.

Then there is the problem of prejudice toward the speaker. A guy with spiked hair, 2 earrings and wall to wall tattoos is not the kind of person I hang with but he may have the key to one of my problems if I would just listen deeply. Listen to the message not the messenger. Even people you don't care for need to be listened to. I need to be open minded to open my ears. Closed mind, closed ears. My attitude has a lot to do with my ability to listen deeply also. If I can remain teachable then everyone who talks to me can teach me something. I have been taught, God speaks to me through other people so how dare I tune them out. I may miss God's message if I don't listen to my brothers and sisters. God gave us a giant clue when he designed our bodies. First, He gave us 2 ears to hear in stereo and one mouth with many functions other than talking. In my opinion listening is more important than talking.

Today I pray for a quiet mind and humility so my listening skills improve and I receive rather than transmit.

June 29

WHAT IS IN YOUR CRUCIBLE?

From a reading in *A New Day*: **Relationships are like crucibles in which our <u>character defects</u> rise to the surface.** So true. In the quiet of morning meditation and prayer, just you and your Higher Power everything is serene and peaceful ... Ahhh. Then add another human being into the mix and there goes serenity. Chances are other people are not on the same wavelength. They will do things and say things we don't like. There are a few folks that make my character defects bubble up just by seeing them. Past history of resentments and hurts cook in my frontal lobes and my eyes send out lightning bolts. When my buttons are pushed, I have to remind myself they are my buttons. I can remove the buttons or at least not activate them when pushed. One of my character defects is to push back when I am pushed verbally or physically. Not a good idea in most cases. I am not a pussy cat but I have learned when to hold back.

All alcoholics are characters, that's why I love them so much. We are all interesting to say the least. It is not surprising we have character defects to excess just like we do everything to excess aye? Now that we have inventoried all our defects we can be positive about what is in our crucible. We know our defects, we can keep our arrows in the quiver without shooting them. Takes some practice not to spoil our relationships and be understanding rather than be understood. I inventory my relationships and look at where my character defects have done harm. As my character improves so do my relationships improve. We never will be perfect but each 24 hours can bring progress. Relationships can be the mirror of positive changes we have made. Listen for the compliment and gratefully accept it. Character defects need not be permanent unless we are unwilling to change. I try to stay open minded toward positive change.

Some of my defects have disappeared but they crop up from the dead occasionally, so I try to stay vigilant.

June 30

SHHH … IT'S A SECRET

The last few days the readings have been about the big secret of a happy life. I know it is a secret because people don't seem to know these facts of joy and fulfillment. Life is a big pain and misery to some of us when the key to the lock is right in front of us. I have my guys read the 3rd, 7th and 11 Steps prayers every morning, as I do. There are some hints to the secret in all three: Hint #1 from the 3rd Step prayer: **Take away my difficulties, that victory over them may bear witness to those <u>I would help</u> of Thy power...**" Hint #2 from the 7th Step prayer: **"I pray that you now remove from me every single defect of character which stands in the way of my usefulness to <u>you and my fellows</u>."** Then a super big hint from 11th Step prayer Hint #3: **"that where there is**

hatred, I may bring love...” On and on what you can bring to wrong, discord, error, doubt, despair, shadows and sadness. The message is clear and repeated several times, It's not about you. It's about helping others.

The secret is not meant to be a secret at all, it is out there in black and white. If you are depressed and discontent, it probably is because you are thinking only of yourself, your expectations, your problems, your resentments. You, you, you. If you get into service, in and out of the rooms, help someone who is bedridden, help another alcoholic by just being there to listen. It may take some practice just like any other skill. In your morning meditation plan an activity to get out of yourself and be useful, helpful, loving to that person who needs it. In my experience the joy of living is in giving freely of myself, my time, my resources. It feels wonderful and I know the secret very well. This entire program is about working on that selfishness we all had when we came into our first meeting. The goal is complete selflessness, never to be achieved but we certainly can be a little less self-absorbed as we accumulate a few more 24 hours.

No strings are attached to my giving of my time to be truly happy, joyous and free.

July 1

OLD AGE

One of the benefits of living in Thailand is that old age is revered and honored. When I go through immigration there is a "Gold Lane" for old folks over 70. (I'm overqualified.) The graphic shows a bent over dude with a cane. In restaurants I get served first because I am the oldest. I accept my old age and I am happy I made it this far. Way beyond my expiration date. In my home group we have had 6 guys pass on and all of them were younger than me. I am very grateful for my old age. After spending a month in the US, I see the culture is quite different. I was invisible there and people talked to me like I was a baby. I just don't give them permission to make me irrelevant.

If I truly live this program one day at a time then I am ageless. If I stay in the now for 24 hours then it doesn't matter what my birth certificate says. If I let my age limit my 24 hours, I am cheating myself out of some joy and freedom. Alcohol limited me into a big nothing but now that I am free from bondage, the sky's the limit. Oh sure, I can't run a 4-minute mile anymore because my knees can't take it but I can walk a mile and I have all day to do it. There are two beautiful girls next door age 7 and 3. We have watched them grow from birth into smart fun people. I can talk to them as equals. They ask me amazing questions and in turn they teach me how to use an iPod. A win-win deal.

While in Mystic visiting my kids, we have been blessed to have the use of the house next door to my son. It is a million-dollar 6-bedroom 2-story mansion. The owner is a 96-year-old lady who can't manage living in the house by herself so the place is vacant most of the year. Her four kids are in their seventies and have been waiting a long time to split the proceeds of the house. We got a chance to spend some time with this lovely lady. There is nothing wrong with her at all except she needs a little help. Her assisted care apartment was magnificent. She was so bright and had nothing but love in her heart. She was delighted that we stayed in her house and made good use of her castle. We have exchanged some emails and they are so loving I am truly inspired to stay the course of how many 24 hours God decides to bless me with. It was a spiritual experience I can't really describe in words.

I have lived so long it has afforded me the opportunity to make every mistake possible. I am willing to share that with you in the hopes you avoid the pitfalls.

July 2

TAKING A HOSTAGE

A guy I work with told me that his wife is trying to leave him. He was hiding her car keys so she wouldn't leave. I told him; why don't you just handcuff her to the stove so she can't escape. In other words, take her hostage. He looked at me like I was crazy. I pointed out that you can release someone with love. If it is meant to be then she will come back of her own free will. Alcoholics of our kind are manipulators and control freaks. We want people we have a relationship with to behave in a way to our liking. We know what is best for them and it is upsetting if they rebel from our guidance. It is especially important in our AA relationships to allow others to be wrong and realize everyone has their own unique path. We need not impose our program on others. One very good friend of mine, now passed on, allowed his sponsor to not only help him do the Steps but also controlled his finances, gave him an allowance out of his own bank account, and even asked permission to get married. Foul ball. Bottom line the sponsor robbed his bank account and refused his "blessing" on the marriage. My friend allowed himself to be taken hostage. In love relationships, we alcoholics need to examine our selfishness. Oh yeah, we are selfish to the bone. Love is not selfish. Love is a mutual, equal emotion with no strings attached. Both parties should be free from bondage from the significant other.

Some of us suffer from a character defect I call "broken wing syndrome." If I find a bird with a broken wing, I can help heal the broken wing in the hopes the bird will stay with me forever in gratitude for my heroic act. So we find someone who is weak in some area, be it a low self-esteem, or poverty, or a handicap and "fix" it by intervention and then make that person a hostage. We then impose our will on this poor person. A great movie with James Caan and Kathy Bates (ugh.) shows exactly what I am talking about. Caan was a famous author and Bates was a devoted fan. She gets him into her house for a visit and chains him up and breaks his ankles, all the while professing her deep love for Caan and his writing. Of course, you need not physically detain someone to make them a hostage, you can use intimidation, dependency, threats and fear. You will never find happiness if you depend on the actions of others to make you happy. If we have expectations of behavior from others, they will never live up to your standards. If you want to be really free, then you must allow others freedom. Hostage taking is a lose-lose game.

Alcohol took me hostage for years, now I am a free man. I will never allow myself to be taken hostage again.

THE MAGIC CUP

The true story of two teachers who worked together we will call Mr. J and Mr. C. Mr. J was in AA and Mr. C was also an alcoholic but was not in the program and had no idea what AA was all about. C was often sick before class and his kids would come in the bathroom and beat on the stall asking if he was alright. J and C saw each other every day in the teacher's lounge for coffee. J had a coffee cup he used every day from a local AA convention from years past. It had a circle and triangle with Unity Recovery Service written on it. It was clear that J was happy with his job and bright eyed. C was foggy and hung over much of the time. C looked J's cup over several times and asked about the origin. J explained about his participation in AA and a few nights a week he went to AA meetings after work. Finally, C asked J if he could come to "one of those meetings." Mr. C got sober and a few years later he was the speaker at an AA convention in front of 500 people carrying the message with his beautiful family in attendance. I can tell you it was one of most inspiring speeches I have ever heard. The ripple effect of that magic cup is just one more story of attraction rather than promotion.

In my own case, I had to prepare my house for sale in Hawaii since it was on the chopping block due to my divorce. My drinking buddy who used to pull me out of bars for my own good was a house painter. He knew I was in AA and had been sober awhile when he agreed to paint my house. He was embarrassed to drink in front of me so he hid an igloo of beer in the backyard while he worked. We would chat every afternoon when he finished and the way he tells the story is: I left AA books all over the place to intimidate him. That was not the case but finally he asked if I would take him to "a" meeting. My house painter has been sober 21 years now and is a close friend to this day. My flooring guy who laid new tile for me same story minus the meetings and he is still sober. I met a fellow member who was homeless and I gave him a bedroom in exchange for help upgrading my house for sale. That was a big win-win situation and he was only a few months behind me in sobriety and we went to meetings together until the house sold. The ripples of this program come from all sorts of sources and none of them are recruitment or promotion and advertising.

I wish you a magic cup in your recovery and finding folks to help just like we got helped.

July 4

TRUE INDEPENDENCE

I can recall the days when I thought independence meant to be free from bosses and rules. To ask for help from no one was my goal. Just be a lean, mean fighting machine, free to act as I wanted, when I wanted. Wow was I upside down. I am no longer lean or mean and the fighting is over. True independence today is depending on my Higher Power to guide my thoughts and actions on a daily basis. I depend on my fellowship and performing the 12 Steps. True independence is admitting I need help to be a better person to handle my difficulties and select the right path. I need help to be really free. That lone wolf attitude just didn't work for me. Now I don't cross the street without a second opinion.

I lost my freedom completely to the bottle. Drinking as much as I could 24/7 without any static from anybody was my idea of freedom. Drink by drink was brick by brick to the walls of my prison. I lost my freedom once and I know how precious my independence from alcohol is to my life today. I will work hard to never lose my freedom. My freedom is not free. I need to be in service and help others to keep my sky blue. I can fly with the eagles and sleep with the angels if I do the work required to secure independence. Today freedom is faith and love. I have faith if I try to do the next right thing God will be in charge of the result and He has a plan for me. If I have love in my heart then it will show on my face and my actions. Love will come back to me from those I come in contact with on a daily basis.

As I spend time with my son, I see he is totally free even though he has the use of only one finger and no voice. He can move his wheelchair anywhere he wants to go with one finger. He can write and text with one finger, so he can communicate and he is very happy for another day of life. Now that's freedom.

July 5

THERE GOES GOD

In my morning hour of prayer and meditation I have a spiritual awakening sometime during that hour that gives me inspiration for the day. This morning I got that boost on the very first minute reading the *Daily Reflections*. **"I try to remember now that the people I meet in the course of my day are as close to God as I am ever going to get while on this earth."** Wow, that hit me. I need to remember God is in everyone and I need to see thru my prejudices. We are all God's kids. When I pass a disagreeable person, I need to say "There goes God," and realize I can't see it in that person so I should work to find some harmony with my brothers and sisters on this planet. I am not going to meet my Higher Power in person but in my daily comings and goings God is there in those folks who cross my path. I remember very vividly the time in my group's conscience we discussed a very disruptive person who attended our meetings. We had a whole list of complaints on this guy. One of our members, who has since passed on, said, "God has sent xxxx to us for some reason and we need to find out why."

In our life of love and tolerance All Lives Matter not just a special group. I try to expand my thoughts without borders. I spent a good portion of my adult life planning the demise of the Soviet Union but in my AA life I quite often hug a Russian. They are just some other brothers. As the world gets smaller, I need to open my arms to different cultures, different philosophy and embrace what I don't understand. I need to have faith. God is not my enemy and as Buddha has taught me. **"Blood stains cannot be cleaned with more blood, they can only be cleaned with love."** If somebody does a hateful thing to me my first reaction is to retaliate. That solves nothing. It just escalates the situation. An eye for an eye way of thinking and acting will lead to worldwide blindness. It takes some creative thinking to defuse volatile encounters. The time of prayer and meditation helps me do it. I ask my Higher Power in that first morning hour to give me patience and understanding that is mentioned in the 11th Step prayer. If I act with love, I will receive love back has been my experience.

Try that on for size as you walk around, as you cross paths with fellow earth travelers, "There goes God."

July 6

EGO REVISITED

At one of our family reunions, a lifelong friend of 50 years came straight from Costa Rica via Ohio to join the family fun. Most of my family had met this guy over the years. This friend and I met in pilot training in 1966 but not in the classroom or the cockpit. We met in the bar and we were of like egos. Loud, boastful, competitive and drunk. He was a captain already with a combat tour under his belt and I was top gun from my class and he was a class behind me. We crossed paths throughout combat and careers in the military and stayed close friends. I realized on seeing him again yesterday we have taken very different paths in life. As soon as he arrived, he needed a drink and never stopped talking for the next 8 hours. His ego still has no ceiling. In the old days I would be drinking, interrupting him and competing for the floor in loud egotistical yak yak. OMG I could see myself as I was before I came to AA and went through "the change." Funny, he sent me a text as he was inbound to Mystic, "Hey Mike, Mr. AA, I will need a drink as soon as I get there. When he came to Hawaii in 2003, he saw my morning meditation books on the kitchen table. He read from some of them and said, "Mike you need to read this shit." How right he was on that. He respects my sobriety and I respect his drinking; he is not an alcoholic.

After a few hours of his boasting of his accomplishments I could see myself doing the same thing in years past. How awful I was in blowing my horn. Yikes. The new me resisted the urge to chime in with a like story. Hell, he never gave me a chance to talk anyway. Some of the stories I heard so many times I can't count. Thank God my ego is at rest. A friend is someone you know everything about and love them anyway. So, yes, I love this loud egotistical friend for life. I just know not to let my gorilla out of the cage, take a drink and start shooting off my mouth. I will be quiet for a few days and watch my former self in action. We are the same age, many divorces, kids all over the map, but so different since I found a new design for living. A life without alcohol or an inflated ego. I got right sized by doing the 12 Steps and continuing my recovery for all these years. It is OK to be silent and let my daily actions do the talking. My good friend lost his oldest son recently and a sister so we are partners in grief. He has brought joy to my son by his fun-loving way of telling jokes, playing the harmonica. It is easy to forgive his egotistical rants.

It is a blessing to see my former self in living color and makes me grateful for my new path of Happy Destiny.

July 7

BEATING YOURSELF UP

All of us who are trying to follow a spiritual life often make the mistake of being too hard on ourselves. Self-condemnation slows us down and causes depression and inner discontent. God doesn't expect more out of us than we can do. We forget "progress not perfection." We can only be human with limitations. Sometimes we must step back or sideways and even fall down now and again. High standards are a good thing as long as they are realistic. Getting impatient with ourselves is foolish since we are doing our best even though it is not always up to our own expectations. "We relax, we do not struggle." I love that line. The fox condemns the trap not himself. All of us run into traps on the road of life and we get caught occasionally and we suffer a setback. Blaming ourselves is just non-productive. When you need a friend the most, that friend should be you. Making yourself a villain is the last thing you want. Yes, it is good to try to reach goals and improve ourselves but a positive balance is better than the negativity of self-flagellation.

If this becomes a problem maybe it is time to look at your relationship with yourself. I vividly remember screaming at myself out loud about what a hopeless wreck I was and I could not stop pouring alcohol down my throat. I hated myself and I had lost all my friends. It was impossible to be a friend to myself when I desperately needed one. Once I put the drink down, I slowly began to look myself in the mirror more than five seconds and stopped yelling at the ugly image I saw. Doing the 12 Steps made grateful and I began to like how far I had come and how wonderful my life was. Then on to acceptance. I accept myself warts and all. Character defects yes but some major accomplishments. I wasn't a dirt bag after all. Slowly I found a new friend. Myself. A good friend is one who knows all about you and loves you anyway. Nobody knows me better and I love myself today. I am a work in progress so much improvement is required but the timetable is mine and my Higher Power's.

If I am going to keep myself as a close friend, why would I turn on myself and create an adversary? I need all the friends I can get in rough seas so I will not fight with myself anymore.

July 8

UPON AWAKENING

When you look at the Golden Gate Bridge in all its beauty it started with a single thought. Our waking hours are a continuous stream of thoughts. All actions come from thoughts hopefully. We know for us that action without thought is dangerous. Our thought life is something we can control and that is why the morning meditation is so important. For me, it controls my thought process and gives my brain a positive start for the next 24 hours. When I retire at night, I thank God for another gift of a wonderful day and it carries over into my sleep and dreams. I can program my brain for a night with the angels. Rest from thoughts. Upon awakening there is a rush of thoughts that need to be slowed down thus the meditation. Whoa, let's go slow and positive. "Ask God to direct our thought life" and proceed into a plan of action just for the 24 hours ahead. I don't need to build a bridge I just need to do some right things and be in service to my fellow man.

I learned to feed my thought machine good stuff. My readings, my prayers all channel my thought life in the right direction. If my thought diet is healthy then there is a good chance my actions will be the correct ones. In my morning meeting with the committee rolling around in my brain "we" come up with an action plan that includes service, charity, learning, fellowship, encouragement to someone. I leave the house with a smile and a happy disposition every day. I know life is going to happen "out there" so I have a good start to handle any negative events. When something bad happens, I know I need to use my thought process slowly and carefully. No longer do I pull the trigger and act without proper thought. Unloading the gun and removing the trigger is better than a regret or a resentment. I seek a reason to laugh, be humorous and show my happiness. I express my gratitude to those I love for their support. I try to be soft in my speech and subtract sarcasm and negativity from my communication. It all starts with a single thought of gratitude.

My thoughts can spin in both directions, so the spin cycle is up to me, thus I choose a positive spin.

July 9

FREEDOM FROM ME

One of my morning prayers has a line: "I seek strength, not to be greater than my brother, but to fight my greatest enemy, **myself.**" All the recent readings have been about freedom from fear, faith and trust. All of these have to be found within. We seem to get in our own way and nobody trips us up like ourselves. I ask God every morning to help me get out of myself. The further away from me, the better off I am. Thinking of others, being in service in and out of AA helps keep me out of my own head. My brain is a bad neighborhood if I stay in it too long. I try to just drive past my expectations and personal desires into a safe area out there somewhere. If I am alone (dangerous) upset with relationships, full of dashed expectations I am on my pity pot until I fall into depression and all my actions tend to be wrong. Soon I feel like the cockroach in the toilet bowl, down, down, into oblivion. The bondage of self is the worst feeling one can have.

I seek help in my 3rd and 7th Step prayers every morning to achieve freedom from me. I can't get away from me no matter how fast or how far away I go, there I am. Yikes. It's me again, the problem and not the solution. The solution is with my Higher Power and action not thought. Do the next right thing and leave the results up to God without expectations. Fear will take over my life if I let it creep into my thoughts and mushroom into a big bogey man. I need to remind myself of my powerlessness every day and limit my scope to the now and let go of the past and give the future to God. Those of you who are single and away from family are especially vulnerable to being into self too much. I am fortunate to be in a family and I can focus outward. The fellowship and meetings are really good for us. In a meeting you have to be quiet for 55 minutes out of an hour and your problems look pretty silly compared to the burden others must bear. Sponsoring other people is wonderful for the soul. It is love, sharing and the right stuff all in one package.

Working the Steps with someone else is freedom from me.

July 10

DEADLY SINS

Character defects month can't slip by without a review of the Seven Deadly Sins. The 12 X 12 goes into great detail, but I will just touch on them for your thought.

ANGER It can drive us to kill another human being, but anger is also a tool to keep us safe and alert. It protects us but to excess we become insane and since we are insane already us alcoholics don't do well with anger. I know in my own case I say and do the wrong things when angry. "The luxury of normal people but we can't afford it."

ENVY It can poison our own banquet. They always use the color "green" when discussing envy as in the color of someone else's money. Low self-esteem is usually a root cause of desiring something you don't deserve or haven't earned.

SLOTH As in delaying the 4th Step. We are all terrible about sloth. It is OK to take it easy once in a while but to do nothing when action is required is a killer. Faith without action is dead. I don't want to talk about it anymore or I will sign off early. Yikes. Guilty as charged.

LUST We alcoholics go to extremes at everything we do and we let our natural desires take off and go overboard. When you sleep with somebody else's wife you are harming at least 3 people. They have a 12 Step program for folks with this problem. I don't want to talk about this one anymore either.

GREED We alcoholics are selfish to the bone. We want more than we deserve, it is deep within our character defects. When we seek greed and start stealing or cheating in our business deals we can get in big trouble. Our 12 Steps get us in the giving mode versus the taking mode.

GLUTTONY Some of us trade one addiction for another and food is the easiest choice. I know I can eat myself into poor health. I have done it so many times and the recovery time is not worth the pleasure time. Five happy minutes with Haagen Dazs ice cream costs me one hour of pain on the treadmill. I have learned not to eat all the French fries they serve me.

PRIDE All the Steps help us get "right sized" and not blow ourselves out of proportion. Humility that comes with our program can keep this awful defect in check. Arrogance just makes us want to puke. We don't like it in others because we remember how we were in our boastful drunken antics of the past.

Any one of these can kill us. As in deadly. There was a time I was playing with all 7 at the same time.

July 11

BOTTOMS

Why there is so much talk about "high bottom" and "low bottom" drunks is beyond me. I don't care what kind of a bottom you had. It takes what it takes to finally surrender. For some having your daughter bail you out of jail is enough to hit a bottom. For others that lose their job, their house, lose a limb or kill somebody with their car to find a bottom. Whatever it is that drives you into the rooms of AA is a golden moment. We are blessed. So many of our fellow drunks die or just don't get it no matter how low they go. I learned to keep my bottom green so I don't forget how bad my bottom was. I never want a repeat. I get it thank you God. I need to remember the fear that ruled my waking moments, I was afraid to answer the phone or pick up the mail. A car stopping at my house could be a cop or a summons. Booze quit working, food stopped working, my body was shutting down. The feeling of despair and loneliness I can recall as if it were yesterday. Doom and gloom were the order of the day. No car, no mobility, no money, no hope.

Down deep I had a concept of God. I prayed only 2 times in 30 years. Once when I was in the hands of the North Vietnamese in Laos and once again in Afghanistan in the hands of secret police armed enemies, hell bent on killing me. My prayers were answered by God and He pulled my fat out of the fire both times. Did I give thanks after escaping with my life? No of course not, I got drunk. Now in my deep dark bottom I was in as much trouble as I was in combat. This time the enemy was me. I opened my mind just a sliver because suicide was not an option. Down deep in my childhood value system I knew I did not have the right to take my own life. What was I to do? Prayer was the last option. I said, "God help me I can't go on like this, I need help!" Asking for outside help was off my radar my entire life but I was in a black hole. The first meeting of AA I also keep as green as my bottom. The hope I felt, the unconditional love of the group pulled me into sunlight. The difference was like black and white, night and day. My little prayer was answered again only this time I began calling on my Higher Power daily rather than when a gun was pointed at my head.

Memory is a funny thing. We tend to remember the good stuff but I need to remember my bottom so as not to ever go there again.

July 12

TRUE PARTNERSHIP

When I was "out there" I had many relationships and partnerships, all bad. Better yet, in some cases, hostile. How about sharing a house with a woman who was divorcing me? It made dating a very delicate matter. I was relationship bankrupt, so all my relationships were wrong. The reason, I was wrong, my attitude was wrong, my priorities were wrong. I looked at relationships as what could I get out of it, what's the payoff to me? At my very first meeting in AA, I got a sponsor, a partnership, a home group another partnership and a host of friendly helpful relationships, some of which last to this day. Take a home group for example, I am in service, I contribute myself, my time, my heart and what do I get back? Help when I need it, spiritual messages on a daily basis and lots of love many laughs and a true sense of belonging. A win-win situation. Previously it was a lose-lose deal or I lose-you win game. I went from zero to hundreds of friends all over the world. I have a ton of partnerships all good because my attitude has changed. I put love and care into my relationships these days. I expect no payoff but I get lots of love back and that makes me happy, joyous and free.

True partnerships take some work on our part. A good relationship needs to be nourished, I have learned. I tell my friends how much they mean to me. I write a note of love and appreciation to my wife every day. She loves her note and she shows me she loves me by all the things she does for me and our family. I tell my home group guys how much I appreciate them and how grateful we have our daily meeting. I give every living creature I meet a smile. Costs nothing but the response lights up my life. I have a host of Thai friends who I see in my daily routine. We joke and share a kind word or two every day. It's good for the soul. I am uncle/brother-in law/cousin to over 100 Thai family up in my wife's village. The love I feel is beyond words from my family-by-marriage.

They accept this foreigner, lock, stock and barrel. They all say "I have a good heart," well OK I owe my heart to AA and the Steps, that's where the "good" came from. They respect my sobriety, which was a surprise to some of them. I start my day with a good relationship with God and all the rest turns out wonderful.

I have found, if you want friends, be a friend. All of you are my friends.

July 13

SHARING

Often heard around AA someone will say, "Thank you for sharing" which is meant to be sarcastic. Like, "I didn't need to hear that." To me sharing is very important and not to be taken lightly. Sharing our experience, strength and hope is the core of most meetings. It says right in the Big Book on page 164, "Admit your faults to Him and to your fellows." To me that means sharing. In my opinion it is like a mini 5th Step when you share your faults, mistakes and character defects with the group in meetings. It has the added benefit of working on your humility at the same time. When I share I am not trying to impress anyone with my knowledge or say things they want to hear. Quoting the Big Book with a touch of arrogance makes me want to puke. Preaching is another problem in some meetings. As we all know, if preaching worked there would be no AA. You can't tell an alcoholic a damn thing. He will listen to your experience especially when he can identify with the same problem. A word of caution, I am careful to share at group level what may help another alcoholic but sensitive personal issues I save for my sponsor or a spiritual advisor.

We talk about anonymity all the time but to be realistic it is a goal not always achieved. Things I have said in meetings have come back to me from people who were not at the meeting where I shared. Many times. I have had AA members say, "I heard you were not at the meeting today." Wrong deal according to our tradition. Who is and is not at a certain meeting needs to stay inside that meeting, especially what is said.

Happens all the time, innocently enough. My home group has a group conscience that everyone in the room has a chance to share. AA math: I talk for 5 minutes in a one-hour meeting and everyone follows my example, only 10/11 people can share but there are 25 folks in the meeting. Our group deals with selfish sharing all the time at the expense of the group conscience.

I read the Daily Reflections every morning in my hour of prayer and meditation, so I have an idea of what I am going to share if given the opportunity. Putting some thought into your share may help someone down the road. I have had people tell me what I shared in a meeting was a great help to them. I usually can't even remember what it is I said. Share from the heart and leave the results up to God.

Thanks for letting me share my experience, strength and hope with you.

July 14

TAKING YOURSELF TOO SERIOUSLY

Learning to laugh at ourselves may be a new deal to some of us. We are the biggest joke of all so might as well relax and laugh. When I was a kid, I was so serious and being laughed at hurt me to the core. When the choir teacher told me, in front of the entire class, "Michael you don't have to sing," because I ruined the whole group song. All the kids laughed at me and I was so crushed I never forgot that day. I had many other "incidents" which caused me grief because I was ridiculed. It took years to build up my ego but then I went too far and became ego driven. Big egos can't stand to be laughed at. Of course, I took myself way too seriously until I hit my bottom and my ego was smashed (no pun intended). I was pathetic and life was, indeed, unmanageable. I heard laughter in my very first meeting of AA and it was foreign to my ears. It had been a long time since I smiled or laughed. But I have been smiling and laughing every day since that first meeting.

Today my friends laugh at my hairline but I tell them God made a few perfect heads and the rest He covered with hair. They kid me about being "old." That is funny. I tell them they will be lucky to be as old as I am. I thank God I made it this far. I am younger now than when I hit my bottom 23 years ago. Close to death, overweight, liver shot etc. Actually, there is no reason to take myself seriously anymore. I crack myself up. Humility brings a certain peace to the soul. No need to prove yourself or inflate your accomplishments. It is what it is. I don't need to be right on every subject. I don't need to be the boss, the leader. I need to help others and get in service if I feel too serious. Being too serious is a symptom of an ego problem. When I review my character defects it is clear there is no reason to feel better than anybody else. I try to stay "right sized." I can laugh at my mistakes and pratfalls, which are many. I see humor in my everyday life and a hearty open mouth yuk is good for your health.

I do take my sobriety seriously. It is a life and death deal. Be sober first and then laugh.

July 15

OLD YOU VS. NEW YOU

One guy I was working with asked me, "Hey I am sober, isn't that enough?" My answer, no it is just a good start, a basic requirement. Ok he says a few years later, "Hey, I did my inventory and Step 5 isn't that enough already?" My answer, no, it is just the opener for the real work. Again, a requirement but not a rest stop. In Step One we surrender and in Step 6 we need to surrender again to the fact we have character defects which need to be changed or we will most certainly go back to drinking or worse. We need to admit we have been going down the wrong path for so long it seems OK to us. It takes some courage to change but change I must. Most important word in Step 6 is entirely ready. Just like we had to admit to our innermost selves we were alcoholic, we have to admit we need a complete makeover from top to bottom. Again this cannot be an overnight deal. How many years did it take to screw up our characters? Slow progress is all we can hope for. Most of my character defects were calcified in stone. Some will follow me into the grave no doubt.

Your spiritual path goes up a notch as we approach Step 6 & 7. We realize we need our Higher Power even more than just praying for sobriety. I hear so many fellow members, who are sober for years in some cases, but angry miserable, hateful blobs. They have failed to change. They have difficulty admitting they are wrong and can't see past their own ego. They are content with their character as is. I came to realize the old me was keeping me from the Sunlight of The Spirit. I was in a dark pit and this process gave me hope I could start a whole new life. A do-over big time! God will help me do this. All I have to do is admit my failings and God will remove those blocks to helping others. I can tell you for certain that is exactly what has happened to me. I have changed. I embrace the changes and look for more all the time. The New me is 100% improvement over the old me like day and night. I can truthfully say I am a new person. Where else can you get a new lease on life?

The old me gets out of the cage occasionally but the new me can spot the problem before I can slip backwards. Forward Ho!

July 16

TIME

When I did my 5th Step with my sponsor, I said, "At least I never stole anything, I was not a thief." Oh yeah, says my sponsor, "You were a thief of time. How much time did you steal from your family while you were in selfish pursuits?" OMG yes, I was a thief. I have a whole new attitude about time thanks to this program. Every day is a gift from God, today is the only cash I have so I try to spend it wisely. There is nothing I can do about time wasted or time stolen, but I can employ time management and stop using time selfishly. I stopped long range planning since it robs me of the present. I have no idea how much more time God will grant me, but I thank God for another day on earth every morning and every evening. I have friends whose lives were taken in an instant. No notice...lights out. Most of my friends who have passed away have been about 10 years younger than me. I didn't start growing until I got sober so my view of time is that it is more valuable than gold. You cannot buy time or save it or depend on it. It is indeed precious.

Time can be your enemy or your friend, depending on your attitude and mindset. I know people who are always late, behind schedule, missing airplanes and appointments. They seem to be behind the power curve all day, every day. This leads to frustration, poor relationships, loss of money, anxiety and heartburn. Bottom line a waste of time by making time your enemy. My day starts with an hour of prayer and meditation so part of the hour there is time for time management. I try to do things ahead of schedule. I don't wait to the last day to start doing my taxes or wait until my birthday to renew my driver's license. I don't come to meetings late. I don't come to doctor's appointments late even if I know I will sit for 30 minutes waiting. I would rather wait for somebody than have them wait for me. If I have wait time, I can get some extra mediation or read or enjoy some quiet time. Time is my friend and I savor extra gaps in activity. I have never been bored. That is a waste. Time helping someone else seems to add to enjoyment of time spent.

Part of my declutter program is to eliminate time wasters. The TV was my worst time waster and negative people came in second place. Time is my only currency today. I try to spend it wisely.

July 17

MEMBERSHIP

When I went to my first AA meeting, I asked, "Who's the boss?" They told me there are no bosses in AA. What? How do you stay organized without a chief and some Indians to do the work? Do I need to sign a book that I attended the meeting? No such book exists in AA. OK can I have a membership card? There are no membership cards, you are a member if you say you are. If you have the desire to stop drinking then that is all you need. What? This entire fellowship baffled me at the beginning. No rules. Only "suggestions." I saw treatment center papers to show attendance, but I was told that is not AA. That is the courts and rehab center requirements not really the business of AA. Wow I became a believer in the AA way. I look in my pocket and my credit cards say Member since 1999. My insurance company Member since 1965 and they treat me like s**t. Hell they don't have meetings or luncheons. Screw their membership. I am a full-fledged AA member in service, attendance and spirit.

Now I have learned if it is good enough for AA it is good enough for me. I have adopted the AA way in so many other outside activities of my life. I dropped my membership from many organizations. For example, Legion China Post #1 in Exile. It was an ego driven with no real charter; all BS full of special ops wannabes. Now Rotary Club is a worthy service club but they do have an attendance book and you can't miss many meetings or you are out. AA has no such requirement. You can miss meetings for years and still be a member (not recommended). I dropped being a "member" of anything I wasn't an active service participant. This was all part of my de-cutter program to streamline my life. I do belong to the VFW to help Thai widows with benefits. I belong to a warrior group because I contribute money to a scholarship fund for Lao refugee college hopefuls. In other words, I only belong to positive useful organizations. I do not belong to a political party. I follow the AA Preamble in my personal life.

Being a "member" does mean **I am responsible. When anyone, anywhere, reaches out for help, I want the hand of AA always to be there. And for that I am responsible.**

July 18

EVERYTHING IS PROGRESSIVE

We all know that our disease is progressive and if we pick up a drink after a period of sobriety the fun meter does not go back to the beginning. In fact, we might as well been drinking all that time. I have seen this to be true in so many of my friends they are amazed how quick they are trashed worse than ever before. Progressive yes but so is our sobriety. We can't just sit still and watch the world go by or we are regressing. I learned I need to progress in my recovery, find new ways to do service, learn new prayers, help more people. You all know how I go on and on about my gratitude list but it is so important to use that list as part of your recovery program. Not just to gaze at all your blessings and sing a happy song about how lucky you are, but use that list as battery power to do new positive things. I know if I am done growing, I am done. I remind myself to be teachable and look for new teachers every day. When a friend of mine goes back to drinking it teaches me the horror of a relapse and the danger of losing my life for not keeping sobriety my #1 priority.

Life is progressive just like my hairline. I can't stop the process. The wrinkles get more and deeper, teeth fall out, eyes go blurry and I forget what else. I know I need to be proactive in my actions and keep up with the sands of time in my hourglass. I have miles to go before I sleep and if I just tread water I am in danger of drowning. My spiritual condition needs a daily tune-up and positive action. I can't progress on yesterday's service or yesterday's meeting. In my 10th Step I look for negatives in my life that can be turned into positives. I can write a forgotten friend. I can forgive an enemy and give the bastard a big hug next chance I get. I read new ideas and search for positive messages in all my comings and goings. I hope my spiritual bank account can handle any bad stuff that comes my way. Tragedy and sickness are part of life, as it progresses, I need to learn from these bad times and turn them into positives.

Adversity introduces a person to him/herself and the way the storms are weathered shows what character we have.

July 19

SPIRITUALITY FIRST

I found it is very true EVERYTHING follows spiritual progress. When I stumbled into my first meeting, I was bankrupt in every department. Physically at death's door with high blood pressure, overweight and a herniated esophagus that would not allow anything larger than a pea go into my stomach. Emotionally bankrupt from loss of employment, loss of friends, loss of all my relationships, loss of all sanity. I was lost at sea without a paddle or a means of navigation. I was at my first meeting because it was required by a pre-divorce agreement. Financially bankrupt to the tune of $300,000 in debt with a minus $2000 a month cash drain. All the credit cards were maxed and the smoke and mirrors of moving credit around was at an end. No more wiggle room and no cash for booze. Yikes. Then, of course, spirituality was a foreign word, it was the worse bankruptcy of all. Alcohol was my higher power; God was something I remember from back in Catholic high school. All I could do is go to meetings at the very beginning. Learn some prayers, get a sponsor and read literature. I didn't realize it at the time but I was entering the spiritual realm.

What happened to me was the spiritual bankruptcy was the first bankrupt area to come around. I didn't plan it that way, but it was a result of just showing up every day at a meeting and working my first three steps. The next thing was relationships began to form with AA friends and a sponsor. I could see my insanity as I did my spiritual prayers and meditation every morning. Then my blood pressure came down as I lost weight from good diet and exercise. I was able to stay sober for a trip to the hospital where they put a big black hose down my throat and opened up my esophagus. I could eat real food again for the first time in years. My emotions were now in check and I could get off the roller coaster of life and get relative peace and serenity. The last bankruptcy to go was the financial disaster I put myself into. I was sober awhile and after a meeting one day, I said, "God I cannot go another day without a job!" and the phone rang. I was on a construction site the next day making way more than I was worth. Just like the reading says, spiritual progress comes first.

The good news is the spiritual bankruptcy is the easiest to address. Once you tap into your Higher Power all good stuff follows.

July 20

HOW TO EAT AN ELEPHANT

We all came into this program with elephants. Monster wreckage, amends pages long, health issues ignored, relationships destroyed, in other words, elephants so big they seemed unmanageable. One of the first things I heard was "one day at a time" which I just couldn't grasp. After all there is a 5-year plan and yearly planner to carry around like a bible. All those ideas had to be smashed until the lights went on. Just focus on 24 hours...that's all. Do a little today and be happy with progress not completion. If I looked at all my problems at once it would choke the life out of me. So, what would I do? There is so much, I do nothing. How insane is that? If your job is to empty the ocean with a tea cup, you better get busy. Just think about how long you were "out there" and you want to clean up the mess overnight? Not going to happen. My fractured math says to make the scales come back to even, I need to work this program vigorously for the same amount of time I was driving my bulldozer through life. I have a few years just to break even. After that I can start adding credits that may keep me out of hell where all my old friends are. Just how do you eat an elephant? Simple really, one bite at a time. One amends at a time, one character defect at a time, one prayer at a time, one step at a time but do them and leave the results up to God. If you view your "elephant" with fear and inaction, then sloth will run you into the ground. When you do your daily 10th Step, be sure to examine the good stuff you did today. Inventory is not just negative stuff it is everything, the good, and the bad. OK that's today, forget about tomorrow until your morning prayer and meditation then start a new list of good positive things just for one day. I have learned to think small, think short. Little bitty bites of my elephants. It took years but some of my elephants have been consumed. It comes as a surprise when suddenly you handle a situation cool and neat whereas in the past you would have lost your temper. You will really like the new you as you handle life one bite at a time. The trick to progress is to not let new elephants join the herd you already have.

3 PARTS OF FORGIVENESS

As a former combat pilot, the litmus test of forgiveness of other people is Hanoi Jane aka: Jane Fonda. During our war against North Vietnam she went to the capital city of our enemy, posed behind an anti-aircraft gun and cause much pain to the US POWs who would not visit her. There are many other stories about her visit. Now 45+ years later there is still heavy resentment from some folks and forgiveness is off the table. In the fighter pilot bathrooms, you may find a Jane Fonda target pasted to the urinal. OK do I forgive her? First of all, it is not for me to forgive. I have no relationship with this woman. Who am I to judge the actions of a person I have no relationship with? I am playing God by condemning her. If she needs forgiveness it is up to God. She has tried to make amends and this is not enough for some who will not let it go. What she did is none of my business. I don't have to like it or send her a Christmas card but forgiveness of others I have no problem doing. If I drop the judgment then forgiveness follows.

I don't have a list of people I need to forgive. God has forgiven them already so who am I to put in my 2 cents?

The second part is a lot harder. Getting forgiveness from others for what we have done or should have done. Hopefully we have everyone who fits this category on our amends list and once we make the face to face amends forgiveness may or may not come as a result of our efforts. The amends is not begging for forgiveness anyway, it is owning up to our part of damage done to the person to whom we are making amends. You have no control over whether forgiveness is forthcoming from anybody else. You do your part and leave the results up to God. I have been super blessed in the process of being sober all these years and continued amends I have received forgiveness beyond what I deserve. A wonderful gift of the program.

I don't have a list of people who should forgive me but haven't.

The third and the hardest part of forgiveness is forgiving yourself. I still struggle with this from time to time. I regret some trash out of my mouth that did permanent harm, decisions that changed the lives of others for the worse etc., etc. Years have been wasted while I was practicing my disease and driving a bulldozer through life.

I know God does not have me on His list of the unforgiven. I try to do positive things to balance the scales. Some more work here.

July 22

THE EASIER SOFTER WAY

When I was young, I sought the hard, tougher way. I worked hard, studied hard and it paid off. Once I achieved all I could, and no more promotions were available I decided I could play. I went the other way, to me every day was R&R. I could sneak drinks in at lunch time and even spike my coffee at 9 a.m. Everybody could smell the evidence, but I didn't care. I felt like I deserved to do whatever I wanted. This was the start of my bottom. I was making all the wrong choices. My picker was broken. I picked the wrong partners, the wrong places to drink, the wrong time to drive drunk, the wrong, easier, softer path. Instead of being fun and smooth it got rocky and troublesome. My pursuit of happiness was all wrong. It was alcohol dependent and self-centered. I painted myself into corner and there was no way out, or so I thought. Somehow, I thought I deserved to let loose as a reward for past accomplishments, but I got punished instead.

When I found this program just before my don't need "rewards" almost killed me, I found my way again. It was hard at first because I was so sick and the wreckage was still burning but I soon learned I had, in fact, found the easier softer way. The Steps rehabbed me into relative sanity. I unloaded the heavy weight of my past. I dropped the bag and found freedom. I learned powerlessness. I stopped being responsible for the troubles of the world. I stopped being guilty over things of which I had no control. I had only one inventory to work on, just mine and not a cast of thousands. It is so much easier to handle 24 hours than the entire history of my life. It is softer to help others than to pursue selfish goals. It is easier to be just me and not something that I am not. No more mask, no more lies. I don't make choices by myself anymore, I have a Higher Power who helps me in my decisions. The results speak for themselves.

Today my reward is to see a newcomer "get it" and to enjoy the gifts God has blessed me with.

July 23

ATTITUDE

One of the very few Broadway plays I saw in New York was a play called "Snoopy" after the cartoon dog in Peanuts. They had a great song called "Attitude" and it still sticks to me. Of course, Snoopy had a very positive attitude. One prayer I read every single morning says:

Today I pray that I may understand there are some things I cannot change:

I cannot change the weather, the tick of the clock, the past.

I can change my attitude.

I can change my priorities.

I can change my bad habits into good ones."

I shortened it up to make my point. So few things we can control but life is still going to happen and not always to my liking. My attitude toward those people, places and things which are out of my control is one of acceptance. I know God is the Master Planner and everything that happens is supposed to happen. A disagreeable person is there to teach me love and tolerance. If I am in a bad mood then something is wrong with my attitude. I look at my gratitude list and how in the world can I be upset or depressed?

I know I have a very positive attitude and it is all due to the attitude adjustment hour first thing in the morning. I read all positive spiritual readings, positive prayers, positive meditation. The mind and heart are fed tons of positive input before setting out into the real world. Now do I stay on a upbeat, positive attitude all day? Not always. Hours of a positive outlook can go up in smoke in a nanosecond under attack by an enemy. The difference today is I need not engage and worsen a bad situation by reacting and making it escalate. I have learned to step aside and let the thrust of the enemy go past me. I believe good things are going to happen to me and most of the time only good things do. I know folks who expect the worst and that's what they get.

My attitude can be changed immediately as many times during the day as necessary. I am the captain of my attitude.

July 24

WRITE IT DOWN

One management technique I learned a long time ago is to make a list in the morning before you head out into the world. There is something magic about writing it down on paper. The action of writing puts a file in your brain and without referring to your list you will be surprised at all the items you can cross off during the course of your day. The same thing goes for problems rolling around in your mind. Putting the problem down on paper takes the power out of it. It takes the ghost of fear and exposes it to daylight. I have a good friend who wrote a book about his experiences in Vietnam 45 years after the fact when he was 70 years old. He found it very therapeutic to write his pain down and free his mind and heart from decades of grief. That's what a 4th and 5th Step can do for you.

I have written down several episodes of my life for my children as my promise to them. Besides fulfilling my obligation to them it was very healing to me. I carried around the heavy weight of my past inside my lock box and over the years the weight of it all has taken its toll. I wish I had learned to journal as a recovery technique a lot sooner. I tried to write when I was "out there" and all it did is drive me to another drink. I couldn't handle opening the wounds again. Now in sobriety after a few 24 hours under my belt, I can put what needs to come out down on paper (well in the computer actually but I can print it on paper.) Just like anything else, practice makes perfect. Your writing need not be perfect with all the aides we have in our computers. I quit trying to spell correctly. Not a problem. The point is writing is good for you and can help your recovery, help heal pain, communicate with others. All sorts of benefits. Once you get started the words will flow but you must start.

My little pieces I write to you do me a world of good and occasionally may help one or two of you and that's my job.

July 25

TOTAL HONESTY

When I was a kid my face would turn beet red when I told a lie. After years of practice I was able to lie with a straight face, a skill I needed to make it in my world. When I went to the seminary to be a priest, they had a 5th Step process as part of the steps to the black robes. Every Friday night I had to sit in front of my Father Confessor and tell my sins eyeball to eyeball. Oh man, it took me all week to make up lies for Friday night. I was not going to tell him the truth. No way! Was I going to tell Father Riddlemoser that I was plagued by sexual thoughts when I was auditioning for a life of celibacy? You know the answer. Then I joined the military. A liar's club and a drinking club. This I could do. They lied to me and I lied to them. My entry into pilot training was a lie. I couldn't hear well enough and I was too tall but I scammed my way into the system. My whole life was filled with honesty blowing in the wind. When I came into the program, I didn't know the truth if it hit me in the face. Decades of dishonesty. Lies so complicated I would lose sleep trying to keep all the stories straight in my mind. Who did I tell what?

Our founders knew that honesty had to be addressed right up front. The 4th Step is all about self-honesty. Who are you really? Honestly and completely. The entire fur ball has to be coughed up. No exceptions. History of recovery has taught us, if the whole job isn't done completely, we will probably drink again. That is why honesty has to be accepted as a new way of life. It may take some getting used to after zero honesty for X number of years. Step 5 is all about honesty that can go past just you and your Higher Power. It may be easy to sit in your private room and be honest with yourself but now this giant step is to look someone else in the eye and tell the whole inventory. This may be the hardest pill to swallow for some but necessary for full, total recovery. It is very important to have trust and pick the right person to do this step. Most of us choose our sponsor but a spiritual leader, clergy or someone you trust will do. Probably best to be the same sex in order to cover the sexual inventory. Then you can look everybody in the eye when you converse. You can look yourself in the eye and be happy with what you see.

Now that honesty has become part of my life, I sleep with the angels, no dishonesty to rob me of peaceful rest.

July 26

HEALING

Healing takes time and it is hard not to try to rush the process. I know my operation for a torn bowel was almost 5 years ago, but it is still healing. Wounds of the heart that go back several decades are just now healing. All of us have been wounded in some way. If we stay on the path, we can inch forward in healing one day at a time just like our sobriety. I was told in my amends work to put myself on my amends list. I add prayers for healing to my list of other prayers and remember I am not whole and never will be. It took years for me to dig the hole I was in from drinking so that hole is not going to patched up overnight. It will take some more years before I can pat myself on the back. I have a good friend in my home group who calls this "slowbriety." The wreckage of my past goes deep and long. I have enough inventory of destruction to work on for the rest of my life. Some nasty words out of my mouth have hurt some people I love and they remember those words from 40 years back. Ouch.

I have a friend of mine from combat days who was shot down and spent 2 years in a hospital in 1970 with a broken back and neck. He kept those wounds fresh for 45 years until he passed away a few days ago. He never would let himself heal. He stayed in the combat mode for all these years not letting the battle finish. He never had a relationship, nor a family nor a real normal life. So sad. We have learned, I hope, that the war is over. No more wounds and no need to wound somebody else. We can stop beating ourselves up and begin healing ourselves and the ones we have harmed. Just being a loving, happy useful member of society is the best healing I can give my family and friends when I get the chance to share time and space with them. Now in this new life the secret to happiness is not adding any more hurts that need to be healed. In my morning meditation I ask God to heal me so that I may help others heal.

They tell me my deep dark past is of great value. If that is true, I am one rich SOB.

July 27

THE LAST WORD

Most of the movies you see today lead you down a path and drop you off not finishing the story. They leave the ending up to you. Personally, I think they run out of money and ideas and just pull the plug. Our famous Big Book takes no such chances. Bill and the editors made sure the ending was powerful and meaningful. Page 164 finishes with a flurry and sizzle. Today's reading is about the two magnificent standards of AA. Humility and responsibility. The Last Word in our Big Book is case in point. **"We realize we know only a little."** I am humbled by my lack of knowledge. In the old days I could hold forth on a variety of topics. No more wise guy. The more I learn the more I define the depths of my ignorance. I will keep learning however, even if it is a teacup into the ocean of knowledge. **"God will constantly disclose more to you and**

us." Key point is, our Higher Power will give us the tools, the words, the direction we need when we need it. Constantly...powerful concept and in my experience absolutely true.

"Ask Him in your morning meditation what you can do each day for the man who is still sick" Point being, responsibility for Step 12 requirement to help other achieve sobriety. Step 12 is the reason AA is growing and is a movement in an upward direction. To me "Ask Him in your morning meditation" is a direct order. No wiggle room here. It implies you do this morning thing and ask God for help in your responsibilities. Step 11 page 86 it says, "On awakening let us think about the 24 hours ahead." The Last Word reinforces the morning process of prayer and meditation. I can tell you it has worked wonders for me and the answers do come in that first hour I confer with my Higher Power. **"See to it that your relationship with Him is right, and great events will come to pass for you and countless others."** Since I am one of the countless others, I can testify this to be 100% true. I have shared so many great events with you guys already. **"Clear away the wreckage of your past."** Step 4, 5, 8, 9 and 10. **"We shall be with you in the fellowship of the Spirit."** You are not alone, ever, you are part of this great fellowship in the 4th dimension. How powerful a sentence.

I am on the Road of Happy Destiny, I know I will meet you somewhere, some day on that Road.

July 28

SHOW ME

I go to a meeting most every day and hear a lot of talk. Sharing has its place, but I tend to learn more from action. Reading the Steps out loud OK, but doing them is where it really works best, I have found. Don't tell me about the service you performed 5 years ago. What service are you doing right now? I can see who is in service ... it becomes obvious. Who comes early and sets out the books and chairs, who is secretary, group service representative, who cleans up the room after the meeting. Then there are folks who expect coffee service, cleanliness, literature all from heaven certainly below their dignity to do service. God bless them they are missing a key part of recovery. I believe if you show me how you stay sober, I can learn from the experience. I went on a 12 Step call with another member who I did not know very well but I learned some good ideas for 12 Step work. He got a commitment from the drunken subject that he would stop right now and come to a meeting tomorrow. Agreed by all. Then my partner asked if he could look around the hotel room for a minute. OK. He filled a shopping bag with beer and vodka from the fridge and various locations around the room. You won't be needing this will you? Wow, I would never have thought of making a booze sweep in someone else's house. It worked.

In my own case, I tell my sponsees I would never ask them to do something I don't do. I encourage my guys to go to as many meetings as possible. They will see me there. I show them my gratitude list. It is not talk, it is real and then I give them a 3 X 5 card to write theirs. I insist they try reading and prayer first thing in the morning so I show them my 6 books and 8 prayers I use every morning. Every once in a while, I will have a little test to see if they read that morning. If they don't know the date then I know they didn't do any daily reading. I show them how I did each step and wait for the action to follow. Also, I watch my own habits, during the meetings I don't come late, enter into side conversations, play with my phone, get up and walk out for coffee and bathroom visits, etc. I pay attention to get the gem of the day and sit still and not be a disturbance. People see what you do and, like it or not, you are setting an example of some kind. Hopefully a good one.

I hear some members talking the talk and not walking the walk. Hot air will not enhance recovery.

July 29

FEAR FACTOR

My life has been filled with horrible events and some of them actually happened. My first memory of sheer terror was the Cuban missile crisis, in October 1962, I was working on B-52's headed for Russia loaded with nuclear weapons and there was a real Armageddon about to happen. But it didn't happen. Most fears never happen. We can "what if" ourselves into bondage. Fear sells insurance. I know because I used to sell fear. The media sells fear. Different causes around the world use fear as their currency. Financial fears rule so many of us and when you take a realistic view of this pervasive fear it is unfounded. Fear of death is a prime mover also. I know many guys actually gave up their country and moved to Canada to avoid going to Vietnam. In other words, fear of death. Pretty drastic measure I would say after spending a few years in Vietnam I did not fear death if I kept my altitude and my attitude safe. The probability of having a car accident was greater than dying in Vietnam.

However, in the Big Book it says quite clearly, "For us, to drink is to die." How insane to survive combat and then drink myself to death. Now that would happen if I didn't get with the program. It will happen if I choose to pick up a drink again. I am having too much fun to waste it on some unfounded fear. I still have fear in my life but I process it very differently. I accept the whims and winds of the world that I have zero control over. Some of my friends are expressing fear of depression and loss of money. I lose no sleep over these possibilities since I do not have a say in the process. I have to leave the results up to God and not get an ulcer over stuff in the powerless box.

I was brought up with the fear of God. If I screwed up, I was going to hell. Now God is my friend, my inspiration and we are on the same team. So, for the love of God, fear is in the right perspective.

Everything that happens is supposed to happen, I need not fear events that have not happened.

THE POISON DRIP

Resentment is like taking a poison drip and hoping your enemy dies. Meanwhile he is sleeping peacefully with no thought of you and how he screwed over you.

Once you hold resentment for very long, that person takes up residence in your head, rent free. You become chained to that person and you become a slave. You lose sleep trying to plot revenge and payback. It eats away at your soul and takes you out of the sunlight for sure. Some people drink over resentments and usually the guys who relapse will tell you their story of why they picked up a drink and resentment is in there somewhere. One reason I work on letting my past go is, I can relive old wounds and regurgitate my ancient resentments all over again. Insane. I know I can't afford to hold on to resentments, so I process them as quickly as possible and leave justice up to God.

You are right. I know you are right. There is no doubt about the fact your anger is righteous. Look out...this is the worst kind of resentment. Just because you are right doesn't mean you will achieve a favorable result. Your frustration will go to the point because you know you are on firm ground but the forces against you still win the day. Is it fair? Of course not, but that is what happens in this unjust world we live in. The bad guys win once in a while. When I feel anger building, I try to nip it in the bud by doing something else, pray, go to another meeting, talk to another alcoholic. Some people count to ten or a hundred. Look for a GAP, a God Authorized Pause. The GAP will put some time and distance into the situation. I believe resentments/anger are just plain human foibles. We alcoholics have to be aware we enter the danger zone. Today I can choose not to fall off the deep end.

I try to stay out of the judge and jury business. Life is not fair, I accept that. I win all my fights by avoiding them.

July 31

CHARACTER

Fast Eddie, the great pool player, asks his manager, "Everybody talks about Minnesota Fats and never about me and I am better. What does Fats have that I don't?" The manager replies, "Character."

All of us have a certain character and others tend to judge you positively or negatively by what they see as your character. If you seem to be at odds with 90% of the people you run into maybe it is time to take a hard, honest look at your character. That 4th Step inventory is a good start. You can see patterns in your relationships. You can see where anger ruled your emotions. Most of us have a long list of resentments which cripple us mentally, emotionally and spiritually. Then anger is always related to fear and we are afraid of losing something we have or fear we won't get what we want. Unfulfilled expectations. Then mix in our personality and the result is character for the good, bad and ugly. Some of us have to "fix" other people. I have a good friend who drives me insane by declaring my glasses are "dirty" and he rips them off my head and cleans my glasses free of charge. Yikes.

You can do a character inventory also and take an inner look at such qualities as: honesty, integrity, humility, kindness, openness, availability, generosity, charitableness, playfulness, forgiveness, willingness, trustworthiness, self-respect, sincerity, commitment, encouragement, responsibility, vigilance and patience. If you find a weak link in any of these character qualities, we can do something about it. The character I was yesterday is replaced by the character I am today. Hopefully my character is changing for the better a little bit at a time until I am pleased with my true character. I need to make the man in the mirror happy with the image. I came into this program with enough deformities to work on for the rest of my life. There is not enough time left to be perfect so just a bit of progress will have to do for today.

My character building is a work in progress, the yellow tape is still around the construction site. Approach with caution.

August 1

INDIRECT AMENDS

One guy I was working with showed me his 8th Step list and about half the people on his list were crossed off. He explained that they were dead or unreachable, so he wrote them off. He then declared that half his job was finished but I instructed him that just because a person is dead you are not off the hook for amends. His job was even harder than if he could see all his people in person. Your recovery is at stake here, so a complete amends process is what I recommend. The indirect amends are part of recovery. In some cases, amends can be made to the family of the person deceased. Where money is involved an act of charity can replace restitution owed. It may take some creativity to fulfill your amends requirement so get some help. In my own case I helped a lady in Vietnam rejoin her family in the USA under an obscure amendment which allowed unmarried children in Vietnam to join their refugee parents. She was 42 years old at the time and now she is happily married in Arizona, close to her parents and brother who were also allowed to enter the USA. The actual person I needed to make amends to was unreachable, but I made a big effort first and then did the indirect method.

The entire 12 Steps are working on changing the person I was, a drunk, into a better person sober. This change will ensure that I never pick up a drink again. My idea is to do a complete closet cleaning in order to deal with my past and make amends wherever possible. The persons who I need to make amends to are not available, but I still have amends to do. I must look at what wrongs I did and change my behavior to deal with my relationships in a new way minus the old character defects and that is indirect amends. Helping someone who needs assistance replaces the ones I hurt and can never see again. Now into 20+ years of making amends I have a good start but by no means will I ever be finished. I enjoy the results of my amends' efforts so much that I look for new ways to add to my list. I can tell you the results of my efforts have been amazing and rewarding.

In my case it took me so long to get to the program that the majority of my amends were and still are indirect. So, don't wait too long.

August 2

SELF AMENDS

Most of us have heard the suggestion to put ourselves on our amends list. I agree with that 100%. First, we mend the fences of our neighbors, make restitution, direct and indirect amends, then start to work on our own fence. I think everyone should make their own damage report to see in black and white the neglect we suffered as a result of the years we were "out there." I know I wouldn't go to the dentist half smashed, I wouldn't see a doctor about my closed esophagus because it would require a night in the hospital with no happy hour. I would have to detox to see any doctor and that just wasn't happening. I never fed my mind, never read a book cover to cover when I was drinking. I read the sports page and Andy Capp in the comics because he was a drunk like me. While I was in my disease no growth was taking place, my body, mind and spirit were rotting. Lucky thing that once I got sober my spirit was the first to respond to recovery. Then I started eating right, going to the dentist and regular exercise. Then I began my education starting with the Big Book.

Once you establish a relationship with the real you then repairs can happen. You can become the loving person God created you to be. You can balance the needs of body, mind and spirit because you need all three. You can reverse the damage to some extent and growth can begin again. When I was 8 years old I said I was going to write a book. Well that went out the window with my drinking but I am now working on that book. Estimated date of completion is my 77th birthday. I picked up a tennis racket after 20 years of no exercise until I blew out my knees. I have read 100's of books. I am up to the ones I should have read in the 80's and 90's. Maybe I will take up painting. I encourage you all to expand your vistas, find your bliss and give yourself some artistic outlet. Don't let age stop you from trying new skills, new entertainment and treat yourself once in a while. You deserve it. Be good to yourself.

AMENDS FOR OTHERS

You won't find any of this next rendering on amends in any AA book. This is strictly from my experience. You read my bit on direct amends and indirect amends, this is level 3 amends for other people, especially those in the program. Example: in a meeting when I hear foul language when women are present, I will, after the meeting apologize to them for the lack of common courtesy from my fellow members. Many members feel it is their right to say anything they want in a meeting. So be it for them but I find foul language does not enhance my message. I am sure it is nothing they haven't heard before, but they all appreciated my amends. Example 2: after one meeting a few of us went for breakfast at a local Thai restaurant and one of the guys ordered apple juice. The waitress brought him a glass of juice with ice. This New York person not yet adjusted to Thai ways said angrily: "I asked for apple juice, not ice, take it back." I was shocked and she was shocked by the rough attitude. After our meal, I went back and gave her an additional tip and an apology. Well, to this day I made a friend. Bling gave me a nice hug then and a hug every time I saw her after and great service for the next 3 years. She married and is in Sweden now.

I have so many amends that I should have made over my lifetime that I can never do enough amends. My favorite story is, up country in Khon Kaen a bunch of us were attending an AA function and we had set a dinner at a restaurant on the lake for some fellowship. Well two members got lost and went to the wrong lake and were over an hour late as we all were leaving. They were mad and the first waitress they encountered got all the venom aimed at her service. She was sobbing and took her apron off. When I saw what was happening, I came back and consoled her. She had no idea what this guy's problem was (I never could understand him either) but she was such a nice person I sat down and talked to her away from the bad guys. Turns out she was working to pay for nursing school that she had to drop due to lack of funds. It was such a small amount by US standards I gave her what she needed. A year and a half later I was back in Khon Kaen on another AA event and I ran into Pla. She was like a different person and was a nurse and so happy and grateful. All because I saw a needless verbal abuse by another AA member. I am sure other people have patched the holes I have made in someone's fence when I was in my bulldozer phase.

This amends process reaps such wonderful rewards I keep looking for opportunities. These examples I have given you really come from putting the 11th Step Prayer into action.

August 4

SPIRITUAL MESSAGES

I guess my antennas are always up and running but I see spiritual messages in just about everything I read and in the events of my life. When I try to share what I see as a spiritual message, others quite often just don't see what I see. Even the comics I see stuff to ponder, especially Andy Capp because he is a drunk. The lines are supposed to be funny but I see some pathetic behavior that was just like my past. One recent one, the cops are hauling Andy off out of the bar and he is screaming bloody murder. Why? Because they didn't let him finish his drink still on the bar. Now that would be me. One such random event just happened to me and my wife and I would like to share with you and show you what I mean by harvesting spiritual messages where you would least expect it. We have a couple who lives in the same condo up until a few months back. He came from Australia (64 years old) several years ago. She is a Thai lady quite a bit younger (the norm here in Thailand). They bought a new house and spent a ton of money fixing it up just like they wanted and kept the condo for sale later. The gentleman passed away very suddenly before he ever got a chance to enjoy the new house. OK so where do the messages come from.

We were not close to this couple. The wife was very nice and we had brief conversations in the lobby but the husband never said a word to any of us. We never even had a lunch or dinner together nor visited each other's home. Even so we decided to attend the Buddhist prayer service for the husband. We both felt it was the right thing to do. The first shock was when we arrived at the temple 30 minutes before prayer time and nobody was there. The widow arrived and came over to where we were standing waiting for the door to open and held my wife in her arms and sobbed for a good 10 minutes. Then she held me for another 10 minutes and sobbed some more. Lost my handkerchief to the grieving widow. We attended the service and this man had not one friend in attendance. We were placed up front in the place of honor to light the candles and be the family. We, a casual acquaintance, are now the best friends. This Thai lady is a millionaire but clearly broken hearted and alone. Message #1...we followed our instincts by attending. Clearly that was the right thing to do. We were needed. Message #2 Hard to imagine a life without friends. I have already invited a lot of people to my memorial. I have friends all over the world, literally. I thank God for my friends...real friends. When I hit bottom, I was without any friends and this program has changed all that. Message #3 Money cannot buy you happiness nor can it buy you friends. We all know this but this scene was pretty graphic to prove the point.

I pray your antennae are online ready to receive spiritual messages.

August 5

EQUALITY

I do believe it is a human trait to compare and judge others to find differences not equality. I grew up knowing most of the kids in my class had more money, their family cars were nicer, they had bicycles while I walked, and they had nicer clothes. My parents taught me I was smarter than my classmates, which wasn't true, but we had to be different and better. There is always a pecking order it seems in life. Funny, I was a "leader" my first day in the Air Force of 3 guys because my last name started with "C" then in basic training I was the tallest so I was the squadron commander, so I was thrust into a mold that lasted 30 years. In the USA there is an obsession with equality and some folks burn down their own city in the name of equality. In sports, there is a big argument for equal pay for women and some are equal, but most are not thus the controversy. Our great fellowship by-passes that problem. There is no rank, no boss, no ladder of success to climb. What a relief.

Our society of AA has no one person better than another. All the years of sobriety don't place you ahead of a newcomer with one day. Amazing really. We stop trying to find differences but find our common ground. It matters not how much education you have, no matter how rich you are, what matters is the quality of your sobriety. If you compare your insides to other folks' outsides you will be forever disappointed. All of this works on our selfishness when we realize we are equal in so many ways to our fellow earth travelers. Gandhi stated that he found it ridiculous that one man considers himself better than another man. Unfortunately, the world is not of like mind. I would like to think our fellowship is free of all prejudice and we are open to all no matter how crazy they might be of what religion they practice or what country they come from. I love our group because it has all different languages and accents that make it international. We are just a bunch of alcoholics staying sober and that is equality.

It makes life so much easier to communicate straight across the table and not look down or up to anybody else.

August 6

LOVE AND TOLERANCE

This AA statement had me thinking of my old friend Hank. He passed away some years back but his spirit still lives in our little group. He always talked about "Love and tolerance is our code," and he lived it for sure. I admired how he would accept everyone no matter what or how disruptive they might be. One such disagreeable chap showed up to a meeting for the sole reason to sell his truck. He wanted no part of the recovery process but Hank welcomed him like a lost son. Amazing. As I age I find my tolerance gets less and less when it should be going the other way. I focus on my tolerance and make efforts to widen my arms to even the angry toxic folks I encounter from time to time. I try not to waste my time on negative thinking or worse ... negative actions.

Love is the answer to any question. I try to remember that we are all God's kids and everybody is my brother or sister. I don't have to like all of them but I must love them. I need to find the good in people who I have shunned. God is in all of us and if I can't find it that means there is something I need to learn. I need to open my heart and my mind to the fact I am wrong about someone. It is hard to get out of the judgment mode and leave justice up to God. To me acceptance and love go together. I know I can't change other people, places or things so why not let others be what they are. I need to forgive everybody even if they don't ask for forgiveness. I hope all folks I have harmed will forgive me too. I know I have hurt the people I love the most. All I can do to restore balance is double my love in an active way.

My head is full of enough stuff without having a resentment take up residence free of charge.

August 7

CHANGE

I do believe that resistance to change is a human condition. There is a supermarket close by that keeps changing the aisles and location of everything. It drives me crazy because I can't find what I want without hunting for the new location of chia nuts. I tend to sit in the same chair in every meeting, even if I haven't been there for years. Changing the route of daily travel to work could have saved the life of my Ambassador in Afghanistan, so change can be a good thing. You can fight change, or you can ride with it, go with the flow. I remember when I was newly sober and life was so wonderful. I said, "Don't change anything. If it's not broke don't fix it." Wow was I ever wrong. I was happy with raw sobriety, stopped on Step 3 and was a happy camper. I didn't realize that I needed to change me, all of me. The rest of the Steps are how most of us change the person we were into a fully vested member of society, helping others and out of the selfish mode. I thought I was on cruise control, but I was really going backwards by not continuing the 12 Steps and changing myself.

I now embrace change and work on changing me every day starting with the morning meditation. I know for 30 years no growth was taking place while I was drinking and being 100% selfish. I have so much learning to do to make up for all those lost years. I have so many amends to make for all the time I stole from my family and friends. My sponsor told me in the beginning. "You don't have to change much, just everything." I didn't pay attention to that and it was almost fatal. Now I look for new ways to change, to improve my life, open my eyes to the beauty around me, learn from others. Sometimes I feel like a blind man who just restored his sight. I have missed the obvious so many times. "Did you see that elephant that just walked by?" No. I know that I must keep growing and keep learning or else I am a goner.

I have undergone the change of life and I wish the same for you too.

August 8

DON'T TAKE BACK YOUR GIFT TO GOD

In my morning meditation I say the 3rd Step prayer first thing. I remind myself to try to find out which way God is going and plan to go that way too. I also remind myself I am not in charge. I have this totally happy, joyous life by the grace of God not by my doing for sure. So many times I could have lost my life but God saved me time and time again by His grace. I made the decision to turn my will and life over to the care of God. I would be stupid to reverse that decision. I gave my drinking problem over to God over 8000 days ago and He is doing just fine with that problem. My gift to God is to stay sober today and I will reaffirm that promise again tomorrow. Why in the world would I take back my gift to God? Now I am not sure of all of God's wishes, but I am 100% sure staying sober is what God wants for me. I don't worry about drinking, I don't think about drinking, it just is not on my daily menu or thought process. My focus in on Step 10, 11 and 12. I don't need to do Step 1 again if I truly do a Step 3. People who drink again have, in fact, taken their will and life back from God, bad choice. Once you find a way out why not stay in the Sunlight of the Spirit?

I hear many of my fellows talk in meetings about how happy they are sober but they never talk about service, helping others, Step work or spiritual progress. They are sober and that's it. There is so much more to this program and it gets better once you keep learning and expanding your growth. Every meeting I hear selfish BS mixed in with the gems that keep me growing. My job is to separate the wheat from the chaff.

Part of that 3rd Step prayer says, "Relieve me of the bondage of self, that I may better do thy will." That selfishness we all have is an obstacle to progress in recovery. I work hard to get out of self in all its forms. Thinking of others is so much more productive than selfish pursuits. The further I am away from me the better I feel and the happier I am, too. When I walk out the door I ask myself, "Who is going to be my teacher today?" Sometimes the beauty of nature is my teacher, sometimes Lucy the dog is my teacher and, if I am lucky, one of my fellow travelers will have an enlightening conversation with me. I try to see God's fingerprints on everything and everybody.

God has filled my basket overflowing with gifts, I would not think of taking back my one small gift to Him.

August 9

A 100% PROGRAM

I enjoyed a 3-day Thailand AA Roundup with a great speaker. Lots of meetings and a reunion of many old friends I had not seen in years. The heart of the speaker's talk was about the Steps and the role it has in all of our recovery efforts. I am one of the lucky ones that went "all in" with this program and I don't know how else to do it but the Steps. I learned it is all or nothing. I don't want to be on the outside looking in. Half assed effort brings half ass results, so I want to "get it." Being in service, carrying the message, sponsoring people, going to meetings every chance I get, reading the literature every single morning. Praying my eight prayers, meditation, reaching out is all second nature. I would not dare subtract any of these things to test my program. I do Step 10, 11 and 12 every day. I touch on about four or five more steps somewhere during the day. If I get to share in the meeting, it is a mini 5th Step with my fellows, admitting my faults. You can't audit this program. There is no correspondence course option. You have to do the work in my experience. If you are not willing to take all the Steps, you may stay sober but you will not get the full benefit of the spiritual awakening in Step 12.

Just staying sober is AA 101 but that is not the end, it is the beginning of the cleanup phase: inventory, restitution, service to something outside yourself. To me, sponsoring folks is the best way to get out of yourself and be useful plus it feels real good when the lights go on with the person you are sponsoring. But I would never ask my sponsees to do something I didn't do myself like the Steps for example. Sure, there are other ways, but this way worked for me and thousands of others I know compared to a very few the other way. I have a sober friend who I am friends with but he is not a friend to me. He spends our time together talking about his aches and pains, his job, his relationships but never once asks about me or my family. Then he is done with me. It is clear that he is the center of all his thoughts and once you have become a fully vested member of AA you automatically enjoy friendships which go both ways. In my experience, I could not be the person I am today without following this program 100% every day. I work on my spiritual condition so I get that daily reprieve the book promises.

Just raw sobriety misses the joy of giving back. For those of us who have been given so many gifts, much is expected.

August 10

BE SURPRISED

We all know expectations are really an embryo for a resentment. Having
some idea of what to expect next is a human condition but we can work
on our attitude about these predictions. I know in my early life all the
expectations came from my mother, I wasn't allowed to have my own
expectations. Of course, I was a constant disappointment to my mother
and I had major resentments toward her. I rebelled and gave up trying to
fill her expectations. She carried grandiose plans for me all of her 90
years. The good news is I learned to live life without great expectations.
In my daily morning spiritual work up, I have faith that God will take
care of my future. I need not agonize over what is to come. I let my faith
trump all my fears, I have no control over the future so why make a list
of expectations that will turn into resentments, the number one killer for
us alcoholics. If you want God to laugh, tell him all about your plans. If I
work on the "now" I know the future will be as God intended, not as I
planned it. It is always "now."

My technique for dealing with expectations is to be surprised. If I stay
out of the planning business, then I wait for the flower to open its pedals
and enjoy the surprising beauty and color. I try to wear the world as a
loose garment and be flexible to my surroundings. Let it rain! Let it
snow. Let it be hot. Let it be cold. I am just happy I can enjoy feeling,
hot or cold. Most of all I need to apply this to my fellow human beings. I
can't control them so why have expectations for them. When they say
something nice or do something nice to me, ta da! Surprise. I got a letter
from the IRS last week. I didn't panic and fear an audit because I haven't
done anything wrong. I fearlessly ripped it open. Surprise. Last year they
paid me $22 interest for a slow return and I need to add the interest on
this year's income. They can expect to see it carefully noted on my next
return.

I used to lose sleep over what the future would bring to my doorstep.
Now I sleep with the angels and let God surprise me tomorrow.

August 11

BALANCING SELFISHNESS

We all know that alcoholism is the most selfish of all diseases. At the end we were all consumed by feeding the monster that took over our lives and that took 100% attention. Nobody else and nothing else mattered more than our selfish needs. All those years of selfishness probably won't be wiped away overnight. Thinking of others was a brand new concept. Our selfishness is in our blood, in our bone marrow to the core. No wonder the Big Book calls selfishness the "root of all of our problems." Many of my morning prayers address selfishness head on and the 11th Step, St. Francis prayer most of all, "to comfort, than to be comforted, to love, than to be loved." The 3rd Step prayer "Relieve me of the bondage of self." And of course, the Steps themselves, clean up and make restitution, help others all aimed at that selfish center we all have. I know I need to work on my ego, my selfishness daily and that's what my quiet hour affords me every single day. Am I completely selfless? Not by a long shot. I would be a Buddha if I could achieve a state of total selflessness.

Given that sainthood is off the table, what should I do about my selfishness? I have been suggested a balance in my study of the subject. I need to have enough selfishness to stay sober, no matter what. If I lose my sobriety, I am no good to anyone, least of all myself. I have promised my Higher Power every day that I will stay sober for another 24 hours, the next morning I write a new contract saying the same thing so I do not ever want to break my promise to God. I need to do whatever is necessary to stay sober. I need to feed my body, mind and spirit. I don't need to steal off someone else's plate to feed my hunger. I can find a balance of helping others while I help myself at the same time. I don't need material trappings to show others I am better or richer or smarter. I need to be presentable so a newcomer can see I am clean, groomed and OK to approach. I always take a look at my actions because at times the surface says good deeds are happening but often deep down there is a hidden selfish motive all wrapped up in sugar.

If we chip away at our selfishness day after day, we will eventually find a happy balance.

August 12

AM I MY BROTHER'S KEEPER?

The answer to the question, am I my brother's keeper? You bet I am. I better be because this program is about giving back. This gold mine is not for me to keep, it is to pass on to my brothers. I need to watch my brothers for signs they are slipping away and placing themselves in danger. Coming to less meetings, not sharing anymore, coming late and leaving early and the lack of a smile are all warning signs. It is my duty to notice and offer assistance. The assistance may be rejected but that's OK as long as that person knows you are there for them.

I look at the meeting room just like a combat flying squadron. It's the place where we do planning, training and have our coffee and fellowship. Then we go out on missions (experience life) and some members just don't make it back from a mission. A bottle of gin is just as deadly as an AK-47 round. Our squadron mates may or may not make it back to the rooms. As a senior member, I need to be ready and available to do a rescue and bring my lost brother back. Wounds and all. (I always loved that Boys town slogan: He's not heavy, he is my brother.) Right now in my "squadron" (home group), we have about 25% lost in the woods. I pray they make it back.

I am my brother's keeper, even if he doesn't appreciate it.

August 13

FUN

Fun is one of my favorite topics because I am not very good at it yet. That prayer I mentioned before about taking time to read also has a line that goes like this:

Take time to play

It is the secret of perpetual youth

I didn't get much play or fun as a kid. The homework and chores took priority over getting outside and playing baseball. Even when I was allowed to play a sport it was painful. Competition was stressful and I never hooked up with a winning team. No win, no fun was the mindset. Getting one over on my parents was my idea of fun. Skipping out on school was as much fun I could muster. I quickly learned once I broke into adult life that "fun" was going to a bar. Work hard, play hard was our motto in the military but it really translated to drink hard. I could do that. So yes, there were some fun times drinking. I remember when flying in combat and all of us pilots would be in a long day of getting shot at and someone would hit the mic button and scream "Are we having fun yet?" Of course, we were not but it broke the tension and made us thirsty for that first beer. It took many years of drinking before trouble started ruining the fun.

What I am trying to say is I certainly had a warped idea of fun. When I got sober, I hurt so bad that "fun" was off the table. I could not define the word. In my early sobriety one lady would ask me where was I going to play today? Huh? What's that? I soon learned I needed to start from square one on lighting up and adding fun stuff to the daily routine. I used to enjoy tennis but my knees can't take it, I have a set of golf clubs gathering dust (maybe tomorrow) does playing solitaire on the computer count? I enjoy the company of good people and fun conversation over a nice meal. That didn't happen in the bar. Since our Higher Power does want us to be happy, joyous and free then it is a good idea to add play to our "Body, Mind and Spirit" concept. I do want to stay young forever so I enjoy the cute little 3-year-old neighbor girl who pays us a visit every so often. She knows how to play and it cracks me up.

I am still learning to have fun after 50 years of not having much that didn't include drinking... pathetic, aye?

August 14

KEEPING IT SIMPLE

Today's reading about the last conversation between our two founders has a lesson for us all, "Let's keep it simple." In my past life, I was always in chaos and turmoil. I could hide in all the confusion and every day was crisis management. Life was stressful and gave me high marks on my report card. The more stress you could handle the more promotions. What a crock. Now I give myself marks for stress avoidance instead of damage control. I used to complicate my life by trying to keep about 10 plates all spinning at the same time. I would volunteer for everything, get involved in activities that ate my time up to the detriment of my family, my health and my peace of mind. I loved a good fight. I would take on the government, the military, congress, city hall whoever was in my sights. The bad news is that sometimes I would win. That just put gasoline on the fire to find a bigger fight. What a waste of time and energy. Now I have learned I need not fight anybody or anything anymore. What a relief.

To my new way of thinking, simplicity is real creativity. When my head is spinning and life seems overwhelming, I look down at my feet. Hey, I am not going anywhere. I take a deep breath and start over from square one. OK what's important here? What are the priorities? What do I have control over? That alone knocks any problem down considerably. For tough issues, I pray and be quiet. I put my hard issues in the overnight cooker and in my morning meditation the answer pops out like magic. My Higher Power is at work 24/7 and can present me solutions if I keep it simple and be quiet so I can hear the message. You have heard me say this before, but again, I declutter my life as much as possible. No wallet (got a few cards loose in my pocket) 2 keys (house and car) no smartphone, no Facebook, no political party, no electronic toys, and no organizational positions. I have learned serenity is listening to the silence. I am a reformed adrenaline junkie.

Living one day at a time makes life very simple. Now it is easy to handle. KISS, keep it simple stupid.

August 15

BODY

Most of you know I quote a Hazelden book called *Body, Mind and Spirit* quite often. (Highly recommend) I firmly believe to follow this program you need to work on all three. You cannot carry a great spiritual message if you are dead from ignoring your health. Most of us have abused our one and only body we were issued at birth when we were "out there." For myself, I was 80 pounds heavier than today, high blood pressure, a blockage in my esophagus that would not allow a pea to pass, on and on the list goes. I always joked that if my body is a temple then I am Angkor Wat, ancient and decaying. We don't talk very much about the physical problems we have caused by our disease but the damage we have done may take us out sooner than our "normie" friends. I know I have outlived my hair, my teeth, my hearing, my eyesight and some more stuff I don't want to talk about. We are powerless over our: heritage, height, skin, eye color, sex, age, voice and gene pool. But we are not powerless over what we ingest, our exercise routine (if any) our sleep habits and health care in general. I promised my Higher Power I would not drink today, and I also promised to take care of what is left of my temple.

I cannot help others if I am sickly and in such poor health, it turns people away. I see some long-term sober members who are in bad shape due to their own choices, be it smoking, carrying a big gut or unsafe behavior. I am very careful to eat: fruit, grain, fresh vegetables, low fat items, little fish and chicken, no red meat, vitamin supplements, rare sweet stuff, small portions of all of it. I stay away from buffets because it is like getting drunk on food to me. Try as I might to just take a little bit of this and that, my plate weighs about 5 pounds. I get on my stationary bike for one hour every day. I never skip a day of eating, so I never skip a day of exercise. Sleep OMG, I abused the gift of sleep all my life. Passing out does not count as sleep. I never slept right for all the years in the military. I used to carry my problems into my pillow and my mind never got a rest from the chaos of my daily life. Now today, with zero resentments and all the love in my life, I sleep with the angels and get the rest my old carcass requires.

You are saying, how can I talk about "body"? What are my credentials? Hey, I am alive and a good number of my age group is not around to give you a lecture. So there.

August 16

MIND

The second theme of my recommended reading *Body, Mind and Spirit* is a follow up from my last epistle. The Mind. I have been taught recovery is largely a matter of subtraction not addition. For example, I need to subtract my fears, my guilt, my regrets and my resentments from my mind to achieve any kind of peace and serenity. I need to be subtracting character defects without adding new ones. When I got here my mind was full of garbage, bad ideas, unnecessary data and confusion. I came to realize all my old ideas didn't work and a thorough closet cleaning was needed. I had to start over from scratch learning how to live by reading the Big Book, listening to my sponsor, listening to the shares in meetings and reading my morning meditation books every single day. After 8000 straight mind control exercises my life has changed, my mind has been re-programmed with good stuff. I have to feed my body daily so to I must feed my mind every day to keep it from spinning out uncontrollably. My brain is defective, it needs constant repair and maintenance. My attitude, one of the few things I can control, needs daily adjustment.

We are in an age of amazing quantities of information and data. We are drowning in available information. TV, computer technology, electronic devices show us the road to take, read us books, allow us to see faces of people halfway around the world as we chat with them. For me, I need to filter all this information flow and tailor what goes in my mind. For example, I don't leave CNN on all day and let the events of the world upset me. All that bad news of terror is simply out of my control and it fills my head with sorrow and sadness. I choose to open my mind to helpful information. For example, when I go into a book store I naturally gravitate toward the inspirational/spiritual section where I can find a book which will lift my spirits and inspire me. I read at least one hour every day to match my one hour of exercise. There is a prayer I say every morning called "Take Time" one line from that prayer is:

Take time to read

It is the fountain of wisdom.

When I was drinking, wisdom was off the table. I treat the inputs to my mind like gold. If I start a non-productive book, I throw it away; if I am watching a terrible movie, I get up and leave. Garbage in garbage out. Inspiration in inspiration out.

August 17

SPIRIT

The third part of "Body, Mind and Spirit" is IMHO the most important of all, spirit. Our program is a spiritual one, not a religious sect, but a fellowship. I have found my happiness is found in getting away from myself and being useful to the outside world. My happiness is not attached to one single material possession. My first thoughts and my first hour of every day (no exceptions) is one of the spirit. It is a great start of each day to attack my selfishness head on. I do this by feeding my spirit, asking for God's help, asking for guidance, thinking of others. If I didn't have my attitude adjustment hour, I would be doing for me, milking my needs, my wants my desires. Me, me, me, I, I, I, and start the self-centered process. My prayers are all about love and tolerance, rendering a smile to every living thing I encounter, resentment prevention, humility, faith, hope and charity. My spirit is fed only good stuff for about the first 4 hours of each day.

I supplement my spirit by reading spiritual books, by feeding my mind and I feed my body with fresh fruit and whole grains. Body Mind and Spirit are all connected in one system I try to balance all three because if I neglect one the whole system crashes. For best results, I have found, strive for improvement in all three. The status quo is like going backwards. I look for new readings to expand my mind, I find new health tips about food and supplements all the time. If I quit learning I am done. My spirit is always up, sometimes more than others but it is from a baseline of happy, joyous and free. My gratitude list shows me I am truly blessed and doing for others doubles my joy. A healthy body and mind results in a wonderful spiritual high.

We stand in The Sunlight of The Spirit, the warmest feeling on this planet.

August 18

CHOICES

Do you remember when you had zero choices? I sure do. It was a long time ago, but it is still green in my memory, sitting in my self-imposed prison with no choice but to keep drinking. The alcohol had stopped working. It was killing me and yet I could not stop poisoning myself to death. So miserable was my life, no freedom whatsoever, my work was torture but I needed the money to feed the gorilla inside my soul. The monster had me by the throat and the dance of death was on. Alcohol gave me wings to fly then it took away my sky. I was grounded as I built a brick shit house to keep out the bogey man and keep myself from the outside world. No choices, no freedom, no life, no friends, no job, no car, no fun. Yikes I am getting goosebumps writing my own history lesson. I knocked down those bricks one by one, step by step. (So many groups are called "Steps to Freedom") I put the gorilla back in the cage, he is still there but I don't feed him anymore.

One of my better Air Force jobs was to bring some pilot POWs from Vietnam back into the blue suit and out of Hanoi Hilton. Most of them had been in enemy jails for 5 to 8 years. They were given the lid to the cookie jar and could pick any assignment they wanted. Well, that sounds great, but after all those years of no choices, no decisions they would change their minds daily and drove the personnel troops nuts. The same with us, we lost our right to freedom of choice, we lost normal thought processes. Now we live in the Sunlight of the Spirit and can make all sorts of choices. We haven't had a good track record of making the right choices so that is why, in the morning meditation, we communicate with our Higher Power and get some assistance in making some good decisions. This wonderful freedom has great responsibilities attached to it. Those choices need to be screened for selfishness, incorrect motives and thought all the way through to the end. Just one drink and the gorilla is out of the cage and the dance is on and will not be over until the gorilla says it's over.

Today I can choose between good, better and best. It's all good.

August 19

TURNING POINTS

Most of us have had our lives changed drastically at different turning points. I know I turned right at times, and if I went left, I would be dead. My Higher Power has been looking out for me 24/7 my entire life. What I had thought was a horrible turn of events was the best possible outcome. I was 18 years old and considering joining the Hell's Angels or joining the military. I needed to get out of my childhood home fast, so the military won out. Instead of a 4 year hitch it turned out to be 30 years. In the Air Force I got sent to Maine because I didn't know there was a guy selling assignments. I got the worst place but it made me study and go to college in order to get out of the snow. I received a free college education as a result. I made my own turning point to get into pilot training by cheating on a flight physical. I am too tall in the saddle and my hearing was shot. I skipped a survival class and if I had been on time I would have been sent to Korea instead of Vietnam. My entire career would be very different than what really happened. I am sure as you look at your history you have many turning points but none as important as the one where one day you were drinking and the next day you were not.

I remember very vividly the realization drinking was killing me, but I could not *not* drink. I had to keep alcohol in my body and I knew I was a trapped rat with nowhere to go. I was screwed without a clue. Suicide was not an option by what little spiritual values I had left. My soon to be ex-wife forced me into signing an agreement that I would enter a rehab program. Yikes. My life was over. The intake folks gave me a date about 10 days down the road and a sheet to be signed at three AA meetings. They gave me a copy of the schedule of meetings and I waited until the 10 days were almost up. I sure had no clue what AA was going to do to me, but I was sure it would be humiliating and painful. Maybe they would berate me publicly. I was at the turning point, either find a meeting or run away. I found a meeting far from my home and super early in the morning. It was the most significant event of my entire life. That turning point was perfect for me. I got a Big Book, a service position, a sponsor and a home group all in the first hour and I have never had to look back.

I believe God has given me two guardian angels to watch over me, one day shift and one night shift. They both would like to retire.

August 20

A SMOKING HOLE

Every year when I read about "First A Foundation" I laugh out loud. It is a nice parable, but I had to start with a smoking hole deep below the surface. It was nice and dark, no sunrise, no sunset and no way out. The hole had that yellow "police crime scene" tape and blinking caution lights that said "do not enter." I was all alone singing the blues at the bottom of the pit I had dug for myself. Songs like, *Ain't No Sunshine When She's Gone*. Before I could even think about a foundation, I needed to dig myself out (with the help of my Higher Power) and fill in the hole. I had to pound a lot of sand and mud. I had six lawyers to handle: court appearances, financial ruin, job firings, medical problems. I went to a lot of meetings, got in service, worked with my sponsor, shovel full by shovel full I, with a lot of help, filled in the hole so I could lay a slab of concrete the readings talk about. It took about a year to pull down the yellow caution tape and allow others to enter the construction site. Step work in progress then.

Now 8,000 days later the house has been built on a solid foundation of Step work, trials and errors, setbacks and victories. I would like to think my house of sobriety is earthquake proof, hurricane and tsunami protected and comfortable at the same time. Room by room the house became a mansion, four stories up the steps to the penthouse (read the 4th Dimension). The house has been decorated by the guys I had the privilege to sponsor. I have a beautiful view of every sunrise from my 4th floor perch. Now the house is pretty old so it requires daily maintenance and care. My 11th Step meeting with prayer and meditation is my maintenance hour and attitude adjustment. My daily 9 a.m. meeting is my "home improvement" program where I get new ideas to enhance the property. I live in a tough neighborhood (a lot of alcoholics) and occasionally there is a drive by shooting (read resentments the #1 killer) and I have to patch some holes but the structure always remains intact (read sober).

I can still smell the smoke from that smoking hole I started with and I keep that memory green so I don't fall back in the pit.

August 21

PERSONALITIES

Life would be pretty boring if we were all principle and no personality. Yes, principle first then personality. All of us are a product of our upbringing, our core values, our religion (if any at all), our experience (drunk and sober), our work history, our country of birth. So, we are certainly unique. Nobody is exactly like you. No two personalities are the same. Now the problem is to relate with creatures very different than us. Sort of like rock polishing, as we run into our fellow earth travelers. We can try to dominate others with our personality or adjust to others so we can communicate evenly and be of help to others if necessary. I know I will not like everybody and as much as I would like to be popular, I know not everyone will like me. There is a guy in the fellowship that hasn't spoken to me in 3 years and I see him every day he comes to a meeting. I am OK with that. His personality is everything I don't want to be. It is true what you don't like in others is what you don't like in yourself. He is sober so that is more important than saying hello to me.

The Steps help me develop principles that become part of my everyday life. I have been at it long enough that it comes naturally and I don't have to look at a cheat sheet to see if I am following all the good principles I have been taught in AA. However, morning meditation is part of daily attitude adjustment to all the personalities I have encountered in the last 24 hours. I review how I handled my interface with others. Was my ego showing? Was I unselfish? Did I give the other person due respect? Did I dominate the conversation? I notice I tend to gravitate toward happy positive people because they bring my spirits up. The grouch will sink my attitude in a heartbeat. To follow the noble principle of helping others sometimes means finding a way to accommodate a disagreeable person. I have learned to stuff my personality in a sock in order to be of assistance. Thanks to the 12 Steps I have undergone a complete personality makeover.

I don't like the old "me" and now I can still be a character in the game based on solid principles.

August 22

PEACE

How can we talk about peace when there are so many wars around the world ongoing? Almost every day somebody opens fire in a church, movie theater, or a shopping mall. These events, as terrible as they are, are out of our control. If we let world events bother us and ruin our attitude we will never be at peace. The whole world has been going to hell in a handbasket ever since I was born during WWII and will be forever. In my morning spiritual work out, I pass out the duties for the day, wars and shootings I leave up to God. Inner peace and happiness that's my job. I got fired from my position as master of the universe. Now I am only in charge of my little piece of the world. I remind myself of my powerlessness and how little I can do to change people, places and things. As I do my 10th Step and 11th Step I am at peace with who I am, where I am, and what I am doing for the next 24 hours. That inner peace I feel is the only peace I have control over. I enjoy the calm of the early morning at soak up the quiet. God has blessed me with a full basket so there are no missing parts to my peace.

If you are not at peace then maybe it is time to work on the blockage to your inner peace. Wreckage of the past, unresolved relationship problems, restitution not made, fears of all kinds can rob us of peace and joy. This time of year, I take time to clean my closet both the physical kind and my spiritual one. I pull out my stack of paperwork (if you don't watch paperwork carefully, it multiplies at night) and throw away things that were important in 1976 but are now useless. I update my "croak" file so when I pass on it won't be a pain to my family to unravel. When the time comes to check out, I will be at peace and I want everybody connected to me to be at peace. I have been involved in cleaning up the mess my fellow vets have left behind for the last 4 years. I have learned what situations are dangerous to my peace and avoid them like the plague. I have found doing random acts of kindness every day enhance my sense of peacefulness. I will walk a mile for a smile.

Peace of mind and heart I have found to be good for your health. Simplicity is so peaceful and rewarding.

August 23

DOWN TALKING

A good rule is "don't talk down to an alcoholic" one of my favorite topics. I read a book in college that changed my life and the way I communicate. Most of you have heard of it: *I'm OK You're OK* by Dr. Harris (recommended). At the time I read it I had been in the military for 7 years and I talked "up" to people who outranked me and "down" to those I outranked. I learned I need not talk up or down but communicate straight across as equals. That fits our program perfectly because we have no rank in AA and length of sobriety is meaningless in communicating one person to another. I talk to my kids as if they we were the same age and not as parent to child. They appreciate that trait in old Pop. It is really important when working with another alcoholic not to look down my nose because I have some long-term sobriety. I only have today based on my spiritual condition just like the guy I am helping. We are partners in recovery. It is not boss and rookie. Making a new guy feel inferior has no benefit whatever. I like the fact no one is better or worse than another in our fellowship.

My rule is not to talk down to anybody anywhere. It is so much easier to find a comfortable way of communicating that doesn't change person to person. Add a smile with you communicating and magic happens. You can talk heart to heart instead of head to head or better yet ego to ego. It is one of my character defects that I just don't like to be addressed in a condescending manner. I usually retaliate but I am getting better. I have learned to accept some folks talk down to me but it is nothing personal, they talk down to everybody. So that's the way they are. This guy in AA was chairperson for a project and I was a committee member. He talked down to me for a whole year but to his credit, he allowed me to be the MC of the event without screwing with me. I had a lunch for the entire committee but he was too arrogant to show. His loss. He will be talking down to everybody until the day he dies. I tend to make friendships with those who communicate as equals. Our fellowship has no tolerance for preachers and demigods. You still hear crap like "I spilled more than you ever drank."

If you learn to communicate from the heart, the message will have a good opportunity to get through.

August 24

AMBITION

I have noticed that my definitions of words have changed over time in recovery. Words like humility, ambition, serenity are all different now than 20+ years back. My entire life I was driven by blind ambition, I would do whatever it took to climb the ladder of success, even if it meant putting myself in harm's way to advance. I would focus on the next goal of the climb and make it the top priority. When I look back at my behavior my achievements are all tainted by the wreckage of my self-centeredness and selfish pursuits. Yes, I advanced. And yes, I did earn a lot of accolades. But at what cost? When I look back at my past, I can see I was drunk with ambition. One more rung on the ladder was never enough, there was always new dragon to slay. A monster ego was part of the equation to success and unbridled ambition. Thank God the ambition machine has been retired for good. No more hoops to jump through, no more tests of strength. Just another bozo on the bus.

I still have fire and ambition today but it has a whole different thrust and definition today. I have ambition for my kids and grandkids, my sponsees, my home group, I have subtracted ego from the equation and the process of the 12 Steps light my afterburners. I have no more bells to answer, no more jumping for the telephone on one ring. I have reordered my priorities to align myself with some new principles that include love first and foremost over selfish wants. Words like humility and serenity are part of my everyday language, before those words had zero meaning. I ask the question "Who will this help?" before I launch out on a project. If I have a selfish motive hidden away in my actions, I try to nip it in the bud. I still have the adrenaline rush in my ambitions as I make the way down the Road of Happy Destiny.

I have always had a lot of airspeed but lacked direction. Now my Higher Power points the way and I provide the throttle.

August 25

WORRY

That the birds of worry and care

fly above your head

This you cannot change

But that they build nests in your hair

This you can prevent

~ Chinese Proverb

Worry is a normal human activity but when it becomes paralyzing it is dangerous. I went through a long 6-month period of "worry" with my close friend relapsing again and again. The yo-yo effect wore me out with worry. He will relapse, and when he does, I worry he won't come out alive. When I evaluate my worry, it is really projecting into the future which we know is a waste of time. It is also concern over things out of my control. I know that I am powerless over people, places and things but still I worry. If I could learn to care without the worry part that would be a neat trick, aye?

In my youth my household was a "house of worry." My father called my mother a "worry wart" and she remained the Queen of Worry for her entire 90 years. Her final act was to kick the hospital orderly for removing her wig. She always was worried about how she looked even on her deathbed. We grew up with "what will the neighbors think?" I would like to think that worry has taken a back seat along with guilt, fear and intimidation in my life of recovery. As I look at the "Promises" I see not only have they come true for me but that the absence of worry is a big part of the Promises. Worry can rob all your waking hours and cause you to lose sleep. I know if I am really doing the Steps, I leave the worry part over to my Higher Power. Everything will turn out the way God intends it no matter how much I worry.

The birds of worry are still there, but since I have no more hair, there is no chance they can build a nest.

August 26

SUGGESTIONS

Most people do not like to be told what to do. But for us alcoholics who sorely need adult supervision, we really hate to be told anything. In my own personal life, I made it a point to be a "rebel without a cause" and fight the rules and regulations. Hard to believe I spent a full career in the military with regulations even on the shape of a mustache. Not only was my mustache out of limits but so was my flying and military bearing. I made a fine art of pushing the envelope without getting into enough trouble to get me kicked out. Funny thing, I got away with it and thought that was my destiny to be wild. Of course, the booze lubricated the machine. Our Founders knew about guys like us and did not lay down a bunch or rules and commandments. They presented us with "suggestions" like the 12 Steps and for me? The attraction of the members who went before me inspired me to take the 12 "suggestions." After a lifetime of fighting the establishment, I followed the book and did what was suggested to me. For example: "If you want to get sober, we suggest you stop drinking!" Good idea, aye?

In terms of a parachute use, if you are going to jump out of an airplane, they suggest you pull the ripcord on your chute. I wore a parachute on my back off and on for 30 years and I only came close to using it once. Wherever I went I always visited the parachute rigging shop and introduced myself to the guy who packed my chute. I knew that my life might depend on a well packed chute, so I thanked the person who packed mine. Nowadays I thank my Higher Power for packing my parachute in my morning meditation and am happy to report the 12 "suggestions" are a part of my life. My life has changed as a result and am super happy customer. I have quit fighting city hall and everything else. War over.

Thanks to a great packing job, I have enjoyed soft landings every day for a long time.

August 27

REALITY

Wouldn't it be nice to live in Disneyland 24/7 and stay in Fantasyland forever? When I was drinking, reality was so far off the table I couldn't recognize fact from fiction. I think the honesty we strive for in our program is tied to our ability to deal with reality. When I was hitting my bottom, I would begin my day at 6 a.m. by turning on the TV, tune out the rest of the world and put responsibility on permanent hold. I was a sports fan, in reality I was a drink fan so the beer would be in my hand with a ballgame on the tube to give me some authenticity to my drunken behavior. I would stay on self-imposed house arrest drinking, because DUI's are real, work had a bunch of sober people asking real questions I couldn't answer. In short, reality sucked. Life was as I imagined it to be, fantasy not as it really was. You can escape reality only so long until it comes knocking at the door and ringing your phone until you answer. When I hit that turning point was I going to live or was I going to die, the truth hurt so bad. My first meeting of AA was a reality check big time. Thank you, God.

The 12 Steps have a reality factor in each one.

Fact: I am an alcoholic.

Fact: My life was unmanageable (stated nicely).

Fact: I couldn't do it by myself, I needed help.

Fact: I needed to find a Power outside myself, let's call Him God.

Fact: I needed to repair the damage done by my drinking.

Fact: I needed to inventory myself and find the real me.

266

Fact: I needed to be of service and help others, carry the message.

Today I can embrace reality and enjoy it for what it is warts and all. I have been able to find realities that were stuffed in a closet for 30 years, connect with relatives that were off my radar for decades. It is what it is. My days of running away from responsibility and reality are over. My daily prayer and meditation are a reality check I have come to cherish.

August 28

HUMILITY & HUMOR

I have come a long way from being in the world's most elite organization as world's best fighter pilot just short of being a general. None of the hype was true and it is now ancient history. The big office is gone, the staff has left for greener pastures and nobody salutes me anymore. I learned right away in AA my former status is of no interest to the fellowship. My actions in the program and in service positions were the new focus. In AA there is no rank so that works for my humility. Everybody's date of rank is today, that works very good on those who have decades of sobriety, to keep them from becoming demigods and bleeding deacons. If you need applause don't look for it in AA, go join a theater group and audition for a part. Nothing is beneath my dignity in AA, cleaning coffee cups, picking up dog poop in front of the meeting room, putting out chairs, cleaning the toilet, all good service work for the group. Humility is not being less than or more than but just being me and being in service. I get right sized every morning when I seek God's will, not mine.

This is of course, a serious program of life or death but we can laugh about our shortcomings and failings. Part of humility is humor as part of my sharing. I find we are all the biggest joke in town. A very funny guy, Victor Borge, said the shortest distance between two people is laughter. I not only agree, but in my experience, think it is a great equalizer. The playing field is fair, flat and even in humor. But some healthy rules apply to humor. I never make someone else the butt of my little jokes, I only refer to my trips and pratfalls. My past is a treasure chest of funny experiences. Real growth can be measured in how far I have come from comic stupidity of the past, to a useful member of society. When I work with a sponsee if I can't make him laugh it is very difficult for me to gain understanding. I always tell my home group I am very proud of my humility. Never understood why they laugh at that.

My first service position at 2 years old was to take out the garbage. Today I still hold that same position. Talk about a glass ceiling and no upward mobility.

August 29

IN THE ZONE

Some readings talk about not praying, letting the program slip and getting angry with God. I am blessed to never experienced these things but, I am not able to stay on a spiritual high all the time. I do not forget to pray because I don't forget to breathe and eat. Not praying would be the same as holding my breath and starving to death. Even though I pray every day the intensity and actual concentration varies greatly. I catch myself reading my prayers, but my mind begins to wander. My mind has no clutch and is like a puppy on the loose with no boundaries. I have to stop myself and start over when this happens and try to get back on track. Sometimes you are standing in the Sunlight of The Spirit and some clouds come by and it gets dark. Just like life itself everything has ups and downs or cycles. Spiritual work is not straight lined either. Our moods are certainly not always bright and cheerful but they are pretty positive most of the time if we are doing this thing right.

What I have found in my experience is knowing I have cycles I try to ride the waves. Just yesterday someone remarked about how happy I looked. That's because I was able to work with some other alcoholics and did some good I think. I was super happy in my heart that I was doing the next right thing and was out of myself and doing Step 12 work. The rest of the day I did a dozen things that needed attention. I call these times being "In the Zone" just like a ball player who goes crazy and scores record points in record time. Same feeling. When I get on one of these "highs" I try to do as much as possible while I am in the zone before it passes. And it will pass just like when I am depressed. "This Too Will Pass" is on the wall at every meeting I go to. The flip side of this is to bring myself out of a pity pot when my expectations are not met. I do extra prayers and extra readings sometimes or call a good friend who makes me laugh. All my problems are luxury ones, I don't stay in a down cycle very long. Sometimes I can pull out of a dive in a matter of seconds. I know backing off my spiritual path is dangerous so I stay out of the danger zone. (Play music from "Top Gun.")

My message is to learn your cycles and use them to your advantage, press your bets when you are winning and know when to fold.

August 30

LONELINESS

"Almost without exception, alcoholics are tortured by loneliness."

This reading today is so true. Imagine going to bars to fill that void of loneliness. Insane. Bars make money on alcoholics like me. They don't pay the overhead with the guy who sips one beer for 4 hours and watches the ballgame. Guys like me come in and order a beer, a Bloody Mary and a martini. The bartender puts out 3 napkins and looks for my group. He soon discovers I am a group of one. You see I want something spicy to take the cotton out of my mouth (tabasco) I am thirsty, and I want to get to the serious drinking soon (gin). So why waste time ordering one by one. Makes sense aye? Then all smart bars have peanuts and pretzels to feed the thirst so you order more. Then they put mirrors behind the bar at all angles because they know all about loneliness in alcoholics. You can sit there and look at yourself so you won't be so lonely. The bartender usually will cut you off if you start an argument with the guy in the mirror. "What are you looking at pal?" If you are lucky there will be a fellow drunk and you can be entertained by nonsense. Better yet you isolate in four walls and drink all by yourself. Pathetic.

I was alone because of my actions and sickness. I pushed everyone away from me yet I wanted company. I didn't like myself or what I was doing to myself but I was stuck with only me. Yikes, a dilemma with no solution. I am so far from loneliness now it is hard to remember what it was like. I used to feel alone in a big group of people. The answer to that problem was to juice up before entering the crowd. Now I am comfortable all the time, alone or in any gathering. I love my alone time in the morning while I confer with my Higher Power and pray. In fact, I need alone time every day. I go to my 9 a.m. meeting almost every day so I certainly am not alone with that bunch of pirates. I have one-on-one time with my wife and my sponsees and that is treasure time. HALT, don't get hungry, angry, lonely and tired. They usually all go together but this way of life prevents HALT.

For more than 20 years I have not experienced one moment of loneliness but take one drink and I will go back to those horrible dark days of incomprehensible demoralization.

August 31

ABSOLUTE REQUIREMENT FOR WILLINGNESS

Our founders were so wise in designing the 12 Steps as "suggestions," and ease into the hard to do steps very carefully. You never have to interface with another human being until Step 5. Of course, Step 4 is preparing for the hurdle of facing someone eye to eye and sharing your life. Step 8, the focus of this month, is simple enough in part. Make a list. No big deal, right? You aren't doing anything with the list just yet, just writing it all down like in Step 4. The focus of Step 8 is willingness. This is one of those open-ended qualities which is hard to measure. The HOW of our program Honesty Open mindedness and Willingness have no ceiling, no upper limit and no measure. So how much is a pound of willingness? Can you buy some? Can you borrow some? No, but you can pray for more willingness. None of us are 100% willing in all categories. We need to evaluate our willingness to change, to put the list into action coming up in Step 9. This list of persons harmed is just a piece of waste paper without the willingness to take action.

Step 9 is the first step anyone other than your 5th Step person is involved. This is a giant leap coming up that may require some painful personal contacts. Step 8 is our chance to prepare ourselves for the task ahead by focusing on our willingness first. Those people on your list were harmed for sure but you were harmed also. This step is considering others, but the step is about you becoming a complete human being again. It is unfinished business required for a full recovery. My goal is to be the best person possible, so I need to be willing to take the necessary steps, no matter how painful or costly. Little pieces of my soul were scattered all over God's green earth before I did Step 8 and 9. It required some research to find some and a plane ride to see others. When I looked at my list I also realized there was different weight attached to those on my list. A simple "I am sorry for what I did" just does not cut the mustard for abuse and harms done over years and years. I must be willing to examine my inventory before launching into Step 9.

I am happy to report soul retrieval through the amends portion of the Steps. I will be making amends for the rest of my life.

Willingness is one more item on my gratitude list and I hope on yours also.

September 1

BYE BYE MATERIAL WORLD

It is no secret in order to reach new spiritual heights you have to put aside material trappings. The ultimate in Buddha's nirvana is a state of selflessness completely detached from material possessions. In my life I have known some very wealthy people and even one billionaire. All of them found life difficult and were unhappy. The responsibility that goes with high positions and wealth is very heavy. The billionaire wanted to use his wealth for a very noble cause, to free American POWs held in

North Vietnam but he was frustrated for many years in his mission. He was a very angry, unhappy human being. I have a good friend who made four-star general, the highest rank in the military. He confided to me he was so unhappy he retired as soon as he could. His life was not his own, he had to answer the phone in one ring 24 hours a day. He had to suit up and work about 16 hours a day, travel about 20 days a month. Ugh. Most of us come from nations that measure success by wealth. Wow, is that totally wrong or what? You can't buy happiness as we have learned by personal experience.

I look at all material things God has given us to enjoy life as stewardship. I am a steward of the car, the house, the clothes I wear, all of it through the grace of God. I don't own these things, in fact I don't own anything but my soul, my thoughts and my actions. The material stuff is on loan for my use temporarily. I came in naked, no hair no teeth, and I will go out naked no hair no teeth. Oh, I could buy a Rolex but I would rather spend the money on my grandson in college. I don't need to know the time from a 10K timepiece. I don't care what time it is and it's displayed on my cheap phone, the TV, the bank and just about everywhere. If you drive a Bentley and it breaks down in the desert it is a piece of junk. A new car is fun for a couple of days but soon it is just a ride. The 12 Steps get us to the point of helping others and a level of happiness beyond our best dreams. When you are helping someone else, giving in some way, you forget about your "stuff." You might as well kiss your favorite possessions goodbye because sooner or later they will all be gone. That is my point about decluttering your life. I have only 3 keys and I don't own the car, the house or the mailbox that the keys open. I could not be happier with the gifts God has given me. I have all I need so I want nothing more.

Financial wellbeing follows spiritual progress every time, no exceptions.

September 2

ONE TWO THREE WALTZ

After having a nice visit with my "grandpa" sponsor I realized a missing part of my early program. My sponsor, my sponsee and "grandpa" sponsor used to chair a beginner's meeting in the military hospital in Honolulu. We did Steps 1,2 and 3 every week over and over. It never got boring and I learned you can never get enough of 1-2-3. Back to basics every week was part of my program for 8-9 years and it did me a world of good. We all know there are no "graduates" from our program, so hardening our foundation pays big dividends down the road. One of my biggest lessons in AA came from doing Step 2 for this beginner's meeting for years. I came to believe.

I keep coming back and I keep believing. IMHO if you don't believe in God you need to go to the Grand Canyon. I went for the first time on the ground (flew over it many times) and the awe of centuries of God's handiwork took my breath away. To see the earth sliced open 5000 feet deep and the colors of millions of years exposed for inspection make one grasp perspective. Our lives only last one minute in the grand scheme and our size is but a grain of sand. Hard to think we are the center of the universe when you stand on the edge of this natural site. GOD great outdoors. Doing Steps 1-2-3 keep me "right sized" and humble. All the growth steps of 10, 11 and 12 all have the foundation of those first three necessary steps.

At one of my meetings if someone has come for their very first meeting, we make Step One the topic and my battery gets charges every time. I love to be at someone's first meeting.

September 3

GRATITUDE LIST

I love to ask folks who have been sober awhile if they have a gratitude list. "Sure, of course I do." OK can I see it? Then all kinds of answers:

273

oh, it's back in my other home, I made one years ago, it's in my head yada, yada. In other words, their list is largely theoretical and for sure they don't use it on a regular basis. Once a year in my home group they get my gratitude list pitch. I show them my list on a 3 X 5 card all 64 items. They can see it is used, worn and real. It's not back home it is in my hand ready for inspection. (a few of them have the guts to read my list). Then I provide a handful of 3 X 5 cards and invite them to make a list right now, today. I always get a couple of takers and some years later they thank me for getting them into a gratitude list. We can only handle one attitude at a time so let that be "An attitude of gratitude." It is impossible to be resentful and grateful at the same time.

When I wake up at sunrise or before every morning, I am usually in a deep dream in some place like Laos or Afghanistan. First, I am surprised I am alive and grateful for life itself. Then I realize I am in Thailand. Wow, this is exactly the place I want to be. More gratitude. This is all before I do my 11 Step every morning. My well-worn gratitude list comes out of my prayer book and sits beside my coffee cup. Thirty-six items that are priceless, blessing from God, the fruit of sobriety, the reward of doing all 12 Steps. How can I possibly think anything is missing in my life? My basket runneth over. Stuff like love, loyalty, freedom, serenity, mobility, health. What store can you buy any of those things? This list is a daily part of my recovery routine, it is real and it works wonders to graphically see the long list of gifts I enjoy daily. It is amazing to me so few people use their list. Why make it if you are going to forget it?

When I am done with my morning prayer and meditation, I hold up my list before I put it back and know I can light a match to the list if I pick up that first drink. Gone.

September 4

MAINTENANCE

My AA grandmother Alice taught me not to refer to the last three Steps as maintenance steps. You will find some literature that says just that and you will hear it in meetings during sharing. Alice used to say, "Mike, your car needs maintenance. If you don't do maintenance the car will quit on you. You and your program are not like a car. Your car doesn't grow, in fact it is dying with age and losing value with time. Your program needs to grow, or it will die. Those last three steps are growth steps." Remember my old bit about the Steps? Give up, own up, clean up and grow up. Over the years I can still hear her voice preaching the importance of growth. I know in my former life I used to say, "If it's not broke don't fix it." Well in my first year of sobriety I applied this incorrect axiom to my program. I was in service, enjoying my six meetings a week, I went into cruise control and didn't fix it because it wasn't broke. Oh yes it was. I am an alcoholic and I am broken no matter how many years I accumulate. I need to fix it daily. (If I was a car, I would be a Ford=Fix Or Repair Daily.)

After learning a hard lesson of resting on yesterday's sobriety and not growing, I was moving backwards. Either I am moving away from my last drink or I am moving toward my next drink. I am moving whether I like it or not. Morning meditation, prayer and inventory starts the growth process every day. My attitude needs adjusting daily and sometimes hourly. The thing about growth is it has no upper limit, no finish line. The more I learn the more I learn how much I don't know. In my life I spent about 35 years with zero growth until body, mind and spirit were totally trashed. This sobriety path of following the 12 Steps has restored all those broken parts and made them better than ever before. I have a lot of catching up to do for those 35 years I was somewhere between.

September 5

CONTROVERSY

I try not to cause controversy, I don't buy into controversial situations, I am not in the controversy business. First, I am no good at it. Some people love a good verbal fight because they think they are good at it. They have a come-back for every argument. They have a desire to be right. I reserve the right to be wrong. My opinion is absolutely worthless, especially if I don't have the power to change whatever I am contesting. I respect other opinions without commenting on them. I certainly don't push my opinions on somebody else. I know I can't change them or their mind. Life is so much easier without conflict. I would much rather have a good laugh than acid reflux from anger and resentment. I remember the old days when I was the expert on every subject. Now I try to act as if everyone is enlightened except me. I know only a little and just enough to be dangerous.

Discussions on politics, religion, etc.... are dead ends for me. Nobody comes out a "winner." Why waste time talking about things completely out of your control? My friends insist on arguing about one political party over another. Who cares? I have relatives that want me to sign up and pledge money for causes that don't concern me. I remember when I was a big campaigner to get our POW's back from the Hanoi Hilton prison. I was insane in my behavior and angry Congress would not answer my letters and I almost lost my career fighting for this cause. I shunned my family and my job in righteous frenzy. Turns out the POWs came home in due time at great expense to the entire country of Vietnam. The only campaign I involve myself in today is working with a fellow alcoholic to help him find sobriety. No controversy there. When I feel the urge to join in an argument, I examine my motives and I find ego at the root of my urge. I know to shut the f*** up!

September 6

IN THE MORNING

On page 164 in the Big Book it states, "Ask Him in your morning meditation..." and in the 11th Step discussion it says the same thing page 86. "On awakening let us think about the 24 hours ahead. We consider our plans for the day. Before we begin, we ask God to direct our thinking." Why the morning? Why not when you feel like it or evening before sleep? All I know for sure is my experience. When I first started, I decided to follow directions for the first time in my life. I spent my entire life fighting City Hall, regulations, rules, laws and I was taught from the very first meeting to quit fighting and go with the flow, follow the herd. Since my old way did not work, I decided to give Good Orderly Direction (GOD) a try. I was also taught we have a "spiritual bank account" and the bank opens early for deposits. Now, today, after several thousands of awakenings in a row, it works wonders for me and my recovery.

Why? In my experience, my mind can spin up to 7500 RPM in a heartbeat. I stop my mind from spinning by my 8 prayers and 7 books I read every morning. It is my mind control. It gets me out of my own head and into some spiritual writings. It fills my awakening brain with hundreds of positive thoughts before the crush of the world becomes part of my day. I absolutely love early mornings, no TV, no phone calls, no dogs or even birds just yet, just quiet and sunrise. Ahhh. This time allows my heart to have a voice before my head starts talking. I know my heart is good and my brain is very defective. I can't hear God, my Higher Power communicate with me if I am talking. I force my brain to shut up. I start my day with about one hour of reading, prayer and meditation without fail no matter where I am. The answers to my questions always come in the morning just like it says in the Big Book. I can verify the BB is 100% right on by my own experience. I know following the directions from those who have gone before me will lead me down the Road of Happy Destiny.

If you are waking up to CNN, you are filling your mind with stuff you have no control over. Try quiet mornings, you will like it.

September 7

MAN OF FAITH

When I was in Catholic grammar school, my first service position was President of the Altar Boys. I was so proud, but I soon found out that it was a scheduling task more than anything else. I was stuck with the mass nobody wanted at 6:30 a.m. plus I would get a call 10 minutes before some service because one of my boys didn't show up. I had to get on my bicycle and get to St. Leo's stat. I knew down deep I was a rotten little bastard, so the next step was to be a priest. I wanted to be a man of Faith with the hopes I would straighten out as I matured. Looking back, I can see I was an alcoholic who had not yet found the bottle. Well, they found me out real quick in the seminary and I got defrocked. Had I become a priest I am sure I would be an alcoholic one and probably cause a scandal with a divorcee in counseling. I got sent home with "An extreme case of worldliness" and dropped my connection to Faith altogether. Faith and spirituality never came to my mind for the next 35 years.

I tried to be a badass but my buddy already in a gang got stabbed so that seemed not too good a route. The well-known drinking club called the Air Force was the ultimate answer for me. I ran away from home leaving a mess behind that took 40 years to hatch. (another story for later) I found the bottle to match my character real fast. I got to be a badass in a way by being an egotistical fighter pilot and a good guy when necessary to get promoted and drink with wild abandon. Perfect. It worked for a while but when I reached a high point of fame, power and promotions, the beauty beside me in a big blue Caddie, I could not drown out the emptiness in my soul. I was missing faith, spirituality, honesty, integrity and character. It wasn't until I made into AA that I even thought about God, faith and a spiritual path. All new territory for me but slowly my fears were cancelled by my ever-growing faith in my Higher Power.

I did become a man of faith after all but without the backwards collar. Celibacy would have been a problem for sure.

September 8

WHO CAN I FIX TODAY?

When I was a young dad I tried to "fix" my kids into a mold of my design. I envisioned greatness for my children. The more I tried to fix them the more they fought me. I caught my daughter smoking at age 13, in fact she burnt a hole in her jacket pocket trying to hide a lit cigarette. I said, "I'll fix this." I took the entire pack and tore off the filters and made her smoke the whole pack from the fuzzy end. Well she is 50 years old now and still smokes every day. That worked well aye? I had college lined up for another daughter and she got pregnant. The stories go on but the point is I could no more "fix" my kids than the man in the moon. Guess what, they all turned into super stars in different areas all by their own doing with no help from dear old dad. I learned I cannot change anybody against their will no matter my relationship to the person. It takes such effort to tinker with other people's behavior and most likely you will not like the results.

Who can I fix today? Me and only me. I can change my attitude and my priorities There is enough work there to keep me busy for the rest of my life. If I see somebody that needs fixing, I say, "not me" and let them find their own path without my direction. I am out of the boss mode, the parent mode, out of the leadership role. I need to sweep my side of the street and stay out of other folks' inventory. If what they do upsets me too much, I stay out of their way because no matter what I do they are not going to change. If a relationship has gone sour, I can say "I release you with love" and exit stage right. In my morning "tune up" I review my inventory and maybe there is nothing which needs fixing every day but for sure there are always things I can do better. I can seek out a long-lost friend, write a thank you letter, go visit a sick friend. I try to find at least one thing I can improve on.

Some people make me angry. It is not their problem, it's mine. I can fix that.

September 9

ANGER

"Anger is the dubious luxury of normal people," so if you are normal go ahead and rage on. I know I am not normal; I am an alcoholic and anger is very dangerous. We alcoholics do everything to excess, it is natural that we take a normal human reaction like anger and go way too far with it. In my experience, I start small and start building a list of wrongs that make me angry until I explode with some insane behavior. Once my anger is out of the box there is no return. The worst kind of anger is justified anger. You know you are right and setting things straight becomes an obsession. Knowing myself very well I have learned to stay away from angry people and stupid institutions which defy logic. I can feel the anger in me when it starts and I take myself into a "time out" and let my heart talk to my head. Is blowing my stack going to help the situation? No, is the answer I get without fail. Can I change people, places and things? No, of course not. So why blow a gasket and hurt myself?

From my background, if you shoot at me, I will shoot back. I had to toss out that old behavior real quick. Buddha taught me when an opponent comes at you with a thrust you simply step aside and let the thrust go by and not engage. Very hard for me to do. If somebody pushes me, I instinctively push back. I have learned not to join in the dance of death. When somebody throws you the ball you don't have to catch it. Now being a doormat is not acceptable either but picking your battles becomes an art form. It takes a cool head and if I have a knee jerk reaction for every situation, I lose the battle. I pray for the GAP, God Authorized Pause. The longer the GAP the better. Sort of like counting to 10. In my case 100 would be better. There is a guy in the fellowship who has berated me openly in meetings, come between me and my sponsees, takes too long in his shares at the expense of the group conscience etc... You can see me building a list to fuel my anger toward this guy who is a detriment to AA in my opinion. Can I change him? Absolutely not. I accept him for what he is, and I can try to set an opposing example by the way I conduct myself. I should thank him.

All of us have a flash point and being aware of it helps prevent hate and discontent.

September 10

GREED RULES

We focus on the addiction of drugs and alcohol, but greed is also addictive. Greed can cause an appetite never to be satisfied. The accumulation of wealth and possessions take us further away from the spiritual world. Usually greed has an ego factor and a fear factor. I never had a chance to be into power and greed because I was too poor to collect nice possessions and stealing stuff was frowned on in my chosen profession. Later in my career, I was able to buy a brand-new Caddie off the showroom floor. I told everybody it was my prize for surviving Afghanistan, but the truth was it was all ego. I felt like I had arrived, but you can only adjust the power seats so many times and drive it only as fast as all the rest of junk cars on the road. Soon the "prize" is just a vehicle to get from A to B and the warm fuzzy of the first day wears off fast. The Caddie hit bottom the same time I did. My recovery car was a 15-year-old Chevette with a broken window but it went to meetings and that's all I needed. I never had the urge to get a luxury car or a luxury anything after I picked a spiritual path rather than a material one.

There is popular movie where the lead actor gives an amazing speech on the benefits of greed. It is a power to be reckoned with for sure, but it implies your acquisitions are someone else's loss. Greed can be ruthless, harmful besides rubbing all our principles the wrong direction. I have known a lot of super rich people in my travels. They all have a security problem. They double lock everything including computers, phones, houses, offices, boats etc.... Most have a bodyguard. My Higher Power is my bodyguard and I only have three keys in my pocket. The power people are so afraid of losing what they have and not making the next conquest they are fear driven along with the greed. They hide assets for taxes as an art form and let us poor folks pick up the tab. The biggest thing they all have in common is they are not happy. Back to the old rule we all know; giving makes you happy not taking. The lure of wealth looks so attractive until you get there.

Greed rules lives just like alcohol, but our program has put us on a new spiritual plane that pulls us away from shiny objects and gets us closer to God.

September 11

NO STRINGS ATTACHED

I remember praying to God when my fat was in the fire and saying, "Dear God get me out of this mess please and I promise I will be good for the rest of my life." Imagine trying to bargain with God? Of course, as soon as I was out of trouble, I forgot my promise and got drunk. In my former life before sobriety, everything had a string. I expected a return on all my actions, Whatever I did had a string attached and I would pull the string when necessary. This latest reading about love with no strings attached, made me think for a couple of days. I realized that my life now has no strings attached, not only to love, but to everything in my life. It makes living so much easier not having to keep book on "returns owed to me." My prayers now are of gratitude to God for all the blessings I have way beyond what I deserve. How can I ask for anything? God gives me what I need so I need no "wish list."

When it comes to love, I found giving freely with no expectations prevents resentments and declutters my brain. I used to sit in front of the TV set drinking my beer on Father's Day and do a slow burn over the kids who did not send a card or call me on "my day." I would not enjoy the phone calls I did get or appreciate the love they expressed. The secret is, have a lot of kids and some of them will love you and some won't remember birthdays and Father's Day but that's okay. I missed a lot of their birthdays and Christmases when I was in some foreign country I didn't belong in. Now my life is full of love, unconditional love. I have been in service to AA from Day 1 and I expect no applause or thanks. It's a good thing I have that attitude because my rewards have been in the act of giving and not in thanks. Once in a blue moon I get some thanks for my service and that's a plus and a surprise.

When I write these little ramblings, I hope you feel the love and you need not respond. Go ahead and hit that delete button it won't hurt my feelings.

September 12

MAKE IT SIMPLE

There is a guy who claims us alcoholics like to pole vault over mouse turds. In other words, we complicate stuff that does not need to so difficult. We like to think we are complex characters with many complicated problems. We forget we are the ones who caused the chaos in the first place. I used to give a 4th Step workshop in Hawaii and one guy wanted to know what kind of paper he needed then what kind of writing instrument. Clearly, he was looking to avoid the action. I told him use the Nike slogan, Just Do It! Last I heard he never did get sober. Most of the obstacles to our recovery are imagined and not real. Driven by all kinds of fear we put up "I can't" signs on the road to progress. I suggest knocking those signs down and try. Leave the results up to God.

Remember my bit on the thief of time? Well the flipside is, don't let people, places and things steal your time. Simplify your life by bypassing the folks eating up your time. You need those minutes and hours for progress. How many hours did I sit in a bar with a bunch of idiots trying to solve the problems of the world? I have wasted years and years in the company of people who didn't care about me or what I had to say. One of my goals in life is to declutter my life. I have reduced a bulging 4 drawer filing cabinet down to 12-inch stack. Mostly important documents for when I die. (I don't want to complicate my wife's life either.) I only have three keys, no wallet, one car, one house, no job. Very uncomplicated.

I stay out of family drama and work on staying out of AA drama. Keep It Simple is a slogan on the wall in our meeting room. Dr. Bob suggested we keep it simple so that's good enough for me.

Making complicated stuff simple is real creativity.

September 13

DESIGN FOR LIVING

When I first read the line "A new life has been given us or, if you prefer (a design for living) that really works," from page 28 in the Big Book. I had to think about it for a long time until the lights came on. And yes, it's 100% true in my own experience. This is a very powerful sentence. My life before had no plan at all. I just went from one crisis to the next disaster. There was no plan, no blueprint, just damage control. When I was a young troop, new to the military prior to becoming an alcoholic, my mother asked for "my plan." I wrote down 30 years of goals and a timeline with missions to accomplish. I made all the benchmarks I wrote down and then some. But the plan ran out and no more goal setting, no more timelines with zero design. If my life was artwork it would be a Salvador Dali painting, the one with the clock melting off the table all distorted.

We get a second chance to do life right. Sure enough, the Steps and principles are, in fact, a design. When the road gets bumpy, we need to go back to the design and check the blueprint for where we went wrong and get back in step. Every morning in my meditation I have a chat with the Designer to see what path is on tap for today. Do I have love and tolerance all the time? Of course not. Do I still get resentments? You bet I do. However, I at least know when I get off the design I can stop before the damage gets unmanageable. I can start my day over again if need be. I no longer wander around without direction. And yes, it works in my experience and in so many of my fellow members. The 10 Commandments told me what not to do whereas the Steps tell me what to do.

Today I have a purpose and some responsibilities all through this wonderful fellowship.

September 14

FAITH

"God did not bring you this far to drop you on your head, have faith." So said a wise older lady in the program. She said this to me after listening to me whine about my problems. I got a dose of faith and never forgot the lesson. Faith is one of those things that has no upper limit, no ceiling. It can always be stronger. Faith is on my gratitude list and my faith whispers, "This too shall pass," in my ear all the time. If I try to get ahead of God and his plan, then I am in for a disappointment. I learned God's plan is one I don't understand all the time but everything that happens is supposed to happen. I need to have faith and patience to let the plan unfold the way God intended not the way I want it. God speed is not my speed.

Like so many other spiritual assets, I need to work on faith every day in my morning prayer and step work. I can close my eyes and fall backwards, and I know my Higher Power will catch me from harm. If something doesn't seem right, I know there is a message I need to find in the discord. Some errors I can correct, others are none of my business. I can't stop all the evil in the world but I can work on my evil thoughts and change my attitude. I have faith the others in the program before me know the right path. I trust their teachings and I trust my instincts. My recovery has been progressive and my faith is part and parcel of the progression. My faith has no time gaps, it is on call 24 hours a day.

Faith trumps fear every time. When fear knocks on the door, faith answers and no one is there.

September 15

GIVING BACK

We have all heard that we have to give it away to keep it. This gold mine has a cardinal rule, whatever nuggets of gold we mine from this program must be given back to others in order to keep mining the endless amount of gold to be received. The more we give away the more we get in return. It is an upward spiral that leads to the best part of this whole process. It is hard for some to get out of the "take" mode and get into the "give" mode. Some of us are so selfish it is almost impossible to reach out and give something away with no expectation of a return. As I have said so many times before, this whole program works on the selfishness we all have right down to our bone marrow. The attitude of giving is a learned skill just like learning Greek. We do have control over our attitude and finding ways to give back is within our scope of doable actions.

Doing random acts of kindness is really a lot of fun once you look for opportunities. As I walk around I will give way, even though I have the right of way, and often a smile is all the reward I need to light my fire. If somebody wants to borrow my pen, I give them the pen (I always have 2 pens in my pocket at all times). I will drop off a cup of coffee to the guy in the local store who is stuck behind the register for hours at a time with no customers early in the morning. I tip the guy in the parking lot who directs my safe backing up. On and on throughout the day. Just little stuff but I am alert to every opportunity. Of course, when it comes to the program, I give a piece of my experience, strength and hope to every meeting when I get a chance to share. My problem is although I try to give it all back, I receive more and more gold and it multiplies to the point of being difficult to give it all back. But I have fun trying.

In my morning spiritual hour, I devote time to thinking about giving back. It works pretty good.

September 16

YOU GOTTA HAVE FIRE

Recently someone asked me if I didn't get bored coming to a meeting every day, reading the same 164 pages over and over, and listening to some verbal garbage from sick puppies. The answer is, No, hell no. I've never had a boring moment in this program. Sure, unpleasant things have happened and painful confrontations, but every day has brought new understandings and new lessons. Some lessons need repeating but are never boring. I have a passion for this program, a desire to do whatever it takes to stay sober and help others. Seeing somebody "get it," to see the lights come on in their eyes, lights my fire. Nothing about this program is ho hum. My God, we have a do-over in life and it is fun, rewarding and a heart full of joy each day no matter what. I just don't understand a lack of enthusiasm with some folks. You gotta have some fire to be attractive to the newcomer who is still suffering. Every guy I sponsored said the same thing, "Mike you are so happy and I am not, will you help me?" Simple.

How do I light my fire and keep it lit? Simple answer again. I do the 11th Step every single morning, no exceptions. A spiritual awakening upon awakening. My readings are all positive, my gratitude list is awesome, my prayers are my daily bread, my Higher Power gives me inspiration every morning. I light a fire under my attitude, one of the very few things I can change in this world. I have a very good friend who just hated his job with a passion. Dreaded every day until he could get home to his beer. Then he got sober and got a job he loves. The same job. If you don't have fire in your furnace, I suggest you think about a way to change your attitude or change your situation to turn up the heat in your life. I have been in afterburn for 25 years and I refuel every morning in my hour of prayer and meditation. I am not going to suffer burner blow out.

It is just like the football coach who gives an inspirational speech to fire up the team for the game. HOO HAA helmets in the air. So all that steam built up will be lost when the thundering herd gets ready to charge the field of play and the locker room door is locked. Just make sure the locker room door is open after getting everybody all worked up (if you know what I mean).

September 17

PINCH HITTER

In my old life, I never prayed until my fat was in the fire. Only when I was desperate would I call on God for help. In other words, I used God as a pinch hitter when all other avenues were closed. Today, I always pray in my morning quiet hour of prayer and meditation. The new way is one of thanking God every day for my wonderful life and all the gifts in my basket from His grace. Funny, I don't seem to be in trouble as much and don't need a pinch hitter like in the old days. I used to pray to be rescued and promise all kinds of things to God. Promises I now can keep. When I used God to pinch hit He always came through 100% with the winning hit. Finally, I realized I needed to make God the captain of the team and not sit on the bench for emergencies. Life is not an emergency anymore thanks to sobriety and the 12 Steps.

When I pray now, it is not for things I need or a wish list. I already have what I want. My list of gifts is what I want. No bucket list. I don't want a Rolex; I don't care what time it is. (Time is on my phone, computer, TV, the wall. Why a watch?) I don't want a BMW I am not going anywhere. My prayers help me with the daily ups and downs life dishes out. The roller coaster ride is over and the mood swings that go with it. Most of the time my spirit resides in the serenity zone and those things I have no control over don't get under my skin. So that is about everything. Only my attitude is mine to control. Prayer is attitude adjustment as far as I am concerned.

A lot of folks don't even have God as a pinch hitter. At least I learned where the talent was on my team, eventually.

September 18

SINGLE PRODUCT

Today I was thinking about Famous Amos Cookies. A single product, chocolate chip cookies, that made Amos a millionaire several times over.

All you get is a brown bag of cookies, no coffee, no juice just expensive chocolate chip cookies at a Famous Amos stand. Same story with Colonel Sanders and his recipe of herbs and spices for his fried chicken. He went to 100 folks before he finally sold the idea of this one product, a recipe really. Now I do believe you might find a KFC on the moon. I know they are very popular in Thailand, in every city. What we in AA have with singleness of purpose. One product, sobriety. Our founders knew very well it could not franchise AA and open recovery centers and hire AA qualified doctors. "Keep it simple," said Dr. Bob and how wise he was. This is a people to people program with no moving parts or equipment (maybe literature is all). One alcoholic talking to another alcoholic and the result equals sobriety.

There is no property, no AA buildings, water parks, no entry fee, no dues, no president as the Traditions carefully explain. The Traditions set the tone for AA to grow and keep growing. I have seen AA triple in my neighborhood in the last 10 years. It is a pure no-frills deal. I also believe it is God centered and has clean pure motives without a profit motive in sight. The product keeps cycling because the second part is to help other alcoholics gain sobriety and that keeps us sober, so round and round we go. This one product brings us a happy, joyous and free life as a result of staying sober and cleaning up our past and carrying the message as long as we live. It only requires we give of ourselves, no money needed. just our time and our hearts.

I know this program will be around for my great, great grandchildren only better as time goes by.

September 19

TRUST

One of the miracles of this program is trust. Remember when you didn't trust anybody or anything, least of all yourself. Now in the sober life, trust, just like faith, gets stronger all the time. These days I trust everybody until they prove untrustworthy but in my experience about

95% of people are trustworthy. It is much easier than the old method of trusting nobody. Sure, I get surprised once in a while, but it is rare to have the trust broken. A lot of that is from the company I keep. I don't deal with lawyers and politicians during most days. The biggest chunk of trust lies with my Higher Power. He has a plan for me and I have learned to trust the process. Sometimes I cannot see the big picture and am unhappy with people, places and things but in time I know it all works out for the best. When I pray, I don't ask God for anything. I ask for the patience to stay the course and trust His will not mine. The gifts I have received from my Higher Power were not asked for but were by-products of trying to do the next right thing.

In my old age I have learned to trust the lessons of those who have gone before me. I don't have to try drugs to know it is a dead end for me even though I never used drugs. I know I cannot be a professional gambler because of the lessons of bankrupt guys in the program who have tried it. I learn from my mistakes but there are a lot of mistakes out there I need not make for a "learning" experience. If you tell me I will get burned by doing something, I trust you completely. I read to learn things without having to experience them. I can trust myself today. I can pass up an extra piece of cake even though nobody is looking. I trust myself around 100 bottles of booze within a arms reach. I know God knows all I do and all I think. I know God trusts me to do the right thing.

I sometimes get annoyed when someone doesn't trust me but that is their problem not mine.

September 20

FORWARD GRATITUDE

I think we can never talk too much about gratitude. Since we can only handle one attitude at a time then let my only attitude be of gratitude. My list gives me a positive boost every time I look at it. It keeps me humble and is full of hope. I try to keep my gratitude moving forward and not focus on yesterday's accomplishments. The question needs to be; what have I done today to help my fellow earth travelers? What service did I provide my group today? What meeting did I go to today? In my morning meditation I try to remember all the people who helped me when I was crawling around in the gutter. In other words, my wonderful state of happiness was built on the shoulders of a lot of loving helpers. Am I doing the same as they all did for me or am I happy to sit on my past actions? My gratitude has a wide arc and everything on my list is part of my life today not yesterday.

This disease is progressive but so is recovery. Since gratitude is a big part of my recovery, I need to keep my engine moving forward. My day today is full of hope for tomorrow. I am sure everything will get better and better as long as I keep moving in the right direction. I know God brought me along this far and failure is not an option. I do not want to let my Higher Power down, myself down, or all the folks who depend on my positive actions down. I never want to go back to zero again. God has given me a second chance at life. I am not going to blow it on complacency, sloth and apathy. I put some logs on the fire every day and keep the heat on my program.

I could never repay all the people who have been part of my recovery, but I can try.

September 21

MEANINGFUL RELATIONSHIPS

I remember when I was working on a deep bottom all alone in my house in Hawaii. I hated to shave because I had to first down two bloody Mary's so I wouldn't cut myself and second I had to look at myself and I would curse myself out loud. I hated me and knew no way out of my black pit. The only relationship that gave me any comfort was with Stephanie. She was my ever-faithful dog who loved me unconditionally drunk or sober. I would sit with glass in hand pouring more alcohol into my wreck of a body and Stephanie would put her head on my lap and look up at me as if to say, "What is the matter with you anyway?" She would help me no doubt if she could. My life had lost its meaning, so a meaningful relationship was off the table. "Bar" relationships were without substance for sure. Once I put the drink down I was taught I had to fix me first before I could start to form any kind of relationship. The members of the fellowship told me they would love me until I could love myself. It took a while to understand what they were saying was true.

To be able to be honest, look everybody in the eye, and to have a loving open heart was the key to good relationships for me. Now I have thousands of relationships of family, friends, fellowship members and just plain passing acquaintances. From zero to a thousand by doing the Steps and changing the person I was, to the person I am today. My smile is my passport to opening the door to a new relationship be it a vendor on the street or a newcomer to the fellowship. I can give of myself today without any expectation of a payback. Of course, there are some poor relationships in my life, a couple of family members and some fellowship people. I am open to a relationship with these folks when they are ready. If it never happens, I accept that also. Love is the answer to hurt feelings and broken relationships.

Today I can shave without cursing myself, it's not pretty but at least there is an image looking back with a smile.

September 22

ROUGH SEAS

In every life some rain must fall. I experience storms and rough seas from time to time. Not turmoil in my life but for those around me. My best friend lost his sobriety after almost 20 years of continuous sobriety and thought he was back on track. Wrong. After 14 days sober he went out again and the storm began again. Hopefully he can pull out of it with help of his group and a sponsor. It is day #2 today and I just talked with him. It really hurts to see the pain and problems of active alcoholism in someone close to you. A number of our group are bedridden and one with a heart attack, quad bypass and a stroke at the same time. I am wearing my oxygen mask so I can help my brothers in need of support. "Ask Him in your morning meditation what you can do each day for the man who is still sick," page 164 Big Book. No problem there for me lately. There is plenty to do.

Whatever rough times are ahead for me I know AA will support and assist me. I would like to think there is nothing that would make me pick up a drink. I re-learned what I know to be true through my good friend.

1. It never gets better, only worse.

2. The alcohol does not work anymore. No starting over. No fun at all.

3. If you pick up a drink after 20 years it is like you drank the whole time you were sober.

4. You might not make it back alive. (My friend OD'd almost died and was hospitalized twice.)

I am certainly grateful for my sobriety and don't want to go through the rough times I see in my friend. I can't keep him sober or anybody else but myself. God has given me a new lease on life and I don't want waste the wonderful opportunity.

This is a life or death deal, trust me on this my friends. Stay well please.

September 23

DARK SIDE

As we all know we have a dark side to our character. I know I was living on the dark side of the moon when I was in my disease. My favorite story is the one about the old Indian chief giving advice to his grandson. The young boy asks, "Grandpa can you give me the secret to a good life?" To which the old chief replied, "My boy there are two wolves that live in our hearts, a black wolf who is mean and evil and a white wolf who is kind and good. Only one can survive in your heart as you get older." The grandson then asks, "Grandpa how do you know which one will survive?" The old man replied, "Only the one you feed will survive."

I know growing up I was the president of the altar boys but I really did not want to be a goodie two shoes. I wanted to be a gang member and a tough guy, but I was too skinny and chicken shit to pull it off. I was neither here nor there, trying to keep both wolves alive. Luckily, I found the Air Force where I could wear a good guy suit and be a badass at the same time. Perfect. At the end, they tore off all my buttons and broke my sword and there was no blue suit to hide the black wolf in residence. As all of us know so very well when we hit bottom the black wolf almost consumed us. The Steps slowly fed the white wolf back into our hearts but a little part of us has a dark side that may never go away completely. The trick is to feed the white wolf daily with good action and a loving heart.

I still cheer the bad guys in movies and want them to get away with all the loot. I am aware of my dark side and avoid situations where my worst character defects bubble to the surface.

September 24

ARE YOU READY?

Now that you have listed all the stuff in your inventory what are you going to do about it? Are you ready to change? Are you willing to do a makeover? Are you humble enough to accept the "real" you? If so then you are ready to get into long term sobriety and change the person you were when you were drinking so you are a new prime time individual who has undergone a psychic transformation. Now all these years later do I still have character defects? You bet I do and maybe some will be there forever. The difference now is I know what they are and I can prepare myself in situations that expose my defects of character. Here goes my confession of the last two days as an example: I had to go to Bangkok (which is a NASCAR challenge to start with) to assist a military widow get her due benefits. I knew I had to deal with two institutions and I don't like to deal with cold heartless institutions. It brings out the worst in me. I did an extra prayer and asked God's help to make it through the day without choking somebody to death.

The first stop was to the military compound in Bangkok to make this widow a military ID card she is authorized. The office that does the ID cards is famous for being closed without notice and the ID card machine is broken half the time. The office is only open a couple of days for two hours only. I prepared myself for closure or some excuse. To my surprise the guy showed up at 8 a.m. ready to go and even though the widow's situation was complicated we had the ID card by 8:15. Great, now on to the US Embassy (I have a 40 year resentment against this institution) to turn in the widow's paperwork for her benefits a 5 minute task at best. I had made an appointment for her and we were checked out carefully at the check in window. They gave her a pass and she was good to go. I went to assist her and they informed me I could not enter. I had to have an appointment also. I explained I am an American citizen trying to enter the US American services section. I also explained this widow does not speak English nor does she know what is happening or the forms she must turn in, not a clue without my help. No dice, no entry for this American. I lost it my friends. The widow sat inside clueless for two hours while I stood in the rain outside the Embassy. Finally, somebody inside came to her rescue and I got a lesson in patience. There is my confession, even with prayer and knowledge, I had a negative attitude toward this mission it all turned out OK without my help.

Some character defects will always be waiting to leap out for a special occasion but today I can see them as lessons for growth.

September 25

FAILURE IS NOT AN OPTION

If you play baseball and fail 7 out of 10 times to get a hit you are batting .300 and a star player. In aerial combat however you must win every air to air encounter or else you are dead. A pilot of a record or 40 kills and one loss is on a plaque somewhere. I look at our encounter with alcohol the same way. Failure is not an option. As I reported last time my close friend relapsed within weeks of his 20-year chip. He shot himself out of the sky. In aerial combat if you get shot down several options can occur A.) You are dead, B.) you land in enemy territory and become a POW (read here you are still drinking), C.) You land in friendly territory and get rescued (read you get back in the program and start over). Well my good friend landed at the airport this morning after an 18-hour day from California and I rescued him from his ordeal and have him back in friendly territory. He is lucky to get Option C because he was very close to Option A. Game over!

I don't know why but us alcoholics need to hear the same things over and over and we still forget the basics. My buddy had some dental surgery and the doctor gave him pain meds. He abused the dosage and went back for some more and the doctor obliged with an additional script and a bottle of vodka followed the empty pill bottle and the gorilla was out of the cage. He reports that he went back into insanity as if he had been drinking 20 years without stopping. Progressive disease we know we have heard once again somebody has proven this axiom to be true. No fun was had and it stopped working 20 years ago and it still doesn't work. Anyway, bottom line he is back alive, day 8 going to a meeting tomorrow and honest about his relapse. I told him I respect him even more for stepping up to event and putting it in the history books and he is sober today. All any of us has is today.

Failure is not an option because you cannot help anybody if you are dead.

September 26

RELAPSE

I have been spending some time dealing with a good close friend who relapsed. In ways more painful than a death. This guy was not a newbie in and out. We are talking 20 years of continuous sobriety gone up in smoke. Nobody will look down their nose at this guy because for the grace of God goes any one of us. I have no idea what would make me drink. I would like to think there is nothing in this world would make me abandon my sobriety. To tell you the truth it made me mad. I wondered why I didn't see something wrong in my friend's behavior. Was I not a good enough friend he would share his difficulties with me? Was I too busy to be available? After doing my own inventory I realized, of course, I cannot keep anyone else sober. I need to set a sober example on a daily basis.

There is only one way to handle a relapse in my opinion and that is to start over. Day 1, Step 1, Meeting #1 and eat your pride and ego. Slip is too nice a term. I like crash and burn better. It is flirting with death and more dangerous than an Evel Knievel stunt. I hope and pray my friend makes it back into recovery and sets his feet on the Road of Happy Destiny again. He was in service, went to a lot of meetings, had a sponsor, sponsored other guys, the whole 9 yards and still not enough to do the job. Of course, I stand by to help him as many other of his friends in the program. It makes me even more grateful for my own sobriety. I put my own oxygen mask on first before I can help somebody else get their oxygen.

Relapse is not part of recovery. It is part of dying a horrible death.

September 27

REVENGE

There was a great movie about a guy who destroyed his house bit by bit trying to kill a mouse who was a happy resident of his house. The mouse just moved to the new house without a scratch. I guess the lesson I learned is, revenge is not for me, it is up to God to judge and get vengeance. Remember my story about the one-star general who had a major resentment when I pulled strings to get assigned to his shop. Well he got his chance to knock me out of the military, but he wanted to humiliate and punish me. I was able to retire much to his chagrin, he also thought I would retire at reduced rank but his math was faulty. He was so focused on revenge he put a desk out in the hallway with my name tag on it to rub my nose in the dirt. Again, he was frustrated because I had enough leave time to go until my retirement date so I never had to sit at the desk. The fallout for this general was the bigger boss, a two-star general I knew very well told me because of his over the top vengeance this little one-star would never make another promotion. Sure enough, my tormentor had to retire himself shortly after trying to squash me.

Best to leave revenge to Sean Connery and *The Avengers*. Carrying our resentments into action most likely will backfire on us. I know in Laos when a friend of mine got shot down and killed I went out halfcocked to seek revenge. I missed the real bad guys who did the damage and ended up with a few bullet holes myself and provided 2 kills in one day to my enemy. A lesson I never forgot. When I let my anger go into action, I become insane. In my experience my anger never leads to a good result. I need to remind myself that I cannot control other people and what they do. I don't have to like it. But then again, I need not react. Revenge is for the movies. Clint Eastwood is all about revenge. If you need revenge go see a movie.

Revenge is best served cold. I need not gloat over eventual revenge such as my one-star buddy above.

September 28

LARGELY THEORETICAL

When I ask old timers if they have a gratitude list most of them will say yes but they can't produce it. To me that is largely theoretical. My entire program can become largely theoretical if I let it. If I stop being in service, stop going to meetings, stop sponsoring people then my program is hollow and without much commitment. Oh sure, I can stay sober. But just plain sobriety is not enough for me. It is an "all in" deal as far as I am concerned. The whole enchilada. I don't know what part of my program I can skip that will put me in danger so why take a chance? I have learned to enjoy the different aspects of this program and the joys of doing the work. I am overpaid in results and gifts from doing the footwork. When I work with a newcomer, I show him the books I read every morning, I attend meetings regularly, I am in service as they can readily see as I pick up the garbage people leave behind when the meeting is over. They can see I chair different group conscience meetings. I show him my gratitude list to read. This is real stuff not theory.

I used to treat old-timers with great honor and respect as if they out ranked me. I have changed my attitude because even though they may have decades of sobriety they stopped doing the things which got them sober in the first place. "Service is for the younger guys." "I used to sponsor a lot of guys but I don't have the time for that anymore." Largely theoretical which is a nice way of saying BS. I admire men of action today not in history. I can't stay sober on yesterday's prayers or yesterday's meeting. I need to do something right now today to keep my afterburner lit. I can't give this program away if my program is half ass. Don't tell me, show me, is my attitude toward action in this program. Everybody has a different program so I don't get into somebody else's rice bowl if their program is largely theoretical. I do what I do as an example. My sponsees can take it or leave it. I will say the ones who have taken my example are happy, joyous and free.

I am out of the theory business altogether and stick to concrete action.

September 29

DARKEST BEFORE THE DAWN

All of us get our faith tested from time to time. No matter how much you have in your spiritual bank account you can go to a zero balance in a heartbeat. I know my faith has always been rewarded but it has often been dark and bleak on the horizon before the storm passes. I work on my faith just like I work out on my exercise bike. I try to connect with my Higher Power every morning as the sun comes up. You can never do too much to increase your faith, there is no upper limit, no ceiling. Fears of all kind lie in the weeds ready to pounce on me but if I stay in the sunlight of The Spirit those fears are just shadows and have no power. Lack of power is my dilemma and my Higher Power has all the power, so I need to keep connected. I will never forget when I was having a rough spell some years back, one of the older ladies in my group said, "Mike, God didn't bring you this far to drop you on your head."

For some reason one of the common traits of us alcoholics is to make mountains out of mole hills. We can weave horrible scenarios out of very simple situations. It is wise to talk to other alcoholics and your sponsor when you are in the soup. Others can see your mess much clearer from the outside looking in. You can't see the forest because there are so many trees. One thing I do when handling a tough situation is, at night, I give the problem over to God so I can sleep and when dawn breaks the solution is right there in my frontal lobes. I am amazed I couldn't see my way out in the darkest part of the night. I have to remind myself I am indeed powerless and God has a plan He chose not to share with me just yet. But I know everything happens for a reason and my little tiny brain can't always know reason. Faith has to trump the dark moments of my life. The sun will shine again very soon.

My gratitude list is my best medicine for a bad day. God is not picking on me, He has truly blessed me and you too.

September 30

FAMILY RELATIONSHIPS

I think family relationships hurt the most when there is a problem. I guess when flesh and blood are involved the pain goes straight to the heart. Every family has members who are difficult. We have to remember as alcoholics we are two different people. The pre-sober days and the sober person of today. You are X miles down the personal road to recovery, but every family member has a different timetable to recover from you. Some people in the family are happy you are sober others may not yet be able to forgive you for harms done to them. When we were sick puppies, we made the family sick to some extent. It is amazing how deep family resentments go and for long periods of time also. The reason this topic came up is my sister who cut off all siblings for 8 years running. She wanted to attend a cousins wedding but she wanted control of the agenda and seating arrangement. She made it clear that she was to be separated from her 2 sisters. She drove the mother and father of the bride so crazy it became a big drama and ended when my sister cut off her relationship with the cousins and did not attend.

I am sure you have family stories that top that one. The selfishness of some can ruin an entire happy occasion that should be a loving event. I have a son who has not spoken or contacted me in 8 years. That really hurts. His mother has passed and she was his enabler to do drugs and deal. Once he was loose, he ended up in jail and has abandoned his daughter. The only thing I can do is hope and pray he returns to a recovery program and makes amends to all he has harmed. I can't force him to become a member of normal society, I can only set an example for my grandkids as a sane sober family member. Both my sister and my son owe me thousands of dollars, but I wrote all that off years ago for a kind word and a genuine hug.

I choose to focus on the loving relationships I do have with my extended family. A gift beyond measure.

October 1

RELIGION

I never talk about religion because I don't belong to any organized group and certainly am not a missionary for any religion. I read recently about AA not being a cure all which is my point. I know quite a few people in AA who are also involved in church or synagogue and handle both with no conflict of principle. I have a Thai brother in-law who is sober for 25 years without AA or any program. He was the terror of the entire village before he quit and is now a respected member of northern Thailand and

Laos. AA works for me and many of us but it is not the only method of sobriety. The point is to be open minded and take good points from wherever they appear be it the bible or a preacher or a teacher.

I have a good friend in the US who is a deacon in his church and is very religious. He asked me where I worship. I told him my kitchen table every morning. He argued that I need to be in a house of God. I told him my house is a house of God. Further I told him God resides in my soul and not in a different location down the street. He just could not grasp my way of thinking. I showed him my books and my routine every morning. I pointed out he goes to church on Sunday, but I go to my Higher Power every day. I am in his "pagan" box. He puts out hate mail about the Muslim religion and how they are the enemy. When I told him that blood stains are not cleaned by more blood but can only be cleaned by love, he nearly tossed me out. He thinks I am a traitor for living in Thailand where a small minority are Muslim. The point is, religious people don't necessarily need to be spiritual and vice versa. We have a program which allows us to design our own spiritual path. In my case I don't choose to add religion to the mix. If you do, well and good.

Spirituality is between your Higher Power and you. Religion is an invention of man and monitored by humans.

October 2

BEHIND BARS

One of my closest friends in the program has spent most of his adult life behind bars. I listen to his stories and am grateful not having prison time on my resume. I did spend a few hours in a holding cell after a DUI arrest in Hawaii and they even left the door open. When my Vietnamese wife came to bail me out the cop at my cell said, "Hey pal now the real trouble starts." How right he was. So being afraid to drive, since I was drunk all the time, I was confined to the bedroom with a TV and had bathroom privileges but that's about all. The Viet Cong (affectionate name for my wife) would put a tray of food in the room and keep my whiskey glass full. So drink by drink, like brick by brick, I imprisoned myself under house arrest. The house would have 10-12 Vietnamese people having a grand time while I remained in my confined space as a prisoner of King Alcohol. Pathetic I lost the war a second time.

My biggest fear in Vietnam was being shot down and taken prisoner. I knew there was not going to be Happy Hour for my arrival as a POW and down deep I knew I would be detoxing in a very nasty place. I worked hard to get my fellow pilots out of Hanoi Hilton but for the grace of God I would be among them if I survived at all. Hard to believe we lose all our freedom exercising the freedom to drink all we want. What a difference life has become using the Steps to unlock the cell door and go anywhere on the face of the planet. One drink and all that freedom evaporates and if not behind bars I would go back to house arrest at best or death at worst. There are all kinds of confinement besides physical: emotional, mental and spiritual confinement and all of it self-imposed.

My Higher Power is my parole officer and I check in with Him every morning.

October 3

DREAMS

It is said that nothing happens without it being imagined first. Even Einstein thought knowledge is great but imagination is more important. I know when we were kids, we had wild dreams. We could be Superman or Steve Canyon, a fireman or a soldier. Slowly these dreams fade away into material dreams of great wealth, winning the lottery, being the president. In my own case I got to fly an Air Force jet while I was in college and even though I had no aspirations to be a pilot, I acquired a new dream to become a pilot. I set my sights on my goal and after many lies, cheating and scamming my dream came true. I looked at the romantic part of being a pilot and soon found out I would be shot at as part of the deal so there was a nightmare side to this dream. Then alcohol gave me wings to fly and finally alcohol took away my sky. As a drunk you really don't dream anymore, you pass out. If there is any dreaming it is a nightmare of horrible guilt and fear of being found out and caught. Dreaming and imagination were off the table for about 30 years in my experience.

In sobriety, I have learned to dream again. I can do a thousand things that were impossible while I was a drunk. In recent years I can remember my nightly dreams and most of them are wonderful. Widescreen, Dolby sound with amazing color and detail. They don't always make sense but I believe my conscience mind is able to connect with the sub-conscience more and more. This is the result of cleaning up my inventory and working through the layers my wreckage has accumulated. Eleven years ago, I was doing my prayer and meditation and a new dream started. Move to Thailand, follow your bliss was cooking in my imagination and through the miracle of sobriety I was able to make my dream come true. I could not be happier. There is nowhere else I would rather be. If I didn't have AA, my home group and cyberspace to keep in touch with my family I couldn't do this.

I had a dream last night that I was putting on a display of Thai culture with books and Thai silk in some conference room in New York. I had an address and kind people helped me to the right place. The details of my travel and the setting were true art. I also had another dream I was teaching one of my sponsees how to land a C-141 (which don't exist anymore) and he didn't do too well but we landed safely in time for a fighter pilot party (no drinking). This happens every night. My very own theater.

I hope and pray you all get to live your dream as I have.

October 4

APATHY, SLOTH, LAZINESS

One of our program sayings is "Take It Easy" but not too easy is my plea. I was the chairman for a group meeting and about 50% took the trouble to show up and participate. One forgot the time, one doesn't care, one is too lazy to make an excuse, one only comes when he has an issue. It amazes me how some people don't live up to a commitment. How do they do that? I have never missed a group meeting in 21 years. These slow down and stop attitudes are very dangerous to my way of thinking. Apathy is a kind of selfishness that shuts out the outside world and pretty soon you don't care about anything. Skip a meeting or two, what the heck why not just skip them all together. I'll wait until next week. Prayer, oh well, I will wait until the spirit moves me. Read the literature, I have read it all already. This kind of thinking is insidious, and if I am not vigilant, I put myself in harm's way.

Procrastination is a killer. Put it off and maybe it will go away was one of my pre-sober theme songs and character defects. The problem is, it didn't go away it just got worse. Finally, after some years in the program I learned to act now and face problems head on rather than wish them away. Step work should be done as soon as possible. One of my amends I put off until the person I needed to talk to was dead. My sponsor told me that doesn't take me off the hook. "When we were wrong promptly admitted it," the words in Step 10. To me that is directive in nature and promptly carries over into my character and all my affairs. I make a list of, "Do It Now" stuff in my morning work up. The day gets busy and the mere act or writing a list somehow the stuff that needs to be done, gets done. I sleep better when my To Do list is complete.

I was going to skip today's offering, but I take my own advice once in a while.

October 5

I'M A PICKLE

I used to be a cucumber but I drank and drank, soaking myself in brine alcohol until it finally took. It worked, I am a pickle forever and will never be a cucumber again. "Once an alcoholic always an alcoholic," is something we hear all the time but some of us believe otherwise. The bad news about this disease is it tells me I don't have this disease. After so many 24 hours sober you feel great and want to enjoy all the freedoms life has to offer. You are OK, you are cured or so your mind tells you. The worse news is, you wasted all the sober time, as if you were drinking all the time. You don't get to start over and work up to a new bottom. You hit the skids so fast your head will swim. I have seen it happen so many times and not one successful case of a slow bottom is in my experience. Bummer. For me being a pickle is OK, I accept my status as a sober pickle never to touch a drop of alcohol as long as I live. Life as a cucumber wasn't so great anyway.

I look at my pickleness like I do my hairline. I will never have a head of hair again. It is gone with the wind. My freedoms have one big caveat, no booze. I certainly don't want to visit another bottom if I make it back alive. I know I have one more drunk in me, but I am not sure I have one more recovery in me. Why flirt with death and destruction? I know I need to keep my last drunk green in my mind and remember how sick I was at the end. I can't let my mind play tricks on me and have a toast at a family wedding or any other "cucumber" activity. I am different than normal folks, but I accept my green color and stay vigilant.

Yes, I am a pickle but I don't have to get into a pickle.

October 6

LEARNING

My favorite line from page 164 is, "We know only a little." So true, how limited my knowledge and how humble it makes me when I define another vast empty space in my tiny brain. I try to let everyone I meet be my "teacher" in some way. I learn so much from others and my vast education has nothing to do with learning. Experience has been the main teacher in my life and even long in tooth my experience is so limited. I cannot claim to be an expert on any subject. I have been successful in staying sober, but I am only one person. I don't have the formula to keep anybody else sober. I am an expert on some aircraft but the ones I flew are all in the boneyard. All those years in the classroom may have been better spent gaining some life experience. I do know, for me, the learning is never over. If I keep my mind open, I can learn new things every day. The information highway is right there at our fingertips.

I know when I am talking, no learning is taking place. A good reason to keep my big mouth shut. If I think I know it all, my mind is closed and being wrong has happened enough that I should be more of a listener. Most of us are very poor listeners and we miss many learning opportunities through bad listening skills. I also know when I was drinking no learning was taking place. There is a big, empty 30-year spot in my brain. They tell me a peanut farmer was US president and the Terminator was governor of California. That can't be possible can it? If I pretend everyone in the room is enlightened except me, I have a good start at learning new ideas from others. I am smart enough to know I am not smart at all.

For me if the learning is done, I am done.

October 7

RETIRED FIGHTER

In my very first meeting, the speaker said, "We don't have to fight anyone or anything anymore." What? The air went out of my lungs, this was very foreign to me. Of course, life is one big fight. Right? You have to fight to get to the top, you have to fight for your rights, you have to fight City Hall, IRS, DMV, AT&T, etc... I spent my whole life fighting, it was in my job description, freedom fighter, fighter pilot, fighter coordinator, combat controller. Now you tell me I don't have to fight. What a relief, I wasn't any good at fighting anyway. I was fighting everybody in my path and worst of all, I was fighting myself and losing every battle. Of all my enemies the dude in the mirror was the one I could not conquer. My favorite from Buddha: "A warrior who has conquered a thousand enemies in a thousand battles is not a true warrior until he conquers himself." Wow.

In that first meeting, I surrendered my fight status and hung up the fight game. No more struggle. I stopped wasting my energy in fights I could not win and accept people, places and things as they were. I can't punch someone into good behavior. All those faceless, nameless, heartless government offices deserve my wrath, but I have learned to stay calm and cool and pick my battles wisely and without resentment. The real trick is to avoid a fight when you see one brewing. That macho crap has to go out the window. To sidestep a thrust of an aggressor may be the best option. Verbally, I have learned to stay out of angry disagreements and keep my mouth shut when others are shouting and waving their arms. Exit stage left whenever possible is my motto, I don't need to be a witness or a participant.

I am a retired fighter. My record isn't too good, so I won't brag about the few victories. But I have conquered myself.

October 8

PRAYER

I am a big fan of prayer. It works. Simple as that. I remember my only prayer at the beginning of this journey was, "God help me please." And sure enough, He did. Now my first and last prayer each day is short and simple. "Thank you, God." In my first hour of 11th Step, I have many prayers which I have shared quite a few with you guys. 3, 7 and 11 for starters.

Today my life is fairly free of emergencies, so I pray from an attitude of gratitude. I also ask for direction and guidance. I can tell you from personal experience that prayer works in all circumstances.

When I was first sober and out of work, I was 2000 dollars a month in negative cash flow and efforts to find work at my advanced age proved fruitless. I sat down at my desk after my morning meeting and prayed out loud, "God, I cannot go another day without employment." Right then the phone rang and it was a former student from University of Phoenix. "Hey Mike, we need a safety guy on our new project, we just fired the one we had. Are you available?" Why yes it so happens I am between jobs right now. Bottom line, I got an interview in an hour's time and was hired by noon. The job pulled me out of financial ruin and led to a follow up job until I could retire. Hard evidence that prayer works.

There is no wrong way to pray and prayer changes the person praying in my experience.

October 9

IT'S NOT FAIR

Most of us have a sense of justice and fairness. You hear young kids say, "It's not fair," when they feel they aren't getting their share of the pie. After youth is gone, we learn life is not fair at all. Bad guys have just as much chance of winning the lottery as good guys. Super nice people get cancer and die while some criminals live a full life without getting caught. Life is not fair and it never was meant to be fair so I don't hold my breath waiting for the scales of justice to level the playing field. Now that is not to say I don't follow the rules of fairness in my activities and try to be honest in my actions. We all have expectations of fairness, such as when we are in line at a ticket counter and someone cuts in front of the line we get upset and may act out to this person. Living in Asia I have learned cutting in line is normal behavior, it stills get a rise in my blood pressure but not so much I lose my temper.

I tell my guys. Life is not fair Thank God. If life was fair most of us would be dead, in jail, in a nuthouse or wet brain. Us AA types have beaten the fairness rule many times over. We are so lucky to have survived the hazards of our drinking and have a second chance at life. I am eternally grateful that in my disease I didn't kill anyone in a black out as some members did who I know. I have been able to repair a lot of the damage I caused by staying alive instead of crashing into a tree when I was drunk. Why did I get this program and a lot of good folks never made it to sobriety? Fair? Certainly not. I know I need to use my good fortune to the best possible end God intends for me.

I can never make the scales of justice even, but I can do a little bit each day to put some weight on the good side. Justice is blindfolded for a reason.

Life is not fair, and I am OK with that.

October 10

LETTING GO

All of us have all heard "Let Go Let God," but the process is not so simple. What I have taught myself is, I own nothing material and nobody belongs to me. I am a steward of some stuff God has given me but only temporarily. I have family but I don't "own" them. I have my children but they are God's kids not mine. I have had to let go of the fact my son is not long for this world with ALS but that letting go does not mean to stop loving him, encouraging him and supporting his family. Another idea I have learned is everything will be just fine without my input. When I was learning to fly aircraft, I was pushing and pulling the controls with tight fists and clenched teeth, this airplane was going to do what I told it to do. My instructor told me to let go of the controls and put my feet flat on the floor. You could hear the aircraft give a sigh of relief and it settled in straight and level without me touching the controls. A lesson in life I never forgot. When I let go everything turns out better.

Here is one of my prayers on Letting Go.

Higher Power, help me to understand:

To let go does not mean to stop caring. It means I can't do it for someone else.

To let go is not to enable, but to allow learning from natural consequences.

To let go is to admit powerlessness, which means the outcome is not in my hands.

To let go is not to try to change or blame another, it's to make the most of myself.

To let go is not to fix but be supportive.

To let go is not to judge but to allow another to be a human being.

To let go is not to protect, it's to permit another to face reality.

To let go is not to deny but to accept.

To let go is not to nag, scold, or argue but instead to search out my own shortcomings and correct them.

To let go is not to adjust everything to my desires but to take each day as it comes and cherish myself in it.

Sweet, aye? All I know is my old ideas led me nowhere. I let go of my old way of life for this one.

October 11

COINCIDENCE

There is a school of thought that says everything happens is supposed to happen. In other words, there are no coincidences. Some of the events happen out of the blue and are often God shots which startle us and give us a jolt. It seems God made me tall and bald for a reason, you can't pass me on the street and say, "Hey Mike, I didn't see you" I keep running into folks in the program who are back drinking. Some even get mad at me but they really are upset with themselves. A head full of AA and a belly full of booze make a person sick and they all have a bad attitude. One such incident was up in Nong Khai on the Mekong River. This gent who was a regular at our morning meeting was sitting all by himself, the only customer at this outdoor bar. He had the biggest yard and a half frosty beer on the table and you could see the look of satisfaction on his face. He was off the map of civilization and nobody could see him. When he spotted me just a few feet away from his table he looked at the beer, too big to hide and said "Oh s**t!" He was not happy to see me and I basically ruined his evening. He told me a year later, the beer tasted terrible and he couldn't finish it.

Well he came back to the rooms of AA and is sober today as far as I know until another "coincidence" happens again. This same guy observed me going to my morning meeting for a year, every day from the back of some bar on the route I took. Just last week I was taking a fellow member to the hospital and quite by coincidence I ran into a lady who was happy to see me after 4 years and announce she had been sober for 90 days. The fact she knew I was in the program was also a coincidence. I was able to encourage her to come to a meeting and gave her directions. As I trudge the road, I may be the only version of the Big Book that someone sees. You never know who is watching you and you may be an example for good or bad without any clue you are on sobriety Candid Camera.

I believe coincidences are God's way of being anonymous.

October 12

THE PAST

We all know the past is one of those things we can't change, but the past is all we have. The future is largely unknown, and the present is just a heartbeat and it's also the past. Most of us had events in our past that were dramatic or tragic and they are not going to go away. Even though we may have pushed them out of our thinking and put these events in the "forget about it" box. In my own case, and you all probably have similar experiences, many things shaped my life like a family tragedy, a bad accident, death up close and personal. I tried to put these happenings in the hurt locker and not focus on them and just hope cold storage would make it all go away. It didn't work that way for me. All that stuff rotted away in my heart and stayed there until I finally learned to pull all that garbage out, let it thaw and deal with the entire mess.

These past events came out in my 4th and 5th Step but they needed special attention. I have made some extensive amends trips retracing my past and it was so healing and beneficial I recommend the same for you and dealing with your past. I went to a battle site in Laos, where I had to fight for my life. I made it out but several others did not survive the day in question. It was just a patch of dirt 40 years after, a horrendous scene and there was nothing there, no bronze plaque commemorating the battle, nothing but the bogey man in my brain. Very healing trip.

The thing about the past, once you bank some years of sobriety you have a sober past that is so much richer than the drunk career past. In recent history I have been able to let my subconscious mind leak into my conscience mind in the form of dreams. Amazing how much stuff is stored in our brain.

If the past is valuable, I am one rich dude my friends.

October 13

SELFISHNESS KILLS

There is some pretty strong language in our Big Book. For example: "And with us to drink is to die." (page 66) What part of dead do we not understand? This latest reading from page 62, "Above everything, we alcoholics must be rid of this selfishness, we must or it kills us!" How much stronger can the message be? No matter how long we have worked this program, selfishness is part of our makeup. The best we can do is be aware of it and keep working on our selfish ways. I have witnessed gross acts of total selfishness by members with 40-50 years of sobriety. One of the goals of Buddhism is selflessness and it is part of nirvana. When we hit our bottom, it was all about us and we didn't like ourselves so it was pretty dark at the end of our drinking. Then we get better, but selfishness takes on new character. We have to be selfish enough to put our sobriety at the top of our endeavors above all else. We need to find the balance between necessary selfishness and harmful selfishness. Not an easy task.

When I examine my motives for my actions most of the time several motives are in play. I am good at wrapping several noble motives around a selfish motive. Rationalization is a neat trick we play on ourselves to sugar coat the truth. When I really look at the 12 Steps, I can see they all work wonders on this selfishness we have all the way to the bone. In Step 12 when I am carrying the message it is 90% unselfish because I am not thinking about "me." There is 10% selfish because I know I need to give it away to keep it and I want to keep what I have. Selfish, OK. Every day I try to put myself in perspective, a grain of sand on the beach of life, just another bozo on the bus. I know for me, selfishness kills love, it kills the attractiveness to others, it kills growth, it kills the Sunlight of The Spirit. I don't want to kill any of these things and I sure don't want to kill myself.

Whenever you are feeling, bad, angry, hurt, look to selfishness first and see if that is the problem.

October 14

ENCOURAGE ANOTHER

One of my daily prayers is "Life Is A Celebration," and one line in the prayer is "encourage another." So, it is in my daily thoughts but not always in action. I try to be encouraging whenever I can but it must be the real deal and not phony. Actually, it is just another expression of love when you care enough about a person to give them some hopeful words and support their dreams. I know in my youth I received very little encouragement, I had to learn how to do it later in life. This is one positive thing you can do for someone else with absolutely no resources. A kind word costs you nothing but can mean so much to someone who needs a boost. I think once I made it into the rooms of AA, I got my first real shot of encouragement. "Keep coming back. We will love you until you can love yourself."

One "old timer" used to tell me to be quiet and listen but then he would put his arm around me and tell me I am doing good. Frank H met me in LA in my first year and took me to a local meeting of about 200 people. He told the speaker he could speak next week and he put me up in front of strangers. I said, "Frank you told me to be quiet!' He said, "Mike now you have something to say." It was great and since I didn't have time to think about what to say, everything came from the heart. That encouragement stayed with me to this day and I try to do the same whenever I can. The act of encouragement gives me a boost also. To see it work in the eyes of another person is reward enough for me.

"Having come to believe that I keep what I share, every time I encourage, I receive courage." (Daily Reflections)

October 15

FUNNY BONE

I remember my very first AA meeting at 7 a.m. I was observing the group from the next room before I would decide if I was going in. They were laughing. Are you kidding me? I was in serious trouble and had not laughed in a very long time. This was serious business and I was ready for my punishment. How can they be laughing? I tried to escape to a more suitable meeting and this guy stopped me and said, "You are in the right place." How did he know? I wasn't sure this was true. During that meeting there were lots of yuks and pretty soon I was laughing too. Now I have had some laughter as part of my daily diet. "Laughter is the shortest distance between two people." This disease we have is fatal, but we can laugh our way down the yellow brick road until the final curtain. As you guys know my son has Lou Gehrig's disease and there is no cure. Now we just found out my son-in-law has Stage IV cancer in his lungs, liver and bones so he has not long to live either. We are powerless over both these situations but our family will face them head-on with a smile and good cheer. Our family funerals are great, not black veils and weeping, but love, laughter and celebration of life.

We need to realize we are funny animals really. We do stupid stuff, human failings and need not be too serious about it all. I laugh at myself all the time. Rule 62 "Don't take yourself too seriously," is part of our AA folklore. Part of humility is not letting pride wipe a smile off our face. We are the biggest joke of all. My group has a great sense of humor and yours probably does too. Laughter is good for your health, seriously. It opens the lungs and clears out the cobwebs.

Why do they call it a funny bone when it hurts to hit it?

October 16

BE STILL

When I was a kid and my mother would tell me to "be still." I hated to comply. I was anything but still, perpetual motion and so went most of my life. You can't hit a moving target, I used to say proudly. In the Oakland Tribune newspaper, we got every day at our house it had a column "Be Still and Know." I was in college before I realized it was written by Norman Vincent Peale the godfather of positive thinking. I used to read it but never understood the message old Norman was trying to convey and it never inspired me to "be still." I was more interested in the ad next to his about Tempest Storm staring on stage nightly. My goal was to grow up and see Ms. Storm as soon as possible. Funny how we change through this process because now I really look forward to opportunities to be still.

That morning routine has become my habit just like the Big Book tells me to do. It all starts with being still. No music, no TV, no phones, no chit chat, no movement just quiet. Being still allows the brain to not be working on physical efforts or material stuff only spiritual thoughts. This is my goal of being still. Being still allows my heart to start thinking and gives my brain a rest. If my brain is going to be the message from my heart I need to be still and listen carefully. When my brain gets sidetracked, I have to start all over again. It is amazing how quick my defective brain can spin up to 4500 RPM and put me in outer space mentally. I have to come back to earth, look at my feet not going anywhere and be still.

I think I finally understand what Rev. Vincent Peale was trying to tell me. (BTW I never did get to see Tempest Storm on stage).

October 17

COMMUNICATION

One of my all-time favorite lines from the movies is in "Cool Hand Luke" where the warden of the prison is standing over inmate Paul Newman and says in a deep Southern drawl: "Now what we have here is a failure to communicate." And so goes the human condition. So often we don't communicate at all or we incorrectly communicate or worse, we think we communicated but it was not received the way we intended. This process involves at least two parties, the sender and the receiver, that's a problem right away. The two parties are often not on the same wavelength. I know in my emails they are often misunderstood no matter how hard I try to be clear. What I meant to be a joke is not funny at all to the receiving party. Emails don't have a tone of voice or eye contact. In verbal communications most of us, myself included, are poor listeners. I work on my listening skills but I give myself a C minus. I anticipate what is coming next or I let my mind wander and think about what I am going to say in return. My head is in two conversations at once. Mine and his/hers. Then I get upset when it is clear the other person isn't listening to me.

There is the whole range of non-verbal communication. I try to keep my big mouth shut at every opportunity, but my face and gestures speak volumes about how I feel so the message gets sent even though my lips are not moving. I try to be careful about a poker face, but I am not. I would lose big time at poker where the slightest tick gives away your hand. I might as well lay my cards on the table. I can't hide my feelings very well at all. If my job is to carry the message in Step 12, I must improve my communication skills to do the best job for the man who is still suffering. In my relationships in and out of AA I can never be a "perfect" communicator. However, I can be honest and correct myself when I mis-communicate. At least people can see that I am sincere even if my message is a bit garbled.

I work hard on my failures to communicate and am still a student.

October 18

DECLUTTER YOUR LIFE

If you really turn your life over to the care of God then it is a good start to simplify your life. The Middle East, the economy, winter storms, leave that up to God to handle, you only have to get dressed and make a meeting. Simple aye? The impossible I leave up to my Higher Power and I get busy with the possible. Clutter stresses me out so there are no old newspapers on the table, the drawers are shut, the floor is clean, there are no dirty clothes in a pile somewhere. Also, there are no amends not made, no inventory swept under the rug and no prayers not made. I don't have a smartphone that is smarter than me in my pocket. I want to call and text and that's enough, simple. I have no wallet. A couple of cards like a driver's license, ID card is all I need. Paperwork, OMG, that stuff multiplies at night. Stuff that is important today is not tomorrow and needs to get tossed or it becomes overwhelming.

I guess my point is, clutter clogs up the system and slows your progress. It is like plaque buildup, insidious and distracting. Makes things simple is real creativity. I try to declutter my mind thru my morning routine of prayer and meditation. I want my life to be aerodynamic, so the daily ride is smooth as possible. I avoid situations which clutter up my day and rob me of time. To my way of thinking, freedom is part of this streamlining. You can choose what apps you really need and discard the junk that is all around you. My first job at 2 years old was to take out the garbage and now it is my only daily chore I still love to do. Garbage in the news, garbage in my computer, garbage out of other people's mouth, garbage on TV. It's everywhere but I toss it, avoid it, sidestep it. All that garbage gets heavy too,

You may have started by stop reading my little blurb for today... hmm.

October 19

LITTLE THINGS

It's not the elephants that will get you, it's the piss ants. I know I can
handle the loud concert in my backyard better than a mosquito that keeps
me up all night. The point is, if you don't pay attention to the little
stuff the nits will eat your lunch. I have learned not to let little stuff build
up to the point it becomes a big pile of stuff. Especially in relationships,
if you let little things go by the boards someday you will blow up when
all the little things get too much to handle. Better to pay attention to keep
small stuff small or deal with it before it grows. On the positive side,
paying attention to detail can make life go smoother.

I am sure you have heard the saying, "God is in the details!" Back to my
previous bit on nature. You can see God's handiwork in each orchid,
twenty different parts with different colors to make one beautiful flower
for our enjoyment. The detail of the Grand Canyon with messages of
beauty and example of our powerlessness and a perspective of how
insignificant we are. I look for God in every flower, that is easy to see,
but I need to find God in every human being I encounter. Some folks you
need to look really hard. I can see God in a dog easier than I can in some
of my brothers and sisters in the human family. God is in the details of
the words in my morning prayers and readings. I get messages from my
Higher Power as I collect the details of the first hour of every day. I carry
these little nuggets with me to make the next 23 hours, happy joyous and
free.

If I go through my day in a hurry, I miss God's details and His messages.

October 20

RENT FREE

Do you ever think of the time and space in your brain as valuable?
Priceless actually, but we still put garbage in there and fill it with junk
and negative thinking from time to time. I try to think of it as my

personal safety deposit box and spend a considerable amount of time reading positive stuff and filter my waking hours as best I can with golden thoughts and constructive thinking. Not always easy of course. Fear, for example, can take up 100% of our available space and not pay rent. It can paralyze us and make us sick. We can play worst case scenarios until we are stuck going nowhere. "What if all my money is gone? What if she leaves me? What if my boss cans me tomorrow? What if what if the sky falls?" When these false events play a trick on our brain, we lose a lot of freedom and ability to make good choices. We become a prisoner of fear, a slave.

Then of course, resentment, let the guy who drives you crazy take up residence in your head rent free, you play 10 plans to wipe him out without getting caught. You rehearse what you will say to this idiot when you have the chance. You can't sleep because your brain is spinning around with anger at this awful human being. Meanwhile he is sleeping like a baby and can't remember your name. What is really bad? When you have a whole bunch of resentments at the same time, her, her lawyer, her friends, my lawyer, my so-called friends, the legal system, etc... Yikes, there is no room in there for one clear thought.

The space between my ears is all I have so if a book is no good, I toss it, if the movie is bad, I leave, if there are loud grumpy people around, I am out of there. I fill my space with good, happy conversations, good art, music, positive reading, some fun stuff. If I put garbage in, I will get garbage out.

What's rolling around in your head without paying rent?

October 21

THIS TOO SHALL PASS

Everything happening to us seems so important. It is hard to take the longer view and ask the question, "will this be important a year from now? A week from now?" Probably not. I am watching a football game right now but I can't remember who won last week. What is going on right now seems earth shattering. When we are in pain it feels like it will last forever and it doesn't, when we are having pleasure, we want it to last forever and it doesn't. When I am in the dentist chair for 2 hours, it is really only 15 noisy minutes on the clock. A dish of coffee ice cream can make my day but really it is gone in 5 minutes and I pay the price of 2 more hours on the exercise bike to lose the effect of the ice cream on my body. Everything will pass on God's time, not ours.

We too shall pass, God knows when. Some folks live as if they will live forever. I live as though I will die tomorrow. Sooner or later I will be right. I don't want to leave amends not made so I do my inventory right now and keep my side of the street clean. I am not so selfish as to leave my family with a mess. My family has a "croak file" on me and they know what to do when I pass. I don't know if there is an afterlife but if there is I want a clean rap sheet. I want to report in with as many days sober as possible. I want to answer the question "who have you helped?" with a long list and hope it passes muster!

You guys will vouch for me, right?

October 22

THE GAP

When I was a teenage hot rod guy I used to set the gap on the spark plugs in my 1951 Mercury. Now I set a different gap in my everyday affairs. The GAP is the time between when somebody says something to me or some event happens to me and I react to those events. This pause I call the GAP. God Authorized Pause. No longer am I in a hurry to react to an insult or verbal attack. In the past, I had a hair trigger and would shoot back when attacked. Once we react without thinking, often we say something or do something rash which we regret and can't take it back. Once it is out of our mouth it is on the table. Worse is to do something physical which can lead to a hostile exchange. The longer this GAP the better off I will be and the others involved. Saying nothing is the best policy sometimes. I never say the right things in heat of a confrontation anyway. My best line comes a day later after it is all over.

Why is this GAP so important? Love and tolerance reside in my heart and not always in my head. I need to have a meeting of my heart and my head with God's help and give my heart a chance to weigh in and cool the hot spot. This takes a bit of time thus the GAP. Often my heart will say, "shut up and consider the outcomes," and once the spin in my brain slows to a level of reasoning, a better respónse results. I don't have to win every battle, when somebody pushes me, I don't have to push back. We need not get walked on like a doormat but there is no rush to win the point. In martial arts, they teach you an angry thrust is best handled by stepping aside and letting the thrust go by. Not always easy. I pray for the GAP every day because my aggressive personality comes out in many situations.

OK so I get it about the GAP, now to work on my face until the GAP has passed. Hmm.

October 23

TEAMWORK

Most us were very alone when we hit bottom and the concept of teamwork was Greek to us. Once we became part of the group, slowly we learned we are in the lifeboat together and everybody has to row the boat to survive. This AA team is unlike any other. No superstars and nobody gets to sit on the bench. We have a common goal, to stay sober and help others do the same. We are so lucky to be on such a "team." Every meeting is a team meeting. All our talents are in the mix for the good of the team and not any one individual. We need each other and the sum is greater than the parts. I think of baseball with Barry Bonds on the SF Giants but really there was no team at all. Barry put a big easy chair in the locker room away from the rest of the players and did not socialize with any of the rest of the team. So, it was Barry Bonds and the guys and the team went nowhere while Barry Bonds hit home runs in a losing cause. Justice finally caught up with Barry in a drugging scandal and the

Giants became a team again. Teamwork takes communication, love, tolerance and forgiveness if you want a winner.

I did not have much experience with teamwork with some notable exceptions in the military. One such experience was in a seminar setting with 55 seminars in competition. Our seminar had no super stars, but somehow, we gelled as a team, and we came out on top of all 55 seminars. In AA I took on chairmanship of the Thai Roundup a few years back. My team had a Thai member which was essential for our negations with hotels etc... We had a guy in the art business for logos, printed advertisements etc... We had a business guy to take care of finances, a traveler who snagged a famous speaker, a good speaker to do the MC stuff and I was just the facilitator to put it all together. Not one cross word or angry disagreements or problems of any sort happened in the entire year of planning. The Roundup went off perfectly with no complaints and it was a great experience plus we were deep in service to 500 AA members.

The trick is to pick the right team who will use your talents, good luck!

October 24

ARE WE HAVING FUN YET?

When I was kid, fun was off the table. Homework and chores had priority so "fun" never happened. I looked forward to being an adult but even my father never had fun either. My mother would never allow him to go fishing. When I was 14 years old in the seminary to be a priest, I went into town to see a movie for fun. Well, I got caught and kicked out of the seminary and returned home in sackcloth and ashes. Certainly, when I joined the military, now I was on my own, I could learn to have fun with the big boys. It became clear that "fun" meant alcohol was involved. In basic training the Air Force loaded us into a blue bus and took us to the Coors brewery and we all drank ourselves silly. OK I can do this, I guess I was having fun.

Then I graduated into the fighter pilot ranks with the real big boys. In the fighter pilot bars someone would scream, "Are we having fun yet?" which translated into, "Are we drunk yet?" It was always met with groans and profanity, so I guess the answer was always "No." Bar games like Mig Sweep, where everybody held arms and ran around knocking everybody and everything over was fun, I guess. Dead Bug was very dangerous game where someone yelled, "Dead Bug," and everybody hit the deck. The last man standing had to buy the bar (several hundred dollars sometimes) and lots of cracked heads and broken chairs were the result. Somehow, I thought this not to be an adult activity and certainly not "fun." When drinking and bar games were no longer available, I had to learn how to have "fun" from scratch. A necessary part of life. I am still working on it and seek new avenues for "fun." I thought when I put down my last drink fun would never happen again in my life, how truly wrong that was.

Driving 9,000 miles and visiting family and friends in 26 states was my latest "fun" activity.

October 25

STEP ZERO

Yeah, I know there are only 12 Steps to our program but I have listened to a few folks who talk about Step Zero. That is the step you admit to your innermost self that you are alcoholic before you even tackle Step One. I have thought about it for few years now and here is my take on Step Zero from my own inventory and experience. My dark bottom was long before steps came into my cognizance. I knew I was sick, I knew alcohol just plain did not work. I could not *not* drink, my body screamed for more and more alcohol and it did less and less. I felt terrible, was overweight, high blood pressure, could not eat anything larger than a pea and saw no end to my downward spiral. I was screwed and knew down deep something had to change. Ground Zero for me. AA was not even in my vocabulary yet. The heat was on me, and I wanted out and to stop the forces invading my space. Suicide looked like the only door open to me, but I had enough moral upbringings, which told me I don't have the right to take my God given life.

For years I knew I was an alcoholic, but I said, "So what?" You have to do something about it, dude, is so what. I did some soul searching and yes, I admitted I was an alcoholic but the next part of my Step Zero was I had no clue on what to do next so I must get help. Asking for help was just not in my makeup or experience anywhere. A key part in my Step Zero was admitting I needed outside help. I wanted to die but I wanted it to be romantic. Die with a glass of Jack Daniels and a beautiful girl under my arm and a smile on my face. Well it just doesn't get romantic. At the end, you just get sick. No girl could stand me, I couldn't afford Jack Daniels and the smile got whipped off my puss for quite some time. The first move after Step Zero was to make it to a treatment interview that my wife (soon to be ex-wife) forced on me. I admitted in the interview that I was an alcoholic and they accepted me into outpatient treatment. All the treatment folks did is steer me to AA meetings. I did Step One after a very spiritual Step Zero.

There you have it, my take on Step Zero. I am a believer now.

October 26

MIND CONTROL

None of us likes to be controlled so the thought of brainwashing pushes our buttons. I remember one of my first meetings when another newcomer complained that this program is nothing more than brainwashing and an old timer retorted, "Son, your brain needs washing." Too much laughter but the point was made. All of us need a good scrub in the brain department. Our thinking got us in this mess so how are we going to think our way out? My thinking was full of old ideas and they got me nowhere. I needed a brain transplant really. If this program is a kind of brainwashing, I am all in and need all the help I can get. I came to realize I needed a complete reprogramming from top to bottom.

Once we grasp the concept of powerlessness, we learn our attitude is one thing we can change. Is that not mind control? To change my attitude is a mental process and it takes some work and prayer for best results IMHO. I know my brain is defective from years of wrong thinking and abuse. God only knows how many brain cells I killed by my drinking. Luckily some are still linked together to help somebody else. Maybe one more gin and all those connectors in my skull would quit holding hands and I would be a wet brain. Knowing that my brain is not the best and never will be I work on keeping it in shape with good readings and a daily attitude adjustment. I try to let my heart talk to my brain and keep life between the white lines. My brain can spin up to Mach 3 for no good reason and I have to look at my feet to see I am going nowhere.

Body, mind and spirit are all connected but the mind is the director.

October 27

REGRETS

Having regret is just plain human. Sure, we don't want to regret the past or shut the door on it. We know we cannot rewrite history so carrying regrets around like a millstone around your neck is non-productive. These regrets we all have can be used in our rehab and new life to great benefit. For example: one of my big regrets was all the time I stole from my kids when they were young and I was well into my disease. Okay, what can I do about it? I have made a point to spend quality time on long visits with all my available children once a year (minus health setbacks) for the last 20 years. Actually, they need it more now than those years I regret stealing their time. I am their only living parent and the grand parents are gone also. It is my version of a living amends and a very real expression of love. It has been a win-win activity born out of a regret. I am closer to my kids than ever before in my life. It replaced the lose-lose days of the past.

As we look at all our regrets, we can ask what is the desired learning outcome from these events. We do not want to repeat painful history so we collect some valuable lessons of what not to do. You can reverse the activity you regret and do something positive going forward. Do you regret not following your bliss, such as artwork you enjoyed in school? Well go to an art store and buy some oil paints and some art paper and let loose. I won't laugh and no one else will either, it will be good for your soul. I used to play a pretty good game of golf in 1964 in college but dropped out for 50 years. I just bought a nice set of golf clubs for both the wife and I. We won't force Tiger Woods into retirement but it's a fun thing we can do together. Doing something about regrets is possible.

Maybe we should give regrets a new name, speed bumps on the road of life.

October 28

WHEN GOD CLOSES A DOOR

Someone wrote "When God closes a door, He always opens a window." In my experience, this is very true. Doors close all the time, a job ends, a relationship blows up or a car gets stolen. The trick is to find the open window. Often, we are blinded by fear we don't see clearly and bang on the closed door in the hope it will open again or burn up with resentment at the closed door. We sit and stare at the blocked door and in the old days, drink over it. When my door to drinking closed I thought there was no way out. I was just plain screwed. I could not be more wrong and all the closed doors of my past I failed to see the open window much of the time.

Faith there is another path when the one in front of you has a big boulder is the key for me. I now have faith God has not brought me this far to drop me on my head. I learned to pray for guidance to find the light at the end of the tunnel. I know when I was on the ground in an enemy airfield with an airplane out of gas it looked like all my doors were shut forever. Somehow through prayer and inspiration from God I was able to find gas and refuel under gunfire in order to make it off the hostile runway and write this little piece. Now I check for open windows before the door closes and prepare myself mentally for an emergency exit. I have found the window is much better than the door was anyway. I just need to forget the door and be happy God has always provided a window into the Sunlight and a better life.

Sometimes there are many windows open and the problem is to pick the right one.

October 29

LIFE IS EASY

I let myself get plagued by small stuff and it is all small stuff. When I finally was able to understand the real meaning of "powerlessness" my life became very easy. I was always in turmoil over all the universe's problems as if I was in some way responsible. Once I saw I am powerless over just about 99% of what I encounter on a daily basis, then I am relieved of all this needless teeth grinding and hand wringing. Why aircraft disappear from 35,000 feet is really beyond my responsibility, maybe I could have saved those lives but I was not at the controls. Why 145 kids in Pakistan get gunned down is something I could not stop, I wish I could, but I can't. I feel terrible about the daily bad news from around the world, but I keep all those things in my powerless box, way in the background of my consciousness. When my head is spinning, I look down at my feet and realize I am not going anywhere. Prayer and meditation stop the spin cycle for me.

Breaking down life into 24-hour segments makes it easier, combined with all those things over which I have no control. It frees up my day to do good stuff and have fun, enjoy life. I cannot stop the tick of the clock, I cannot control people, places and things but I don't have to like it. I try not to focus on those negative happenings that cross my path. I can pick my friends, I stay away from grumpy, nasty people. If I don't like the weather I can move (which I did). My attitude is probably the most important item I am not powerless over. If I don't feel right, I know I have an attitude problem and I can fix it. If I am disturbed, I know I am taking myself too seriously. I begin to think I am better than being just another Bozo on the bus. My ego can puff little stuff into thunderstorms if I don't keep myself in proportion to a grain of sand on the beach of life.

Every day requires an attitude adjustment. Life is only hard when I make it hard.

October 30

SERVICE = LOVE

We talk a lot about service as a key element of our program. The three sides of the triangle: Recovery, Unity and Service. Most of us think of service as attending a home group and making coffee or being secretary of a meeting but really service extends to all areas of our life. A fellow in a meeting recently, a guy whom I respect a lot, said service is just another word for love. Wow. I thought about it and thought there was a familiar ring to that. Of course, it was the saying from Mother Teresa.

Here it is again. I know I have used it before but it bears repeating.

The fruit of silence

is prayer

The fruit of prayer is faith

The fruit of faith is love

The fruit of love is service

The fruit of service is peace

Mother Teresa

Just doing things for others is an act of love and it has the great reward of promoting positive living. Love is contagious and causes an upward spiral. I have been blessed in my life to have opportunities for service of all kinds. I enjoy it, seek it and try to improve on it. Love is the answer to all the ills of this world.

October 31

ADVICE & JUDGMENT

Many of our readings have been about advice and judgment especially when dealing with newcomers. Personally, I try to stay out of the advice business altogether. Being a senior citizen is not always easy. I have a lot of experience, a lot of it bad experience, so why should I not spread my wisdom? When I am asked for advice, I try to put it in my own framework, "This is what I did, or this is what I didn't do," instead of preaching, "You need to do this, or else." I learned to let people make their own mistakes and not try to save the world by inserting my input into their life. Now if someone is about to be hit by a train, I will pull them off the tracks but that hasn't happened lately. I don't mind saying, "I don't know," when asked advice about something I am fuzzy on or have limited knowledge. Lawyers charge big bucks for advice. Mine is given freely, if asked, you get what you pay for. The founders of AA knew that advice does not work.

"If you don't take the first drink, you won't get drunk." To me that is a stone-cold fact and not advice.

Judgment is just plain human. We make an instant judgment when we meet someone. "Wow this guy is dressed like a slob, looks like he had too much to drink, he is putting out negative vibes, etc ..." We also like to think we are excellent judge of people. I have been proven wrong so many times I try to stay out of the judgment business. I collect more information and then make a judgment, also wrong many times. The guys I thought could not stay sober have and the guys with the light on and the golden words don't stay sober. I can't judge what's going on in someone else head or his heart. I think it is okay to have some judgment but I keep it to myself. I don't need to gossip about my crazy evaluation of another person.

I try to be selective in my advice and keep my judgments to myself.

November 1

LISTS

The topic of lists has been rolling around in my warped brain for a while. You will always find two lists in my pocket, my gratitude list and my daily to-do list. I've been listening to folks talk about "Bucket lists" a list of things they want to do or places they want to see before they die. Since we have no idea when we are going to die, I find this list non-productive for me at least. I have no bucket list. If I die tonight, I will not feel cheated or missing a single thing in this life. In fact, I have been blessed way beyond what I deserve. I have a world atlas and looking at the planet there is no place I really need to visit. If I go somewhere it is to see someone I love. I am where I want to be. Then there is the famous Shit List, people who I have resentments against. I learned to wipe (no pun intended) that list clean. When I did have such a list most of the people on it didn't know they were on my shit list or would they care one way or another. Resent someone and they are living in your head rent free in a very negative way. It is like taking poison and hoping the other person will die. Forget that list also.

I don't have a "wish list or a "want list" either. I want what I have already. My prayers don't ask God for anything material for myself, my cup runneth over.

I do have "a people to pray for list" in my pocket I already expounded on before. That is a good list to help me think of others. There is one list however that is part of my daily life. My gratitude list. The 44 items on this list does so many things for me right now today. It makes me happy to review the gifts God blessed me with. It makes me humble as part of being grateful. It fills my heart with love and serenity. It keeps me positive in a negative world. It keeps me out of the storms of controversy. I see daily life as heaven because I am not so sure about what happens after death. My resume might not pass muster so I have been busy trying to pad my good vs. bad listing in the sky. Happy joyous and free, it's all on the list.

In my experience, writing it down seems to be the first step in making it happen. My to-do list is forgotten until the next day and usually all has been accomplished, magic.

November 2

THINKING OF OTHERS

Every year when the reading about "Thinking of Others" I think about Rick, a great friend in sobriety now long passed away. When we had our daily morning conversation before the meeting started, he would often say, "Mike I am happy you are thinking of others." In his share he always mentioned, "Thinking of others." When Rick was diagnosed with cancer beyond fixing, it was easy for me to think about Rick and tell him he will not be alone through his condition. For one year I stayed in the caregiving mode with a lot of help from his wife and another guy in the fellowship. It was a wonderful year of giving of myself and a terrible year to see Rick go from a robust 60 to a dying 100-year-old man. Both of us were combat vets in addition to AA so I was able to have proper military honors and benefits come to him and his family. I learned many things about death and dying, cancer, overseas death procedures and have written much about the process. Living is a much better way and less paperwork.

In the reading, the writer admits he often thinks of himself first and thinking of others does not come naturally. If you read the emergency procedures when you fly it says, "If the oxygen masks come down from the overhead please put on your mask first before you try to help a child or others." Same with sobriety, you need to take care of your own sobriety or you may not be able to help others. There is some balance which has to be reached in this business of helping others. I know from my own experience I feel better when I am not thinking about me and I think about you. I have a list of people on my prayer list in my pocket and refer to it daily. It helps me keep others in the foreground and my needs in the background. When I give to others, I get paid back much more than I deserve.

The further I get away from me the better I feel. Thinking of others makes me happier.

November 3

EXPERIENCE

Life is a little upside down when you think about it. The tests in life come first and the lessons are learned after the test is over. Experience may be the only teacher we can ever depend on. When we do 12 Step work, we say we share "Our experience, strength and hope." Our own experience is the only asset we have in this process. All of us have different paths and experience obviously and all of us are "unique." My years on this planet gave me a treasure chest full of experience but only a small portion of it is useful in helping others. I learned to tone back my combat experiences because those who have no combat experience cannot relate to the stories. Even my fellow pilots cannot relate to some of my experiences because they had a different set of rules. The war was different over time. However, most agree I was insane. The second step promises to restore me to sanity, good luck. I was never sane in the first place.

When working with a new guy I found it useful to keep my mouth shut and not talk about my experience until I hear his experience then I try to find a common ground that says, "I understand, I know, I have been there too." Only then will experience be an aid to carrying the message of hope. I always try to tell funny stories of my past to relax the guy listening. I can laugh at myself but am careful not to laugh at the experience of others. They might not see the humor in their pratfalls just yet. When I do my inventory of experience I must say, "Thank You God for bringing me this far." I sure did not get cheated in this life for experience. What a ride. Now my job in this program is to put this gift to good use and help others. As I share my experiences with you, it is my prayer that some of it is useful.

Life is a banquet and most poor suckers are starving to death ~ Auntie Mame

November 4

NO PRICE TAG

I've been thinking about the reading on *Love Has No Price Tag*. Love is one of those pure emotions connected to the heart and of course, has no price tag. We know love cannot be bought or sold. It is priceless like so many other things on our gratitude list. Actually, the best things in life have no price tag. As the path gets narrower, I know all my worldly possessions will be toast. I came in with nothing and will leave with nothing. I can only hope the love I have shown to friends and family will live on. I learned the material world needs to be replaced by a spiritual world for me to fully live in the 12th Step. There is a spiritual answer to all my problems, I can't buy the results which are up to God anyway.

So many folks know the price of everything and the value of nothing. So many of us attach happiness to a fancy car, a nice house and a fat bank account. If that is true then why do famous people with all those items I mention, commit suicide? I have found love, spirituality and happiness to be all one ball of wax. I am so happy this program of ours is not about money in any way. All the help in the world is available free, given freely and shared freely. I give of myself for free and I am overpaid in dividends. In my world money is never an issue. God provided me with everything I need to do my job of carrying the message of love wherever I go. I am old and everything I have is old (including this computer) and that's OK with me. I don't need a Rolls or a Rolex but I am on a roll.

This message is written to you absolutely free of charge and with love.

WHO PACKS YOUR PARACHUTE?

I just love the term "suggested steps," just like it is suggested you pull your rip cord on your parachute for best results. I used to wear a parachute on my back as part of my flying equipment and it was "suggested" we check it out before each flight because you never know when you might need to depart a broken burning airplane. Luckily in all my flying, all my takeoffs and landings came out equal. Every time I flew, I looked at the big "D" ring that opened the chute and wondered if today would be the day I would have to pull it. It was a leap of faith the chute would open correctly and a nylon letdown would happen safely. If an emergency did happen the most important person in the world at that point is the nameless, faceless guy who packed my parachute. Would I seek him/her out and thank the person after surviving a jump?

I think about my life today and I do the "suggestions" because I know they work. I still have faith my spiritual parachute will work because I know my Higher Power packs my chute every day. I don't see Him but I know He is there and any emergency I have will be OK once I pull the ripcord (read pray). I know that God will help me in all my rough circumstances. I wear this program just like I wore my chute when I flew. I would not take off without my equipment and I don't try life without my Higher Power. When disaster strikes, I know I have a reserve with me to stay alive and safe for one more day. All I have to do is keep my chute in good working order by a daily workout on my spiritual condition and all my landings have been very soft.

Ask yourself who packs your chute and thank whomever that is, happy landings.

November 6

JUST ANOTHER BOZO ON THE BUS

Many of us have a problem with humility and what it really means. Often confused with humiliation, humility to me is being "right sized" not better than or less than anybody else. We all have the same rank and the same date of rank, today only. Nobody is president, we have no bosses (we have some bossy people). Often heard in meetings, "I am just another Bozo on the bus." Great visual because a bus is pretty humble and melting into the general population is humble. I always add, "this Bozo sits in the middle, not in the front or the back as a statement just right in the middle with no meaning. I will try to be a worker among workers, just a trusted servant not a leader, we do not govern and that's a good thing.

A lot of readings are about the "limelight" and the dangers it poses to us. I have had my opportunities in the limelight and I did not handle it well as a drunk. I had my run with the big dogs and now is the time to stay on the porch. The limelight is addictive and there is never enough applause, never enough praise. Now being "right sized" I need only impress myself by doing the next right thing. Others may criticize or praise but their opinion is none of my business. I know my ego needs a daily review to make sure it does not Edge God Out EGO. A look at our powerlessness helps a lot and the gratitude list reminds us all of our gifts come from the grace of God, in other words, humility.

Being just another bozo is being "right-sized" not the worst, not the best, but just plain old me. OK, I am off to catch the bus. My Porsche is in the shop.

November 7

RELAX

People used to tell me to "relax" quite often and I hated it. I would tell them they need to relax from telling me to relax. My life before I got sober had no relax in it. Life was turmoil, chaos and trouble but finally I came to realize most of it was my own doing and my choices. I put myself in the way of every storm available. Relax? You have to be kidding me? Even drinking is supposed to be a relaxation activity but how can you relax when keeping it together so as not make a fool out of yourself and get arrested. When I did my step work and morning mediation became second nature, I learned you must relax for best results. How can you quiet the mind without relaxing? Impossible. The Big Book says, "We relax we don't struggle," so true. Acceptance of life as it is means no more fighting, no more struggle.

To relax can be learned and it was not in my vocabulary, it was just one more tool I needed to learn from zero experience. Now maybe I relax too much at times when I should take action. I have found doing nothing is often the best policy. It has been many years since anyone has told me "to relax" so I guess I have mastered it somewhat. Getting old forces you to relax or you pop a joint. God knows where the road leads and He does not need my help and knowing that helps me relax all the more. Staying out of other people's lives is hard to do for family and friends but praying for God's will is all you can do at times. I find the more I relax the more my mind opens to new ideas and new options I never saw before. These periods of relaxation bring about moments of inspiration.

All the great athletes are very relaxed in their skill of their sport. When I played golf, I was wound up like a spring, humans, flora and wildlife were in danger when I struck the ball. I relaxed and sold my clubs.

November 8

LET GO LET GOD WITH LOVE

All of us have learned we must let go of many things, let go of our bottle, let go of slippery friends, let go of destructive relationships. Some folks leave claw marks on everything they let go of. There are many ways to let go or you get dragged down. Turning it over to God for His care and His will is great but what about your attitude? You can let go with resentment, hate and discontent or let go with love. I recommend (you saw this coming, right?) letting go with love. Especially true in relationships. In my own experience, to release with love and wish the best for the other person is not only healing it keeps the door open for a spiritual connection if not a physical one. My first wife, the mother of 4 of my children and I had a wonderful relationship even though we were divorced for many years. We bonded in a way much more important than high school puppy love. I was blessed to be able to be by her side when she passed with cancer and help her in a real way when she no longer could work.

In my family we just had a big event. My cousin in California with whom I am very close just became a grandfather for the first time. His daughter just gave birth to a baby girl. So what, you say? Well for the first time in this family, the baby girl is half black. The father whom I just met on my last trip is a great guy with a great family. There was a baby shower at my cousin's house and you could not help but notice some older black ladies in attendance. (Grandma and great Grandma) The beauty of all of this is my family has let go of old ideas and old prejudice which was the sin of our fathers now departed. Total acceptance by the entire family minus any snide comments or looks. To me that is letting go with love in a very open way. I was proud of my family and our new addition to the family.

I am ready to let go of anything at any time, nothing belongs to me anyway.

November 9

BEND BUT DON'T BREAK

Along the theme of "go with the flow" in the recent readings, I learned the idea of bend but don't break like a reed in the water moving with the tide and currents. By "break" I mean lose my temper or act rashly to events or people. We often have to endure undesirable people or unfortunate events but must be calm and "bend' until the situation passes.

Reminding ourselves we have no control over people, places and things. We can only control our attitude toward the bad times. I learned a long time ago, I am in the minority in my opinion so I would be in constant turmoil to push my thoughts onto any group. I quietly disagree in my own head but do not enter into controversy. A smile while disagreeing helps confuse the opponents. The things I have left unsaid are much better unsaid. In fact, keeping my mouth shut at every opportunity works very well. It is better to be thought a fool than open my mouth and remove all doubt.

One of my favorite posters is a pack of bloodhounds on a hunt, ears all perked up and right in the middle of the pack is the fox trying to look just like the pack of hounds. The caption is: "Go with the Herd." I really identify with the fox, not really fitting in but trying to be one of the hound dogs. Always afraid of being found out and eventually be consumed by the enemy. When the group I am in makes a decision it usually is not to my liking but I have learned to bend and put its importance in perspective. Who cares a year from now? Who cares next week in some cases? In the military, we often had bad bosses, so we had a saying, "Outlast the Bastards." And sure enough, the bastards moved on or got found out. Patience is the key.

I have found flexibility to be very attractive. Knowing when to pick your battles is an art form so backing up is OK until you hit one of your boundaries.

November 10

INFERIORITY COMPLEX

I know a lot of you use the Hazelden 24 Hours A Day book, and if not, I highly recommend it to add to your morning reading. All the old timers I met in my early sobriety used it as a notebook with birthdays and margin notes. The very first meeting in Honolulu the fellowship used the book for meetings as topics for sharing. Yea, I know it is not AA approved but you can find useful literature outside the AA bookshelf. I like the daily questions in each reading and sometimes I answer out loud. November 8th was: "Have I lost my inferiority complex?" In my home group I mentioned this question in my share but I said, the real question is, "Have I lost my superiority complex?" Got a good laugh. November 10th the question was: "Am I less self-centered?" IMHO the two go together. Most of us are in the self-hatred mode when we hit bottom. "I can't stand myself but all I think about is me." "I am an egomaniac with an inferiority complex." Only an alcoholic could understand these statements. It takes some quality sobriety and time to rebuild self-esteem. We beat ourselves up at the beginning of this journey and really it is a waste of time and very unproductive. It is just another example of our selfishness. This is absolutely a selfish disease.

Once we grasp the idea, we are not bad people getting good, we are sick people getting well. We are viewing ourselves in a better light. The biggest step is to do the thorough moral inventory and step back and look at ourselves. We learn not to compare ourselves to anybody else. We are not trying to find ways we are better than the other guy nor are we looking for how we are less than our fellows. We get right-sized for us, nobody else. Not more than not less than. Inferior to whom, superior to whom? In morning prayer, we measure up to our Higher Power by doing the best we can, by doing the next right thing. God knows who you are and you will too, eventually. What other people think of you and how they measure you is none of your business. The hell with what they think. You know are what you are. In time, you will love yourself. I was taught that you can't expect somebody to love you if you don't love yourself.

If we do the Steps, we will not have any complexes and self-centeredness will slip away.

November 11

SPOT CHECK INVENTORY

I have learned Step 10 is not a once over deal, it is a constant process. In the last few weeks with family drama happenings all around me, I need to keep my tongue in my mouth, my ideas on hold, and my emotions in check. Since I have not been able to attend meetings while traveling, Step 10 is part of my "road show." I have this wonderful recovery program that works for me and when surrounded by folks not in any program it is difficult to watch them flounder away with problems that a Step program could solve. But I have to remember I don't sponsor any family members and I can only be an example. Even though I am busy with family I find quiet time in the morning to do my Step 10 and make a report card on myself how I handled family interaction and drama. I consider the day's activity ahead and try to gird my loins ahead of time and think of the character defects I may have a chance to improve on.

I had one family member who jumped into my inventory. All of us AA types hate to have someone else do our inventory but I had to bite my tongue when it happened to me. I wanted to tell this guy I didn't need his help. He also tried to get a debate going about world events and I told him I don't keep up with world news I have no control over them and they will upset me needlessly. This was unacceptable to him and he found someone else to argue with. He stopped talking to me and that was good for the both of us. He has been a negative person forever and I am not going to change him. In my 10th Step I avoided giving up my principles but I could have done a better job of explaining my attitude. I came to the realization living in Thailand is very good for me. My family in the USA doesn't need my help.

Whenever there is a lot of interaction and argument, I do not feel comfortable I excuse myself quietly and do a mini Step 10 and return to the fray with a smile.

341

November 12

BEATING YOURSELF UP

All of us who are trying to follow a spiritual life often make the mistake of being too hard on ourselves. Self-condemnation slows us down and causes depression and inner discontent. God doesn't expect more out of us than we can do. We forget "progress not perfection." We can only be human with limitations. Sometimes we have to step back or sideways and even fall down now and again. High standards are a good thing as long as they are realistic. Getting impatient with ourselves is foolish since we are doing our best not always up to our own expectations. "We relax, we do not struggle." I love that line. The fox condemns the trap not himself. All of us run into "traps" on the road of life and we get caught occasionally and we suffer a setback. Blaming ourselves is just non-productive. When you need a friend, the friend should be you. Making yourself a villain is the last thing you want. Yes, it is good to try to reach goals and improve ourselves but a positive balance is better than the negativity of self-flagellation.

OK, if this becomes a problem maybe it is time to look at your relationship with yourself. I vividly remember screaming at myself out loud about what a hopeless wreck I was. I could not stop pouring alcohol down my throat. I hated myself and I had lost all my friends. It was impossible to be a friend to myself when I desperately needed one. Once I put the drink down, I slowly began to look myself in the mirror more than 5 seconds and stopped yelling at the ugly image I saw. Doing the 12 Steps made me grateful and I began to like how far I had come and how wonderful my life was. Then on to acceptance. I accept myself warts and all. Character defects yes but some major accomplishments. I wasn't a dirt bag after all. Slowly I found a new friend. Me. A good friend is one who knows all about you and loves you anyway. Nobody knows me better and I love myself today. I am a work in progress so much improvement is required but the timetable is mine and my Higher Power's.

If I am going to keep myself as a close friend why would I turn on myself and create an adversary? I need all the friends I can get in rough

342

seas so I will not fight with myself anymore.

November 13

SELFISH FROM BIRTH

I enjoy driving and opted to drive to reconnect to my home country after 10 years in Thailand. Plenty of time to meditate during the 3,500 miles. Some things that struck me were the entire country is in decay on the highway. It was work zone after work zone, reduced speed, one lane traffic, orange cones and signs, threats of double fines and jail for driving error. The population of the USA is, in general terms, overweight. I joined them as eating always included fries with everything you order. The truck drivers used to be knights of the road, no more. I got pushed around and run off the road by trucks blocking lanes of traffic at slow speeds to overtake another even slower truck. Luckily, I was not in any hurry so I rolled with the punches. In fact, the whole trip was an exercise in tolerance and patience.

The biggest impression I had was the vastness of America and the abundance of farmland growing wheat, corn, vegetables enough to feed the whole planet yet people are starving elsewhere. God gave us a full basket and we as a nation have not found a way to share all our gifts properly. I grew up in selfishness in a nation built on material wellbeing. Success was measured in material ways from birth and since alcoholics are engaged in a selfish disease, we Americans come by it honestly. There were some hours of driving that not one house or one person was in sight. To say the earth is overcrowded is just plain wrong. The USA has plenty of room but selfishness keeps us from sharing it. Doing my own inventory, I realize that my selfishness from birth is something I need to work on to reverse the material focus to a more spiritual one.

Living in a country which is not so blessed in wealth as the USA is good for my recovery. My Thai family up in the village is a very happy loving family and no BMW's in sight. They are the most unselfish people I have ever met.

November 14

SO, YOU WANT TO BE A MILLIONAIRE?

I went to a meeting in a fire station 12 time zones away from home with 70 people (a convention where I come from). I felt very much at home and ran into a guy who remembered me from a Honolulu Wailana Coffee Shop and another gent who remembered me from a Bourbon Street meeting in Bangkok. AA is a small world after all. Then in the evening, I went to a house of my son and daughter-in-law's friend that was "millionaires only." The house was a city block large, 8 servants working the party, the house was like an art gallery that could handle 100 people, indoor swimming pool, button down be-jeweled guests. I never felt more uncomfortable in my life. Clearly, I did not belong and was happy to escape before the alcohol worked on all the millionaires. I thank God when I prayed for riches God gave me poverty instead so I might achieve humility and gratitude for other blessings which made me much richer in other areas than money and property. I realized that Mystic has so few AA meetings because millionaires don't make it to the rooms of AA very easily.

If a famous person came to my door and offered me $10 million to do a Budweiser beer commercial, I would turn him down. I would lose much more than money if I picked up a beer. I don't need a million dollars and all the fears of someone taxing it all away. I would break a promise to my Higher Power and to myself, not to pick up a drink as long as I live. I can't afford even one drink. When I am surrounded by millionaires, I don't want what they have. The boats, the houses and luxury cars, are not necessary in my life. We are the lucky ones, rich in spirituality, rich in love, rich in serenity, rich in service to others. This program provided all I need to meet my basic needs in order to do God's will for me. Priceless.

It is harder for a rich man to get to heaven than it is for a camel to make it through the eye of a needle. ~ Bible

November 15

LOVE WITHOUT BORDERS

I had a great visit with my good friend and sponsee who came down from Mass to CT for a big hug and lots of "talk story." We drank together (amazing stories) in Honolulu and we got sober together. I was newly sober and had all my AA books out on my kitchen table and my sponsee was painting my house getting ready to sell. He swears I put the books out to push him into the program. Not my intent and I had no idea Bear had a cooler of beer in the back of the house to assist him through a day of painting. One day he mustered up enough courage to talk to me about his drinking. He said, "Mike if you can get sober, I sure can." When we were drinking buddies, Bear was the one who drug me out of Honolulu bars before I spent every dime and he put an end to some foolishness. So at least I could serve as a bad example of someone who got sober. We had a long friendship that has no location because both of us have left Hawaii. Bear has made it through massive medical problems, loss of loved ones and has not picked up a drink in over 17+ years. Our bond of love has no location. We have remained in contact all these years no matter our physical location.

I tried to get my sponsee into Step 5 to no avail until he had to be admitted to a hospital for an emergency operation. It was Christmas 2001 and he had tubes and wires out of every orifice of his body. So, we did a 5th Step finally when he couldn't move and escape.

When I made a meeting in Mystic, Conn., the secretary didn't show up just like home, there was a "preacher" just like home, one guy talked way too long just like home. Wherever you go on this globe AA is waiting for you to show up and get plugged in and it is the same with little differences. This Mystic group holds hands and says the Lord's Prayer at the end. Unheard of in Thailand but I sure enjoyed the change and the sameness both.

November 16

QUALITY VS. QUANTITY

I am happy to report there are more meetings in my little Thai town than there are in Mystic CT. I want to share my family happenings and the spiritual message I get from the entire experience. The first story is about the physical therapist my son with ALS has been dealing with. Luckily my doctor granddaughter was here to put a stop to damaging procedures this person was doing to my son. She was treating my son as if he was needing to get stronger and build his muscle tone but it doesn't work that way with ALS. The muscles are not going to get better so range of motion is the only good thing that can happen to an ALS patient. My granddaughter put a stop to things which could shorten my son's life. Since he is the only survivor of his test group, the doctors can only put the finger on his positive attitude that has given him some quality and quantity.

The family problem we face now is that my son is enjoying walking around, driving and drinking beer. To him that is quality. But if he falls, which he has done 5 times we know of, and he breaks a leg, hip or arm, it will not heal and cut what life he has left in half. One family member would have him stay home in his wheelchair, look out the window and extend his life. Other family members would let him do what he wants to do even if it is dangerous. My son clearly wants quality days and not more days. Eventually he will need a feeding tube to stay alive, which he doesn't want, or all the other procedures necessary for a longer run at life. A tough balancing problem for the family and the conflict of differing opinions. I have a spiritual path that tells me God's will not mine. I pray for to my Higher Power for the help to find the right choices.

I am in awe of my own family and their harmony of love for each other. I am truly blessed.

BRINGING THE MESSAGE HOME

I guess all these years of following the program and doing the Steps have paid off big time with my family. Even though none of my family is in the program some stuff has rubbed off on them from my actions and attitude. I have heard my son (the one with ALS) talking to his friends about some of the things he has learned from his father. One day at a time is the number #1 principal in his attitude, enjoying every single day to the fullest knowing his days are numbered. He tells everyone he refuses to get stressed out. His father taught him not to be concerned about those things which he has no control over. The one thing he really gets a big laugh over is "What people think of me is none of my business." On the other hand, my other son who needs to be in recovery, is not buying into his father's program or its principles but I need to continue to show him my path and just maybe he will be open to changing his life also.

My 31-year-old doctor granddaughter has spent a couple of days with me and we have had some quality time together. Last night she gave me a priceless compliment. She said she really appreciated my calm way of handling family situations, my positive attitude and acceptance of everybody in the family. She told me she enjoys my company and thinks I am a fun guy.

I learned I need not weigh in on everything that happens in family conflicts and my opinion can stay in my brain and not out of my mouth. The love and tolerance I need to deal with my AA group applies to my family also. I want the best for them, of course, but I cannot control them in any way. I have found living this program rubs off on others in a good way.

Being happy joyous and free is contagious.

November 18

THE WOUNDED SOUL

This business of recovery has so many benefits and blessings. We have done damage to our bodies and some of it can be reversed by new healthy choices of diet, exercise and neglected medical care. However, some things with our bodies cannot be changed like ALS that my son has or just plain age-related decay. For some of us the biggest wound is to our soul. The wreckage of the past has scarred our souls but those wounds can be healed. The first step is to get your soul back. You can retrieve your soul by good spiritual conditioning as a result of the Steps. Once you put all the missing pieces back then it is easier to heal the wounded soul. In my own inventory, I was "out there" for a long time and spread my wreckage over a large area of the map. When I did my deep amends, I traveled thousands of miles on my personal journey of soul retrieval. I feel whole again but still wounded and scarred.

On this family trip I have been sharing with all of you, it's an amazing healing journey for my wounded soul. I will see every member of my family who is available and have quality time with all of them. I listened to a story from one of my sons about a motorcycle accident that could have killed him. First time I ever heard of this incident, a major event in his life. I missed that whole piece of his life because I took myself out of the picture many years back. As I looked around the table, I realized I missed a big portion of the life of every person in my family. I was missing in action by choice and made myself unavailable. Today I am part of the family again and the healing to my soul is like heaven. I have been able to bond with my children, my grandkids, my sisters, my in-laws, my cousins and all of their significant others. What a blessing.

One more drink and I could have missed all of this. The damage to the soul can be healed. Be good to yourself.

November 19

ACCEPTANCE PROMOTES LOVE

Acceptance is the key. We have heard this many times, but I would like to add, it promotes love. As you know, my son is in later stages of Lou Gehrig's disease (ALS) but he has acceptance of his condition and has a great positive attitude. He has maintained his sense of humor and is a joy to be around even though he has a hard time speaking, walking, eating. My family is at his house since his mobility is limited and the family has accepted the facts of the situation and don't treat my son in a condescending way at all. My son doesn't want people to feel sorry for him or act differently because of his condition. His acceptance is making everyone else accept what is. The family has traveled from Alaska, California, Florida, Vermont, Texas, and Thailand of course to be together in a very meaningful display of love.

This family reunion would never have taken place if my son had a bad attitude and not accepted his fate. If he was a negative person, nobody would travel thousands of miles to be unhappy. I thank God for my amazing family and the way they have rallied together. I have already told you about my daughter who gave up her house in Dallas and her job to be with her brother until he passes. Her actions have shown the rest of us a love beyond the norm.

All of my son's group of 24 ALS patients have passed but him. His ability to be positive is the only thing the doctors can pinpoint to his longevity. He is living one day at a time and enjoying each day to the fullest. It is a lesson to the entire family and it has bonded us all in love by acceptance of the situation.

November 20

SUICIDE

So, we lost another one of us. This one, rich and famous. Maybe Robin W or Phil H sat next to you in a meeting somewhere, two guys who had

20 years of sobriety at one time but got off track and they both committed suicide. It brings home the message that material wealth and fame do not keep you sober. Only the God of your understanding can stop you from putting a belt around your neck. I hammer the point of our selfishness a lot, but excuse me, suicide is the most selfish act of all. Leave a mess for your loved ones to clean up and deny them the chance to help you recover. All of us have had suicidal thoughts, speaking for myself, I have engaged in suicidal behavior in my profession and volunteering my life in pursuit of selfish goals. Right now, I am with my sibling that made a serious suicide attempt a few years back. I am enjoying her company and we have had more time together now than all the 50 years before. She told me yesterday that my phone call when she was in the hospital changed her thinking and made a world of difference to her.

My phone call was straight program. Even though she is not an alcoholic she had all the negative thinking, depression and other garbage we suffered at our bottom. Now she is enjoying the family and with an attitude of gratitude. She keeps saying, "I almost missed all of this." Life sucks from time to time no doubt about it but it passes just like pain. We owe God a pause for the storm to pass. God gave us the gift of life and taking it away by ourselves gets ahead of God. Bad idea.

Suicide is a permanent solution to a temporary problem.

November 21

ROMANTIC PACKAGING

I remember being a kid at Christmas and piling up a stack of presents along with my 3 sisters. First, we would compare who had the biggest stack. I finally realized a box with a shirt is bigger than a dress box for a little girl. When it was all over there was a pile of paper, boxes and ribbon and a tiny collection of ugly socks and checkered shirts I hated. Bummer. The package is more exciting than the contents was the lesson I learned. Then all the advertising on TV associated toothpaste with romance. Crest will hook you up with the right girl. I guess somebody believes that BS because they keep selling romance with stuff which has no connection. When we shop for a car, we look at the sleek body lines, the color, the brand name. Hey, guess what? You drive the car from the inside not the outside. A better attribute might be to find out how this tin can handles in a crash.

We are suckers for romance and packaging. Same with people. Who are you going to elect president? A young energetic, bright eyed idealist or an over-the-hill grey haired stiff-armed old man? I saw a new car ad on TV for Honda, it has a handsome couple dressed to the max going to an auction where the knockout lady acquires a diamond necklace (worth 4 Hondas). The message is sex, romance, wealth and classy life in a Honda. This is not a BMW it's a Honda. Get real. How often we chase the dream girl and enjoy the romance, sooner or later somebody has to take out the garbage and clean the house. I try to look beyond the advertising, the hype, the romance, the slick package and get a grip on reality before it hits me in the chops.

I have a friend in the program who runs a fancy upscale bar. I had no idea there were so many different flavors of vodka. His bar had backlighting on all the colorful bottles as a shrine to alcohol. I told the guy it was all very pretty but I see skull and crossbones on every bottle.

Trust me on this, the first drink is poison no matter how much romance and attractive packaging they promise. It is a lie for us.

November 22

GETTING KICKED

Wow, it is amazing how the readings hit a cord right on cue. Today's reading about "slips" and going back to drinking. I think slip is too nice a word. More like pulling the trigger in Russian roulette. I have seen so many of my brothers "slip" into the grave. The door is always open but there is no guarantee you can make it back to the rooms. One of our group, with some years of sobriety, just went out drinking. He sent me a text that he was sorry to disappoint me and his sponsor. Hell, he is only disappointing himself. Nobody else can make you drink and nobody else can make you stay sober. This guy's sponsor is my best friend here and he is crushed. We love the guys we sponsor and want the best for them. Staying sober is Life 101. You never know what is rolling around in the mind and heart of an alcoholic. My friend and I could not believe a person going to meetings daily, in service and sponsoring other people could possibly pick up a drink. Impossible. Wrong.

So now what. Once you are out there, life is a mess, a head full of AA and a belly full of booze is bad chemistry. It will screw up your drinking fun forever. With solid sobriety we face problems head on, stuff happens to all of us. How could we forget a drink or a drug will not make the pain go away or do any problem solving? Our "forgetter muscle" has no zip left. Our Higher Power needs to be a God of our understanding and not a relationship as a higher power. I can attest to this first hand. I lost one year of sobriety to a relationship that crashed and I crashed along with it. Luckily, I stopped right away and got with my sponsor and went to a meeting the next morning. No more "slips" for me. It scared the hell out of me, so it did kick me upstairs just like the reading says. It turned a negative into a big positive.

OK, so you got kicked, upstairs or downstairs, it's up to you!

November 23

GIVING THANKS

Every day is a day to give thanks, not just one day a year. Every day is a holiday if you make it one. Up to you. Here in Thailand on average there are 10 different countries represented in my group. American holidays are not even mentioned. It should be called Thanksgetting instead of Thanksgiving. Most families practice gluttony by eating too much, drinking beer and watching ball games. They really don't get off the couch and give anything except opinions. One of the reasons I love Thailand is giving is part of the culture. Buddha provides seven items to give with absolutely no resources: 1. Give one's service, helping physically. 2. Spiritual offering, giving a sympathetic heart. 3. Offering of the eyes, as in a warm glance to transmit tranquility. 4. A smile. 5. Kind words of comfort and encouragement to others. 6. Offer your seat to others for their rest. 7. Offering shelter and let others stay in your home. The manner of giving is also important. To give with a selfish motive of a payoff is not a true offering according to Buddha.

The practice of offering rids us of selfishness and we all know alcoholism is a very selfish disease.

Just saying "thanks" is good but doing some action to show thanks is even better. A grateful heart is a happy heart, I can tell you from my own experience. My gratitude list makes me happy, the process of giving back makes me happy and to see others "get it" in the program is a joy that makes me happy. The further away from me the happier I am. I forget my pains and troubles when I am giving. If I am uncomfortable or upset all I have to do is look at my natural selfish tendency and sure enough there it is. Gratitude combats my selfish side and giving of myself takes it away altogether. I get my gratitude from my loving Father, my Higher Power has bestowed on me gifts way more valuable than gold or money. My Higher Power wants me to be happy joyous and free and I am.

I thank my Higher Power in my daily prayers of gratitude and I receive His grace and enjoy the Sunlight of the Spirit 24/7.

November 24

I WANNA BE PRESIDENT

When I was growing up my mother had her expectations that her only son should be president. I started slow with becoming president of the altar boys at St Leo's. (I was able to pick the Mexican weddings to serve, they paid the most in a white envelope) I kept trying to 12 Step Father Keane from drinking too much wine at 7 a.m. mass but it didn't work out well. Then I was class president in my junior year but became unpopular for busting chops over smoking behind the gym. For the rest of my life I was commander, director or some such title until I joined AA and I was stripped of all my titles and given only one, alcoholic. That's all I aspire to be. I have reached my glass ceiling. When I came to AA and found there was no president, no leadership, I was surprised at first but now see the beauty of our fellowship.

I had to change all my old ideas. My mother was willing to settle for senator but I pointed out that an alcoholic serial groom with four divorces just wouldn't fly politically. I was a large disappointment to her. God bless her soul.

Americans are really funny about organization. Put 12 people in a room, lock the door in a classroom with a blackboard and tell them nothing, no direction. Those 12 will elect a spokesman, write on the board "Why are we here?" Start listing possible reasons. Leaders will emerge and someone will be a devil's advocate, and a few will do a crossword and not participate in the process. It's a riot. We are programmed to organize, and our program works opposite of what we have been doing all our lives. Trusted servants, not leaders, turn on the lights and lead the meetings but not for too long. We get rotated out before our ego claims ownership of a particular service we perform.

Our founders knew what type character defects most of us have and wrote the traditions to suit our fellowship best.

November 25

EVERYBODY IS A TEACHER

We hear all the time the phrase "Remain teachable." I truly believe and try to view everyone I meet as a teacher. It is hard sometimes but there is always a lesson hidden in every crossing of another's path. When I see someone less fortunate it teaches me to be grateful. When I am uncomfortable about someone's actions, it teaches me to be tolerant. If someone makes me wait, it teaches me patience. Even a child teaches me to have fun and play, not to take life too seriously. Folks who give me resentments are big teachers with many lessons. They may be just like me in some ways and I need to do my own inventory instead of my enemy's. If I look for the grain of truth in my opponent's argument, I can learn something. If I stay in the learning mode it helps my open-mindedness.

If everybody is a teacher and I am the student it helps me in the relationship department as well. I always treated my teachers with respect. Why not treat all these daily teachers the same? I didn't like all my teachers in school, but I still had to learn the material. It is OK to dislike the teacher and love the lesson. In my 10th Step every day I ask myself, "What lessons did I learn and what lessons did I miss altogether?" My character defects are often a block to learning, so in my spiritual floss job I can take an honest look at my part in all the situations I find myself.

I sure hope I can remain a teacher and not a preacher.

November 26

TALK, TALK, TALK

Doesn't an over talkative person drive you up the wall? I was having dinner with three other people I had not seen in a couple of years and I noticed they were all done eating and I was only half done. Talk, talk, talk was me trying to catch up with lost time and becoming one of those people I don't like. God gave us some clues about talking. He gave us two ears and only one mouth, which is multi-purpose, whereas the ears have only one purpose. If you need to get a word in edgewise, give the other guy something to eat and you will get your chance. Talking can be a very selfish thing because you are taking center stage and all others are placed in the listen mode. Talk, talk, talk can take away valuable time from your friends. Most meetings we go to the members are good stewards of the lock but it is really annoying when you get blah, blah, blah at the expense of others. The big problem with talking is your ears are shut off, no learning is taking place.

I recently shared all of us AA types have selfishness to the bone. One member crosstalked me and objected to my little bit. He swore he was not selfish and used up 20 minutes of the hour telling us all how unselfish he was. Seven more people did not get to share. OK now there is some balance to this, you need to talk to share your feelings. I am not advocating silence but it is better to be thought a fool than open my mouth and remove all doubt. I try to ask God to direct my sharing so it is of some value to others. Words are important and choosing the right ones can change someone's life especially in recovery. Time in a meeting is valuable and getting lost in a story that has nothing to do with recovery is theft really.

Action, action, action, trumps talk, talk, talk.

November 27

DID YOU SEE THAT?

I am amazed at the new trend of people focused on their phones so much that an elephant could go right by and they would not notice. I know we are not very good listeners, but we aren't very good watchers either. I love the prayer "I will only pass this way once so God let me do the best I can with this opportunity." There is so much beauty all around us and we miss a lot of it by losing our focus. I see folks with their field of vision down to one degree and they miss the flowers and they miss making eye contact with other earth travelers and rendering a smile and a kind word thus communicating some love. I try to keep my antenna up and running, not having an iPhone helps, but the point is to pay attention to my surroundings to enhance my daily life.

The same goes for people in our horizon. Some years back I noticed a janitor who worked in the office building where I worked for years. He walked with a limp and was past the age where he should be retired. He always had a nice smile and a twinkle in his eyes. One day I sat down next to him on his break and had a chat I will never forget. Turns out the limp was from losing a leg in Normandy on D-Day in WWII. He was working because he wanted to keep active, not because he had to make a buck. He had great stories and was delightful to talk to. When I left, he told me that I was the first person who talked to him in 5 years. We had a wave and wink relationship until I moved on.

Too often our senses are dulled by electronic life and distractions. God has provided unbridled beauty and our job is to see it.

November 28

YOU CAN'T IF YOU SAY YOU CAN'T

How many times I have heard, "I can't get sober." By golly they can't. If you define your own limitations then you own your limits. If you have made up your mind you can't do something then end of story, you can't. Now, of course, there is a reasonable factor in all of this. No, you can't leap over tall buildings and stop a speeding bullet. But I can do reasonable things if I make up my mind to do them. Of course, all of us are sober so we all had a turning point where we stopped and stayed stopped. With the help of God and other folks in the fellowship we made it past the roadblock to our sobriety. When we were drinking, we could not stop. What about other stuff in our lives? It is my belief we make our own fence or wall and we rarely if ever go outside the fence we put up. We get comfortable.

It is more exciting to try things outside the box and expand our horizons. Ever paint a picture with oils? I self-limit myself and say I can't paint. Well, I have never tried it and maybe there is talent under my bushel that has not seen the light of day. I have had an oil in mind for years, simple with only 2 colors but I need to get action to my thoughts. Our creativity was snuffed out when we were drinking, so now, we have our faculties back it is time to look at our "cant's." Can I beat Tiger Woods? I see some of his putts miss so bad I know I could do better.

All action begins with a thought and if you cancel out your own thoughts nothing is ever going to happen but try to be the little engine of your childhood, "I think I can, I think I can" and you probably will.

November 29

WHAT'S IMPORTANT

All of us, quite naturally, place high importance on what we are doing right now. At times we have so many plates spinning on a stick we are in danger of them all breaking. It is not easy but I have learned to apply the time test to what is important. I ask the question, "Will this be important a year from now?" Probably not important next week. I remember losing an entire folder of tax paperwork on my move from Hawaii to Thailand. I went crazy trying to find that folder at all my stops. Time went by and all that paperwork was never needed but I lost my serenity over that darn folder.

Sometimes we need to step away from "right now" stuff and take a long view of our importance factor. This is why early morning quiet time is key to setting today's priorities. If you look through eyes of love and apply the inner voice, advice you receive in your goal setting, the good stuff will trump the not so important stuff. Once I get out of balance then stupid things rob my time and I end up frustrated and angry. Life should not be an emergency.

You are alive, you have choices, you have freedom that's important.

November 30

OTHER STUFF

When you get sober the good news is you get your feelings back, the bad news is you get your feelings back and all the "other stuff" is waiting for you. It didn't go away while you stepped out of life for however long you were in a bottom. In fact, "other stuff" multiplies when you don't watch it. When I came out of my fog, I realized my health was in terrible shape, overweight, high blood pressure, etc. ... I also had PTSD which drinking does NOT help. Luckily, I found a University of Hawaii program from the VA that worked on my PTSD only after I was sober. It was wonderful and a ton of junk came out of my locker box and was removed. It is like peeling layers of an onion. One problem gets solved and there is another one underneath. When will it end? I am 20+ years into my onion and it still stinks. But at least I am working on the next layer.

Getting sober and staying sober is such a joyful accomplishment we can only pat ourselves on the back for a short pause and then get back to work. Many of us need to seek professional help in other areas for "other stuff" because AA is not a cure all and we are not doctors or shrinks. When I was growing up, I took a lot of science and math courses and not a one on relationships. I knew nothing about relationships when I got sober, I was a baby in that area. If you are in a dysfunctional setting long enough you think that is normal because you don't know any different. When you finally pop out of that eggshell you were in, you discover a whole new world. It is a wonderful world and we almost missed it completely.

All this "other stuff" can get us off track and divert us from our primary purpose. The hour of morning prayer and meditation can give us a good starting point each day.

December 1

WE'RE RICH

You have all seen those stories of lottery winners becoming instant millionaires. Their arms in the air, "We are rich!" We are just as rich as those folks, maybe not in cash but in other ways much more important. I read if you went to bed without being hungry, you have a computer and a bank account you are in the top 1% of all people on the globe. Food shortage is a big problem worldwide but for us too much food and wrong food is our problem. I need to send some of my meals to Africa. We tend to look upward to the rich and famous instead of the masses of very poor fellow human beings on our planet. We are lucky to be born in the country we were raised, able to find work, be nourished very well and become a 1%er. The gratitude for this good fortune brings humility along with the gifts we enjoy and take as a given, even a right. I don't ever feel "entitled" or demand my "rights."

OK then, in your position, in this one percent we are addicts and alcoholics who are sober. Wow, what percent of alcoholics are into their disease and not in recovery. How lucky we are to be in a super small percentage again.

We have won the lotto big time and for me, I am choked up with gratitude. Then to go even further we learn in this program to move away from material wealth into the spiritual sunlight until we reach peace and serenity which is more valuable than gold. We know all the money in the world does not bring happiness. A full spiritual bank account is like hitting the lotto not once but every day. I can write a check to cover any bad days and still be flush.

We have progressed further than hundreds of our fellows out there. We are blessed and rich way beyond our wildest dreams, enjoy.

December 2

CHANGE YOUR RELATIONSHIPS
TO YOUR PROBLEMS

We all have problems, that's life. We can't avoid problems especially when they are not our doing. Those government agencies, our fellow workers, bad weather, broken cars are out of our control. However, we can change our relationships to these rocks on the road of life. We can view these events as teaching points or a challenge, if you will. These problems will go away and you will be better off taking something positive out of the experience. What I do when I have a "challenge" is think of a friend who has much bigger problem and shrink my view of my difficulties to not such a big deal. We all tend to exaggerate our problems because of our selfish focus. "Poor me." Most of our problems are luxury problems. "Somebody scratched my BMW!"

360

I mentioned the way I handle physical pain before but here I go again. If am in pain, like in the dentist chair for example, I think of my friend Bud being tortured on a daily basis in a North Vietnamese prison camp. I visualize being hung upside down with my limbs tied together behind my back. A little raw nerve at the dentist is small stuff compared to what others have suffered. Thinking about Bud has helped me at the hospital countless times. When my pain passes, I get to go home. In the Buddhist tradition, there is a prayer that goes like this: "Grant that I may be given appropriate difficulties and sufferings on this journey so that my heart may be truly awakened and my practice of liberation and universal compassion may be truly fulfilled."

Whatever problems I have ever had, I know someone who has double my trouble. We can take advantage of these opportunities for further growth.

December 3

TOXIC PEOPLE

Some people are annoying, some obnoxious, some overbearing, some negative but with love and tolerance they can be OK. However, when you run into a toxic person some action is needed for peace and serenity. You are not going to change a toxic person so don't even try. Usually a toxic person loves confrontation, negative attention is better than no attention at all. These people have an answer for everything so whatever argument you present there is a counter point and a confrontation most likely will lead nowhere and may even get physical. In my own family a member has cut herself off from her siblings, mother and extended family. They are all wrong and she is right. She is of course God. When the mother of my children passed away, this family member floated into the afterlife and had a conversation with my dead wife and reported back her findings. She then poisoned my children in their time of grief with her personal problems.

This toxic family member did not attend her own mother's funeral and had a big part in a sibling suicide attempt and did nothing to take the sting out. You may have someone in your life who is toxic for you and what I have learned is to let go of this person with love. This family member is toxic to me but loved by her husband so it is not a 100% affliction, thank God. Earth is a big place and there is room for everybody, so I give my toxic folks a space away from my space. Live and let live. This toxic relative of mine has not spoken to me or the rest of the family in nine years, Great! Being 12 time zones away helps too.

There are some toxic people in AA also. AA is not "Wellness Anonymous." Sober, but sick in many other areas, so I steer clear. Beware and be gone.

December 4

FREEDOM IS NOT FREE

I am grateful for all my freedoms on a daily basis and remember it was others who gave me the gifts of freedom. I owe a debt which can never be repaid but I can use my freedom responsibly and with humility. I was a prisoner of King Alcohol for a couple of decades and it was the help of other kind folks that pulled me out of the pit I was in. Finding a Higher Power was key but some wise members showed me how to find the necessary steps to a new concept of a Higher Power. Funny how I come from a land of freedom and lost all my freedom by practicing the freedom to drink as much as I could whenever I wanted. Insane but true. Every bottle was like another brick added to my cell until there was no more light coming in. Once I surrendered, the brick walls came down in bunches and now I choose not to drink plus a lot of other things I choose not to do. It all had a price and the pain I caused others while I was being insane will be a lifelong endeavor to repair.

I let some things get into my freedom box, like resentments. If you resent somebody, they are in your head without paying rent. You become a slave to the resentment and your adversary is sleeping soundly while you toss and turn all night. I know better, but a guy got under my skin. I let it happen and I am responsible for fighting this person in a dance of death with no end. My freedom to be happy and approachable to others gets shut down in times like this. Only I can put me back into bondage. That makes no sense at all. My gratitude list puts me back in the free zone. Freedom is down there twice lest I forget the loss of my freedom from years past.

I must remember, a lot of people in my country gave their lives so others could be free. So, my freedom was not free at all.

December 5

BEING RIGHT

Amazing how some folks will fight to the death over being right. It can be an obsession just like anything else. Since there is no bonus for being right, no prize, no blue ribbon what's the big deal? One of my prayers says, "It is important what is right not who is right." What seems right to me is often not right to somebody else. They are convinced they are right and I am not going to change their mind. The trick I learned, a long time ago, is to let go of being right. Nobody cares if I am right or wrong anyway. I just surrender the point to my opponent and let them be right. It gets easier over time. I suppose it is an ego thing, a matter of pride. Since I have been in ego deflation mode for a long time now, giving up being right is OK with me.

Not to be a doormat, sometimes for safety reasons, may require some collection of evidence to show the right path to an idiot who needs direction. Our 11th Step prayer has some thoughts about correction error but with humility. If it is necessary to be right, a dose of humility might make it digestible to the person opposing you. I do, secretly, enjoy the other person realizing they are wrong, admitting it and telling me so. It happens rarely and I usually cover my smile with my hands. I want to be happy and right, if possible.

It is better to be kind than right, right?

December 6

GOOD BETTER BEST

How often do we settle for "good enough" instead of doing something better? One of my favorite tennis players is Venus Williams. At 37, she is still up with the best players in the world. She has won all the big slams and made millions of dollars but she is still working on her game. Venus need not prove anything to the world, only to herself. She played a very close match a couple of days ago it could have gone either way, but she lost. The writers harassed her about retirement after the match but she said, "You guys have been trying to retire me for 10 years, I am looking for ways to improve." You go girl. We can be champions also by constantly trying to improve ourselves. When I help somebody, that's good. But if they start drinking again, I look at my assistance and wonder if I could not have been better. When I do my inventory, I can say "That was OK but maybe not the best so what can I do next time to be better."

I am not promoting perfectionism but doing the best we are capable of is not always perfect, but it is our "personal best." Doing our best is rewarding even if it takes more time and resources. It is a product of positive thinking to add plus signs to our actions. It takes some tenacity to keep making upward changes even in losses. A bad experience can be a positive one if we learned something from it and use what we learned at the next opportunity for failure. My sponsor told me once, "At least you can serve as a bad example." Thank you, I think?

I know not to ever declare myself "best" at anything but I can claim to be getting better and better.

December 7

PILLS

A good friend in the program lost his sobriety of 20+ years over prescription drugs. I heard of so many cases of folks with a lot of time losing it all over pills. It is a slippery slope when you actually need drugs for whatever and the doctor prescribes them. But we know in our heart of hearts, when we abuse the drugs and it becomes mind altering instead of healing a problem. You can get a doctor to prescribe anything under the sun. You might have to try a few doctors, but there is one out there who will send you to happy, happyland. A doctor is not on your sobriety team, your program and the fellowship are. Most doctors do not really understand alcoholism/addiction like we do. It is our responsibility to be the head of our medical team.

Now the good news about my friend, he called it upon himself and reset his sobriety date to zero. He knew he had crossed the line and probably nobody would be the wiser but since this is a program of rigorous honesty he came forth. He is back in meetings and helping other people like he always did. In my experience some popular drugs just don't work well on alcoholics. Xanax is a 10 for 10 failure with guys I know for example. Prozac is another one which affects people quite differently. I am not an expert on drugs, but I sure am afraid of what I have witnessed in others. I will just be my special brand of crazy and be happy with that.

Pills are solid fuel alcohol and deadly too. There is no chemical solution to a spiritual problem.

December 8

REST

When we engage in meditation it is like zeroing all the dials, stopping our minds from spinning. Well the same thing goes for our body when we give it a rest. It feels good to stop moving. I had to learn how to rest just like I had to learn "fun" and so many other strange things which were off the table when I was drinking. (Passing out is not rest BTW.) When things get busy in our lives, we need to plan rest during the chaos. Most problems will still be there after we rest a bit. The rest recharges our energy and brains. "No time for rest" was our family motto when I was growing up. I was made to feel guilty for "resting." Now I owe it to myself to be the best "me" takes periods of rest.

If I am in an intense situation, like a wedding party with a 100 people, I go find a quiet spot to give myself a rest from 20 people all talking at the same time, shaking hands, posing for pictures. Ugh. Maybe you can handle it, but I lose my serenity. I am not at my best if I get tired and rundown. If I take a break from the madding crowd my chances of enjoying myself are doubled. I have found the older I get the more rest I need. Rest is not something with time leftover, rest is part of the game plan so I can have some quality with my time. "Give it a rest!" can be good advice. Take it easy, but not too easy.

December 9

THE MASK

We all know how a clown paints on a big smile or an oversized frown, you don't see the real person under the makeup. We often do the same thing by wearing a mask to put out an image that really is not us at all. I used to hide behind a uniform that said, "I am a big daddy in this business, so don't mess with me." But behind my mask was a fearful person afraid of being found out. In fact, I had a whole collection of masks, a macho mask for the bars, a smart mask for my staff, a love mask for the family, a humble mask for the authorities, etc... I had so many masks I lost who I really was or wasn't.

Taking off all those masks is a big step in freedom. No more pretending, no more lies, no more posturing. I don't have to try to please everybody. If you like me that's great and if you don't like me that is OK too. The important thing is to approve of myself. I need to look in the mirror and get the real picture not one I would like to be. What you see is what you get. The flip side is not to rip the mask off my fellow man, so many of them depend on the mask they wear to cope with life. It is not my job to de-mask them. Let Zorro wear his.

I try to remember a mask can suffocate. Life is so much better without having to remember the lines to my act. What you see is what you get. Rigorous honesty.

December 10

GOD: GREAT OUT DOORS

Almost everyone I have worked with had or has a "God" problem. They were all surprised when I said, "Good I don't have to reprogram you." Better to start from zero than to clean out old ideas like the ones I came in with. They were also surprised when I told them they didn't have to believe in God to get this program. Just believe in something outside yourself which you can call "Higher Power." Then over time they develop a work in progress "Higher Power." I have heard GOD is more digestible as Good Orderly Direction. Personally, I call my Higher Power "God" because it is my personal belief. I see God in everybody and everything.

A few years ago, at my morning meeting, a visitor said his "GOD" is the Great Out Doors. Wow! He saw God in all of nature and its creatures. I am in awe of all the varieties of flowers and the rainbow of colors they come in. I am in awe of the animals in our world that have special functions and a special design to survive. Who made this master plan? I can't believe it just "happened." I choose to believe God is the Master Planner and I need to try to follow the "plan." If you like, just add one more letter and say "GOOD" since all the religions in the world have doing "good" as part of their teachings. The main thing I tell myself is "I don't know who God is but it isn't me."

The main thing is to see God in your own way and think of God as your friend, loving and on your team.

December 11

PERFECT STORM

I don't know about you, but when bad things happen in my life, they seem to bunch up into a s**t storm. When this happens, I look up to the heavens and say, "OK God, what is it that I am not doing right? Let's talk about this." Then I pray and try to re-start my day. In my first homegroup in Hawaii there was an elderly lady that used to sit next to me during the meeting. Lita taught me many things. For example, one meeting I was reading a newspaper before the meeting started and Lita said, "Mike there is not a thing in that paper that will help you stay sober." I haven't read a newspaper since. One meeting I was fretting about all my problems during a s**t storm and Lita said, "Mike, don't worry. God will never give you more than you can handle!" I will never forget that and have passed it on too many people.

Funny, the longer I stay with the program the less frequent the "storms" but I have been in enough storms to watch myself and not lose it. If you do an 11th Step every morning it sort of puts up a shelter against a storm or at least gives you a head start. Then when the lightning hits you know to pray and ask for help. You are never alone so call for assistance before your dinghy capsizes. If the house is on fire don't answer the phone, get a hose. In other words, look at your priorities and adjust then based on the urgency of your "storm." When I think something bad is happening to me it always turns out the way it was supposed to turn out and it is a good thing.

Wishing you blue sky and clear sailing.

December 12

MY FAMILY DOESN'T UNDERSTAND ME

Once we get sober and undergo a great change in our lives, we are surprised everyone is not in tune with the new you. You might have changed but they haven't. You need to remember we were the ones who spoiled the family harmony and made everybody else sick. Maybe they still remember five years back when you ruined Christmas by falling drunk into the tree. Maybe they still remember your cousin's wedding when you delivered a speech about the groom, telling raunchy stories with four letter words. They may come around to the new you in time, on their timetable, not yours. I still run into folks that haven't seen me in years and they treat me like the drunk I was. Good reminder for me, my amends are never done.

I make living amends with my family at every opportunity and it is still not near enough. I was able to make amends every year for 15 years to the mother of my children. Even though she was my ex-wife, we saw each other almost every year and I was able to help her in her last few years with her cancer and financial situation. My kids have seen me sober for 20+ years but they still tell drunk stories when they reminisce at family reunions. They love the story of flying down the windiest street in San Francisco like a roller coaster with drunk dad at the wheel. I don't remember it that way but they do. Three against one. I recently wrote a story about my time in Afghanistan and preparing for the trip. I asked my son's help in recalling some detail. Now this was 1977 and he remembered how upset I was going to Afghan gatherings in Washington DC because there was no alcohol.

The family is never going to understand me, it's not their job. It is my job to understand rather than be understood.

December 13

THE HOUSE THAT GOD BUILT

Spiritually speaking, I live in a mansion which is always under construction with new additions every year. It has a strong foundation and a wonderful view (attitude) in all directions. It is full of art and music all throughout. There is a limo in the driveway with a driver (God) and I am not allowed to touch the steering wheel. This mansion and associated goodies is in my mind and it is truly the house God built. My earthly life is not nearly as wonderful. have lost all interest in material trappings. No jewelry, no toys, no iPad, iPod, iPhone, only 3 pair of shoes and no suits, ties, no tux, no uniforms, nada. Simplicity is very spiritual to me. I don't know how I could be happier with my surroundings without levitating.

At one point, I had a mansion, 2 story, 7-bedroom, marble floors, swimming pool, horseshoe driveway with rose garden, a car with a driver and an expense account for entertainment of hundreds of people. I was miserable. I had a smoking hole spiritually, emptiness beyond description. I was spiritually bankrupt. I was so happy to leave the mansion in my rearview mirror. It wasn't mine anyway. It all belonged to the job, not by my earning. A fancy house does not bring happiness I can attest. Now the simple life I live is paid for 100% for the first time in my life. The sunlight of the Spirit lights up my life and powers the mansion God built for me to use temporarily. It is portable, flexible, durable. Who could ask for anything more?

God re-built my entire life from the ground up. I reside in my Father's house that He has built. This is my heaven, my happiness.

December 14

GO WITH THE FLOW

All my life I fought city hall, swam upstream and flew with a headwind. Going with the flow is against my very nature. I wanted to be different, be off road and unique. I had to learn the easier, softer way was to let the tide take me in and send me out. I can see the folks who went before me are happy, joyous and free so I jump into their flow and go with it. I picked a crowd who was staying sober and did what they did and so I stayed sober too. This program does not match the tune, "I Did It My Way." It worked for Frank Sinatra but creativity in doing the Steps is not recommended. The Steps are in order for a reason and as much as I love shortcuts, I found doing what I am told works better than a shortcut which may get me lost forever. Going with the herd is against my grain but now I have surrendered to the flow it has worked out very well thank you.

When I was flying a little Bird Dog in Vietnam, I could get up into the wind stream with a head wind, put down the flaps and actually hover in ground speed. I took a whole clip of AK-47 fire doing that. Lesson learned; you need to keep moving or you are in danger. I have also learned to loosen my grip on the neck of life and quit trying to choke it to death. If I let go and let God, the natural flow of events doesn't need my input. God sends me this little note, "Mike, I won't be needing your help today. Thank you." The secret is to find God's flow and get in the stream where I belong.

As I sit in my dingy paddling as hard as I can, I realize I am not making progress. It was time to change my destination from "nowhere" to the Road of Happy Destiny. So much easier and I am not tired anymore.

December 15

SPIRITUAL HEALTH

When I was drinking, the only "health" I thought about was the shakes, the bloody shaving process, the headaches, etc... I never focused on emotional health or spiritual health because there was nothing to talk about. When the program taught me I was spiritually sick, in fact bankrupt then I began to learn about spiritual wellbeing. The concept of a spiritual bank account was discussed at my very first AA meeting and it hit the target. Then it became clear, physical, emotional, and spiritual health were all connected. If one of those three go south the whole barrel can go rotten if you let it.

Sometimes your physical health is out of your control, like when you fall on a concrete stair and need an operation. Then emotionally, some family members cause us concern, like one of your kids self-destructing, and you are powerless to stop the train wreck. But spiritual health is totally under your control and you can never get too much "good health" because there is no ceiling on spiritual growth. The sky's the limit. In my experience, when physical health and emotional health are not the best, if you work on spiritual health it will bring the other two into line. I have gone into meetings with a bad headache and a bad attitude and when the hour is over, I feel great again. Magic.

Unlike a physical workout, I can't overdo or hurt myself by too much spiritual health workouts. Spiritual growth has taken me to a dimension I had no idea was possible.

December 16

MATH SOLUTION: HAPPINESS X GRATITUDE

Time for some of Mike's fractured math.

Wants = What I Have = What I Need. They are all equal.

I don't have any wants that I don't already have. I have everything I need and more, so there is no wish list, no letters to Santa. This means I have no expectations or disappointments. What I do have is gifts way past my achievements which I don't deserve. I want what I have and will try to live up to a standard of doing the right things. All of this =happiness.

Happiness is not something I expect. I don't chase happiness it comes as a natural by-product of service to others and doing the next right thing over and over again. Unfulfilled expectations make for unhappy states of mind. Math here Infinity.

OK, let's get into an upward spiral. We all know about downward spirals having watched our lives go down the toilet. To reach nirvana we must be grateful for all the gifts we possess (check your gratitude "list") and it makes us happy. Being happy brings us back to gratitude and it keeps multiplying in an upward spiral until we experience a spiritual high. As we subtract material wants and needs then this multiplier effect works faster and better until we fly with the angels. Take a rocket ride to the stars with a gratitude X happiness fuel mixture.

Try my math and see if it doesn't solve some of your problems.

December 17

THE ADVENTURES OF A SNOWFLAKE

One of the worst speeches I ever endured has stuck with me for 45 years. This guy was an expert on rivers and could name every river in the world with details you don't need to know. But he had the story of a snowflake that blew into Minnesota from Canada and turned into a drop of water in a little stream and made its way down several rivers (he named carefully) and hit a rock. If the water drop went left it would go to Ohio and if the drop went right it would travel the Mississippi River into the Gulf of Mexico. So goes our lives as we bump into turning points in our lives, the course we take can be quite different. I know in my life some rocks took me to an unintended destination.

I threw a letter of reprimand back into my boss's desk rather than sign it, I ended up in Afghanistan as a result and almost got killed. But when I escaped a beating at the hands of Afghan secret police, I landed an assignment in Hawaii. I got sober in Hawaii by making the best first meeting ever. Saved my life. I was going to turn and run from the first meeting until the right guy grabbed me by the arm and told me I was in the right place. I stayed. All of us have turning points where we could go right or left. The way we hit the rock will change our lives forever. It is my belief that God has a hand in those turning points and we should have faith the path we are on is the right one. I am thankful to God to be down this river floating along in my dingy, merrily down the stream.

I am sure as you review your history you have pivotal turning points which took you over the rapids instead of merrily down the stream. No matter how many wrong turns we make, if we land in the rooms of AA everything will be alright.

December 18

GIVING IS THE ANSWER

When I was a kid at Christmas, I would have a wish list in my hopes for a great Christmas. It was all take and no give. The big day would finally arrive and it was a huge disappointment. The big stack of presents amounted to a lot of ugly shirts I would never wear and red socks to embarrass me for life. A turning point came when I got a $100 bonus check from my part time job in the wallpaper shop. I spent the entire $100 on my sisters, parents and girlfriend. I still remember the feeling of giving was so good that I became a "giver" instead of a "taker" back then as a teenager. No more disappointments at Christmas. I spent the next 50 years in some sort of service as a commitment to giving.

The 12th month, the 12th Step is all about giving. It comes at the end of the road. You can't take anything with you at the end of the show so you might as well give it away. I have been giving you all the gift of silence lately and nobody has complained so Merry Christmas from my computer to yours. Giving with love is the most rewarding. Expect zero return and you will never have a resentment for the gifts you have given away. That includes love.

This is Christmas time in Thailand and I played Santa with big baskets of goodies for some folks I see every day in my travels. It is fun and the marketplace where I buy the baskets, one by one were amazed by this crazy person coming in and out of the store at 8 a.m.

Today I give you all the gift of my words in hopes they are meaningful to someone out there. I enjoy writing them and hope you enjoy reading them, with love.

December 19

DON'T LEAVE BEFORE THE MIRACLE

Miracles happen all the time, but we miss them quite often. One of our group who has been in a coma for six weeks and has missed several sunrises. No more, he has snapped out of the coma and is alert and awake. He is cognizant but cannot speak. He is not out of the woods by any means but where there is life, there is hope.

When I first got sober, an old timer told me not to leave before the miracle. Not sure if he meant the meeting or the program but both apply. Yesterday my home group had only two guys besides me at meeting time. The secretary for the day didn't show up and one of the two that were there put his head back on the chair and shut his eyes. My gut feeling was to leave but I thought about "Doctor Bob's Coffee Pot" that my sponsor does when he has one or more alcoholics visiting. I have been to Doctor Bob's Coffee Pot when it was just the two of us and my sponsor runs the meeting the same as if 20 people were there. A lesson I will never forget.

So with that inspiration, I decided to chair the meeting with one interested and one uninterested member besides myself. During "How It Works" one more visitor showed up and by the time that was finished we had two more for a total of six. This would be a convention for Dr. Bob. One of the visitors had not been to a meeting in some time and really needed to be in the room. It was a great meeting (a miracle) and the entire hour was used for sharing.

I did a 5th Step later in the afternoon and the guy I was working with shared that I pushed him into service when he really didn't want to stay. That was two years ago and he is still sober and working the Steps. Miracle? Yeah, I think so.

December 20

AWAKE

Every day is about giving thanks, not just a special season like Christmas. Every day is a family time to share gratitude for the gifts we all are blessed with. Now month 12 and focus on Step 12, Spiritual Awakening. I am so happy to be awake. Every sunrise chokes me up with gratitude for another day of life. All the daily problems are so small they really are not problems. It's just life. Just the process of awakening is a very spiritual experience. If you have been close to not having another sunrise you know what I mean. One of our home group members has been 6 weeks without an awakening. Our prayers are with him as a respirator keeps him alive, waiting for a miracle.

When Buddha was asked the question, "Are you God?" His answer was, "No." Then are you man? His answer was, "No." The question then was, "What are you then?" The answer was, "I am awake." Now I think I understand his answer better than the first time I heard Buddha's answer:

Being awake to life, Being awake to self-awareness, Being awake to doing the next right thing, Being awake to God being with us, Being awake to a connection with our fellow human beings, Being awake to events are supposed to happen the way they do happen. And being awake to serenity and peace. In my morning wake up, my first thoughts are of gratitude for another day of life and a good night's rest. Every morning is a spiritual awakening.

As I watch the red and purple of today's sunrise, I am without words, I am awake, thank you God.

December 21

EXPOSE A FRIEND FOR HIS RICHES

Nothing can be more rewarding than a good friend to share the rough times and the celebrations alike. This reading struck me, and I will share it with you: **"The greatest good you can do for another is not just to share your riches, but to reveal to him his own."**

How often do we talk to our friends and just share our own experiences and daily activities? Yes, it's a good thing and the other person does the same. But do you ever focus on a gift that friend has and how you treasure the friendship? Do you expose him for all the riches he probably doesn't see himself? To encourage someone to stop hiding their light under a bushel basket can light a fire. Think about your best friend and ask yourself if you have put a spotlight on his valuable attributes?

I know the definition of a good friend is you know all there is to know about a person but love them anyway. It's the flip side but a boost from a close friend is worth 100 criticisms. Sure we should tell our friends when they are off track. But at the same time tell them when they are on track.

In my own case, I have been writing more lately to live up to my promise to my kids. "What Daddy did during the war." I have been very critical of my own writing but I have a good friend who is a writer and he told me I was a great writer. Even if it isn't true it gave me a shot of enthusiasm which I needed to keep writing. It was painful but I finished a three-part series on Afghanistan during my two years there. It was like a 4th Step.

December 22

WHAT PORT ARE YOU SAILING FOR?

One of my readings had this thought, "If you do not know which port you are sailing to then there is no wind that is the right wind." If you have lost your compass, broken the mast and out of gas you are not sailing anywhere anyway.

I remember entire years of my life where I was afloat in a dinghy without a rudder, without an engine, bobbing up and down in an ocean with no name. I didn't know where I was going and didn't care. The wind blew me around and it was never the right wind because I did not know how to adjust my sail. How awful those years were. A total waste. I was not useful to anyone, least of all myself.

Today I have a port in sight. It is called nirvana, it is serenity. I adjust my sail daily toward that port. Every day I try to improve my navigation through what life gives me. Life on life's terms. Some people would throw me off course, so I avoid them. Some people have been this route before and offer me assistance and I listen to them. I get a weather report from my Higher Power every morning, so I am ready to face the next 24 hours with the knowledge that everything happening is supposed to happen. The wind is in my face and fear is in my wake

I pray for guidance to set the right goals to sail to the right port and adjust my sails as needed to complete the journey.

December 23

SPIRITUAL MATH

I have some friends who think all matters under the sun can be expressed in a formula. When I was studying Differential Calculus, I tended to believe it. As life unfolded, I never used algebra, geometry, calculus or the $400 math calculator I bought back in college. I use a free, small calculator that adds and subtracts and it is all I ever needed. So goes my spiritual life. Add more prayer subtract my resentments. Add good things to my daily routine and subtract time wasters. For example: when I get on the computer and I am between projects, I used to play solitaire. At the end of each game it asks: "Play again?" and I do. Result, hours are wasted that I could have used for much higher spiritual gain than a stupid game.

This change in my behavior came as a result of my 10 days of 11 Step work while in the hospital. I had a chance to review my inventory and playing hours of solitaire came to mind. I have not played a game since leaving the hospital a month ago. I know if I open the game, I will start my bad habit all over again. My diet had to change as a result of my operation and it was all for the good. I was drinking 3 big cups of coffee in the morning and one more in the afternoon. The doctor only allowed me a half cup all day. I found I am OK with a half cup in the morning. It is enough to open my eyes. I used to eat spicy, pepper hot Thai food. Not good for my tender repaired gut. All of this is good stuff which comes out of a bad situation.

As far as my character, it is mostly subtraction taking place. I know God will remove the defects which block me from helping other people. I pray for the release of those bondages of self.

December 24

BUILD A BRIDGE INSTEAD OF A FENCE

Jan was born in Holland but spent most of his life in the USA and finally a good portion of the last 20 years in Thailand, delighting all who know him. Jan didn't get sober until he was 58 years old so he did have 25 years of continuous sobriety. He would burst into the meeting room well before starting time (I like that) and shout Happy, Happy, Happy. I love music, sweet music! Jan went to all the different meetings, not just one home group. He would make me smile and laugh with his joyful rant. Jan never said a bad word about anybody or anything.

Not a negative word ever came out of his mouth. He built only bridges and no fences which is my topic.

Remember my take on eye contact and how poorly we humans are at eye contact with each other? Dogs do a better job than people. Well another human trait is to erect a fence where a bridge would do better. In the days of the wild west, the pioneers would stake out a piece of land and fence it in and call the enclosed area "mine," Do not cross or I will shoot you. It is a mindset that comes natural to us. We have a nice house and then we put bars on the windows so nobody can break in while we are on vacation. We install an alarm system, get a pit bull for the backyard and try to feel safe with our .357 in our lap when we take a nap. In the case of two countries, Laos and Thailand, the Mekong River acted as a fence. In fact, when we flew from Laos to Thailand, we would radio our ground control, "We just crossed the fence" meaning we crossed the border into Thailand. Laos and Thailand have much in common, the people ethnically are very close, the language is 80% overlap so you can communicate well, no matter which country you are in. Finally, the two countries have 2500 years of Buddhism in their blood. Many temples (wats) line both sides of the Mekong.

The point is to make loving connections. Bridge the gap between two people or two nations. I tore down the imaginary fence I built around myself.

TAKE TIME TO LAUGH

One of my Daily Prayers is called "Take Time," it talks about taking time to pray, time to play, time to work. I focused on this one:

Take time to laugh

For it is the music of the soul

Beautiful. I was 10 days into my accident and one of my good friends came to visit. He made me laugh for the first time in 2 weeks. It felt so good, so refreshing, it cleared out some cobwebs. Laughter has always been part of my life. It is the shortest distance between two people. Now I say this prayer every morning but the next morning I focused on the line. Music! I have a broken CD player kaput for two years. Now everybody is MP3. Always behind. I still have my 8-track of Crystal Gayle.

I called up a good friend from my home group and had him buy some external speakers for my computer. My hearing is so bad I cannot hear anything from the tiny speaker. Another friend who spent some years in Afghanistan downloaded 20,000 songs into an external drive. He bought this computer for me and as a special favor he downloaded all these into my computer. So, I had all this music at my fingertips and never heard a song. Now, I have music, music, music.

Laughter is my music and since I have no musical talent I found out I can make people laugh and it is the shortest distance between two people. Getting a good laugh is chicken soup for my soul.

December 26

UNITY

Some recent readings have been about unity and the necessity to stay unified for the survival of AA. When I think about it, it applies to everything, family, work, countries, world organization. World peace would take unity. Wars over which religion you believe in would be over. Seeking oneness is a great goal. I have to have total tolerance and love of others to obtain unity. Live and let live, no killing over politics, race, religion.

Time to pray every day is so important. If you are too busy to take time out for yourself, you need to stop, smell the coffee, give your dog a big hug. Be true to thine self. When I was in the hospital and could not sleep, I would wait for hourly blood pressure check and grab my books and do my reading and prayer at 1 a.m., 3 a.m., maybe 5 a.m. at the latest. My day went great every time I did this. Good news about this test or another, x-ray shows improvement, most functions are in the normal range. All good news to my ears. The entire hospital staff operated in unison. This, my friends, was unity in action. Four doctors with one goal, make Mike live and get well. I have no idea if they had a team meeting or had a computer connection but all four knew about each blood test and each x-ray. They were poetry in action, simply amazing. I was able to surrender to their care and not fight or question each move. They would say, we need to do a C-scan, I would say OK let's go. And go we did.

Being on the right team working together for a common goal is so rewarding. My true friends were by my side, what a gift. Am I ever blessed.

December 27

MOTHER LODE

One of my favorite readings is the one about a gold miner who discovered the Mother Lode and he will mine gold for the rest of his life provided he gives away the entire product. Beautiful. This is exactly what our new life has given us. We have won the lotto. The gold we mine on a daily basis is not for us to keep but an opportunity to pass it on. If we could attain a level of selflessness it would be nirvana. The treasurers of life are right there for us all this time, but we never did dig deep enough to strike gold. Plus, we have only scratched the surface, the more we mine the more gold we find. The more we give away, the better we feel.

Life and happiness in life are a matter of attitude and perception. I am so happy to be in the gold mining business. It came after a dark starving period of my life which appeared to be hopeless and doomed. A sliver of light and one ounce of willingness is all it took to open the mine shaft. Now my job is to give it all back. Every ounce. My problem is, I receive so many dividends from giving, my basket runneth over with blessing and gifts. The joy of giving away gold is reward enough for me. I will walk a mile for a smile.

I enjoy going to meetings and picking up golden nuggets of wisdom to pass on later. I have many arrows in my quiver.

December 28

EVER CHANGING PRAYER

When I was kid making my way through religious training, prayer was equal to punishment. The priest would say: "Your penance will be 10 Our Fathers and 10 Hail Mary's." This was my introduction to prayer. Then I was taught to pray for what I wanted. Might as well write a letter to Santa Claus was my thought about this tactic. Then as I got older, I learned to pray when I got into trouble, which became often. When I got sober, my prayer was for help to get the heat off. God please get everybody off my butt. God please help me stop shaking. God please help me stay sober for 24 hours. Guess what? All those prayers were answered. The Steps told me prayer was part of the deal and I was willing to do whatever would save my life and stop the pain. Not only were the prayers answered but my problems went away and life became worth living first, then fun, then total happiness.

Now my prayer is not asking for myself. Now it is pure thanks and gratitude. God gives me all I could possibly put in my basket without making a wish list. The thrust of my prayers has changed drastically over the years. I say some of the same prayers every morning for 20 years. All those prayers are very different from when I started 25 years ago. The words are not different. I am different. I am the one who changed. Sometimes the change is so small it is hard to see a difference but my Higher Power sees it and challenges me to change even further. I will never stop changing for fear of going backwards

Prayer does not change God, but changes the person doing the praying.

December 29

SOBER AND MISERABLE

I often hear raw sobriety in meetings. Some members are happy with personal sobriety but never move on to helping others, sponsoring, being in service or dealing with anybody outside themselves. Yes, being sober is basic, AA 101, an absolute requirement but then after achieving sobriety maybe it is time to clean up and grow up, ya think? You hear in AA all the time "I am not much but I am all I think about." If you are sober and still miserable my guess is it is all about you. Once you start giving, being in service, the magic happens, you become happy, joyous and free. I don't believe God wants us to be miserable. Nobody is going to ask me for help if I am miserable and grouchy.

A newcomer is not going to be attracted to the program by unhappy members. If I get sober and am not having fun, then what's the point? I insist on having fun, enjoying life, laughing until my sides hurt, finding love in every relationship. Raw sobriety is a form of cruise control. I need to learn more, read more, help more people, reach out more, expand my horizons every day. No breaks, no recess. My disease is doing pushups just waiting for me to screw up. I have been beat up enough, thank you. I am so happy doing what I have been doing all these years I keep looking for ways to add to my menu. I know I need to be enthusiastic all the time to carry the message of hope and happiness.

Helping others is the Rx for misery. Getting out of yourself makes you forget your troubles and it's good for your health too.

December 30

AIN'T NO BIG DEAL

In sobriety, we don't make everything a big deal like we did in the old days. **There are no big deals.** Something about us alcoholics is we can make a mountain out of a mole hill. Just go to an AA business meeting and watch people get their panties all ruffled over the smallest thing. Amazing. Luckily, I have a good friend in the fellowship who has been my partner in many AA projects and service. I tend to fuss and fume over details and timelines and my co-worker just shrugs and tells me, "Ain't no big deal." It always calms me down and makes me realize I am powerless over people, places and things.

It is easy to see most big deals are of our own making and have nothing to do with reality. When we make things larger than life, it was usually because of our need to feel important or to fill our desire for attention. We like to be heroes and save people from the fire, but we were the ones that started the fire. I need to remember I am no big deal either. Just another Bozo on the bus.

Will it matter 100 years from now? Will it matter tomorrow? Probably not. Now sobriety, that is a big deal. You lose sobriety and there are no deals at all, big or small.

December 31

PROGRESS NOT PERFECTION

I remember being pushed into "perfection" by my mother. I came home with seven A's and one B. We didn't talk about the A's, that was expected, oh no, we talked about the B and my not living up to my potential. Pretty soon striving for perfection was so exhausting I went the other direction. Then I got used to the guilt of not being the best of everything. Drinking was a great way to push guilt off the table. One of the amazing gifts of this program is the saying in "How It Works." "We claim spiritual progress not spiritual perfection." Only God is perfect and sometimes a big fat "C" is good enough (It chokes me to say that). If progress is taken on a daily basis, you need not produce a work of art in one day but just do a small corner of the canvas. If you want to empty the ocean with a tea cup, you find a big cup and you get started.

I remember when I accepted the idea of body, mind and spirit. I looked at my 260 lbs. and thought it too far gone to even try. Then I said to myself, progress no matter how small. Today I tip the scales at 185lbs. so 75 lbs. went little by little. Sometimes no change could be measured for weeks at a time, but I was in the habit of working out and I stayed the course. Just finished my hour today. The same thing works for my knowledge, my character defects, my amends. Step by step, one phone call more, one book added. I will never ever be perfect at anything and that's OK with me. My mother has passed on so I don't have to appease her anymore. Today I am the best me I can be for today, tomorrow we will add some good stuff to the program.

You added another day, another year of continuous sobriety if nothing else. HAPPY NEW DAY!

THE GREAT ESCAPE

When you think about it, we all performed the greatest escape possible. Escape from the bondage of alcohol and drugs. Now that has been accomplished, how about other escapes? For example: escape from our past, escape from fear, escape from bad relationships. To me the goal of all great escapes is freedom. I remember when I lost my freedom to an armed enemy, twice, it was by the grace of God I escaped. I should have dropped to my knees in gratitude but instead I got drunk, both times. Today I thank God for my freedoms, which are many, every single morning. I remember putting my soon to be ex-wife on an airplane ending a horrible relationship. (I never saw her again BTW) As soon as they closed the door to that aircraft, I jumped up 6 feet in the air and clicked my heels, "I'm free, I'm free!" So what did I do? Go to the bar and start another horrible relationship within the hour. The reason the relationship with my ex was bad, I was in in it. When I did my inventory, I could see I was the "horrible" part and my freedom was lost by my own doing.

Almost all of my bondage and loss of freedom was my own fault. Even though I deserved jail, I was never behind bars, but I was on self-imposed house arrest. Hiding in a dark house full of fear. Fear the phone would ring with more bad news. Fear of the mail with a summons or bill I couldn't pay. Fear the police would knock on my door. I was terrified to drive because I had so much alcohol in my body, a cop would lock me up if I got stopped for sure. I had no escape plan! I craved my freedom and it was gone. I might as well have been in state lockup without a key. My Higher Power had the key and it was by the grace of God I found my way to that first meeting and started my journey to true freedom. I didn't need to escape from jail, or from bad relationships, I needed to escape from ME. I was the jailer. I realized God wants us to be happy joyous and free in order to not only enjoy life but to be helpful to others. To get in the give mode instead of the take mode.

Today I still enjoy a great escape from boredom and look for new ways to fly free and soar with the eagles. I don't take any of my precious freedoms for granted any more. I thank God for setting me free.

APPENDIX 1
MORNING PRAYERS

I PROMISE MYSELF

Today I pray:

To promise myself to be so strong that nothing can disturb my peace of mind.

To talk health, happiness, and prosperity to every person I meet.

To make all my friends feel that there is something in them.

To look at the sunny side of everything and make my optimism come true.

To think only of the best, to work only for the best, and expect only the best.

To be just as enthusiastic about the success of others as I am about my own.

To forget the mistakes of the past and press on to the greater achievements of the future.

To wear a cheerful countenance at all times and give every living creature I meet a smile.

To give so much time to the improvement of myself that I have no time to criticize others.

To be too large for worry, too noble for anger, too strong for fear, and too happy to permit the presence of trouble.

CHANGES

Today I pray that I may understand there
    are some things I cannot change:
I cannot change the weather.
I cannot change the tick of the clock.
I cannot change another person against their
    will.
I cannot change what is right and wrong.

I cannot change the fact that a relationship
   ended.
I can stop worrying over that which I can-
   not change and enjoy living more! I can
   place those things into the hands of the
   One Who is bigger than I. Save energy.
   Let go. Instead of trying to
   change someone else:
I can change my attitude.
I can change my list of priorities.
I can change my bad habits into good ones.
I can move from a place of brokenness
   Into wholeness, into the beautiful per-
   son God created me to become.

TAKE TIME

Today I pray that I can:
Take time to think.
   It is the source of power.
Take time to play.
   It is the secret of perpetual youth.
Take time to read.
   It is the fountain of wisdom.
Take time to pray.
   It is the greatest Power on earth.
Take time to be friendly.
   It is the road to happiness.
Take time to laugh.
   It is the music of the soul.
Take time to give.
   It is too short a day to be selfish.
Take time to work.
   It is the price of success.
Take time to do charity.
   It is the key to Heaven.

LIFE IS A CELEBRATION

Lord, help me today to:
Mend a quarrel.
Seek out a forgotten friend.
Dismiss suspicion and replace it with trust.
Write a friendly letter.
Share a treasure.
Give a soft answer.
Encourage another.
Manifest my loyalty in word and deed.
Keep a promise.
Find the time.
Forego a grudge.
Forgive an enemy.
Listen.
Acknowledge any wrongdoing.
Try to understand.
Examine my demands on others.
Think of someone else first.
Be kind.
Be gentle.
Laugh a little.
Smile more.
Be happy.
Show my gratitude.
Welcome a stranger.
Speak your love.
Speak it again.
Live it again.
LIFE IS A CELEBRATION!

THIRD STEP PRAYER

God I offer myself to Thee to build with me and do with me as thou wilt. Relieve me of the bondage of self, that I may better do thy will. Take away my difficulties, that victory over them may bear witness to those I would help of Thy power, Thy love, and Thy way of life. May I do Thy will always.

Amen

(Big Book, page 63)

7th STEP PRAYER

My Creator, I am now willing that you should have all of me, good and bad.
I pray that you now remove from me every single defect of character which stands in the way of my usefulness to you and my fellows.
Grant me strength, as I go out from here, to do your bidding.

Amen

(Big Book, page 76)

11th STEP PRAYER

Lord, make me a channel of Thy peace
    -that where there is hatred, I may bring love
    -that where there is wrong, I may bring the spirit of forgiveness
    -that where there is discord, I may bring harmony
    -that where there is error, I may bring truth
    -that where there is doubt, I may bring faith
    -that where there is despair, I may bring hope
    -that where there are shadows, I may bring light
    -that where there is sadness, I may bring joy.

Lord, grant that I may seek rather to comfort, than to be comforted
    -to understand, than to be understood
    -to love, than to be loved.

For it is by self-forgetting that one finds.
    It is by forgiving that one is forgiven.
      It is by dying that one awakens to Eternal life.

Amen

(12 Steps & 12 Traditions, page 99)

Made in the USA
Coppell, TX
31 May 2024

32979019R00231